Lecture Notes in Computer Science   12231

More information about this series at http://www.springer.com/series/7410

Kazumaro Aoki · Akira Kanaoka (Eds.)

Advances in Information and Computer Security

15th International Workshop on Security, IWSEC 2020
Fukui, Japan, September 2–4, 2020
Proceedings

 Springer

Editors
Kazumaro Aoki
Bunkyo University
Chigasaki, Japan

Akira Kanaoka
Toho University
Funabashi, Japan

ISSN 0302-9743   ISSN 1611-3349 (electronic)
Lecture Notes in Computer Science
ISBN 978-3-030-58207-4   ISBN 978-3-030-58208-1 (eBook)
https://doi.org/10.1007/978-3-030-58208-1

LNCS Sublibrary: SL4 – Security and Cryptology

This Springer imprint is published by the registered company Springer Nature Switzerland AG
The registered company address is: Gewerbestrasse 11, 6330 Cham, Switzerland

Preface

The 15th International Workshop on Security (IWSEC 2020) was held online (originally scheduled to be held at Happiring Hall and Fukui International Activities Plaza, Fukui, Japan), from September 2–4, 2020. The workshop was co-organized by ISEC (the Technical Committee on Information Security in Engineering Sciences Society of IEICE) and CSEC (the Special Interest Group on Computer Security of IPSJ).

This year, we categorized topics of interests into two tracks, namely, Cryptography Track (Track A) and Cybersecurity and Privacy Track (Track B) as was done last year; each track is formed by separate Program Committee members. We received 48 submissions, 25 in Track A and 23 in Track B, out of which 1 paper was withdrawn before the review process. After extensive reviews and shepherding, we accepted 15 regular papers (9 from Track A and 6 from Track B) and 1 short paper (from Track B). Each submission was anonymously reviewed by four reviewers on average. These proceedings contain revised versions of the accepted papers. Track A consists of the sessions on symmetric- and public-key cryptography and cryptographic protocols. Track B consists of the sessions on malicious activity detection and security, privacy, and machine learning.

The Best Paper Awards were given to "Efficiency and Accuracy Improvements of Secure Floating-Point Addition over Secret Sharing" by Kota Sasaki and Koji Nuida, and to "Timing Attack on Random Forests for Generating Adversarial Examples" by Yuichiro Dan, Toshiki Shibahara, and Junko Takahashi. The Best Student Paper Award was given also to "Efficiency and Accuracy Improvements of Secure Floating-Point Addition over Secret Sharing" by Kota Sasaki and Koji Nuida, and to "Detection of Malicious PowerShell Using a Word-Level Language Model" by Yui Tajiri and Mamoru Mimura.

This year, many researchers had difficulty in carrying out their daily lives due to COVID-19. It is our pleasure to be able to publish the proceedings of IWSEC 2020 in such circumstances. It is because of those researchers who continued their research despite the difficulty. It is also because there were reviewers who agreed to evaluate the papers. We would like to thank all authors for submitting their papers to the workshop, and also we are deeply grateful to the members of the Program Committee and to the external reviewers for their in-depth reviews and detailed discussions. We must mention that the selection of the papers was an extremely challenging task. Last but not least, we would like to thank the general co-chairs, Shoichi Hirose and Toshihiro Yamauchi, for leading the Organizing Committee, and we would also like to thank the members of the Organizing Committee for ensuring the smooth running of the workshop.

September 2020

Kazumaro Aoki
Akira Kanaoka

IWSEC 2020

15th International Workshop on Security

Organization

Fukui, Japan, September 2–4, 2020

co-organized by

ISEC in ESS of IEICE
(Technical Committee on Information Security in Engineering Sciences Society
of the Institute of Electronics, Information and Communication Engineers)
and
CSEC of IPSJ
(Special Interest Group on Computer Security of Information Processing
Society of Japan)

General Co-chairs

Shoichi Hirose	University of Fukui, Japan
Toshihiro Yamauchi	Okayama University, Japan

Advisory Committee

Hideki Imai	The University of Tokyo, Japan
Kwangjo Kim	Korea Advanced Institute of Science and Technology, Republic of Korea
Christopher Kruegel	University of California, Santa Barbara, USA
Günter Müller	University of Freiburg, Germany
Yuko Murayama	Tsuda University, Japan
Koji Nakao	National Institute of Information and Communications Technology, Japan
Eiji Okamoto	University of Tsukuba, Japan
C. Pandu Rangan	Indian Institute of Technology, Madras, India
Kai Rannenberg	Goethe University Frankfurt, Germany
Ryoichi Sasaki	Tokyo Denki University, Japan

Program Co-chairs

Kazumaro Aoki	Bunkyo University, Japan
Akira Kanaoka	Toho University, Japan

Local Organizing Committee

Masahiro Fujita	Mitsubishi Electric Corporation, Japan
Ryo Fujita	Chuo University, Japan
Yuichi Hayashi	Nara Institute of Science and Technology, Japan
Xuping Huang	Advanced Institute of Industrial Technology, Japan
Yasuhiko Ikematsu	Kyushu University, Japan
Tetsuya Izu	Fujitsu Laboratories Ltd., Japan
Satoru Izumi	Tohoku University, Japan
Kazuya Kakizaki	NEC, Japan
Toru Nakanishi	Hiroshima University, Japan
Ryo Nojima	National Institute of Information and Communications Technology, Japan
Kazuma Ohara	National Institute of Advanced Industrial Science and Technology, Japan
Satsuya Ohata	Digital Garage, Inc., Japan
Toshiya Shimizu	Fujitsu Laboratories Ltd., Japan
Yuji Suga	Internet Initiative Japan Inc., Japan
Yuta Takata	Deloitte Tohmatsu Cyber LLC, Japan
Atsushi Takayasu	The University of Tokyo, Japan
Naoto Yanai	Osaka University, Japan
Sven Wohlgemuth	Hitachi, Ltd., Japan

Program Committee

Track A: Cryptography Track

Kazumaro Aoki	Bunkyo University, Japan
Geoffroy Couteau	IRIF, Paris-Diderot University, CNRS, France
Bernardo David	IT University of Copenhagen, Denmark
Itai Dinur	Ben-Gurion University, Israel
Antonio Faonio	IMDEA Software Institute, Spain
Yuichi Komano	Toshiba Corporation, Japan
Florian Mendel	Infineon Technologies, Germany
Kazuhiko Minematsu	NEC, Japan
Toru Nakanishi	Hiroshima University, Japan
Miyako Ohkubo	NICT, Japan
Thomas Poeppelmann	Infineon Technologies Austria AG, Austria
Yusuke Sakai	AIST, Japan
Jae Hong Seo	Hanyang University, Republic of Korea
Yannick Seurin	Agence Nationale de la Sécurité des Systèmes d'Information, France
Takeshi Sugawara	The University of Electro-Communications, Japan
Willy Susilo	University of Wollongong, Australia
Katsuyuki Takashima	Mitsubishi Electric Corporation, Japan
Atsushi Takayasu	The University of Tokyo, Japan

Mehdi Tibouchi	NTT, Japan
Damien Vergnaud	Sorbonne Université, UPMC, CNRS, France
Yuyu Wang	University of Electronic Science and Technology of China, China
Yohei Watanabe	The University of Electro-Communications, Japan
Bo-Yin Yang	Academia Sinica, Taiwan

Track B: Cybersecurity and Privacy Track

Mitsuaki Akiyama	Nippon Telegraph and Telephone Corporation, Japan
Josep Balasch	KU Leuven, Belgium
Gregory Blanc	Télécom SudParis, France
Herve Debar	Télécom SudParis, France
Josep Domingo-Ferrer	Universitat Rovira i Virgili, Catalonia
Kimmo Halunen	VTT Technical Research Centre of Finland Ltd., Finland
Yuichi Hayashi	Nara Institute of Science and Technology, Japan
Mika Juuti	University of Waterloo, Canada
Akira Kanaoka	Toho University, Japan
Frederic Majorczyk	DGA-MI/CentraleSupelec, France
Ryo Nojima	National Institute of Information and Communications Technology, Japan
Yoshihiro Oyama	University of Tsukuba, Japan
Giorgos Vasiliadis	Foundation for Research and Technology - Hellas, Greece
Takeshi Yagi	NTT Security (Japan) KK, Japan
Takumi Yamamoto	Mitsubishi Electric Corporation, Japan

External Reviewers

Daisuke Fujimoto	Satsuya Ohata
Daniel Heinz	Yuto Otsuki
Julius Hermelink	Martin Schlaeffer
Yohei Hori	Kazumasa Shinagawa
Yuhei Kawakoya	Kuniyasu Suzaki
Hirotaka Kokubo	Tran Viet Xuan Phuong
Shoei Nashimoto	Naoto Yanai

Contents

Symmetric-Key Cryptography 1

On the Design of Bit Permutation Based Ciphers

The Interplay Among S-Box, Bit Permutation and Key-Addition

Sumanta Sarkar[1], Yu Sasaki[2], and Siang Meng Sim[3(✉)]

[1] TCS Innovation Labs, Hyderabad, India
sumanta.sarkar1@tcs.com
[2] NTT Secure Platform Laboratories, Tokyo, Japan
yu.sasaki.sk@hco.ntt.co.jp
[3] DSO National Laboratories, Singapore, Singapore
crypto.s.m.sim@gmail.com

Abstract. Bit permutation based block ciphers, like PRESENT and GIFT, are well-known for their extreme lightweightness in hardware implementation. However, designing such ciphers comes with one major challenge – to ensure strong cryptographic properties simply depending on the combination of three components, namely S-box, a bit permutation and a key addition function. Having a wrong combination of components could lead to weaknesses. In this article, we studied the interaction between these components, improved the theoretical security bound of GIFT and highlighted the potential pitfalls associated with a bit permutation based primitive design. We also conducted analysis on TRIFLE, a first-round candidate for the NIST lightweight cryptography competition, where our findings influenced the elimination of TRIFLE from second-round of the NIST competition. In particular, we showed that internal state bits of TRIFLE can be partially decrypted for a few rounds even without any knowledge of the key.

Keywords: Lightweight cryptography · Block cipher · Bit permutation · S-box · Differential cryptanalysis · Linear cryptanalysis · PRESENT · GIFT · TRIFLE

1 Introduction

Block ciphers are often inspired by the principle of *confusion* and *diffusion* [25]. The Substitution Permutation Network (SPN) has been widely followed in constructing block ciphers, for example, Rijndael [12] that became the block cipher standard AES[1]. Confusion property comes from the substitution layer (SubBytes) which applies some S-boxes in parallel. The output of the substitution layer is processed by two linear operations, namely, byte permutation (ShiftRows)

---

[1] In this article we will use AES instead of Rijndael.

© Springer Nature Switzerland AG 2020
K. Aoki and A. Kanaoka (Eds.): IWSEC 2020, LNCS 12231, pp. 3–22, 2020.
https://doi.org/10.1007/978-3-030-58208-1_1

and matrix multiplication (MixColumns). The *wide-trail* strategy proposed in AES [11] allows designers to measure the strength of SPN ciphers against two basic attacks, namely, differential cryptanalysis [6] and linear cryptanalysis [21]. The core strategy is to count the number of *active* S-boxes for some rounds. The four round propagation [12] shows that the resistance of AES against differential and linear cryptanalysis depends on the permutation layer. Then AES adopted maximum distance separable (MDS) matrices for MixColumns as these matrices have the optimal diffusion property. The key-addition operation introduces secret key material into the internal state of a cipher during computation, and often accompanied with round constant addition which breaks any structural symmetry to avoid attacks like slide attacks [7] and invariant subspace attacks [18]. Extreme lightweight primitive designs like SKINNY [5] and GIFT [3] add key materials to only half of the internal state each round (like Feistel network) to save on the hardware implementation cost.

One of the ISO/IEC 29192-2:2019 lightweight block cipher standards PRESENT [8] followed the SPN, however, in order to reduce the hardware cost it completely removed diffusion matrix. Essentially one round of PRESENT comprises of the S-box layer, a bit permutation and key-addition operation. Such construction is given a more specific name—Substitution-bitPermutation Network (SbPN) [3]. As the bit permutation does not cost anything in hardware (simple wiring), the only cost is the S-box implementation and some XOR gates for the key-addition. The novelty of PRESENT is that it uses 4-bit S-boxes with differential branch number 3, and the output of S-boxes is optimally diffused by a bit permutation. The bit permutation plays a crucial role: despite the absence of diffusion matrices, together with the S-box it ensures strong cryptographic properties. Later GIFT [3] took the design of PRESENT to the next level – strengthens the resistance against linear cryptanalysis, which is the PRESENT Achilles heel, and further reduced the hardware implementation cost. It proposes a new paradigm called *Bad Output must go to Good Input* (BOGI) which allows designers to select S-box lighter than that of PRESENT, and accordingly chooses a bit permutation to maintain strong security. To further reduce the hardware cost, GIFT made an aggressive yet careful move to add key materials to only half of the internal state in each round. Without careful analysis, this is a risky move as a wrong combination with other cipher components could lead to unexpected and undesirable properties.

Over the last decade lightweight cryptography has been enriched with interesting designs and primitive constructions, that it has also drawn the attention of US National Institute of Standards and Technology (NIST). NIST is in the process of standardising lightweight cryptography [22]. To this call NIST has received several authenticated encryption based on GIFT, for example GIFT-COFB [2], HyENA [10], Simple [15] and SUNDAE-GIFT [1]. Moreover, there are also multiple submissions whose designs are inspired by GIFT, in particular a submission called TRIFLE [13] whose underlying block cipher TRIFLE-BC is inspired by GIFT.

A Study on TRIFLE-BC and Motivation of this Paper. TRIFLE-BC constructed its S-box using cellular automata (CA) rules, and combined a PRESENT-like bit permutation with GIFT-128 key-addition. The intention was to maintain low hardware cost while achieving low side-channel protection cost as well.

The first observation on TRIFLE were reported by one of the authors of this paper on April 25, 2019 [23], which was the origin of this research. On June 19, 2019, Liu and Isobe submitted their article on ePrint [19] (later published by SAC 2019 [20]) which included the 44-round key recovery on TRIFLE-BC and 11-round key recovery on TRIFLE (AEAD) by differential cryptanalysis. Soon after we reported our extended analysis to the mailing list on June 26, 2019 [26], which was independently done from [19]. On July 6, 2019, Flórez Gutiérrez reported the 50-round (full-round) key recovery on TRIFLE-BC by linear cryptanalysis [17].

On August 30, 2019, NIST announced the second round candidates and TRIFLE was not selected. On October 7, 2019, NIST released the reasons [27]. ([37], [39] and [16] in NIST's report correspond to [20,23,26] in this paper.)

> *Several observations have been made that highlight undesirable properties in the block cipher TRIFLE-BC. NIST believes that these properties are cause for concern. In particular, the combination of S-box fixed points [37], subspace transitions, ability to decrypt a quarter of the state over two rounds without knowledge of the key, and long single active bit trails [39] could be combined to mount attacks. An iterative differential characteristic on reduced-round TRIFLE-BC that leveraged these properties was independently described by Liu and Isobe [16].*

We believe that a series of our reports was a main reason for NIST not to select TRIFLE for the second round. Note that the full-round linear cryptanalysis [17] was not mentioned by NIST.

Although new cipher design proposals often include their design rationale, the experiences in fail design attempts or consequences of violating certain design criteria are often omitted. This could lead to misunderstanding of the design philosophy and designing ciphers with undesirable properties. While the design principle of SPN is well-understood thanks to the popularisation of Rijndael (AES), SbPN has not gotten much attention.

In this paper, we revisit the design principle of PRESENT and GIFT. As evident from the design rationale of GIFT and PRESENT that in SbPN, the S-box and bit permutation are closely intertwined. Therefore, one has to be careful while adopting SbPN for cipher design, and should choose the components of SbPN appropriately. For instance, some crucial aspects of SbPN have been overlooked by TRIFLE-BC which render weaknesses into the cipher. In this paper we give a critical view on this, and come up with a general guideline for designing such ciphers.

Main Contributions. We revisited the design philosophy of PRESENT and GIFT, looking at the interplay among the S-box, bit permutation and key-addition operations. (1) We enhanced the BOGI paradigm of GIFT, introducing what we called the BOGI+ criteria to improve the theoretical differential/linear bounds of primitives that adopt BOGI paradigm. (2) Using the BOGI+ criteria, we reaffirmed the computer-aided bounds of GIFT with our pen-and-paper analysis. (3) We presented the essence of the SbPN design strategies and lastly (4) highlighted the weaknesses of TRIFLE-BC that this a direct consequence of SbPN design oversight.

Outline of the Paper. First, we give a quick recap of SbPN components in Sect. 2. Next, we analyse the interaction between these components in Sect. 3. We summarise the potential pitfalls when selecting the components in Sect. 4. Finally, we present a case study on TRIFLE-BC in Sect. 4.1 and conclude in Sect. 5.

2   SbPN Components

Definition 1. *[3] Substitution-bit Permutation network (SbPN) is a subclassification of Substitution-Permutation network, where the permutation layer only comprises of bit permutation. An m/n-SbPN cipher is an n-bit cipher in which substitution layer comprises of m-bit (Super-)S-boxes.*

In this work, we focus on bit permutation based ciphers that use 4-bit S-boxes, or $4/n$-SbPN ciphers. For brevity, we use SbPN instead for the rest of this paper.

A round function of an SbPN cipher typically consists of 3 core operations:

SubNibbles. An S-box layer that applies 4-bit S-boxes to all nibbles of the state.

PermBits. A bit permutation layer that bit-wise permutes the state.

AddKey. Key-addition that XORs the round keys (subkeys) to the state.

Depending on the design, the constant-addition operation may either XOR the round constants directly to the internal state or to the key state as part of the key schedule. For most of our discussion, the constant-addition and key schedule are irrelevant, thus we only bring them up only when necessary.

For the rest of this section, we recap some properties of S-boxes (used in SubNibbles), characteristics of bit permutation (used in PermBits) and types of key-addition (used in AddKey).

2.1   Properties of S-Boxes

Let $\mathbb{F}_2^m$ be the vector space formed by the 2^m binary m-tuples. An S-box is a mapping $\mathcal{S} : \mathbb{F}_2^m \to \mathbb{F}_2^m$. We call $\mathcal{S}$ as an $m \times m$ S-box (or simply m-bit S-box). In general S-boxes are chosen to be bijective, however, non-bijective S-box has also been used, e.g., in [14].

Differential and linear cryptanalysis are the basic attacks that the designer needs to take care of. In order to resist the differential cryptanalysis, the S-box should have low *differential uniformity* (DU). Let

$$\mathcal{D}_S(\delta, \Delta) = \{\#x : S(x) \oplus S(x \oplus \delta) = \Delta\}.$$

Then DU of $\mathcal{S}$ is defined as

$$DU(\mathcal{S}) = \max_{\delta \neq 0, \Delta \neq 0} \mathcal{D}_S(\delta, \Delta).$$

If $DU(\mathcal{S}) = k$, then $\mathcal{S}$ is called k-differential uniform. $DU(\mathcal{S})$ values are always even, and 2 is the lowest possible. S-boxes that are 2-differential uniform are called *almost perfect non-linear* (APN). So far APN permutations are only known to exist over $\mathbb{F}_2^m$ when m is odd, and for $m = 6$ when m is even [9]. The differential distribution table (DDT) is the collection of all $\mathcal{D}_S(\delta, \Delta)$ values.

On the other hand in linear cryptanalysis, the attacker exploits the probabilistic linear relations, also called *linear approximations*, between the input plaintext, key, and the ciphertext. Basically the attacker looks for relations

$$\bigoplus_0^{m-1} a_i x_i = \bigoplus_0^{m-1} b_i y_i,$$

that happen with high probability, where $(x_0, \ldots, x_{m-1})$ and $(y_0, \ldots, y_{m-1})$ are the input and output of an S-box respectively, and $(a_0, \ldots, a_{m-1}) \in \mathbb{F}_2^m$ and $(b_0, \ldots, b_{m-1}) \in \mathbb{F}_2^m$ are called input and output mask respectively. The maximum probability for all the non-zero input and output mask pairs is called the *linear probability* of $\mathcal{S}$ denoted as $\mathcal{L}_\mathcal{S}$. For all possible input and output mask pairs the probabilistic bias of the relations is recorded in the *Linear Approximation Table* (LAT).

Definition 2 (4-bit Optimal S-box). *A 4-bit S-box is optimal if both the maximum differential and linear probabilities are 2^{-2}.*

It is important to know the number of *active* S-boxes after a certain number of rounds. For instance, if c is the number of differentially active S-boxes in r rounds, and $DU(\mathcal{S}) = k$, then the complexity of the differential cryptanalysis is at least $(\frac{k}{2^m})^c$. On the other hand if ℓ is the number of linearly active S-boxes and $\mathcal{L}_\mathcal{S} = p$, then the complexity of the linear cryptanalysis is at least p^ℓ.

Additionally, there are two important security notions called *branch numbers*.

Definition 3 (Differential Branch Number). *For an m-bit S-box $\mathcal{S}$, its differential branch number denoted as $DBN(\mathcal{S})$ is defined as*

$$DBN(\mathcal{S}) = \min_{x,y \in \mathbb{F}_2^m, \, x \neq y} \{wt(x \oplus y) + wt(\mathcal{S}(x) \oplus \mathcal{S}(y))\}.$$

In [24], it was proved that $DBN(\mathcal{S}) \leq \lceil \frac{2m}{3} \rceil$. For 4-bit S-boxes, the bound is 3 and it is tight. For example, PRESENT uses a 4-bit S-box with $DBN(\mathcal{S}) = 3$.

Next we define linear branch number for which we first define *correlation coefficient*. For any $\alpha, \beta \in \mathbb{F}_2^m$ the correlation coefficient of $\mathcal{S}$ with respect to (α, β) is given by

$$\mathcal{C}_\mathcal{S}(\alpha, \beta) = \sum_{x \in \mathbb{F}_2^m} (-1)^{\beta \cdot \mathcal{S}(x) + \alpha \cdot x}.$$

Definition 4 (Linear Branch Number). *For an m-bit S-box $\mathcal{S}$, its linear branch number denoted as $LBN(\mathcal{S})$ is defined as*

$$LBN(\mathcal{S}) = \min_{\alpha,\beta\in\mathbb{F}_2^m\setminus\{0\},\,\mathcal{C}_\mathcal{S}(\alpha,\beta)\neq0}\{wt(\alpha) + wt(\beta)\}.$$

In [24], it was also proved that $LBN(\mathcal{S}) \leq m - 1$. In case of 4, the maximum possible LBN is 3. As a bit permutation based block cipher lacks the diffusion layer like MixColumns of AES, one way to increase the number of active S-boxes is to use S-boxes with higher branch numbers.

XOR-Permutation Equivalence. Let $\mathcal{P}$ and $\mathcal{Q}$ be two bit permutations of $\mathbb{F}_2^m$ and $c_i, c_o \in \mathbb{F}_2^m$ are some constants. Then two m-bit S-boxes $\mathcal{S}$ and $\mathcal{S}'$ are said to be XOR-permutation equivalent if the following holds for all $x \in \mathbb{F}_2^m$,

$$\mathcal{S}'(x) = (\mathcal{Q} \circ \mathcal{S} \circ \mathcal{P})(x \oplus c_i) \oplus c_o.$$

Note that any bit permutation of $\mathbb{F}_2^m$ is actually an $m \times m$ permutation matrix.

Several properties remain invariant in the equivalent class. For example, differential uniformity, linear probability, differential branch number and linear branch number are the same for two XOR-permutation equivalent S-boxes.

Hamming Weight 1 Transitions. For any Hamming weight 1 input difference δ that has no transition to Hamming weight 1 output difference Δ, we call it *good input* or otherwise *bad input*. Conversely, any Hamming weight 1 output difference Δ that has no transition from Hamming weight 1 input difference δ, we call it *good output* or otherwise *bad output*. The same analogue applies to the linear masking of an S-box.

Definition 5 (Score of an S-Box). *[3] The row score and column score of an S-box is the number of good input and good output respectively. The score of an S-box is the sum of the row and column score.*

BOGI Paradigm. Given an S-box, one can determine the *score of the S-box*. If the score is at least 4, it is possible to construct a bit permutation that, together with the S-box, guarantees certain security bounds. Refer to [3] for more details.

Remark: One might find that the score metric is similar to the $CarD1_S$ and $CarL1_S$ metric described in [29]. $Car*1_S$ counts the number of times a Hamming weight 1 input causes an Hamming weight 1 output, but it does not capture the position of these transitions. The score metric is a more refined description of the Hamming weight 1 transitions, allowing one to design SbPN cipher with minimally guaranteed security. Consider an S-box S_A with the following differential transitions $1 \rightarrow 2$, $2 \rightarrow 4$, $4 \rightarrow 8$, $8 \rightarrow 1$, and another S-box S_B with $1 \rightarrow 1$, $1 \rightarrow 2$, $2 \rightarrow 1$, $2 \rightarrow 2$. Under the $Car * 1_S$ metric, both S_A and S_B have $CarD1_S = 4$ and are indifferent unless verified with computer-aided tool. Under the score metric, S_A with score 0 is obviously not suitable for SbPN ciphers, while S_B has score 4 and can be used with BOGI paradigm to achieve a minimally guaranteed security bound.

Affine Subspace Transition. Let $a \oplus V$ be a (affine) subspace, where $V \subseteq \mathbb{F}_2^m$ and $a \in \mathbb{F}_2^m$, it is a linear subspace if $a \in V$. If there exists $b \oplus V'$ such that

$$\forall x \in a \oplus V, \quad S(x) \in b \oplus V',$$

then $a \oplus V \to b \oplus V'$ is a (affine) subspace transition through the S-box S.

2.2 Characteristics of Bit Permutation

Apart from "Our observation", this section is an abstract from the design rationale of GIFT [3]. We recommend reading Sect. 3.2 of [3] for a better understanding. For concise, we denote bit-position $4i + x$ as bit x, where $0 \leq i \leq n/4$.

PRESENT Bit Permutation. To analyse the PRESENT bit permutation, the designers partition the 16 S-boxes into 4 groups, namely $\{S_0, S_1, S_2, S_3\}$, $\{S_4, S_5, S_6, S_7\}$, $\{S_8, S_9, S_{10}, S_{11}\}$ and $\{S_{12}, S_{13}, S_{14}, S_{15}\}$, and presented the following four properties [8]: (**1**) The input bits to an S-box come from 4 distinct S-boxes of the same group. (**2**) The input bits to a group of four S-boxes come from 16 different S-boxes. (**3**) The four output bits from a particular S-box enter four distinct S-boxes, each of which belongs to a distinct group of S-boxes in the subsequent round. (**4**) The output bits of S-boxes in distinct groups go to distinct S-boxes.

GIFT Bit Permutation. The designers revisited the analysis on the bit permutation and presented an elegant way to decompose the bit permutation, providing better insights and proposed framework to construct any bit permutation that is a multiple of 16 (and at least 64-bit) [3]. The bit permutation is partitioned into several identical 16-bit permutations, so called the *group mapping*. Each group mapping maps 16-bit output bits of 4 S-boxes to input bits of another 4 S-boxes. The grouping of the S-boxes is denoted as *S-box mapping*.

GIFT *S-Box Mapping:* The S-boxes S_i are partitioned in two ways—Quotient group $Qx = \{S_{4x}, S_{4x+1}, S_{4x+2}, S_{4x+3}\}$ and Remainder group $Rx = \{S_x, S_{q+x}, S_{2q+x}, S_{3q+x}\}$ where $q = n/16$ and $0 \leq x \leq q - 1$. S-box mapping maps Qx to Rx, where the specific bit permutation is defined by the group mapping.

Projecting the S-box mapping description on PRESENT bit permutation, the PRESENT S-box mapping coincide with the S-box mapping for $n = 64$.

Group Mapping: The mapping of the output bits from a Quotient group to the input of a Remainder group in the next round. The output bits from an S-box in the Quotient group goes to 4 distinct S-boxes in the Remainder group.

For GIFT, its group mapping is described in Table 1 and Fig. 1.

$\pi(\cdot)$ is a bijective permutation on $\{0, 1, 2, 3\}$ that is determined by the properties of the DDT (resp. LAT) of the S-box. The only requirement for the permutation is that it must map bad output to good input, hence the name BOGI. Conversely, one may choose an XOR-permutation equivalent S-box that works

Table 1. $\mathcal{G}$-group mapping

		Rx^{r+1}			
		$\mathcal{S}^{r+1}_x$	$\mathcal{S}^{r+1}_{q+x}$	$\mathcal{S}^{r+1}_{2q+x}$	$\mathcal{S}^{r+1}_{3q+x}$
Qx^r	$\mathcal{S}^r_{4x}$	$(0,\pi(0))$	$(1,\pi(1))$	$(2,\pi(2))$	$(3,\pi(3))$
	$\mathcal{S}^r_{4x+1}$	$(1,\pi(1))$	$(2,\pi(2))$	$(3,\pi(3))$	$(0,\pi(0))$
	$\mathcal{S}^r_{4x+2}$	$(2,\pi(2))$	$(3,\pi(3))$	$(0,\pi(0))$	$(1,\pi(1))$
	$\mathcal{S}^r_{4x+3}$	$(3,\pi(3))$	$(0,\pi(0))$	$(1,\pi(1))$	$(2,\pi(2))$

where (l,m) denotes the output bit l of the S-box in the corresponding row will map to the input bit m of the S-box in the corresponding column in the next round.

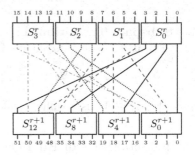

Fig. 1. $\mathcal{G}$-group mapping of GIFT-64

Table 2. $\mathcal{P}$-group mapping

		Rx^{r+1}			
		$\mathcal{S}^{r+1}_x$	$\mathcal{S}^{r+1}_{q+x}$	$\mathcal{S}^{r+1}_{2q+x}$	$\mathcal{S}^{r+1}_{3q+x}$
Qx^r	$\mathcal{S}^r_{4x}$	$(0,0)$	$(1,0)$	$(2,0)$	$(3,0)$
	$\mathcal{S}^r_{4x+1}$	$(0,1)$	$(1,1)$	$(2,1)$	$(3,1)$
	$\mathcal{S}^r_{4x+2}$	$(0,2)$	$(1,2)$	$(2,2)$	$(3,2)$
	$\mathcal{S}^r_{4x+3}$	$(0,3)$	$(1,3)$	$(2,3)$	$(3,3)$

where (l,m) denotes the output bit l of the S-box in the corresponding row will map to the input bit m of the S-box in the corresponding column in the next round.

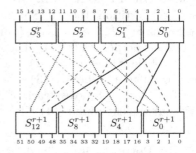

Fig. 2. $\mathcal{P}$-group mapping of PRESENT

with identity permutation $\pi(i) = i$ as in GIFT. For simplicity, we assume π to be identity and denote such group mapping as $\mathcal{G}$-group mapping.

PRESENT bit permutation could also be described in a similar manner (Table 2 and Fig. 2).

We denote PRESENT-like group mappings as $\mathcal{P}$-group mappings. The main difference between $\mathcal{P}$-group and $\mathcal{G}$-group mapping is that the latter always maps bit i to bit $\pi(i)$, while the former has 16 distinct bit position mapping (i,j).

Optimal Bit Permutation. A *full diffusion* is where any single bit flip has an influence over the entire internal state. For an $4/n$-SbPN cipher, suppose a single input bit is flipped, the maximum number of affected bits after r round is 4^r. Thus, a bit permutation is *optimal* if full diffusion (starting from any bit) is achieved in $\lceil \log_4(n) \rceil$ rounds.

Our Observation. The aforementioned 4 properties of PRESENT bit permutation is not sufficient to ensure full diffusion for an 128-bit bit permutation. One could duplicate and concatenate 2 copies of PRESENT bit permutation without interaction, this will satisfy the 4 properties but will never achieve full diffusion because there is no mixing between the two halves of the internal state. The reason that it doesn't work is simple—there is no clear definition on how the S-boxes are grouped.

On the other hand, the GIFT S-box mapping has been shown to be optimal permutation for both 64-bit and 128-bit [3]. *We conjecture that GIFT S-box mapping provides an optimal permutation for any arbitrary block size that is multiple of 16. In addition, we proposed using GIFT S-box mapping as the framework to build 4/n-SbPN ciphers*, especially for 64-bit and 128-bit, and not just satisfying the 4 properties of PRESENT bit permutation.

2.3 Types of Key-Addition

In conventional designs, key materials are added to the entire internal state. In recent lightweight designs, like SKINNY [5] and GIFT [3], the key materials are only added to half of its internal state (so-called partial key-addition). One obvious benefit is to reduce hardware footprint. While one of the drawbacks is having a weaker related-key differential bounds for lower number of rounds.

Related-Key Differential Bounds. In a nutshell, related-key differential cryptanalysis is an attack model where differences can be introduced in the master key. Naturally, if it takes r rounds for the all key materials of the master key to be added to the internal state, the highest related-key differential probability for the first $r-1$ rounds is 1. Since partial key-addition takes more rounds to introduce all the key materials into the internal state, it directly increases r.

Invariant Subspace Analysis. This is a weak key attack, introduced by [18], that exploits subspaces which are preserved through arbitrary number of rounds. A "simple" way to break any subspace structures is through the addition of round constants, as discussed in [4]. However, as seen in [16,26], round constants may not work if the designers are not careful, hence the scare quote for simple. To reduce the dependency of the round constant to prevent invariant subspace attacks, we are interested to analyse the properties of the S-box and key-addition against these attacks. Counter-intuitively, when designing SbPN ciphers, having partial key-addition could actually help finding suitable S-box candidates easier. This is because we can relax some of the conditions necessary for S-boxes to be resistant against invariant subspace attack. Details will be explained in Sect. 3.2.

3   Interaction Between Components

In this section, we discuss the pair combination of the 3 main components of SbPN.

3.1   S-Box and Bit Permutation

One of the most important analysis to be performed for new cipher design is resistance against differential and linear cryptanalysis. A common approach is to use some computer-aided tool to find out the upper bound for the differential probability or linear bias of the SbPN structure. The designers of RECTANGLE [28] (4/64-SbPN cipher) adopted this approach and provided experimental evidence. However, due to the bit-oriented nature of the SbPN structure, analysing larger state size (say 128-bit) and large number of rounds is computationally infeasible.

Another approach is to provide theoretical proof that the combination of a particular S-box and a bit permutation guarantees some upper bound. Such theoretical arguments also serve as a guideline to design primitives with strong cryptographic properties. The designers of PRESENT [8] are one of the first to propose a theoretical argument for 4/64-SbPN. Combining DBN 3 S-boxes with a 64-bit optimal bit permutation, they proved that any 5 consecutive rounds of PRESENT have at least 10 differentially active S-boxes (denoted as 10-AS/5-round).

A third approach is a hybrid method. First, select components satisfying certain cryptographic criteria to guarantee some theoretical upper bound, and then perform the computer-aided analysis to obtain more accurate results. This approach requires much lower computational effort than the first approach and obtain more accurate bounds (usually better bounds) than using the second approach alone. The designers of GIFT [3] first introduced the BOGI paradigm that, with the correct combination of S-box and bit permutation, guarantees at least 7-AS/5-round; and used computer-aided search to show that GIFT achieves at least 18-AS/9-round, the same number of active S-boxes ratio as PRESENT.

Theorem 1. *(BOGI paradigm) If an SbPN construction satisfies all the differential (resp. linear) BOGI criteria, the longest consecutive single active S-box differential (resp. linear) trail is 3. And the $4/n$-SbPN structure has at least 7-AS/5-round, where $n \geq 64$ is multiple of 16.*

Proof. BOGI criteria ensures that there is no consecutive single bit transition (having single active bit input and output), thus the longest consecutive single active S-box trail is 3, only the middle S-box can have single bit transition (1–1–1). Beyond that, there are at least 2 active bits at input of the preceding S-box and output of the succeeding S-box which leads to at least 7 active S-boxes (2–1–1–1–2). For $n \geq 64$, the active bits different S-boxes of the same round will not go to the same S-box because of the Quotient and Remainder grouping. Thus, there are at least 7-AS/5-round (1–1–1–2–2 or 2–2–1–1–1). □

Although S-boxes with DBN = 3 provide strong cryptographic properties (10-AS/5-round) for SbPN structure, it is known that there is no 4-bit optimal S-boxes simultaneously having DBN = 3 and LBN = 3. BOGI paradigm did a trade-off to have good cryptographic properties on both the differential and linear cases simultaneously at a cost of a weaker theoretical bound (7-AS/5-round).

For the rest of this section, we first analyse the various possible differential or linear characteristics, followed by proposing new criteria to improve the theoretic bounds of BOGI paradigm (we called it BOGI+ criteria). Lastly, we apply our results to improve the theoretic bound for GIFT.

Differential/Linear Characteristics with Single Active S-Box. To simplify the discussion, we assume that some $\mathcal{G}$-group mapping with identity π, and all the S-box mappings use this same group mapping.

For any r-round differential/linear characteristic, suppose that there is some round with 1 active S-box. By Theorem 1, the trail will eventually split and have multiple active S-boxes in some round. For the average number of active S-boxes to maintain below the ratio of 2, one of the two patterns must occur:

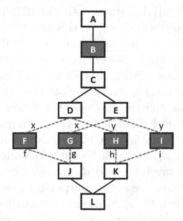
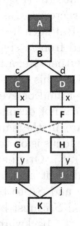

Fig. 3. Net pattern. Each box represents an S-box and red boxes are S-boxes with Hamming weight 1 transition. The solid black lines are the active bits trail and dashed red lines form the special pattern. (Color figure online)

Fig. 4. Cross pattern. Each box represents an S-box and red boxes are S-boxes with Hamming weight 1 transition. The solid black lines are the active bits trail and dashed red lines form the special pattern. (Color figure online)

For the net pattern (Fig. 3), although it propagates to more than 2 active S-boxes at some round, if it manages to converge back to 2 active S-boxes, it can achieve 11-AS/6-round. If it can further converge to 1 single active S-box, then it could lead to an iterative 6-round structure. Thus, the focus is to analyse the conditions for the four Hamming weight 1 transitions to occur between the net pattern. Notice that the 2 active S-boxes, $\mathcal{S}_D$ and $\mathcal{S}_E$, belonged to the same remainder group as they originated from a same S-box $\mathcal{S}_C$. Thus, they are in different quotient groups but in the same position (same row of the group mapping). For them to propagate to 4 S-boxes that belong to only 2 quotient groups, hence allowing converging to occur, $\mathcal{S}_F$ and $\mathcal{S}_G$ must have the active input bit at the same bit position, say bit x. Similarly for $\mathcal{S}_H$ and $\mathcal{S}_I$ at bit y. In addition, since the input bits to S_F and S_H came from a same S-box, we must have $x \neq y$. Finally, for output of S_F and S_G (resp. with the other S-box pair S_H and S_I) to go to the same S-box S_J (resp. S_K), the active output bit positions, say bit f and g, must be different, i.e. $f \neq g$ and $h \neq i$. In summary, such net pattern needs 4 distinct Hamming weight 1 transitions:

$$x \mapsto f, \ x \mapsto g, \ y \mapsto h, \ y \mapsto i.$$

That said, we have the following lemma.

Lemma 1. *Assume an SbPN construction satisfies all the BOGI criteria, any S-box that allows a net pattern has 4 distinct Hamming weight 1 transitions; and both its row and column score at most 2.*

A cross pattern (Fig. 4) could potentially be iterative, resulting in 2-AS/round characteristic, as observed in the differential characteristic of PRESENT and GIFT-64. But such iterative pattern is acceptable as long as this pattern is not propagated from a single active S-box, and does not converge to a single active S-box. Otherwise, a trail can start or end with 3 consecutive single active S-boxes and with this cross pattern as the main body. Such characteristics have $(2r - 3)$-AS/r-round or even $11r$-AS/$7r$-round iterative pattern. Note that the cross pattern cannot occur immediately after the splitting because the S-boxes S_C and S_D are in the same remainder group and different quotient groups. Therefore, the focus is on the conditions for the Hamming weight 1 transition at S_C, S_D and S_I, S_J. Originated from S_B, S_C and S_D are in the same remainder group with different active input bit positions, say bit c and d, and we know $c \neq d$. For S_E and S_F to be in the quotient group, the active output bit positions of S_C and S_D must be the same bit position, bit x. Similar argument for S_I and S_J in the backward direction, i.e. $i \neq j$. In short, for a cross pattern to begin with a single active S-box requires the following 2 Hamming weight 1 transitions:

$$c \mapsto x, \ d \mapsto x.$$

For a cross pattern to converge to a single active S-box, it requires a different pair of Hamming weight 1 transitions:

$$y \mapsto i, \ y \mapsto j.$$

Lemma 2. *Assume an SbPN construction satisfies all the BOGI criteria, any S-box that allows a single active S-box to propagate to a cross pattern has a row score of at most 2; any S-box that has a cross pattern converging to a single active S-box has a column score of at most 2.*

There could be other patterns that eventually converge back to a single S-box, but those patterns will result in a trail with more than 2-AS/round or require an S-box with even lower scores. Suppose the initial split lead to 3 or 4 active S-boxes, with 3 consecutive single active S-boxes, the trail has 3-AS/3-round.

Upon propagating to 3 (resp. 4) active S-boxes, the trail now has 6-AS/4-round (resp. 7-AS/4-round) active S-boxes. Since all 3 (resp. 4) active S-boxes are in different quotient groups, any further propagation to more active S-boxes will result in a trail with more than an average of 2 active S-boxes per round. For all the active S-boxes to have Hamming weight 1 transitions, it would require either the row or column score to be lower than 2.

New Criteria for Guaranteed Good Bounds (BOGI+ Criteria). Here, we introduce new criteria that guarantee higher theoretical bound. As they are built upon BOGI paradigm, we call them the BOGI+ criteria.

Theorem 2. *(BOGI+ criteria) Assume an SbPN construction satisfies all the differential (resp. linear) BOGI criteria, if the differential (resp. linear) property of the S-box satisfies exactly one of the follow criteria:*

- *has a differential (resp. linear) row score of 3,*
- *has a differential (resp. linear) column score of 3,*

then a $4/n$-SbPN structure has at least $(2r-3)$-AS/r-round, where $r \geq 9$.

If both criteria are satisfied, then a $4/nSbPN$ construction has at least $2r$-AS/r-round, where $r \geq 9$.

Proof. For any r-round characteristic, if each round has at least 2 active S-boxes, then we have at least $2r$-AS/r-round and we are done. Otherwise, there exists some round with exactly 1 active S-box.

If both criteria are satisfied, both the net and cross patterns cannot occur, then the longest characteristic with 1 active S-box at some round and has an average below 2-AS/round is 8 round, an example is shown in Fig. 5. Thus for $r \geq 9$, we have at least $2r$-AS/r-round.

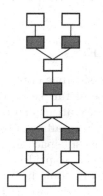

Fig. 5. 14 active S-boxes in a 8-round characteristic. Each box represents an S-box, 1-1 transition S-boxes are in red. (Color figure online)

If exactly one of the two criteria is satisfied, say the S-box has column score 3 but row score 2, by Lemma 1 the net pattern cannot occur. But there could be a characteristic starting with 3 consecutive single active S-boxes, followed by an iterative cross pattern (2-AS/round) without converging back to 1 active S-box (by Lemma 2). This results in an r-round characteristic with $(2r - 3)$ active S-boxes, where $r \geq 9$.

□

Improved Theoretical Bound for GIFT. Using the above results, we can improve the theoretical bound of GIFT. Table 3 and 4 shows the 1-1 bit DDT and 1-1 bit LAT of the GIFT S-box respectively.

Table 3. 1-1 bit DDT of GIFT S-box.

Δ_O

	1	2	4	8
1	0	0	0	2
2	0	0	0	0
Δ_I 4	0	0	0	0
8	0	0	0	0

Table 4. 1-1 bit LAT of GIFT S-box.

β

	1	2	4	8
1	0	0	2	4
2	0	0	0	2
α 4	0	0	0	0
8	0	0	0	0

For the differential case, from Table 3 we see that both the row and column have score 3. By Theorem 2, there are at least 18 differentially active S-boxes in 9 rounds. For the linear case, although the BOGI+ criteria are not satisfied, we know from Lemma 1 that the net pattern is not possible. By enumerating the possible cross patterns based on the LAT of GIFT S-box, we can see that the cross pattern is not possible either[2]. Thus, there are at least 18 linearly active S-boxes in 9 rounds.

3.2   S-Box and Add Round Keys

In [16], the authors studied the resistance criteria of an S-box against invariant subspace attacks [18] for the case of full key-addition. To achieve a high level resistance against invariant subspace attack, an S-box should have the following two conditions [16]: **(1)** There are no affine subspace transitions of dimension more than 2. **(2)** There are no affine subspace transitions of dimension 2 that can be connected (output subspace of one coincides with input subspace of another).

Interestingly, these two conditions could be relaxed when a cipher design uses partial key-addition. Similar to [16], we assume that any subspace is preserved over the linear layer (in our case, the bit permutation layer). First, we give an example before generalising our observation.

---

[2] Due to the page constraints, we omit the case-by-case analysis.

Example 1. Suppose the partial key-addition adds key bits to bit 1 and 2 of every nibble. Consider the following subspace transition of an S-box: $0 \oplus \{0, 2, 4, 6\} \rightarrow 1 \oplus \{0, 2, 4, 6\}$. After the SubNibbles, supposed that the PermBits preserves the affine subspace $1 \oplus \{0, 2, 4, 6\}$, if the AddKey XORs $x \in \{1, 3, 5, 7\}$ to each nibble, the subspace will return to $0 \oplus \{0, 2, 4, 6\}$ and we will have an invariant subspace. However, notice that $1 \oplus \{0, 2, 4, 6\}$ will not be sent back to $0 \oplus \{0, 2, 4, 6\}$ because bit 0 is not updated by the partial key-addition. Hence, this subspace transition posts no threat to the cipher.   △

In summary, we can check if the partial key-addition and/or constant-addition could link any subspace transition from the output back to the input of the S-box. If it doesn't, then this S-box candidate is still resistant against invariant subspace attack. That said, we introduce a third condition for S-boxes to have high resistance against invariant subspace attacks: **(3)** Exceptions can be made if none of the necessary values for connecting the affine subspaces can be attained by the key-addition or add-constant.

3.3   Bit Permutation and Add Round Keys

With the partial key-addition, designers need to take care of how the internal state is masked with the key materials. Without loss of generality, we assume the order of operations to be PermBits – AddKey – SubNibbles, this is because the XOR gates of AddKey can be moved across the bit wiring (PermBits) trivially.

One desirable property is that *none of the internal state bit values can be determined with probability 1 after SubNibbles.* Since S-boxes are applied to the internal state nibble-wise, each nibble should be masked by some key bit prior to the SubNibbles operation. In addition, taking into consideration of efficient software implementation, more specifically the bit-slice implementation, the key materials should be added to the same bit position of each nibble. For example, GIFT-128 adds the key materials to bit 1 and bit 2 of each nibble.

Although this approach works well for $\mathcal{G}$-group mappings, it doesn't work that well with $\mathcal{P}$-group mappings. From the $\mathcal{P}$-group mapping (see Table 2 and Fig. 2), we see that if bit i of each nibble in round $r + 1$ is masked with the some key bits, then only the output of S^r_{4x+i} is masked with those key bits.

This implies that for any partial key-addition that doesn't add key material to bit i, during the backward computation some nibble will have no obscurity and one can inverse the S-box to know the input values trivially.

The problem lies with the nature of $\mathcal{P}$-group mapping having distinct bit position mappings. Having irregular partial key-addition could resolve this issue but it could potentially make the cipher description confusing and software implementation less efficient. On the other hand, a $\mathcal{G}$-group mapping does not have this issue because masking bit i of each nibble implies masking bit $\pi^{-1}(i)$ of each nibble, no nibble will be left unmasked.

In summary, partial key-addition works fine with $\mathcal{G}$-group mapping but not as well with $\mathcal{P}$-group mapping.

4   Highlights on Security Aspects of SbPN Design

We have seen in the previous section that various components have different cause and effect when combined with other components. It creates a "chicken and egg" situation for the order of component selections. As different designers have different design rationale in mind, there is no standard procedure for designing an $4/n$-SbPN cipher that would suit everyone. Nevertheless, having strong cryptographic properties is a common goal for all cipher designers. That said, we summarise our results thus far and classify them according to the relevant cryptanalysis techniques.

Differential/Linear Cryptanalysis. Having an S-box with differential and linear branch number 3 is great for proving high security bounds when combined with either $\mathcal{P}$-group mapping or $\mathcal{G}$-group mapping. But if such option is unavailable, one should minimally select an S-box with score 4 and combine with $\mathcal{G}$-group mapping. If both differential and linear rely on the score 4 property, make sure that π can simultaneously satisfy both the differential and linear BOGI criteria. If that doesn't work, one should search for other S-box candidates.

If there is an abundant choice of S-boxes with score 4, selecting one with row and/or column score 3 will directly improve its theoretical bound. Otherwise, further analysis like computer-aided tool is necessary to get more accurate bounds.

Invariant Subspace Attack and Related-Key Differential. In the process of analysing the affine subspace transition through the S-box, one can consider the position of the key-addition and constant-addition to see if any affine subspaces can be preserved. This could potentially find S-box candidates that otherwise would been discarded by the first two conditions in Sect. 3.2.

A full key-addition tend to have better related-key differential bounds but also makes invariant subspace attack more probable. Nonetheless, with stronger key schedule and further analysis, invariant subspace attack could be mitigated.

Partial Encryption or Decryption. Although partial key-addition could save a substantial amount of hardware resources, one should avoid using $\mathcal{P}$-group mappings together with partial key-addition as it could result determining part of the internal state information without having to guess any key materials.

4.1   A Case Study on TRIFLE-BC

TRIFLE is one of the 56 first-round candidates for the NIST lightweight cryptography standardization process. Its underlying cipher TRIFLE-BC adopts SbPN. The block size and the key size of TRIFLE-BC are 128 bits. It computes 50 rounds in total, and each round consists of the following 3 operations that are of interest to us.

- **SubNibbles** applies the 4-bit S-box 0c9735e46ba2d18f to each nibble.
- **BitPermutation** moves bit-position i to $\lfloor i/4 \rfloor + (i\%4) \times 32$ for $i = 0, 1,\ldots,127$.
- During **AddRoundKey**, a 64-bit round key computed by a key schedule algorithm is XORed to bit 1 and 2 of the state.

A state is often denoted by a 4×32 matrix. The bit i in the vector form, where $0 \le i \le 127$, corresponds to the bit in the $(\lfloor i/4 \rfloor)$-th column from the left and ($i \bmod 4$)-th row from the top.

Long Single Active S-Box Trail. The DBN takes a crucial role to ensure the security of SbPN. However, as pointed out by the designers, DBN = 2 for the TRIFLE S-box, besides there are 4 differential propagation with DBN = 2; $8 \rightarrow 4$, $4 \rightarrow 2$, $2 \rightarrow 1$, and $1 \rightarrow 8$. Clearly, attackers can construct a differential characteristic only with those four transitions, which leads to an r-round differential characteristic only with r active S-boxes.

This property ensures only a weak security. The designers of TRIFLE realized this property, hence tried to mitigate the damage from this property by limiting the probability of each propagation to 2^{-3}. However as independently pointed out by Liu et al. [20], this still allows r-round differential characteristics with probability 2^{-3r+2}, where the factor 2^2 comes from the fact that the first round input and the last round output can have more than 1 active bits, thus the probability can be 2^{-2} for those 2 rounds.

Keyless Partial Decryption. The bad interaction between the partial key-addition and the bit permutation pointed out in Sect. 3.3 actually occurs in TRIFLE-BC.

TRIFLE-BC XORs key material to bit 1 and bit 2 of each nibble while adopting the $\mathcal{P}$-group mapping. While in the forward direction (encryption), 2 of the 4 input bits to every S-box is masked with some secret key material, it is not the case from the backward direction (decryption).

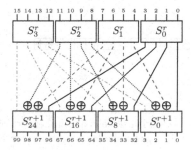

Fig. 6. TRIFLE-BC group mapping (Color figure online)

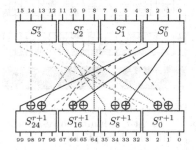

Fig. 7. GIFT-128 group mapping (Color figure online)

As one can see from Fig. 6, 2 of the 4 S-boxes (black and green) in the previous round of TRIFLE-BC is not masked by any key material. Such property does not exist in PRESENT because all bits are masked with some key material. Whereas for GIFT (Fig. 7), bit i is mapped to bit i, thus 2 of the 4 output bits to every S-box is masked with some key material.

Namely, the attacker can compute some inverse S-boxes in round r even without knowing any round key bits in round r as summarized below.

Let X_i^r denote bit i of the state just before SubNibbles at round r. Given 4 bit values in bit positions $\{X_i^{r+1}, X_{i+32}^{r+1}, X_{i+64}^{r+1}, X_{i+96}^{r+1}\}$, where $i \in \{0, 3, 4, 7, 8, 11, 12, 15, 16, 19, 20, 23, 24, 27, 28, 31\}$, the values of $\{X_{4i}^r, X_{4i+1}^r, X_{4i+2}^r, X_{4i+3}^r\}$ are fully determined independently of the key.

By using the above, part of the internal state bits of TRIFLE that can be recovered without subkey guesses during the 3-round decryption are depicted in Fig. 8.

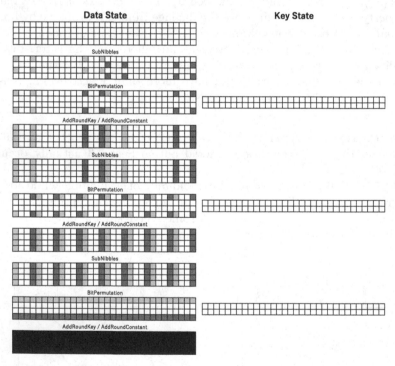

Fig. 8. Partially decrypted state bits without subkey guess. In the data state, row i corresponds to bit i, columns correspond to the S-boxes. Black cells are ciphertext bits and gray cells are decrypted bits without subkey. Different shades of gray is for the convenience to trace the bit permutation.

5   Conclusion

In this article we have provided an extensive insight of SbPN designs. We have introduced BOGI+ criteria which is further refinement of the BOGI criteria as given by GIFT, and with this new criteria we have been able to improve the theoretical bounds of active S-boxes in GIFT. Our analysis goes much deeper and explains the interplay between S-box, bit permutation and key addition and how to choose them for a secure SbPN design. We highly recommend designers to follow our guidelines while creating a new SbPN cipher, and avoid flaws that render weaknesses as observed in a recent SbPN cipher TRIFLE-BC.

Acknowledgements. The authors would like to thank Thomas Peyrin for the meaningful discussion on the study of TRIFLE-BC.

References

1. Banik, S., et al.: SUNDAE-GIFT, submission to NIST lightweight cryptography project (2019)
2. Banik, S., et al.: GIFT-COFB, submission to NIST lightweight cryptography project (2019)
3. Banik, S., Pandey, S.K., Peyrin, T., Sasaki, Y., Sim, S.M., Todo, Y.: GIFT: a small present. In: Fischer, W., Homma, N. (eds.) CHES 2017. LNCS, vol. 10529, pp. 321–345. Springer, Cham (2017). https://doi.org/10.1007/978-3-319-66787-4_16
4. Beierle, C., Canteaut, A., Leander, G., Rotella, Y.: Proving resistance against invariant attacks: how to choose the round constants. In: Katz, J., Shacham, H. (eds.) CRYPTO 2017. LNCS, vol. 10402, pp. 647–678. Springer, Cham (2017). https://doi.org/10.1007/978-3-319-63715-0_22
5. Beierle, C., et al.: The SKINNY family of block ciphers and its low-latency variant MANTIS. In: Robshaw, M., Katz, J. (eds.) CRYPTO 2016. LNCS, vol. 9815, pp. 123–153. Springer, Heidelberg (2016). https://doi.org/10.1007/978-3-662-53008-5_5
6. Biham, E., Shamir, A.: Differential cryptanalysis of the full 16-round DES. In: Brickell, E.F. (ed.) CRYPTO 1992. LNCS, vol. 740, pp. 487–496. Springer, Heidelberg (1993). https://doi.org/10.1007/3-540-48071-4_34
7. Biryukov, A., Wagner, D.: Slide attacks. In: Knudsen, L. (ed.) FSE 1999. LNCS, vol. 1636, pp. 245–259. Springer, Heidelberg (1999). https://doi.org/10.1007/3-540-48519-8_18
8. Bogdanov, A., et al.: PRESENT: an ultra-lightweight block cipher. In: Paillier, P., Verbauwhede, I. (eds.) CHES 2007. LNCS, vol. 4727, pp. 450–466. Springer, Heidelberg (2007). https://doi.org/10.1007/978-3-540-74735-2_31
9. Browning, K., Dillon, J., McQuistan, M., Wolfe, A.: An APN permutation in dimension six. Finite Fields Theory Appl. **518**, 33–42 (2010)
10. Chakraborti, A., Datta, N., Jha, A., Nandi, M.: HyENA, submission to NIST lightweight cryptography project (2019)
11. Daemen, J., Rijmen, V.: AES and the wide trail design strategy. In: Knudsen, L.R. (ed.) EUROCRYPT 2002. LNCS, vol. 2332, pp. 108–109. Springer, Heidelberg (2002). https://doi.org/10.1007/3-540-46035-7_7

12. Daemen, J., Rijmen, V.: The design of Rijndael: AES - the advanced encryption standard. Information Security and Cryptography. Springer, Heidelberg (2002). https://doi.org/10.1007/978-3-662-04722-4
13. Datta, N., Ghoshal, A., Mukhopadhyay, D., Patranabis, S., Picek, S., Sadhukhan, R.: TRIFLE, submission to NIST lightweight cryptography project (2019)
14. DES: Data encryption standard. In: In FIPS PUB 46, Federal Information Processing Standards Publication, pp. 46–52 (1977)
15. Gueron, S., Lindell, Y.: Simple, submission to NIST lightweight cryptography project (2019)
16. Guo, J., Jean, J., Nikolic, I., Qiao, K., Sasaki, Y., Sim, S.M.: Invariant subspace attack against Midori64 and the resistance criteria for S-box designs. IACR Trans. Symmetric Cryptol. **2016**(1), 33–56 (2016)
17. Gutiérrez, A.F.: Official comment: TRIFLE. Email to lwc-forum, July 6, 2019. https://csrc.nist.gov/CSRC/media/Projects/Lightweight-Cryptography/documents/round-1/official-comments/TRIFLE-official-comment.pdf
18. Leander, G., Abdelraheem, M.A., AlKhzaimi, H., Zenner, E.: A cryptanalysis of PRINTCIPHER: the invariant subspace attack. In: Rogaway, P. (ed.) CRYPTO 2011. LNCS, vol. 6841, pp. 206–221. Springer, Heidelberg (2011). https://doi.org/10.1007/978-3-642-22792-9_12
19. Liu, F., Isobe, T.: Iterative differential characteristic of TRIFLE-BC. Cryptology ePrint Archive, Report 2019/727 (2019). https://eprint.iacr.org/2019/727
20. Liu, F., Isobe, T.: Iterative differential characteristic of TRIFLE-BC. In: Paterson, K.G., Stebila, D. (eds.) SAC 2019. LNCS, vol. 11959, pp. 85–100. Springer, Cham (2020). https://doi.org/10.1007/978-3-030-38471-5_4
21. Matsui, M.: Linear cryptanalysis method for DES cipher. In: Helleseth, T. (ed.) EUROCRYPT 1993. LNCS, vol. 765, pp. 386–397. Springer, Heidelberg (1994). https://doi.org/10.1007/3-540-48285-7_33
22. NIST: round 1 of the NIST lightweight cryptography project (2019)
23. Sarkar, S.: Re: TRIFLE S-box has some structural weakness. Email to lwc-forum (2019). https://csrc.nist.gov/CSRC/media/Projects/Lightweight-Cryptography/documents/round-1/official-comments/TRIFLE-official-comment.pdf
24. Sarkar, S., Syed, H.: Bounds on differential and linear branch number of permutations. In: Susilo, W., Yang, G. (eds.) ACISP 2018. LNCS, vol. 10946, pp. 207–224. Springer, Cham (2018). https://doi.org/10.1007/978-3-319-93638-3_13
25. Shannon, C.E.: Communication theory of secrecy systems. Bell Syst. Tech. J. **28**, 656–715 (1949)
26. Sim, S.M.: Official comment: TRIFLE. Email to lwc-forum (2019). https://csrc.nist.gov/CSRC/media/Projects/Lightweight-Cryptography/documents/round-1/official-comments/TRIFLE-official-comment.pdf
27. Turan, M.S., McKay, K., Çalik, Ç., Chang, D., Bassham, L.: Status report on the first round of the NIST lightweight cryptography standardization process. NISTIR 8268 (2019). https://csrc.nist.gov/publications/detail/nistir/8268/final
28. Zhang, W.T., Bao, Z.Z., Lin, D.D., Rijmen, V., Yang, B.H., Verbauwhede, I.: RECTANGLE: a bit-slice lightweight block cipher suitable for multiple platforms. Sci. China Inf. Sci. **58**(12), 1–15 (2015). https://doi.org/10.1007/s11432-015-5459-7
29. Zhang, W., Bao, Z., Rijmen, V., Liu, M.: A new classification of 4-bit optimal S-boxes and its application to PRESENT, RECTANGLE and SPONGENT. In: Leander, G. (ed.) FSE 2015. LNCS, vol. 9054, pp. 494–515. Springer, Heidelberg (2015). https://doi.org/10.1007/978-3-662-48116-5_24

Equivalent Keys of a Nonlinear Filter Generator Using a Power Residue Symbol

Yuta Kodera[1]($^{(\boxtimes)}$) [iD], Yuki Taketa[1] [iD], Takuya Kusaka[1] [iD], Yasuyuki Nogami[1] [iD], and Satoshi Uehara[2] [iD]

[1] Okayama University, 3-1-1, Tsushima-naka, Kita, Okayama 7008530, Japan
{yuta.kodera,yuki_taketa}@s.okayama-u.ac.jp,
{kusaka-t,yasuyuki.nogami}@okayama-u.ac.jp
[2] The University of Kitakyushu, Kitakyushu-shi 808-0135, Japan
uehara@kitakyu-u.ac.jp

Abstract. The existence of equivalent keys for a secret key is an inseparable topic in cryptography. Especially for pseudorandom number generators for cryptographic applications, equivalent keys are not only a specific pair of keys that generate the same sequence but includes the one that gives simply the phase-shifted sequence. In this paper, the authors especially focus on a kind of nonlinear filter generator (NLFG) defined by using a power residue calculation over an odd characteristic. Generally speaking, an evaluation of NLFGs has conducted by the randomness of the sequence itself and the security of keys. Though the previous evaluations of the randomness of the target NLFG are studied and proven theoretically, the security aspects as a cryptosystem still have not discussed. Therefore, this paper would like to begin a new security evaluation by focusing on the existence of equivalent keys for the NLFG. As a result, the authors first show that sequences generated by the NLFG are classified into several types of sequences depending on the choice of a certain parameter. Owing to this, it is found that there exist equivalent keys concerning the parameter corresponding to the above. At the same time, we show that the equivalent keys are possible to eliminate by giving the restriction on the corresponding parameter adequately.

Keywords: Equivalent keys · Nonlinear filter generator · Multi-value NTU sequence

1 Introduction

Pseudorandom number generators (PRNGs), a kind of deterministic generator having the reproducibility for the parameters, are often taken on an inseparable role of cryptographic applications. Especially, stream ciphers [1,2] are the representative ciphering system that exploits random numbers. Since these symmetric ciphering systems require to use the same random numbers for encryption and decryption, they are basically designed based on the deterministic calculation.

© Springer Nature Switzerland AG 2020
K. Aoki and A. Kanaoka (Eds.): IWSEC 2020, LNCS 12231, pp. 23–36, 2020.
https://doi.org/10.1007/978-3-030-58208-1_2

It coincidently induces the risk of having a specific pair of distinct keys that generate the same ciphertext.

Such a pair of keys are called equivalent keys and for example, Küçük reported the existence of equivalent keys [3] to one of the candidates of the competition held in the eSTREAM project [4,5] in practice. In general, PRNGs are evaluated by focusing on several randomnesses such as low correlation with a large period, unpredictability, and uniformity. However, these properties are not always the ones that ensure the sequence is cryptographically adequate having the resistance against this kind of practical vulnerability. In this paper, the authors consider the existence of equivalent keys by targeting a PRNG defined by using a residue calculation based on a power residue symbol. This aims to step up the process of the evaluation by discussing a possible vulnerability.

As a widely adopted construction of a PRNG to resist an attack based on the linear analysis using the Berlekamp-Massey algorithm (BMA) [6], an approach that applies a nonlinear filter function for a linear feedback shift register (LFSR) has been known. Such a PRNG is called a nonlinear filter generator (NLFG) [7] and among them, the ones that apply a function to the respective output of an LFSR is said a geometric sequence. The PRNG dealt with this paper is a kind of geometric sequence whose filter function is defined by using the power residue symbol. More precisely, the authors focus on the Nogami-Tada-Uehara sequence [8,9] that is assembled by a maximum length sequence [10] and the power residue symbol over an odd characteristic field. It is referred to as NTU sequence in what follows. By reviewing the randomness properties [9,11,12], especially for the linear complexity (LC) in [11], the geometric sequence is thought to be potentially a candidate of cryptographic generators.

Therefore, to promote the evaluation for the practical uses, this paper aims to reveal whether there exist equivalent keys or not. As a result, the authors are firstly clarified that the NTU sequences can be classified into several types of sequences depending on the choice of a certain parameter. In addition, the parameter is found to be related to the existence of equivalent keys and in fact, such keys are induced by choosing non-zero constant to the corresponding parameter. In other words, this paper concludes that the NTU sequence is found not to involve equivalent keys by restricting the parameter to the zero. Thus, we recommend using in this manner to keep the security of the sequence without sacrificing the randomness properties. However, there still remains a lot of security evaluations such as inversion attack and those are future works.

2   Preliminaries

This section briefly reviews the notations and the basic finite field theory [13].

2.1   Notations

Let p be an odd prime defining a finite field of order p. The finite field defined under modulo p is the set $\{0, 1, 2, \ldots, p-1\}$ with additive and multiplicative operations and is denoted by $\mathbb{F}_p$ in this paper.

Let $\mathbb{F}_p$ be a prime field defined by p and let $\mathbb{F}_{p^m}$ be an m-dimensional vector space over $\mathbb{F}_p$. The vector space is referred to as an extension field of $\mathbb{F}_p$ having the extension degree m. To distinguish the respective element in $\mathbb{F}_p$ and $\mathbb{F}_{p^m}$, boldface is used to represent an extension field element in what follows.

Every extension field has a basis $\{\beta_i; \beta_i \in \mathbb{F}_{p^m}, 0 \le i < m\}$, and an element a in $\mathbb{F}_{p^m}$ is represented by the linear combination of the basis and a coefficient vector $\{c_i; c_i \in \mathbb{F}_p, 0 \le i < m\}$ as follows:

$$a = \sum_{i=0}^{m-1} c_i \beta_i = c_0 \beta_0 + c_1 \beta_1 + \ldots + c_{m-1} \beta_{m-1}.$$

The sequence consisting of digits, including bits, generated by a pseudorandom number generator is denoted by a capital letter. Let S be a sequence of digits having the period λ. The ith coefficient of the sequence is indicated by s_i, where $0 \le i < \lambda$.

2.2 Trace Function and Power Residue Symbol

For an element $a \in \mathbb{F}_{p^m}$, the *trace* of a, denoted by $\mathrm{Tr}_{\mathbb{F}_{p^m}|\mathbb{F}_p}(a)$, is defined as follows:

Definition 1. *Let a be an element in $\mathbb{F}_{p^m}$. The trace of a is defined to be the sum of conjugates of a as follows:*

$$\mathrm{Tr}_{\mathbb{F}_{p^m}|\mathbb{F}_p}(a) = \sum_{j=0}^{m-1} \phi_j(a) = \sum_{j=0}^{m-1} a^{p^j},$$

where $\phi_j(a)$ denotes the p^jth power of a.

The trace function holds the following notable properties that are used in this paper.

Lemma 1. ([13] Theorem 2.23)

1. *For all $a \in \mathbb{F}_{p^m}$, $\mathrm{Tr}_{\mathbb{F}_{p^m}|\mathbb{F}_p}(a) \in \mathbb{F}_p$,*
2. *For all $a, b \in \mathbb{F}_p$ and $x, y \in \mathbb{F}_{p^m}$, the trace of $(ax + by)$ satisfies*

$$\mathrm{Tr}_{\mathbb{F}_{p^m}|\mathbb{F}_p}(ax + by) = a\mathrm{Tr}_{\mathbb{F}_{p^m}|\mathbb{F}_p}(x) + b\mathrm{Tr}_{\mathbb{F}_{p^m}|\mathbb{F}_p}(y),$$

3. *$\mathrm{Tr}_{\mathbb{F}_{p^m}|\mathbb{F}_p}(a) = am$ for all $a \in \mathbb{F}_p$,*
4. *$\mathrm{Tr}_{\mathbb{F}_{p^m}|\mathbb{F}_p}(a^p) = \mathrm{Tr}_{\mathbb{F}_{p^m}|\mathbb{F}_p}(a)$ for all $a \in \mathbb{F}_{p^m}$,*

Let $\left(\frac{a}{p}\right)_2$ denote the Legendre symbol, a number-theoretic function defined to be equal to ± 1 depending on whether a is a quadratic residue (QR) or quadratic non-residue (QNR) over $\mathbb{F}_p$ as follows:

Definition 2. *For an element $a \in \mathbb{F}_p$, the Legendre symbol is defined by*

$$\left(\frac{a}{p}\right)_2 = a^{\frac{p-1}{2}} \pmod{p} = \begin{cases} 0 & \text{if } a = 0, \\ 1 & \text{if } a(\neq 0) \text{ is a QR in } \mathbb{F}_p, \\ -1 & \text{if } a(\neq 0) \text{ is a QNR in } \mathbb{F}_p. \end{cases} \tag{1}$$

As the natural generalization of quadratic residues and the Legendre symbol, the following power residue symbol can be defined for a positive integer k such that $k|(p-1)$.

Definition 3. *For an element $a \in \mathbb{F}_p$ and a positive integer k such that $k|(p-1)$, the power residue symbol is defined by*

$$\left(\frac{a}{p}\right)_k = a^{\frac{p-1}{k}} \pmod{p} = \begin{cases} 0 & \text{if } a = 0, \\ \epsilon_k^j & \text{otherwise,} \end{cases} \tag{2}$$

where ϵ_k is a primitive kth root of unity in $\mathbb{F}_p$.

An element $a \in \mathbb{F}_p$ is said to be kth power residue (kth PR) if $\left(\frac{a}{p}\right)_k = 1$ and kth power non-residue (kth PNR) otherwise.

2.3 p-ary Maximum Length Sequences

A maximum length sequence (m-sequence) [10] is a class of binary sequences having attractive properties with respect to the period, the statistical uniformity, and the correlation. An m-sequence is generated by a certain type of linear recurrence relation over a finite field, and the m-sequence derived by a linear recurrence relation over odd characteristic field is called a p-ary m-sequence in particular[1].

There is mathematical and practical approaches of having m-sequences, and in common, the necessary and sufficient condition is known that the generating polynomial has to be primitive[2] over $\mathbb{F}_p$.

Let $R = \{r_i; 0 \leq i < p^m - 1\}$ be an m-sequence. The mathematical interpretation concerning R is the sequence of the traces for the continuous powers of a primitive element in $\mathbb{F}_{p^m}$. More formally, R is defined by Eq. (3) for a primitive element $\theta \in \mathbb{F}_{p^m}$, which is a root of a primitive polynomial.

$$R = \left\{ r_i = \mathrm{Tr}_{\mathbb{F}_{p^m}|\mathbb{F}_p}\left(\theta^i\right); 0 \leq i < p^m - 1 \right\}. \tag{3}$$

Since θ is a root of a primitive polynomial $q(x) = x^m + \sum_{i=0}^{m-1} q_i x^i$ $(q_0 \neq 0)$, the following equality holds.

$$\theta^m + q_{m-1}\theta^{m-1} + \cdots + q_0 = 0. \tag{4}$$

---

[1] It is noted that the authors simply refer p-ary m-sequence by m-sequence except for distinguishing them intentionally.

[2] An irreducible polynomial $q(x)$ of degree $m(>0)$ over $\mathbb{F}_p$, satisfying $q|(x^t - 1)$ when t is the smallest positive integer and $t = p^m - 1$, is said to be primitive.

According to Lemma 1, the trace of $\boldsymbol{\theta}^m$ is found to be obtained by transforming Eq. (4) as follows:

$$\mathrm{Tr}_{\mathbb{F}_{p^m}|\mathbb{F}_p}\left(\boldsymbol{\theta}^m\right) = -\sum_{j=0}^{m-1} q_j \mathrm{Tr}_{\mathbb{F}_{p^m}|\mathbb{F}_p}\left(\boldsymbol{\theta}^j\right). \tag{5}$$

It defines the linear recurrence relation that makes us easy to implement an m-sequence and in practice, m-sequences are generated by using LFSRs. It is noted that the m-sequences generated by using Eq. (4) and Eq. (5) are the same sequence if the respective employed primitive element is the same. In this paper, the former representation is especially used for the simplicity of the discussion.

2.4   Nonlinear Filter Generators and Equivalent Keys

Binary sequences having high LC, which is a measure of unpredictability, are one of the essential requirements for cryptographic use and there are several traditional approaches to generate random numbers used as stream ciphers [1,2]. Among them, NLFGs are the one that efficiently yields a sequence of digits having high unpredictability.

The approach of NLFGs is simply applying a nonlinear function to the internal states of single LFSR. In other words, it is defined as a sequence S generated by applying a nonlinear function f to an m-sequence $R = \{r_i; 0 \le i < p^m - 1\}$ as follows:

$$S = \{s_i; s_i = f(r_i, r_{i-1}, \ldots, r_{i-m+1})\}.$$

It is noted that r_j denotes the state of the jth register of an LFSR of length m, where $i \le j \le i + m - 1$. Thus, it potentially enables us to analyze the randomness and the characteristics of the sequence by accounting the property of the nonlinear function.

In general, the traditional randomness property of PRNGs such as long periodicity, low correlation, uniformity, and unpredictability are essential requirements but it is not sufficient for stream ciphers. A reason is that these randomness property does not always guarantee the hardness of recovering the internal states or the key, which are known to be strong attacks against stream ciphers.

Equivalent keys of a stream cipher is a non-negligible pair of distinct keys that yields the same or simply phase shifted sequence. The reason why the authors focus on the equivalent keys is on the fact that the existence of an equivalent key enables an attacker to reduce the sampling space concerning seed values. In other words, there exists an efficient way to reproduce a given sequence faster than the exhaustive manner and a threat of attacks induced by the equivalent keys has to be paid attention if equivalent keys exist. In this sense, the authors purpose to reveal the existence of equivalent keys in the target NLFG and to find a way to avoid the vulnerability if the equivalent keys are existing. In this paper, the authors especially deal with the NLFG whose nonlinear function is defined by using the power residue symbol.

3 Existence of Equivalent Keys Against the NLFG

This section begins by reviewing the target NLFG and discusses the existence of equivalent keys via the classification of the NLFG.

3.1 Definition of the NLFG

The NLFG dealt throughout the paper is a multi-value (including binary) sequence proposed by Nogami, Tada, and Uehara (NTU) in [9]. The design is based on the construction of Chan and Games's theory in [14].

Throughout the research, they have shown the construction of a class of periodic binary sequences that are obtained from p-ary m-sequences and its complexity. More precisely, let $R = \{r_i\}$ be an p-ary m-sequence of period $p^m - 1$ and ρ a function $\rho : \mathbb{F}_p \rightarrow \mathbb{F}_2$, a binary sequence $S = \{s_i; s_i = \rho(r_i), 0 \leq i < p^m - 1\}$ can be constructed with the period at most $p^m - 1$. In addition, Chan and Games have proven that the LC of S, which is a measure of difficulty of predicting the next digits, is endowed by the multiple of $\frac{p^m - 1}{p - 1}$ if ρ satisfies $\rho(0) = 0$.

Based on this and the works [15–18] concerning the Legendre sequence and Sidelnikov sequence, NTU sequences employ the nonlinear function defined below by using the power residue symbol.

Definition 4. *For a positive integer k such that $k|(p-1)$, let ϵ_k be a primitive kth root of unity in $\mathbb{F}_p$. The nonlinear function $f_k(\cdot)$ is defined by*

$$f_k(x) = \begin{cases} 0 & \text{if } x = 0, \\ \log_{\epsilon_k}\left(\frac{x}{p}\right)_k & \text{otherwise,} \end{cases} \tag{6}$$

where $x \in \mathbb{F}_p$.

It is noted that since $\left(\frac{x}{p}\right)_k$ returns a scalar of the form $\epsilon_k^j \in \mathbb{F}_p$ for $0 \leq j < k$, the output of $f_k(x)$ is given by j when $x \neq 0$. In addition, the nonlinear function holds the property $f_k(ab) = f_k(a) + f_k(b)$ due to its logarithmic property.

Originally, though the NTU sequence was proposed in [8] as a binary sequence defined with using the nonlinear function $f_2(\cdot)$, it has been generalized by Nogami et al. in [9] so that the NTU generator can provide multi-values (including binary) sequence having high LC. The multi-value NTU sequence is defined as follows:

Definition 5. *Let $\mathbb{F}_p, \mathbb{F}_{p^m}, k$, and a be an odd characteristic field, mth extension field of $\mathbb{F}_p$, a positive integer such that $k|(p-1)$, and an element in $\mathbb{F}_p$, respectively. For a primitive element $\theta \in \mathbb{F}_{p^m}$ and the nonlinear function $f_k(\cdot)$, multi-value NTU sequence is defined to be an NLFG as follows:*

$$S = \left\{s_i; s_i = f_k\left(\text{Tr}_{\mathbb{F}_{p^m}|\mathbb{F}_p}\left(\theta^i\right) + a\right), 0 \leq i < p^m - 1\right\}. \tag{7}$$

For example, the four-values NTU sequences using the parameters $(p, m, k, a) = (13, 2, 4, 1)$ and the primitive polynomial $q(x) = x^2 + x + 1$ is given by

0, 0, 1, 2, 1, 2, 1, 0, 3, 1, 0, 1, 2, 0, 0, 0, 1, 1, 1, 0, 3, 0, 2, 3, 3, 1, 1, 0,

3, 3, 2, 3, 2, 0, 3, 0, 1, 3, 2, 2, 1, 3, 2, 2, 1, 3, 1, 3, 0, 0, 1, 0, 1, 1, 2, 2,

1, 1, 3, 0, 3, 2, 2, 0, 2, 2, 1, 3, 1, 1, 1, 1, 3, 2, 3, 1, 0, 0, 1, 0, 2, 3, 3, 1,

2, 2, 0, 0, 0, 1, 0, 0, 3, 0, 1, 0, 3, 2, 1, 1, 2, 0, 2, 2, 3, 0, 3, 3, 3, 2, 0, 1,

3, 3, 0, 3, 0, 1, 2, 0, 0, 2, 3, 0, 2, 3, 3, 3, 0, 2, 0, 3, 1, 0, 2, 1, 0, 0, 0, 3,

0, 0, 3, 1, 3, 3, 1, 0, 0, 1, 2, 3, 0, 0, 2, 2, 2, 1, 2, 0, 2, 0, 0, 2, 0, 2, 3, 2,

Throughout the previous works [9,11], and [12], the randomness properties required as a PRNG such as correlation, distribution of digits, and LC have been proven theoretically. For example, the period λ of multi-value NTU sequence is classified into two cases depending on the choice of a as follows:

$$\lambda = \begin{cases} \frac{k(p^m - 1)}{p - 1} & \text{if } a = 0, \\ p^m - 1 & \text{otherwise.} \end{cases} \tag{8}$$

By reviewing these results, the common mathematical mechanism that induces those randomness properties is found. It allows us to consider the existence of equivalent keys and the following sections discuss by focusing on that characteristic. For convenience, the multi-value NTU sequences are simply referred to as NTU sequences in what follows.

3.2 Structure Analysis and Classification of Available Sequences

As seen from the period of NTU sequences in Eq. (8), the parameter a controls the properties of the sequence, and the reason is found by considering the multiplicative relationship between traces. According to Lemma 1, the trace function has linearity over $\mathbb{F}_p$ and since a primitive element $g \in \mathbb{F}_p$ holds the equality $g = \theta^{\frac{p^m - 1}{p - 1}}$ for a primitive element $\theta \in \mathbb{F}_{p^m}$, the following equality holds.

$$\mathrm{Tr}_{\mathbb{F}_{p^m} | \mathbb{F}_p} \left(\theta^{i + \frac{j(p^m - 1)}{p - 1}} \right) = \mathrm{Tr}_{\mathbb{F}_{p^m} | \mathbb{F}_p} \left(\theta^i \times g^j \right)$$
$$= g^j \mathrm{Tr}_{\mathbb{F}_{p^m} | \mathbb{F}_p} \left(\theta^i \right). \tag{9}$$

It is noted that the equality $g = \theta^{\frac{p^m - 1}{p - 1}}$ is immediately endowed by the Fermat's little theorem.

Considering the multiplicative relationship Eq. (9) and the definition of the power residue symbol Definition 3, the NTU sequences are presumed to be classified into $(k + 1)$ types of sequences. For example, let us consider the NTU sequences generated by fixing prime p, extension degree m, the kinds k of values, and primitive polynomial q as $p = 7$, $m = 2$, $k = 3$, and $q(x) = x^2 + 2x + 5$. Let $S_{a,\lambda}$ be an NTU sequence generated by using a, where λ denotes the period of the NTU sequence. Under these settings, the NTU sequences generated by moving $0 \le a < p$ are as follows:

case: $a = 0$

$$S_{0,24} = \{1,1,0,0,0,1,2,1,2,2,1,1,0,2,0,2,0,0,2,2,0,0,1,0\}$$

case: $a = 1$

$$S_{1,48} = \{2,0,1,1,0,2,2,0,2,1,0,0,0,2,1,1,1,0,1,1,0,1,0,0,$$
$$0,2,0,0,0,0,1,2,1,2,2,2,0,1,0,2,0,1,2,2,0,0,2,1\}$$

case: $a = 2$

$$S_{2,48} = \{2,0,2,2,1,2,1,0,1,0,0,0,1,1,2,0,2,0,0,0,1,2,0,0,$$
$$0,2,0,0,1,0,0,2,0,1,2,2,1,0,0,1,0,2,1,1,1,0,2,2\}$$

case: $a = 3$

$$S_{3,48} = \{1,0,2,2,2,1,0,0,0,0,0,0,2,0,2,0,2,1,0,0,2,2,0,1,$$
$$0,1,1,1,2,0,0,1,0,0,1,1,2,0,1,0,1,2,0,0,2,1,1,2\}$$

case: $a = 4$

$$S_{4,48} = \{0,1,1,1,2,0,0,1,0,0,1,1,2,0,1,0,1,2,0,0,2,1,1,2,$$
$$1,0,2,2,2,1,0,0,0,0,0,0,2,0,2,0,2,1,0,0,2,2,0,1\}$$

case: $a = 5$

$$S_{5,48} = \{0,2,0,0,1,0,0,2,0,1,2,2,1,0,0,1,0,2,1,1,1,0,2,2,$$
$$2,0,2,2,1,2,1,0,1,0,0,0,1,1,2,0,2,0,0,0,1,2,0,0\}$$

case: $a = 6$

$$S_{6,48} = \{0,2,0,0,0,0,1,2,1,2,2,2,0,1,0,2,0,1,2,2,0,0,2,1,$$
$$2,0,1,1,0,2,2,0,2,1,0,0,0,2,1,1,1,0,1,1,0,1,0,0\}$$

One can find from the above example that there exist the pairs of sequences that they are cyclically phase-shifted by each other. More precisely, we can classify those seven sequences as shown in Table 1 by regarding that the phase-shifted sequences are the same.

Based on this fact, the following Theorem holds for the NTU sequences.

Theorem 1. *Let θ and ϵ_k be a primitive element in $\mathbb{F}_{p^m}$ and a primitive kth root of unity in $\mathbb{F}_p$, respectively, where k is a positive integer such that $k|(p-1)$. NTU sequences generated by Eq. (7) are distinguished by depending on the choice of a. More precisely, let g be a primitive element in $\mathbb{F}_p$ and let a be represented by $a = g^{kl+h}$ with using positive integers l and h, where $0 \leq l$ and $0 \leq h < k$. For such a positive integer $a \in \mathbb{F}_p$, NTU sequences are classified into $(k+1)$ kinds of classes as follows:*

$$s_i = \begin{cases} f_k\left(\mathrm{Tr}_{\mathbb{F}_{p^m}|\mathbb{F}_p}\left(\theta^i\right)\right) & \text{if } a = 0, \quad (10a) \\ f_k\left(\mathrm{Tr}_{\mathbb{F}_{p^m}|\mathbb{F}_p}\left(\theta^{i-\frac{kl(p^m-1)}{p-1}}\right) + g^h\right) & \text{otherwise.} \quad (10b) \end{cases}$$

Table 1. The classification of the sequences generated by the parameters $p = 7$, $m = 2, k = 3, 0 \leq a \leq 6$, and $q(x) = x^2 + 2x + 5$

The condition of each class	Corresponding sequences
$a = 0$	$S_{0,24}$
$\left(\frac{a}{7}\right)_3 = 1$	$S_{1,24}$ and $S_{6,24}$
$\left(\frac{a}{7}\right)_3 = 4$	$S_{2,24}$ and $S_{5,24}$
$\left(\frac{a}{7}\right)_3 = 2$	$S_{3,24}$ and $S_{4,24}$

Proof. Since the powers of $\boldsymbol{\theta} \in \mathbb{F}_{p^m}$ give a unique representation of every non-zero element in $\mathbb{F}_{p^m}$, a primitive element g of $\mathbb{F}_p$ holds the equality $g^j = \boldsymbol{\theta}^{j\eta}$, where $0 \leq j < p$ and $\eta = \frac{p^m - 1}{p - 1}$. In addition, assume that a given element a of Eq. (7) is represented by using the primitive element g as follows:

$$a = g^{lk+h} = \boldsymbol{\theta}^{(lk+h)\eta}. \tag{11}$$

According to Lemma 1, the trace of $\boldsymbol{\theta}^{j_1\eta+j_2}$ holds the relation Eq. (12), where j_1 and j_2 satisfy $0 \leq j_1 < p - 1$ and $0 \leq j_2 < \eta$, respectively.

$$\mathrm{Tr}_{\mathbb{F}_{p^m}|\mathbb{F}_p}\left(\boldsymbol{\theta}^{j_1\eta+j_2}\right) = g^{j_1}\mathrm{Tr}_{\mathbb{F}_{p^m}|\mathbb{F}_p}\left(\boldsymbol{\theta}^{j_2}\right), \tag{12}$$

Here, consider the transformation of $\left(\mathrm{Tr}_{\mathbb{F}_{p^m}|\mathbb{F}_p}\left(\boldsymbol{\theta}^i\right) + a\right)$ with the primitive element, where $0 \leq i < p^m - 1$. First, assume that $a = 0$. Then, it is obvious that NTU sequences are generated by Eq. (10a).

Second, assume that $a \neq 0$. Since we have Eq. (11), $\left(\mathrm{Tr}_{\mathbb{F}_{p^m}|\mathbb{F}_p}\left(\boldsymbol{\theta}^i\right) + a\right)$ is rewritten into the following form.

$$\begin{aligned}\mathrm{Tr}_{\mathbb{F}_{p^m}|\mathbb{F}_p}\left(\boldsymbol{\theta}^i\right) + a &= \mathrm{Tr}_{\mathbb{F}_{p^m}|\mathbb{F}_p}\left(\boldsymbol{\theta}^i\right) + a \\ &= \mathrm{Tr}_{\mathbb{F}_{p^m}|\mathbb{F}_p}\left(\boldsymbol{\theta}^i\right) + g^{lk+h} \\ &= g^{lk}\left(g^{-lk}\mathrm{Tr}_{\mathbb{F}_{p^m}|\mathbb{F}_p}\left(\boldsymbol{\theta}^i\right) + g^h\right). \end{aligned} \tag{13}$$

Recall that the ith coefficient of NTU sequences are generated by applying the nonlinear function Eq. (6) to Eq. (13), we have

$$f_k\left(\mathrm{Tr}_{\mathbb{F}_{p^m}|\mathbb{F}_p}\left(\boldsymbol{\theta}^i\right) + a\right) = f_k\left(g^{-lk}\mathrm{Tr}_{\mathbb{F}_{p^m}|\mathbb{F}_p}\left(\boldsymbol{\theta}^i\right) + g^h\right). \tag{14}$$

It is noted that since the output of $f_k(\cdot)$ relies on the result of the power residue symbol, the above relationship is obtained by considering the equivalence through the power residue symbol. The readers can refer to the Appendix (A) for the detail of proof having Eq. (14).

Since h satisfies $0 \leq h < k$, there are k kinds of choices for the additive term g^h in Eq. (14) and the relation $g = \boldsymbol{\theta}^{j\eta}$ further endows the following representation.

$$f_k\left(g^{-lk}\mathrm{Tr}_{\mathbb{F}_{p^m}|\mathbb{F}_p}\left(\boldsymbol{\theta}^i\right) + g^h\right) = f_k\left(\mathrm{Tr}_{\mathbb{F}_{p^m}|\mathbb{F}_p}\left(\boldsymbol{\theta}^{i-(lk+h)\eta}\right) + 1\right) + h. \tag{15}$$

It is noted that Eq. (15) is endowed by using the logarithmic property of $f_k(\cdot)$. (see Appendix (B) for the detail.)

Here, recall concerning the variables k, l, and h that they are determined by the choice of a. Since η and g are constant values, the sequences generated by using constant additive terms $a_1 \in \mathbb{F}_p$ and $a_2 \in \mathbb{F}_p$ becomes the phase-shifted sequences by each other if $\left(\frac{a_1}{p}\right)_k = \left(\frac{a_2}{p}\right)_k$.

More precisely, recall from the definition of an m-sequence and the properties Lemma 1 of the trace function that the p-ary m-sequence R generated by a primitive element $\theta \in \mathbb{F}_{p^m}$ is given in the following form.

$$
\begin{aligned}
R = \{ \quad & \mathrm{Tr}_{\mathbb{F}_{p^m}|\mathbb{F}_p}\left(\theta^0\right), \quad \mathrm{Tr}_{\mathbb{F}_{p^m}|\mathbb{F}_p}\left(\theta^1\right), \ldots, \quad \mathrm{Tr}_{\mathbb{F}_{p^m}|\mathbb{F}_p}\left(\theta^{\eta-1}\right), \\
& g\mathrm{Tr}_{\mathbb{F}_{p^m}|\mathbb{F}_p}\left(\theta^0\right), \quad g\mathrm{Tr}_{\mathbb{F}_{p^m}|\mathbb{F}_p}\left(\theta^1\right), \ldots, \quad g\mathrm{Tr}_{\mathbb{F}_{p^m}|\mathbb{F}_p}\left(\theta^{\eta-1}\right), \\
& \qquad\qquad\qquad\qquad\qquad\quad \vdots \\
& g^{p-2}\mathrm{Tr}_{\mathbb{F}_{p^m}|\mathbb{F}_p}\left(\theta^0\right), \; g^{p-2}\mathrm{Tr}_{\mathbb{F}_{p^m}|\mathbb{F}_p}\left(\theta^1\right), \ldots, g^{p-2}\mathrm{Tr}_{\mathbb{F}_{p^m}|\mathbb{F}_p}\left(\theta^{\eta-1}\right)\}.
\end{aligned}
$$

Considering the fact that a primitive element g gives unique representation to a as $a = g^{lk+h}$, the difference of NTU sequences induced by using distinct a is found to be the amount of shift value. In addition, since h is in the range $[0, k)$, there are k kinds of choice for h. By taking into account these facts, the NTU sequences are thought to be the sequence obtained by adding h to the phase-shifted but the same sequence concerning θ. Therefore, we conclude that there exist $(k + 1)$ types of sequences distinguished by concerning a. (Q.E.D.)

3.3   Existence of Equivalent Keys

According to Theorem 1 in Sect. 3.2, the NTU sequences are found to have $(k + 1)$ kind types which is classified depending on the choice of its additive term a. It is obvious that the NTU sequences when $a = 0$ do not have equivalent keys with respect to a, therefore, the following targets and discusses the remaining k types of sequences. Since equivalent keys are a pair of keys (seed values) that generates the same sequence which includes the phase-shifted sequences, the seed value that determine the class of sequence can be equivalent keys.

In fact, if the additive term a in Eq. (7) is not equal to 0, then there are $\frac{p-1}{k}$ numbers of equivalent keys to each a that generate the same class (but phase-shifted) sequence, where k is a positive integer such that $k|(p-1)$ for an odd prime. More precisely, assume that $a_1, a_2 \in \mathbb{F}_p$ be constant values satisfying $\left(\frac{a_1}{p}\right)_k = \left(\frac{a_2}{p}\right)_k$. Since a primitive element $g \in \mathbb{F}_p$ is calculated by a given primitive element $\theta \in \mathbb{F}_{p^m}$ as Eq. (11), the exponents of a_1 and a_2 are uniquely obtained as $a_1 = g^u$ and $a_2 = g^v$, respectively.

As we assumed in the beginning, since $\left(\frac{a_1}{p}\right)_k = \left(\frac{a_2}{p}\right)_k$ is held for a_1 and a_2, u and v have to satisfy $u = v \pmod{k}$. Thus, the NTU sequences (16) and (17) are actually the same sequence generated by Eq. (18).

$$
S_1 = \left\{ s_{1,i}; s_{1,i} = f_k\left(\mathrm{Tr}_{\mathbb{F}_{p^m}|\mathbb{F}_p}\left(\theta^i\right) + a_1\right), 0 \le i < p^m - 1 \right\}, \tag{16}
$$

$$S_2 = \left\{ s_{2,i}; s_{2,i} = f_k \left(\mathrm{Tr}_{\mathbb{F}_{p^m} | \mathbb{F}_p} \left(\theta^i \right) + a_2 \right), 0 \le i < p^m - 1 \right\}, \tag{17}$$

$$S = \left\{ s_i; s_i = f_k \left(\mathrm{Tr}_{\mathbb{F}_{p^m} | \mathbb{F}_p} \left(\theta^j \right) + 1 \right) + u \pmod{k} \right\}. \tag{18}$$

This shrinks the seed space concerning the additive term a, in detail, an attacker can reduce the sampling space of the additive term from p to k to reproduce the same sequence. In other words, the authors think that this mechanism would enable an attacker to reproduce a given sequence faster than the brute-force way.

Therefore, this paper gives alert of the existence of equivalent keys in NTU sequences when the additive term is not the zero. However, the randomness properties, especially for the LC, are thought to be superior as well as other generators. Considering these aspects, NTU sequences are recommended to be used with the restriction $a = 0$ for considerate cryptographic uses.

Since the NTU sequence is considered as a sequence generated by applying the nonlinear filter to an m-sequence under the restriction, the implementation can be optimized by employing LFSRs and a lookup table. In addition, Eq. (8) tells us that the generator enables us to have a large periodic sequence even when the prime number is small by setting an adequately large extension degree. That is why though the comparisons with other generators and further evaluations would be essential, the NTU sequences are thought to have the potential to play an active part in a cryptographic application that needs to perform on resource-limited devices.

4   Conclusion

This paper dealt with the existence of equivalent keys for the multi-value (including binary) nonlinear filter generator. The equivalent keys are known to be the specific pair of keys that can generate the same or the simply phase-shifted sequence and can be a vulnerability for cryptographic purposes in particular. Though the target generator, which is called the NTU sequence, has theoretically known to have nice randomness property, especially for its nonlinearity, the practical aspect such as the existence of equivalent keys has not been discussed. Therefore, the authors focused on the NTU sequence and discussed the possibility of the existence of equivalent keys throughout the paper.

As a result, it was found that the NTU sequences are classified into several types of sequences depending on the choice of its key. In other words, the classification enabled us to reveal that the NTU sequences implicitly involve equivalent keys. However, the authors think that the equivalent keys can be vanished by giving a restriction on the choice of the specific key and the generator itself is useful even for cryptographic use by taking its randomness properties into account. On the other hand, there remain various discussions such as an optimization toward practical implementation and its security against physical attacks. These researches are future works.

Acknowledgment. This work was partly supported by a JSPS KAKENHI Grant-in-Aid for Scientific Research Challenging Research (Pioneering) 19H05579.

Appendix

A) Proof of Eq. (14)

The proof of the equivalence of $\left(\operatorname{Tr}_{\mathbb{F}_{p^m}|\mathbb{F}_p}\left(\boldsymbol{\theta}^i\right)+a\right)$ and $\left(g^{-lk}\operatorname{Tr}_{\mathbb{F}_{p^m}|\mathbb{F}_p}\left(\boldsymbol{\theta}^i\right)+g^h\right)$ through the nonlinear function $f_k\left(\cdot\right)$ is shown, where the variables used below are the same as the proof of Theorem 1. Since we have Eq. (11) and Fermat's little theorem, the following transformation holds for $\operatorname{Tr}_{\mathbb{F}_{p^m}|\mathbb{F}_p}\left(\boldsymbol{\theta}^i\right)+a$.

$$
\left(\frac{\operatorname{Tr}_{\mathbb{F}_{p^m}|\mathbb{F}_p}\left(\boldsymbol{\theta}^i\right)+a}{p}\right)_k = \left(\frac{g^{lk}\left(g^{-lk}\operatorname{Tr}_{\mathbb{F}_{p^m}|\mathbb{F}_p}\left(\boldsymbol{\theta}^i\right)+g^h\right)}{p}\right)_k
$$

$$
= \left\{g^{lk}\left(g^{-lk}\operatorname{Tr}_{\mathbb{F}_{p^m}|\mathbb{F}_p}\left(\boldsymbol{\theta}^i\right)+g^h\right)\right\}^{\frac{p-1}{k}}
$$

$$
= g^{l(p-1)}\left(g^{-lk}\operatorname{Tr}_{\mathbb{F}_{p^m}|\mathbb{F}_p}\left(\boldsymbol{\theta}^i\right)+g^h\right)^{\frac{p-1}{k}}
$$

$$
= \left(g^{-lk}\operatorname{Tr}_{\mathbb{F}_{p^m}|\mathbb{F}_p}\left(\boldsymbol{\theta}^i\right)+g^h\right)^{\frac{p-1}{k}} \quad (\because \ \mathrm{mod}\ p)
$$

$$
= \left(\frac{g^{-lk}\operatorname{Tr}_{\mathbb{F}_{p^m}|\mathbb{F}_p}\left(\boldsymbol{\theta}^i\right)+g^h}{p}\right)_k .
$$

Recall from Eq. (6) that since $f_k\left(\cdot\right)$ applies the logarithmic operation to an output of the power residue symbol, it is found that $f_k\left(x\right)=f_k\left(y\right)$ if the respective result of power residue symbol satisfies $\left(\frac{x}{p}\right)_k = \left(\frac{y}{p}\right)_k$. (Q.E.D.)

B) Proof of Eq. (15)

The proof of how to derive Eq. (15) based on the property of $f_k\left(\cdot\right)$ is shown here. First, recall that since $f_k\left(\cdot\right)$ is defied by $f_k\left(x\right)=\log_{\epsilon_k} x$ for a non-zero input $x \in \mathbb{F}_p$, where ϵ_k is a primitive kth root of unity. Thus, it has the logarithmic property for non-zero values $x, y \in \mathbb{F}_p$ as follows:

$$
f_k\left(xy\right) = \log_{\epsilon_k}\left(\frac{xy}{p}\right)_k
$$

$$
= \log_{\epsilon_k}\left\{\left(\frac{x}{p}\right)_k\left(\frac{y}{p}\right)_k\right\}
$$

$$
= \log_{\epsilon_k}\left(\frac{x}{p}\right)_k + \log_{\epsilon_k}\left(\frac{y}{p}\right)_k
$$

$$
= f_k\left(x\right)+f_k\left(y\right).
$$

By taking into account the above property of $f_k(\cdot)$, $f_k(g^{-lk}\mathrm{Tr}_{\mathbb{F}_{p^m}|\mathbb{F}_p}(\boldsymbol{\theta}^i)$ $+g^h)$ is found to be transformed into Eq. (15) as follows:

$$
\begin{aligned}
f_k\left(g^{-lk}\mathrm{Tr}_{\mathbb{F}_{p^m}|\mathbb{F}_p}\left(\boldsymbol{\theta}^i\right)+g^h\right) &= f_k\left(\mathrm{Tr}_{\mathbb{F}_{p^m}|\mathbb{F}_p}\left(g^{-lk}\boldsymbol{\theta}^i\right)+g^h\right) \\
&= f_k\left(g^h\left(g^{-h}\mathrm{Tr}_{\mathbb{F}_{p^m}|\mathbb{F}_p}\left(g^{-lk}\boldsymbol{\theta}^i\right)+1\right)\right) \\
&= f_k\left(g^h\right)+f_k\left(g^{-h}\mathrm{Tr}_{\mathbb{F}_{p^m}|\mathbb{F}_p}\left(g^{-lk}\boldsymbol{\theta}^i\right)+1\right) \\
&= \log_{\epsilon_k}g^{\frac{h(p-1)}{k}}+f_k\left(\mathrm{Tr}_{\mathbb{F}_{p^m}|\mathbb{F}_p}\left(g^{-lk-h}\boldsymbol{\theta}^i\right)+1\right) \\
&= f_k\left(\mathrm{Tr}_{\mathbb{F}_{p^m}|\mathbb{F}_p}\left(\boldsymbol{\theta}^{i-(lk+h)\eta}\right)+1\right)+h.
\end{aligned}
$$

It is noted that $\eta = \frac{p^m-1}{p-1}$ and $\boldsymbol{\theta}^\eta = g$. (Q.E.D.).

References

1. Rueppel, R.A.: Analysis and Design of Stream Ciphers. Springer, Heidelberg (1986). https://doi.org/10.1007/978-3-642-82865-2
2. Cusick, T.W., Ding, C., Renvall, A.: Stream Cihpers and Number Theory, Revised edn. Elsevier Science, The Netherlands (2004)
3. Küçük, Ö.: Slide resynchronization attack on the initialization of Grain 1.0. eSTEAM, Report 2006/044 (2006). http://www.ecrypt.eu.org/stream/papersdir/2006/044.ps. Accessed 1 Mar 2020
4. Robshaw, M., Billet, O. (eds.): New Stream Cipher Designs. LNCS, vol. 4986. Springer, Heidelberg (2008). https://doi.org/10.1007/978-3-540-68351-3
5. eSTREAM: the ECRYPT stream cipher project. https://www.ecrypt.eu.org/stream/index.html. Accessed 1 Mar 2020
6. Canteaut, A.: Encyclopedia of Cryptography and Security. Springer, Boston, MA (2005). https://doi.org/10.1007/978-1-4419-5906-5
7. Dichtl, M.: On nonlinear filter generators. In: Biham, E. (ed.) FSE 1997. LNCS, vol. 1267, pp. 103–106. Springer, Heidelberg (1997). https://doi.org/10.1007/BFb0052338
8. Nogami, Y., Tada, K., Uehara, S.: A geometric sequence binarized with Legendre symbol over odd characteristic field and its properties. IEICE Trans. Fundam. Electron. Commun. Comput. Sci. **E97–A**(1), 2336–2342 (2014)
9. Nogami, Y., Uehara, S., Tsuchiya, K., Begum, N., Ino, H., Morelos-Zaragoza, R.H.: A multi-value sequence generated by power residue symbol and trace function over odd characteristic field. IEICE Trans. Fundam. Electron. Commun. Comput. Sci. **E99–A**(12), 2226–2237 (2016)
10. Golomb, S.W.: Shift Register Sequences. Aegean Park Press, Laguna Hills (1981)
11. Tsuchiya, K., Ogawa, C., Nogami, Y., Uehara, S.: Linear complexity of generalized NTU sequences. In: IWSDA 2017, pp. 74–78. IEEE (2017)
12. Kodera, Y., et al.: Distribution of digit patterns in multi-value sequence over the odd characteristic field. IEICE Trans. Fundam. Electron. Commun. Comput. Sci. **E101–A**(9), 1525–1536 (2018)
13. Lidl, R., Niederreiter, H.: Introduction to Finite Fields and Their Applications. Cambridge University Press, New York (1986)
14. Chan, A.H., Games, R.A.: On the linear span of binary sequences obtained from q-ary m-sequence, q odd. IEEE Trans. Inf. Theory **36**(3), 548–552 (1990)

15. Zierler, N.: Legendre sequences, pp. 34–71. M.I.T. Lincoln Publications, Group Report (1958)
16. Damgård, I.B.: On the randomness of legendre and jacobi sequences. In: Goldwasser, S. (ed.) CRYPTO 1988. LNCS, vol. 403, pp. 163–172. Springer, New York (1990). https://doi.org/10.1007/0-387-34799-2_13
17. Dai, Z., Yang, J., Gong, G., Wang, P.: On the linear complexity of generalized Legendre sequence. In: SETA 2001, pp. 145–153. Springer, London (2002). https://doi.org/10.1007/978-1-4471-0673-9_10
18. Sidelnikov, V.M.: Some k-value pseudo-random sequences and nearly equidistant codes. Probl. Inf. Transm. **5**(1), 12–16 (1969)

Malicious Activity Detection 1

Detection of Malicious PowerShell Using Word-Level Language Models

Yui Tajiri(✉) and Mamoru Mimura[iD]

National Defense Academy, Yokosuka, Japan
{em58028,mim}@nda.ac.jp

Abstract. There is a growing tendency for cybercriminals to abuse legitimate tools installed on the target computers for cyberattacks. In particular, the use of PowerShell provided by Microsoft has been increasing every year and has become a threat. In previous studies, a method to detect malicious PowerShell commands using character-level deep learning was proposed. The proposed method combines traditional natural language processing and character-level convolutional neural networks. This method, however, requires time for dynamic analysis. This paper proposes a method to classify unknown PowerShell without dynamic analysis. Our method uses feature vectors extracted from malicious and benign PowerShell scripts using word-level language models for classification. The datasets were generated from benign and malicious PowerShell scripts obtained from Hybrid Analysis, and benign PowerShell scripts obtained from GitHub, which are imbalanced. The experimental result shows that the combination of the LSI and XGBoost produces the highest detection rate. The maximum accuracy achieves approximately 0.95 on the imbalanced dataset. Furthermore, over 50% of unknown malicious PowerShell scripts could be detected in time series analysis without dynamic analysis.

Keywords: PowerShell · Latent Semantic Indexing · Doc2Vec · XGBoost

1 Introduction

In recent years, digitalization of social life and economic activity is progressing with the development of information and communication technology. Digitization brings various benefits to society, such as increasing the efficiency of operations and improving the convenience of consumption activities. On the other hand, digitalized critical infrastructures and systems of enterprises and financial institutions have been targeted by cyber criminals, and many damages have occurred. The methods of such cyber attacks are diversifying and becoming more sophisticated year by year, and the attacks that cannot be detected by anti-virus software or intrusion detection systems are increasing.

According to Symantec's latest white paper on cyber threats, cybercriminals are more likely to exploit legitimate tools and operating system features

© Springer Nature Switzerland AG 2020
K. Aoki and A. Kanaoka (Eds.): IWSEC 2020, LNCS 12231, pp. 39–56, 2020.
https://doi.org/10.1007/978-3-030-58208-1_3

installed on the target device [23]. In particular, PowerShell is a powerful tool that can access almost all functions of Windows. As a result, PowerShell is used as a primary tool in both cybercrime and targeted attacks, and malicious PowerShell scripts are on the rise [12]. Moreover, attacks using PowerShell are often performed in combination with different technologies and attack methods such as targeted attacks and ransomware. Thus, the threat of malicious PowerShell is increasing. Many studies attempted to detect malicious JavaScript [14,19] and macro malware [15–18], but a few studies tackled malicious PowerShell.

In previous research on malicious PowerShell detection, Hendler et al. proposed a method of detecting malicious PowerShell commands using deep neural networks [9]. They proposed to combine traditional natural language processing and character-level convolutional neural networks. However, this method requires dynamic analysis. Hence, detection in real time seems to be difficult because dynamic analysis is often time consuming. In addition, dynamic analysis is often costly, since dynamic analysis uses a dedicated environment.

In this paper, we examine malicious PowerShell detection methods without dynamic analysis. With the development of natural language processing technology in recent years, researches applied it to malware detection [10]. However, there is no research on the detection of malicious PowerShell that focuses on natural language processing technology, and many studies focus on deep learning and machine learning. In this paper, we propose a method of detecting malicious PowerShell scripts using natural language processing and machine learning. In this method, a script is statically analyzed, and word-level language models are created to detect malicious PowerShell. The language models are constructed using the new natural language processing technologies such as Latent Semantic Indexing (LSI) [8] and Doc2Vec [11]. Our method constructs the language models from malicious and benign samples (training dataset), then the feature vectors are constructed from training dataset. Thereafter, our method trains classification models to classify unknown PowerShell scripts. We use the datasets that are constructed of PowerShell scripts with time series information. The datasets are separated into training data and test data by the time series information. In this paper, we use the training data as known PowerShell scripts, and the test data as unknown PowerShell scripts.

This paper provides the following contributions:

1. This paper proposes a method to classify unknown PowerShell scripts with word-level language models.
2. The experimental result shows that the combination of the LSI and XGBoost produces the highest detection rate.
3. The maximum accuracy achieves approximately 0.95 on the imbalanced dataset.
4. Over 50% of unknown malicious PowerShell scripts could be detected without dynamic analysis.

The structure of this paper is shown below. Section 2 describes PowerShell, and Sect. 3 introduces related research. Section 4 introduces related techniques used in this study. Section 5 describes the proposed method, and Sect. 6 describes the verification experiment and its results. Section 7 produces some considerations. Finally, we discuss the results and conclude this paper.

2   PowerShell

PowerShell is a command-line shell and scripting language developed by Microsoft. PowerShell is object-oriented and based on the .NET framework and has high flexibility system and powerful functions. PowerShell provides full-access to Windows important function and remote control. In general, PowerShell is used for purposes of automating processes and system administrations. PowerShell is a task automation and configuration management framework from Microsoft, which consists of a command-line shell and associated scripting language. PowerShell provides full access to perform administrative tasks on both local and remote Windows systems. PowerShell is a legitimate tool to provide these powerful functions.

2.1   Abusing PowerShell

On the other hand, these powerful functions regrettably improve flexibility in cyber attacks. For example, cyber criminals can create an illegitimate task in the victim machine without sending malware. Cyber criminals insert the illegitimate task into regular tasks to evade detection. As a result, cyber criminals have become more sophisticated to prevent detection. Thus, PowerShell is increasingly being used as one of the attack tools for cyber criminals.

2.2   Obfuscated PowerShell

Most malicious PowerShell scripts are obfuscated to evade detection. Obfuscation is a process of modifying binary files or source code while preserving function, so that a result of the process prevents humans understanding. Generally, this technique is used to protect copyright of software and prevent tampering. However, obfuscation techniques are often used by attackers to evade malware analysis and detection. It is difficult to understand what is executed by the code without removing obfuscation. Hence, distinguishing malicious PowerShell scripts from obfuscated ones without dynamic analysis is a challenging task. Table 1 shows typical examples of obfuscation methods. Cyber criminals use a combination of these obfuscation methods to evade detection.

3   Related Work

This section describe related studies to detect malicious PowerShell and elucidates the novelty of this paper.

Hendler et al. proposed a malicious PowerShell detection deep neural network-based method:*Deep/Traditional Models Ensemble(D/T Ensemble)* [9]. The *D/T Ensemble* is a detection method that combines deep learning architecture and traditional natural language processing. This method uses 4-layer CNN

Table 1. Examples of typical obfuscation

No.	Overview	Example
1	Base64 encoding	$([Convert]::FromBase64String ('7b0HYBxJliUmL23K... 9k9yGyfDw=='))
2	Insert lengthy space character	po w e r s h e l l . e x e - n o p
3	Mix capital letters and small letters	$nW = NEW-ObJECt SySTem.NeT.WebCLIeNT;
4	Dynamic creating a command	$cmd = "get-"+"Process" Invoke-Expression $cmd
5	Insert escape sequence(')	$dm = ... wI'N3'2'_co'MPUTE RSYS'TEm...
6	ASCII encoding	((...45,72,111,115,116,32,...)| %{ ([Int]$_ -as [char]) }) -Join"

and 3-gram, which have the best detection rates. In this method, dynamic analysis is performed to extract PowerShell commands in preprocessing. To mitigate the obfuscation, Base64 decoding and replacing redundant white space with single space are performed. In addition, character strings with unique values such as IP addresses are replaced with other common characters in order to treat them as the same element. At the end of preprocessing, PowerShell being case-insensitive, all commands are converted to lowercase to generalize the command. Then, the commands are classified using the 4-CNN and 3-gram detectors, and the two detection results are compared. If the result is greater than or equal to a threshold, the maximum score is used, and if it is below the threshold, the average of the two scores is used.

Rubin et al. proposed malicious PowerShell detection methods using contextual embeddings of words [21]. Their methods are based on Microsoft's Antimalware Scan Interface (AMSI) and contextual embeddings of words. Their methods use contextual embeddings of words (Word2Vec, FastText), Token-Char, CNN and RNN, which have the best detection rates with Token-Char-FastText. In this method, AMSI is used to extract deobfuscated PowerShell tokens in preprocessing. Then, this method creates a word embedding model from unlabeled PowerShell scripts and modules. The deep learning models are trained using this model and the training set.

Rusak et al. proposed a method of detecting malicious PowerShell by combining abstract syntax tree (AST) and deep learning [22]. The feature of their method is structural information of the code instead of text-based. AST is often used in programming language processing systems as an intermediate representation of programs such as compilers. This method decodes a script or command encoded in Base64 as preprocessing, and converts it into AST. The root of each AST node is constructed based on the corpus of the PowerShell scripts, and the malware family can be distinguished. In some studies, the method for preprocessing is not clearly described [9, 22].

Ugarte et al. introduced a tool *PowerDrive* to deobfuscate PowerShell [3, 24]. *PowerDrive* is a hybrid multi-stage deobfuscation tool. Ugarte et al. correctly analyzed 95% of the scripts in the dataset. In addition, they provided PowerShell behavior model taxonomy and a comprehensive list of malicious domains [24]. *PowerDrive* is provided on GitHub and has high reproducibility. This study mainly focuses on analyzing obfuscated PowerShell scripts rather than detecting.

Thus, a few studies focused on word-level models and used traditional language models. Moreover, some methods require dynamic analysis. In this paper, we use Doc2Vec and LSI models to automatically extract the features. These sophisticated models may reveal the context of malicious PowerShell scripts, which contributes to classify. Furthermore, our method does not require dynamic analysis.

4   Related Technique

4.1   NLP Technique

NLP digitizes natural languages for processing by computers. In this paper, we use Latent Semantic Indexing and Doc2Vec. In addition, we use Bag-of-Words as baseline for evaluation.

Bag-of-Words. Bag-of-Words (BoW) is a model that converts a document into a vector based on the frequency of words. A document d is represented as in Eq. (1). In Eq. (1), each w represents a word, and n represents an appearance frequency corresponding to w.

$$d = [(w_1, n_{w_1}), (w_2, n_{w_2}), (w_3, n_{w_3}), ..., (w_j, n_{w_j})] \tag{1}$$

In Eq. (1), document d can be represented by a numerical value by fixing the position of n and omitting word w. As a result, the relation between the document and word representing the number of occurrences of the word in each document d can be expressed by a vector (document-word matrix) as in Eq. (2).

$$\hat{d}_i = (n_{w_1}, n_{w_2}, n_{w_3}, ..., n_{w_j}) \tag{2}$$

Thus, BoW converts each document into a vector, which a fixed number of dimensions with a unique number of words.

TFIDF. TFIDF is a method for evaluating the importance of words contained in a document. TFIDF is calculated based on Term Frequency (TF) and Inverse Document Frequency (IDF), as in Eq. (3). In other words, a word that appears more frequently in a certain document and does not appear much in other documents has a larger TFIDF, indicating that the word is a word characterizing the document.

$$tfidf = tf * idf \tag{3}$$

TF stands for a frequency of occurrence of a certain word in a document. The TF is represented $tf(t, d)$ as in Eq. (4), then t means a term in a document, d means a document.

$$tf(t, d) = \frac{n_{t,d}}{\sum_{s \in d} n_{s,d}} \tag{4}$$

IDF is the reciprocal of the document frequency in which a certain word appears. The IDF of a certain word t is represented $idf(t)$ is expressed as in Equation (5). In Eq. (5), N is the total number of documents, then $df(t)$ is the number of documents where the certain term t appears.

$$idf(t) = \log \frac{N}{df(t)} + 1 \tag{5}$$

Latent Semantic Indexing. Latent Semantic Indexing (LSI) analyzes the relevance of documents and words contained in the documents [8]. The LSI can calculate the features of documents and analyze the relevance by performing singular value decomposition on vectors weighted for each component of the document-word matrix obtained by BoW. The derived relevance seems to indicate potential meaning. In general, TFIDF is used to weight each component of the document-word matrix. The TFIDF is expressed by Eq. (6). In Eq. (6), $n_{w,d}$ is the frequency of occurrence of word t in document d, N is the total number of documents, and $df(t)$ means the total number of documents including the word t.

$$tf_{i,j} * idf_i = \frac{n_{t,d}}{\sum_{s \in d} n_{s,d}} * (\log \frac{N}{df(t)} + 1) \tag{6}$$

Then, singular value decomposition is performed on a vector weighted by TFIDF. An element $x_{(i,j)}$ of a matrix X, which is a group of documents, represents TFIDF of a word i in a document j. Each row of the matrix indicates a vector corresponding to one document, and each element indicates a relation with each document. Similarly, a column of the matrix indicates a vector corresponding to one document, and each element indicates relationship with each word. Singular value decomposition of X decomposes into orthogonal matrices U and V, and diagonal matrix Σ. The determinant is expressed by Eq. (7).

$$\begin{aligned} X &= \begin{bmatrix} x_{1,1} \dots x_{1,j} \\ \vdots \ddots \vdots \\ x_{i,1} \dots x_{i,j} \end{bmatrix} \\ &= U \Sigma V^T \\ &= \begin{bmatrix} u_{1,1} \dots u_{1,r} \\ \vdots \ddots \vdots \\ u_{i,1} \dots u_{i,r} \end{bmatrix} * \begin{bmatrix} \sigma_{1,1} \dots 0 \\ \vdots \ddots \vdots \\ 0 \dots \sigma_{r,r} \end{bmatrix} * \begin{bmatrix} v_{1,1} \dots v_{1,r} \\ \vdots \ddots \vdots \\ v_{j,1} \dots v_{j,r} \end{bmatrix} \end{aligned} \tag{7}$$

Doc2Vec. Doc2Vec is one of the implementations of Paragraph Vector [11] proposed by Le et al. Paragraph Vector is an extended version of word2vec [13], a model for generating word feature vectors proposed by Mikolov et al. Paragraph Vector differs from Word2Vec in that the model generates feature vectors for the document, not words. Paragraph Vector has no limit on the length of the input sentence. Hence, the process does not depend on the input length. Paragraph Vector can calculate the similarity and relevance between documents.

4.2 Machine Learning Technique

There are three machine learning techniques used in our method: Support Vector Machine (SVM), RandomForest and XGBoost. We chose these three techniques to compare the compatibility between language models and machine learning techniques.

SVM is a pattern recognition model using supervised learning, and is applied to classification problems and regression problems. SVM is one of the most popular algorithms in the field of machine learning. In addition, SVM is provided as a module in programming languages such as Python [6,20].

RandomForest is a ensemble learning algorithm proposed by Leo Breiman that is the weak learner used a decision tree [5]. RandomForest uses multiple decision trees learned from randomly sampled training data.

XGBoost is an ensemble learning algorithm that combines gradient boosting and Random Forests, and is a classifier with a scalable End-to-End Tree Boosting system [7].

5 Proposed Method

This section details the detection method of malicious PowerShell scripts proposed in this research.

5.1 Outline

Figure 1 shows the overview of our method to classify unknown PowerShell scripts. The training samples and test samples include benign and malicious PowerShell scripts. The procedure of the proposed method is as follows.

① Preprocessing on the training samples: data cleansing, obfuscation counter-measures, and separating strings.
② Constructing a corpus from separated strings.
③ Constructing each language model with BoW, Doc2Vec, and LSI.
④ Training three classifiers: SVM, XGBoost, and RandomForest.
⑤ Preprocessing on the test samples as ①.
⑥ Input the preprocessed and separated test samples to each language model created in ③.
⑦ The test sample is input to each classifier created in ④, and classification is performed.

The details of each procedure will be described in the following sections.

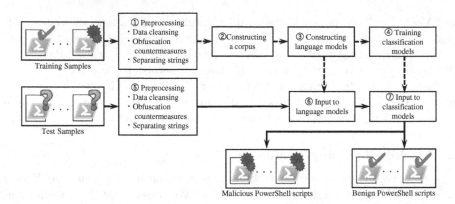

Fig. 1. Overview of the proposed method.

5.2   Preprocessing

Our method performs preprocessing on the dataset to improve the detection rate of obfuscated malware. This process is performed in the parts ① and ⑤ in Fig. 1.

For data cleansing, several patterns are replaced as shown in Table 2. For instance, various IP addresses are replaced with the same word. Thereby, the word can be processed as the same features.

Table 2. Replace strings

Pattern	Replaced word
IP-address ex.) 255.255.0.26	IPAddress
Write code that spans multiple lines on one line	Terminal character of PowerShell ";"/White space (space, tab, line feed)
Character strings after encoding	Replace with one of the features
Mixed uppercase and lowercase scripts	Change to lowercase
URL	Replace with one of the features
File name	Replace with one of the features

For obfuscation countermeasures, several obfuscation patterns are extracted by using regular expression matching. The countermeasures shown in Table 3 are performed.

Finally, PowerShell scripts are separated into words using symbols such as spaces, terminal symbols, and parentheses as delimiters. The symbols are as follows: [ ]{}()+.&"',:.

Table 3. Obfuscation countermeasures

Pattern	Countermeasure	Example
Multiple commands in one line	Separate with PowerShell's terminal character ";" or space character (space, tab, line feed)	Before: $id = (Get-Wmi Object Win32...).UUID; $log = $lk+$uuid; After: $id = (Get-WmiObject Win32...).UUID; $log = $lk+$uuid;
Base64 encoding	Replace with the same word	Before: Base64String('7b0HYBxJli UmL23K... 9k9/yGyf/Dw==') After: Base64String('base64str')
Mixing lowercase and uppercase characters	Unify them into lowercase	Before: $mSEnT = nEW-obJEcT sYstEm.io.mEmOrySTReaM After: $msent = new-object system.io.memorystream

5.3 Training

First, a dictionary of unique words is created from training samples. The training samples are converted into a corpus with the dictionary. Some unique words have an extremely large number of occurrences and some have a small number of occurrences. In general, commonly occurring words are often deleted, because they do not affect the classification. However, the words are retained in this study to maintain context. Next, language models are constructed from the corpus. The language models are Doc2Vec, LSI, and Bag-of-Words.

Thereafter, our method trains the SVM, XGBoost, and RandomForest classifiers using the feature vectors of training samples. The training samples are labeled as malicious or benign.

5.4 Test

Test samples are converted into words with the same process (Sect. 5.2). The feature vectors are extracted from the words with each language model. Thereafter, the trained classifiers are used to classify the feature vectors. Thus, our method classifies PowerShell scripts as malicious or benign, and thereby detects malicious PowerShell scripts.

5.5 Implementation

The proposed method was implemented with Python 2.7 in the environment shown in Table 4. The libraries shown in Table 5 were used to implement machine learning models for natural language processing and classification.

Table 4. Experiment environment

CPU	Core i7-8700K 3.70 GHz
Memory	16 GB
OS	Windows 10 Home
Programming language	Python 2.7

Table 5. Main Python libraries used for experiments

Natural language processing	Bag-of-Words	Gensim −3.7.3[a]
	Doc2Vec	
	LSI	
Machine learning	SVM	Scikit-learn −0.20.4[b]
	RandomForest	
	XGBoost	XGBoost −0.82[c]

[a] https://radimrehurek.com/gensim/index.html
[b] https://scikit-learn.org/stable/
[c] https://xgboost.readthedocs.io/en/latest/index.html

6   Evaluation

6.1   Dataset

The datasets consist of malicious and benign PowerShell scripts. The 310 malicious scripts and 5145 benign scripts were obtained from Hybrid Analysis [2] and GitHub [1].

We used the APIs provided by Hybrid Analysis, and downloaded samples which can be obtained as much as we could. These samples were split into malicious or benign ones by VirusTotal [4]. Besides, we obtained publicly available PowerShell scripts from GitHub.

These malicious PowerShell scripts were categorized by the year when they were firstly posted to Hybrid Analysis. The details of samples are shown in Table 6. In this experiment, we examine whether unknown malicious PowerShell scripts could be detected. Therefore, we consider the date the sample was first posted to Hybrid Analysis as the date of its first appearance. Then treating the 2018 sample as known and the 2019 sample as unknown. Since the scripts obtained from GitHub have no time series information, these scripts are sorted by file name in ascending order and alternately classified in the training set and the test set.

6.2   Evaluation Metrics

The definitions of the evaluation metrics used in this study are described. Table 7 shows the relations between the predicted result and true result. In general, the following four definitions are used as evaluation metrics for the classification

Table 6. Structure of dataset

Hybrid analysis			GitHub
Year	Malicious	Benign	
2018	251	118	5000
2019	59	27	

Table 7. Relations between predicted and actual results

		Actual class	
		Malicious	Benign
Predicted class	Malicious	True Positive (TP)	False Positive (FP)
	Benign	False Negative (FN)	True Negative (TN)

problem. Accuracy is metrics for determining the degree of agreement between the predicted result and the correct answer, and is defined in (8).

$$Accuracy = \frac{TP + TN}{TP + FP + FN + TN} \qquad (8)$$

Precision is the percentage of data that is actually malicious among the data predicted to be malicious, and is defined in (9).

$$Precision = \frac{TP}{TP + FP} \qquad (9)$$

Recall is the percentage of data that is predicted to be malicious among data that is actually malicious, and is defined in (10).

$$Recall = \frac{TP}{TP + FN} \qquad (10)$$

F-measure is an evaluation scale calculated by the harmonic mean of precision and recall, and is defined in (11).

$$F\text{-}measure = \frac{2\,Recall \times Precision}{Recall + Precision} \qquad (11)$$

In this study, we focus on the following two points when evaluating.

1. There is no missing detection for the purpose of detecting malicious Power-Shell scripts.
2. In real environment, malicious PowerShell can be detected.

Therefore, in the verification experiment, we focus on Recall and F-measure.

6.3   Experiment Contents

In this study, two experiments are performed. First, we construct classification models and evaluate the generalization performance of the detectors. Then, we evaluate the detection rate of the unknown PowerShell scripts. To confirm the effects of obfuscation countermeasures, these experiments are conducted with and without obfuscation countermeasures.

The generalization performance is evaluated by 5-Fold cross validation using the 2018 dataset. The parameters for the language models are the initial values of each module. To provide a fair comparison of each language model, the size of the model vector space is fixed. Other parameters are the initial settings of each module.

The detection rate of the unknown PowerShell scripts is evaluated by performing a time series analysis. In the time series analysis, the models are trained using the 2018 dataset, then the 2019 dataset is classified as unknown PowerShell scripts.

6.4   Result

In this section, we show the result of the generalization performance and the detection rate of the unknown PowerShell scripts. As previously described, the datasets consist of 310 malicious PowerShell scripts and 5145 benign PowerShell scripts. Thus, the malicious PowerShell scripts account for approximately only 6% of the total. Therefore, considerable attention should be paid to the results because the datasets are highly imbalanced.

The results of the five cross-validations are described in Fig. 2 and Fig. 3.

First, we focus on the results of the performance of the benign class shown in Fig. 2. The vertical axis indicates the precision, recall, F-measure, and accuracy. The horizontal axis indicates the combinations of language models and classifiers. Without obfuscation countermeasures, the performance of the benign class was fairly good. The maximum accuracy achieves approximately 0.95 on the imbalanced dataset.

To evaluate the performance against the unknown malicious PowerShell scripts, we focus on the recall and F-measure. The malicious recall and F-measure are shown in Fig. 3. The vertical axis indicates the recall and F-measure. The horizontal axis indicates the combinations of language models and classifiers. It seems that the performances with obfuscation countermeasures are higher than ones without the countermeasures. Consequently, the obfuscation countermeasures are demonstrated to be effective. In addition, the LSI and Bag-of-words with unfixed vector dimensions tend to be more accurate. In particular, the combination with LSI and XGBoost has the highest recall among these combinations. The maximum recall and F-measure are 0.57 and 0.65 respectively.

Regarding the time series analysis, the recall and F-measure of the malicious PowerShell are shown in Fig. 4. The vertical axis indicates the recall and F-measure. The horizontal axis indicates the combinations of language models and classifiers. To provide a fair comparison, we focus on the performance with fixed

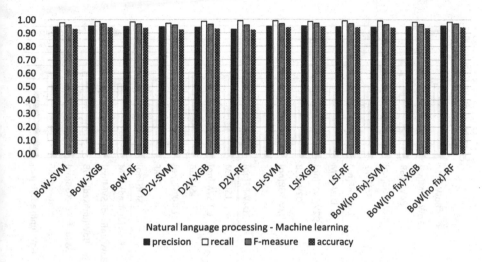

Fig. 2. The performance of the benign class of the 5-fold cross validation without obfuscation countermeasures. The TP in this result is that the classification result of a sample that is actually benign is benign.

vectors. Comparing the maximum recall values for each language model, the LSI achieves 0.55. In contrast, the Doc2Vec and Bag-of-Words produce only 0.36 and 0.22 respectively. Hence, the LSI is effective in detecting unknown malicious PowerShell scripts. Focusing on F-measure, it is 0.54 or more when using any classifier with LSI and obfuscation countermeasures. Consequently, the result indicates the effectiveness of LSI. In regard to the performance with unfixed vectors, the Bag-of-words and XGBoost achieves the highest value. The recall and F-measure are 0.60 and 0.73 respectively. Note that the dimension is different, thereby does not provide a fair comparison.

7   Discussion

7.1   Accuracy

As described in Sect. 6.4, our method with the LSI produced a higher detection rate than other models. Hence, it can be said that LSI is an effective language model.

Besides, the accuracy depends on the combination of the language model and classifier. As an example, we focus on the Doc2Vec model in Fig. 4. Comparing the performance of SVM and RandomForest, the RandomForest produces worse accuracy despite the same language model. Thus, the combination of the language model and classifier affects the classification accuracy. To evaluate each combination of the language model and classifier, we compare the results of the accuracy in the cross validation and time series analysis. Since some combinations produce high accuracy in the cross validation, most of them produce low accuracy in the time series analysis. On the other hand, there are combinations

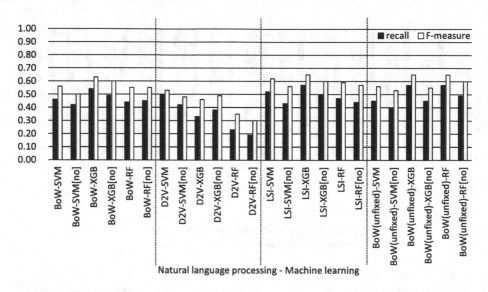

Fig. 3. The malicious performance of the 5-fold cross validation. ("[no]" indicates no-countermeasures.)

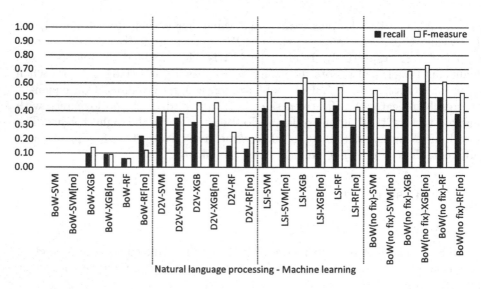

Fig. 4. The performance of the time series analysis. ("[no]" means no-measures.)

that maintain the accuracy in the time series analysis. One of the combination with high accuracy is the LSI and XGBoost. From these results, the best combination seems to be the LSI and XGBoost.

7.2   Comparison with Previous Research

In the previous studies [9,21], their methods were evaluated using AUC and TPR (recall). We compare the detection rate of unknown malicious PowerShell. The TPR with the Bag-of-Words was 0.87 in [9]. In our study, the recall was 0.22 with a fixed dimensionality. Even with unfixed dimensionality, the recall was no more than 0.60. Note that the previous study examined PowerShell commands. Our study examined PowerShell scripts. A PowerShell script consists of multiple commands. Hence, analyzing PowerShell scripts is more complicated. Rubin et al. did not use Bag-of-Words [21]. Therefore, we could not make comparisons in the same natural language processing techniques. We focused on n-grams of traditional natural language processing techniques as a reference for comparison. The TPR with 3-gram was 0.67. The accuracy depends on the datasets. For instance, our datasets are categorized by the year to evaluate the performance against unknown PowerShell scripts. Therefore, we cannot simply compare the accuracy. In addition, their method requires dynamic analysis to obtain code instances. Our method does not require dynamic analysis.

Comparing the datasets, the previous study [9] used a large-scale dataset of 6388 malicious and 60,098 benign samples. In addition, the previous study [21] used a labeled dataset of 5383 malicious and 111593 benign samples. By contrast, the datasets used in this study consists of 310 malicious and 5145 benign samples. The size of our datasets is less than 10% of the previous studies. In addition, the Bag-of-words with unfixed vectors achieved better accuracy than LSI. This result suggests that our method does not contain enough words to construct an efficient language model. Therefore, it would seem that a higher detection rate can be obtained if datasets of the same size are used.

7.3   Practical Use

The experimental result shows the maximum accuracy achieves approximately 0.95 on the imbalanced dataset. This result needs to be interpreted with caution. Recall the malicious ones account for approximately only 6%. In fact, the recall for unknown malicious PowerShell scripts achieves only 0.55. Although performance was not ideal, we nevertheless believe our method can be practical. Because our method does not require dynamic analysis. Furthermore, the actual ratio of malicious and benign samples is imbalanced. This suggests our method produces low false positives. In practical use, false positives should be minimized. Hence, our method can be used to filter out suspicious samples concisely. To extract these samples, the detection rate should be improved.

7.4   Research Ethics

The modules used in this study, such as gensim and scikit-learn, are freely provided and can be used on consumer computers. The PowerShell samples were obtained from popular web sites. Comparing the previous studies, the preprocessing method is more clearly described. Hence, it seems that the proposed method can be easily implemented and produces high reproducibility.

7.5 Limitations

Our study has some limitations. The most important limitation is that we could not obtain enough samples to provide a fair comparison. According to the experimental result, there is room for improvement on our method. To produce more reliable results, multiple datasets with enough samples should be used. Another limitation is that we did not examine the details of the samples. In this experiment, we simply categorized the samples by the year when they were firstly posted to Hybrid Analysis. We did not strictly identify the samples. Hence, we cannot deny that the test samples contain the variants. To evaluate the performance against unknown PowerShell scripts, we should analyze the samples to identify.

8 Conclusion

This paper proposes a method to classify unknown PowerShell scripts by creating feature vectors from malicious and benign PowerShell scripts. Our method constructs word-level language models without dynamic analysis. The experimental result shows that the combination of the LSI and XGBoost produces the highest detection rate. The maximum accuracy achieves approximately 0.95 on the imbalanced dataset. Furthermore, over 50% of unknown malicious PowerShell scripts could be detected without dynamic analysis. Although our study produces higher reproducibility, the accuracy of the conventional method with dynamic analysis is not achieved.

The followings are left as future problems. The first is to obtain many samples. The number of malicious PowerShell samples used in this study is approximately 300, which do not represent the whole distribution. To produce more reliable results, we have to consider how to obtain more samples. The second is analyzing the malware families and detection rates for new malware families. Identifying the malware families and investigating the detection rate for each family will contribute to the improvement of our method. In addition, it is necessary to verify whether a completely new malware family can be detected. The third is analyzing the causes of false positives. This will also contribute to improve the accuracy.

References

1. GitHub. https://github.co.jp/
2. Hybrid Analysis. https://www.hybrid-analysis.com/
3. Powerdrive. https://github.com/denisugarte/PowerDrive
4. Virus Total. https://www.virustotal.com/
5. Breiman, L.: Random forests. Mach. Learn. 45(1), 5–32 (2001). https://doi.org/10.1023/A:1010933404324
6. Chang, C., Lin, C.: LIBSVM: a library for support vector machines. ACM Trans. Intell. Syst. Technol. 2, 27:1–27:27 (2011). https://doi.org/10.1145/1961189.1961199

7. Chen, T., Guestrin, C.: XGBoost: a scalable tree boosting system. In: Proceedings of the 22nd ACM SIGKDD International Conference on Knowledge Discovery and Data Mining, San Francisco, CA, USA, August 13–17, 2016, pp. 785–794 (2016). https://doi.org/10.1145/2939672.2939785

8. Deerwester, S.C., Dumais, S.T., Landauer, T.K., Furnas, G.W., Harshman, R.A.: Indexing by latent semantic analysis. JASIS **41**(6), 391–407 (1990). https://doi. org/10.1002/(SICI)1097-4571(199009)41:6⟨391::AID-ASI1⟩3.0.CO;2-9

9. Hendler, D., Kels, S., Rubin, A.: Detecting malicious PowerShell commands using deep neural networks. In: Proceedings of the 2018 on Asia Conference on Computer and Communications Security, AsiaCCS 2018, Incheon, Republic of Korea, June 04–08, 2018, pp. 187–197 (2018). https://doi.org/10.1145/3196494.3196511

10. Ito, R., Mimura, M.: Detecting unknown malware from ASCII strings with natural language processing techniques. In: 2019 14th Asia Joint Conference on Information Security (AsiaJCIS), pp. 1–8 (2019)

11. Le, Q.V., Mikolov, T.: Distributed representations of sentences and documents. In: Proceedings of the 31th International Conference on Machine Learning, ICML 2014, Beijing, China, 21–26 June 2014, pp. 1188–1196 (2014). http://proceedings. mlr.press/v32/le14.html

12. McAfee: McAfee labs threats report August 2019 (August 2019). https://www. mcafee.com/enterprise/en-us/assets/reports/rp-quarterly-threats-aug-2019.pdf

13. Mikolov, T., Chen, K., Corrado, G., Dean, J.: Efficient estimation of word representations in vector space. In: 1st International Conference on Learning Representations, ICLR 2013, Scottsdale, Arizona, USA, May 2–4, 2013, Workshop Track Proceedings (2013). http://arxiv.org/abs/1301.3781

14. Mimura, M., Suga, Y.: Filtering malicious JavaScript code with doc2vec on an imbalanced dataset. In: 2019 14th Asia Joint Conference on Information Security (AsiaJCIS), pp. 24–31 (2019)

15. Mimura, M., Miura, H.: Detecting unseen malicious VBA macros with NLP techniques. JIP **27**, 555–563 (2019). https://doi.org/10.2197/ipsjjip.27.555

16. Mimura, M., Ohminami, T.: Towards efficient detection of malicious VBA macros with LSI. In: Attrapadung, N., Yagi, T. (eds.) IWSEC 2019. LNCS, vol. 11689, pp. 168–185. Springer, Cham (2019). https://doi.org/10.1007/978-3-030-26834-3_10

17. Mimura, M., Ohminami, T.: Using LSI to detect unknown malicious VBA macros. J. Inf. Process. **28** (2020)

18. Miura, H., Mimura, M., Tanaka, H.: Macros finder: do you remember LOVELETTER? In: Su, C., Kikuchi, H. (eds.) ISPEC 2018. LNCS, vol. 11125, pp. 3–18. Springer, Cham (2018). https://doi.org/10.1007/978-3-319-99807-7_1

19. Ndichu, S., Kim, S., Ozawa, S., Misu, T., Makishima, K.: A machine learning approach to detection of JavaScript-based attacks using AST features and paragraph vectors. Appl. Soft Comput. **84**, 105721 (2019). https://doi.org/10.1016/j.asoc. 2019.105721

20. Pedregosa, F., et al.: Scikit-learn: machine learning in Python. J. Mach. Learn. Res. **12**, 2825–2830 (2011). http://dl.acm.org/citation.cfm?id=2078195

21. Rubin, A., Kels, S., Hendler, D.: AMSI-based detection of malicious PowerShell code using contextual embeddings. arXiv e-prints arXiv:1905.09538 (May 2019)

22. Rusak, G., Al-Dujaili, A., O'Reilly, U.: AST-based deep learning for detecting malicious PowerShell. In: Proceedings of the 2018 ACM SIGSAC Conference on Computer and Communications Security, CCS 2018, Toronto, ON, Canada, October 15–19, 2018, pp. 2276–2278 (2018). https://doi.org/10.1145/3243734.3278496

23. Symantec: Symantec 2019 Internet security threat report (February 2019). https://docs.broadcom.com/docs/istr-24-2019-en
24. Ugarte, D., Maiorca, D., Cara, F., Giacinto, G.: PowerDrive: accurate de-obfuscation and analysis of PowerShell malware. In: Perdisci, R., Maurice, C., Giacinto, G., Almgren, M. (eds.) DIMVA 2019. LNCS, vol. 11543, pp. 240–259. Springer, Cham (2019). https://doi.org/10.1007/978-3-030-22038-9_12

Detection of Running Malware
Before it Becomes Malicious

Sergii Banin[✉] and Geir Olav Dyrkolbotn

Department of Information Security and Communication Technology,
NTNU, Gjøvik, Norway
sergii.banin@ntnu.no

Abstract. As more vulnerabilities are being discovered every year [17], malware constantly evolves forcing improvements and updates of security and malware detection mechanisms. Malware is used directly on the attacked systems, thus anti-virus solutions tend to neutralize malware by not letting it launch or even being stored in the system. However, if malware is launched it is important to stop it as soon as the maliciousness of a new process has been detected. Following the results from [8] in this paper we show, that it is possible to detect running malware before it becomes malicious. We propose a novel malware detection approach that is capable of detecting Windows malware on the earliest stage of execution. The accuracy of more than 99% has been achieved by finding distinctive low-level behavior patterns generated before malware reaches it's entry point. We also study the ability of our approach to detect malware after it reaches it's entry point and to distinguish between benign executables and 10 malware families.

Keywords: Malware detection · Low-level features · Hardware-based features · Information security · Malware analysis · Malware classification

1 Introduction

Every year our society becomes more dependent on computers and computer systems, thus attacks on the personal, industry and infrastructure computers start having more severe consequences [23, 26]. According to NIST the amount of vulnerabilities discovered every year has grown almost 3 times during the years 2015–2019 [17]. At the same time a number of vulnerabilities found on Windows platforms has shown 10% growth [18]. Furthermore, the amount of newly discovered Windows malware has grown 30% during the same period [4]. Such security landscape outlines the need for updates in existing and invention of new malware detection mechanisms.

The research leading to these results has received funding from the Center for Cyber and Information Security, under budget allocation from the Ministry of Justice and Public Security of Norway.

The original version of this chapter was revised: two modifications have been made. The correction to this chapter is available at https://doi.org/10.1007/978-3-030-58208-1_17

K. Aoki and A. Kanaoka (Eds.): IWSEC 2020, LNCS 12231, pp. 57–73, 2020.
https://doi.org/10.1007/978-3-030-58208-1_4

Malware detection methods can be divided based on which features of malware they use for detection: static and dynamic. Static features emerge from the properties of an executable files themselves: file header, opcode and byte n-grams or hashes are known to be used for malware detection [24]. Dynamic features represent the behavior of malware when it runs and can be roughly divided into high- and low-level features [8]. API and system calls, network and file activity are some of the high-level features, while memory access operations, opcodes or hardware performance counters are the low-level features. Basically we perceive behavioral features that emerge from the system's hardware as the low-level ones [7,13,20]. Static features are easier to change for an attacker utilizing techniques such as obfuscation or encryption. However, malware becomes malicious only when it is executed and it is impossible to avoid a behavioral footprint [10]. Even though different techniques such as polymorphism, anti-VM or anti-debug might be used to change high-level behavioral patterns, the functionality of malware remains similar. Moreover, as soon as malware is launched - it is impossible to avoid execution on the system's hardware. That's why in this paper we use low-level features such as memory access patterns for malware detection [9] and classification [7].

Memory access patterns previously were proven to be effective features for malware detection [9] and classification [7]. A memory access pattern is a sequence of read and write operations performed by an executable and will be described in details in Sect. 3. The problem with low-level features is that it is hard for a human analyst to understand the context under which a certain pattern has occurred. A previous work [8] presented an attempt to fill the gap between low-level activity (memory access patterns) and its high-level (more human understandable API calls) representation. During the study it was also found, that under the experimental design used in [8] and [7] most of the recorded behavioral activity emerged not from the main module of an executable (after the Entry Point[1] - AEP) but prior to the moment when instruction pointer (IP) is set to the Entry Point (before the Entry Point - BEP). Without going into much details (see Sect. 2 for details) these findings showed, that it is potentially possible to detect running malicious executable before it starts executing the logic that was put into it by the creator.

To study these findings, in this paper we use a novel approach in behavioral malware analysis. This approach involves analysis of behavioral traces divided into those generated BEP and those generated AEP: *BEP-AEP approach*. More specifically, we show how memory access patterns can be used for malware detection based on the activity produced BEP. To be consistent in our studies we also compare these results to those achieved based on the activity produced AEP: by the malicious code itself. As paper [7] showed a possibility to classify malware into categories (families or types) using memory access patterns, further we investigate the usefulness of *BEP-AEP approach* for distinguishing between

---

[1] In this paper, by Entry Point, we mean the first executed instruction from the main module of executable.

benign executables and different malware families. In order to formalize our future findings we propose the following hypotheses:

Hypothesis 1. *It is possible to detect (distinguish from benign) running malicious executable based on the memory access patterns it produces before it begins to execute malicious code (BEP).*

Hypothesis 2. *It is possible to detect (distinguish from benign) running malicious executable based on the memory access patterns it produces after its Entry Point (AEP).*

And as the logic put into the executable (and makes malware malicious) normally runs AEP we had another hypothesis:

Hypothesis 3. *If Hypotheses 1, 2 are true, then it should be easier (higher classification performance) to detect running malicious executable AEP than BEP.*

To test whether a *BEP-AEP approach* can be used to distinguish between benign and several different categories of malicious executables we had another three hypotheses (directly derived from Hypotheses 1, 2 and 3)

Hypothesis 4. *It is possible to distinguish between several malware categories and benign executables based on the memory access patterns they produce BEP.*

Hypothesis 5. *It is possible to distinguish between several malware categories and benign executables based on the memory access patterns they produce AEP.*

Hypothesis 6. *If Hypotheses 4, 5 are true then it should be easier (higher classification performance) to distinguish between several malware categories and benign executables based on the memory access patterns they produce AEP.*

In order to check the above mentioned hypotheses we decided to perform a series of experiments that consist of several parts. First, we record memory access patterns produced by executables before and after entry point with help of dynamic binary instrumentation framework Intel Pin [12]. Second, we perform feature construction and selection to create different feature vectors. Last, we train several machine learning (ML) algorithms to check our hypotheses by looking at classification performance of machine learning models.

The remainder of the paper is arranged as following: Sect. 2 provides a literature overview, Sect. 3 describes our choice of methods, Sect. 4 explains our experimental setup, in Sect. 5 we provide results and analyze them, in Sect. 6 we discuss our findings and in the Sect. 7 we provide conclusions.

2 Related Works

In this section we provide an overview of papers that are related to this article in terms of features used for malware detection as well as methods to extract those features. The first paper we would like to mention is [3] where authors suggested to use Intel Pin based tool to detect malicious behavior by matching it against predefined security policies. Authors record execution flow of executables and describe it by splitting into basic blocks with additional information about each basic block. Among the different sources of information of the basic blocks they used: file modification system calls, fact of presence of *exec* function call and the fact of presence of memory read and write operations. During the testing phase they managed to achieve average path coverage of more than 93% which later helped them to get as much as 100% detection rate on Windows and Linux systems. Even though their datasets were relatively small this work showed promising capabilities of Intel Pin in the malware research.

The next paper [5] focuses more on the low-level features and their use in malware detection. As the features they used retired and mispredicted branch instructions as well as retired load and stored instructions derived from hardware performance counters. Authors achieved classification precision of more then 90%. Their dataset was also relatively small, but they pointed to the effectiveness of low-level feature in malware detection. Later, the same authors expanded their approach by using additional low-level features (near calls, near branches, cache misses etc.) in the paper [6]. They have also expanded their task to multinomial classification of benign and malicious samples divided into several families. This time they achieved 95% precision on a bigger dataset, what, once again, showed capabilities of low-level features use in malware detection and classification.

In [14] another example of application of hardware-based features is proposed. Extending their work from [19], authors propose hardware malware detector that uses several low-level features such as: frequencies and presence of opcodes from different categories, memory reference distance, presence of a load and store operations, amount of memory reads and writes, unaligned memory accesses as well as taken and immediate branches. Using ensemble specialized and ensemble classifiers authors achieved classification and detection accuracy of around 90% and 96% respectively.

Papers [3,5,14] used information about memory access operations but they didn't use sequences, or patterns, of memory access operations. The first paper where memory access patterns were used for malware detection was [9]. There authors explored a possibility of malware detection based on n-grams of memory access operations. They recorded sequences of memory access operations from malicious and benign executables. After the experiments authors found, that with n-gram size of 96 it is possible to achieve malicious against benign classification accuracy of up to 98%. Later, the same authors explored possibility of a use of memory access n-grams for malware classification [7]. They tested their approach on two datasets label into malware *types* and *families* respectively. After the feature selection they went down to as low as 29 features which allowed them to classify malware types with accuracy of 66% and families with accuracy of 78%. This performance was not as good as pure malicious against benign classification. However, for 10-class classification problem such accuracy showed that this methods (with certain limitations) can be used for malware classification as well. During their studies authors discovered a following problem: memory access patterns provide little context to a human analyst as it is almost impossible to understand which part of the execution flow created a distinctive memory access pattern. To eliminate this knowledge gap, in their next paper [8] they performed an attempt to "correlate" memory access patterns (as low-level features) with API calls (as high-level features). Together with memory access operations they recorded API calls performed by malicious executables. In the end their attempt was not successful: with their methodology they were not able to find any significant "correlation" between memory access patterns and API calls. However, as those events were proven to be independent they showed, that combining API calls and memory access patterns into integrated feature vector results into increased classification performance. On the dataset from [7] they managed to show increased classification accuracy of 70% and of 86% for malware types and families respectively. It was in this paper where they discovered, that most of the behavioral activity they recorded originated from BEP and outlined a need for additional study of such finding.

To the best of our knowledge no one has analyzed the possibility of malware detection and classification based on activity generated BEP. Therefore we think that our paper provides a novel contribution and grounds for further research.

3 Methodology

This section describes the methods used in our work. We begin with a description of the process creation flow on Windows. It has multiple stages and it is important to show where we begin to record a behavioral trace: a set of opcodes with their memory access operations, current function and module name. Second, we explain the way we transform a behavioral trace into the memory access patterns that are later used as features for training the ML models. We also describe how we perform a feature selection. Last, we provide a description of ML methods and evaluation metrics.

3.1 General Overview

As we present BEP-AEP approach in this paper, we have to provide a brief description of a process creation flow the way it is implemented in Windows. The flow of process creation consists of several stages (as described in Windows Internals [28]) and is depicted on the Fig. 1. First, the process and thread objects are created. Then a Windows Subsystem Specific process initialization is performed. Lastly, the execution of the new process begins from the Final Process Initialization (Stage 7 on Fig. 1). During these stages OS initializes a virtual address space that is later used by a process. Virtual address space is divided into private process memory and protected OS memory. The size of virtual address space depends on the OS type. Normally 32-bit Windows will have up to 4 GB while 64-bit - up to 512 GB of virtual address space. The virtual address space contains heap, stack, loaded DLLs, kernel and code of the executable (main module). CPU executes instructions (opcodes) from main module or one of the loaded libraries. Each opcode can be divided into several microoperations. Some microoperations are used for arithmetical-logical operations while some are responsible for memory read and write operations. Whenever execution of an opcode requires a memory related microoperation to be executed, Intel Pin tool will record this into the behavioral trace. Intel Pin tool begins to record the behavioral trace at Stage 7, when a new process is started. In the context of a newly created process, Stage 7 generates a BEP activity and includes (but is not limited to) the following actions: installing of exception chains; checking if the process is debugee and whether prefetching is enabled; initialization of image loader, heap manager; loading of all the necessary DLLs. When it is finished, AEP activity begins from execution of Entry Point in the main module. Some malware samples might use packing, thus will unpack itself in the beginning of its execution. However, it is important to understand, that unpacking will be done with instructions from the main module of executable. Thus, with our approach, unpacking will happen AEP.

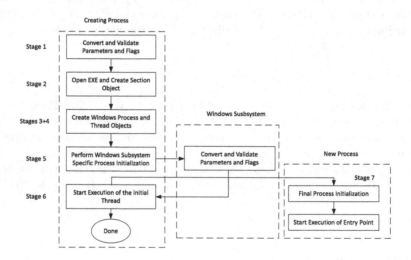

Fig. 1. Process creation flow [28]

3.2   Data Collection

In this subsection we describe the way we record behavioral traces. In order to record memory access traces we wrote a custom tool that was based on the Intel Pin framework [12]. Intel Pin is a binary instrumentation framework that allows to intercept execution flow of a process and extract much of the information related to this process such as: memory access operations, opcode, name of a module from which an opcode is being executed and name of a current routine (if possible to derive). Every executable from our dataset (Subsect. 4.1) was launched together with the Intel Pin tool. The tool records all the data mentioned above into the behavioral trace. The process of each executable was observed from the beginning of its execution. We recorded the behavioral trace until we gathered 1,000,000 (1M) of memory access operations (similar to [9] and [7]) BEP, and then we continued recording AEP - again until we reached 1M of memory access operations. As we worked with real-life malicious and benign executables, we were not always able to record the desired amount of memory access operations. Some samples reached main module before producing the desired 1M of memory access operations BEP, while some finished their work before producing 1M of memory access operations AEP. It is worth mentioning, that some samples didn't produce any traces AEP. All data collection was done in the Virtual Box virtual machine (VM) in order to protect the host system, allow automation and ensure equal launch conditions for all executables.

3.3   Feature Construction and Selection

Before using our data for training the ML models we have to construct and select features. Memory access operations (BEP or AEP respectively) are concatenated into memory access sequence. Based on the methods used in [8] we split memory access sequence produced by an executable into a set of subsequences: n-grams of the length 96. These n-grams are overlapping, so every next n-gram begins from the second element of the previous one. A typical memory access n-gram looks the following way: $RRRWWWWR...WRRRRRRRW$. If we treat R as 0 and W as 1 n-gram of a size $n = 96$ becomes binary sequence with potential feature space of 2^{96}. Even though we do not get this amount of distinctive features, our samples still produce millions of features (see Sect. 5). So we need to perform feature selection in order to reduce feature space, reject uninformative features and be able to train ML models in a feasible time. Smaller feature set also contributes for better understanding of the findings and allows "manual" analysis if necessary [7,8].

The feature selection is performed in two steps. On the first step we go down from millions of features to 50,000 by using Information Gain feature selection method. Information Gain (IG) is an attribute quality measure that reflects "the amount of information, obtained from the attribute A, for determining the class C" [15] and is calculated as following:

$$Gain(A) = -\sum_k p_k \log p_k + \sum_j p_j \sum_k p_{k|j} \log p_{k|j}$$

where p_k is the probability of the class k, p_j is the probability of an attribute to take j_{th} value and $p_{k|j}$ is the conditional probability of class k given j_{th} value of an attribute. On the second step we use Correlation-based feature selection (CFS) [11] from Weka [2] package (CfsSubsetEval). This method selects a subset of features based on the maximum-Relevance-Minimum-Redundancy principle by selecting features that have maximal relevance for representing the target class and minimal mutual correlation [21]. The reason we did not apply this method to the full feature set is computational complexity. In order to perform CFS feature selection one needs to calculate correlation matrix between all features which would require infeasible amount of computational resources and time. We also select 5, 10, 15 and 30 thousands of features with IG. It is important to know, that CFS adds features to the feature set until further increase of its merit is no longer possible. Thereby, in the end we use IG to select the same amount of features as was selected by CFS. By doing so we can directly compare performance of two feature selection methods. After the feature selection process we create data that is later used to train ML models. Basically we generate a table, where each row represents values that features from the feature set take for a certain sample. In our paper similarly to [9] we use *1* if feature (memory access n-gram) is generated by sample and *0* if not.

3.4 Machine Learning Methods and Evaluation Metrics

We use Weka [2] machine learning toolkit to build and evaluate our models. Similarly to [8] we choose the following ML methods to build our models: k-Nearest Neighbors (kNN), RandomForest (RF), Decision Trees (J48), Support Vector Machines (SVM), Naive Bayes (NB) and Artificial Neural Network (ANN) with the default for Weka [2] package parameters. To evaluate quality of models we use 5-fold cross validation [15] and choose the following evaluation metrics for models assessment: accuracy (ACC) as number of correctly identified samples and F1-measure (F1M) which takes into account precision and recall. We omit using False Positives measure as it is not representative for multinomial classification. The F1M values presented in Sect. 5 are average weighted. For the benign against malicious classification our dataset is nearly balanced (see Subsect. 4.1), however while doing multinomial classification we had to deal with imbalanced classes. The problem with imbalanced classes is that evaluation metrics does not reflect real quality of models, since simple guessing on the majority class will give high accuracy. To deal with this problem we apply weights to the samples, so that sums of the weights of samples within each class would be equal.

4   Experimental Setup

In this section we describe our dataset, experimental environment and experimental flow.

4.1   Dataset

As Windows is the most popular desktop platform [16] we focused on analyzing Windows malware. Our dataset consists of two parts: malware samples and benign samples. Benign samples were collected from Portable Apps [22] in September 2019. It is a collection of free Portable software that includes various types of software such as graphical, text and database editors; games; browsers; office, music, audio and other types of Windows software. In total we obtained 2669 PE executables. Malicious samples were taken from *VirusShare_00360* pack downloaded from VirusShare [1]. *VirusShare_00360* contained 65518 samples, out of which 2973 were PE executables. For each sample we downloaded a report from VirusTotal [27] and left samples that belonged to the 10 most common families. Those families are: Fareit, Occamy, Emotet, VBInject, Ursnif, Prepscram, CeeInject, Tiggre, Skeeyah, GandCrab. According to the VirusTotal reports, resulted samples were first seen (first submission date) between March 2018 and March 2019. Not all the samples were launched successfully, and from those that launched not all the samples produced traces AEP (most likely executables lacked some resources, e.g. certain libraries). So the amounts of samples that generated traces BEP and AEP are different. In the Table 1 we present amount of samples of each category that produced traces BEP and AEP.

Table 1. Amount of samples that generated traces BEP and AEP.

	Benign	Malicious	Fareit	Occamy	Emotet	VBInject	Ursnif	Prepscram	CeeInject	Tiggre	Skeeyah	GandCrab
BEP	2098	2005	573	307	196	164	162	143	127	117	115	101
AEP	1717	1755	573	174	188	162	161	143	115	69	73	97

4.2 Experimental Environment

For our experiments we used Virtual Dedicated Server with 4-cores Intel Xeon CPU E5-2630 CPU running at 2.4 GHz and 32 GB of RAM with Ubuntu 18.04 as a main operating system. As a virtualization software we used VirtualBox 6.0.14. We created a Windows 10 VM and disconnected it from the Internet. We have uploaded Intel Pin together with our custom tool into the VM. We also disabled all built-in anti-virus features to make malware run properly and also because they kept interrupting the work of Intel Pin and created a base snapshot which was used for all experiments. We controlled the VM and data collection process with Python 3.7 scripts.

4.3 Experimental Flow

During the data collection phase we begin with starting up a VM. Then we upload an executable to the VM and launch it together with Intel Pin tool. When a behavioral trace is ready we download it from the VM and begin a new experiment with reverting a VM to the base snapshot. It is important to notice that benign executables were uploaded together with their folder. This allowed more of the benign applications to run properly and helped to emulate a more real-life scenario, where benign applications often come with various additional resources they need for normal operations.

5   Results and Analysis

In this section we provide the classification performance of ML models performed under different conditions. We also analyze the results and show how they align with the Hypotheses from Sect. 1.

5.1   Classification Performance

Each table contains performance metrics of ML methods (Subsect. 3.4) achieved with a feature sets (Subsect. 3.3) of a different length (*FSL* stands for feature set length). Some of the cells contain missing values: due to processing limitations of Weka we were not able to obtain all of the results.

In the Tables 2 and 3 the results of malicious against benign classification BEP and AEP are presented. As we can see, under our experimental design it is possible to achieve classification accuracy of 0.999 for BEP and 0.992 for AEP with 10000 features. CFS selected 9 features for BEP and 39 for AEP. Classification performance with use of CFS-selected features is slightly lower than the best result achieved with those selected by IG. At the same time, it is often higher for the same amount of features selected by IG.

Table 2. Malicious vs Benign BEP classification performance.

		kNN		RF		J48		SVM		NB		ANN	
Method	FSL	ACC	F1M	ACC	F1M	ACC	F1M	ACC	F1M	ACC	F1M	ACC	F1M
	50K	0.996	0.996	0.996	0.996	0.997	0.997	0.983	0.983	0.693	0.671	-	-
	30K	0.996	0.996	0.997	0.997	0.998	0.998	0.986	0.986	0.983	0.983	-	-
InfoGain	15K	0.996	0.996	0.998	0.998	0.998	0.998	0.991	0.990	0.983	0.983	-	-
	10K	0.998	0.998	**0.999**	**0.999**	0.998	0.998	0.992	0.991	0.983	0.983	-	-
	5K	0.995	0.995	0.997	0.997	0.997	0.997	0.988	0.988	0.983	0.983	-	-
	9	0.988	0.988	0.988	0.988	0.988	0.988	0.988	0.988	0.988	0.988	0.988	0.988
CFS	9	0.997	0.997	0.997	0.997	0.996	0.996	0.997	0.997	0.988	0.988	0.997	0.997

Table 3. Malicious vs Benign AEP classification performance.

		kNN		RF		J48		SVM		NB		ANN	
Method	FSL	ACC	F1M	ACC	F1M	ACC	F1M	ACC	F1M	ACC	F1M	ACC	F1M
	50K	0.974	0.974	0.985	0.985	0.991	0.991	0.948	0.948	0.735	0.720	-	-
	30K	0.982	0.982	0.990	0.990	0.989	0.989	0.949	0.949	0.795	0.787	-	-
InfoGain	15K	0.990	0.990	**0.992**	**0.992**	0.988	0.988	0.947	0.947	0.795	0.787	-	-
	10K	0.990	0.990	**0.992**	**0.992**	0.989	0.989	0.955	0.955	0.795	0.787	-	-
	5K	0.989	0.989	0.991	0.991	0.988	0.988	0.960	0.960	0.795	0.787	-	-
	39	0.910	0.909	0.910	0.909	0.908	0.908	0.907	0.906	0.844	0.840	0.910	0.909
CFS	39	0.990	0.990	0.990	0.990	0.989	0.989	0.987	0.987	0.982	0.982	0.991	0.991

In the Tables 4 and 5 we present performance of ML models in classifying benign and 10 malicious families using features generated BEP and AEP. In these tables we show classification performance for the imbalanced (*Imb*) and balanced datasets (*Bal*) (Subsect. 3.4). As we can see, performance of multinomial classification is lower than the benign against malicious classification.

By using BEP and AEP features we achieved 0.605 and 0.749 classification accuracy respectively. The main observation that can be derived from these tables is that it is easier to distinguish between benign executables and 10 malware families using features generated AEP than BEP.

Table 4. 10 Malicious families vs Benign BEP classification performance.

Method	FSL		kNN		RF		J48		SVM		NB		ANN	
			ACC	F1M	ACC	F1M	ACC	F1M	ACC	F1M	ACC	F1M	ACC	F1M
InfoGain	50K	Imb	0.812	0.776	0.812	0.775	0.811	0.771	-	-	0.429	0.462	-	-
		Bal	0.601	0.546	**0.605**	0.549	0.596	0.541	-	-	0.403	0.326	-	-
	30K	Imb	0.812	0.777	0.813	0.776	0.808	0.769	0.789	0.740	0.687	0.667	-	-
		Bal	0.598	0.542	0.600	0.543	0.594	0.538	0.549	0.477	0.433	0.355	-	-
	15K	Imb	0.813	0.777	0.815	0.777	0.811	0.772	0.792	0.745	0.689	0.668	-	-
		Bal	0.594	0.538	0.596	0.540	0.594	0.539	0.565	0.501	0.435	0.355	-	-
	10K	Imb	0.813	0.775	0.814	0.776	0.809	0.770	0.798	0.753	0.689	0.668	-	-
		Bal	0.589	0.531	0.593	0.535	0.590	0.531	0.569	0.502	0.435	0.356	-	-
	5K	Imb	0.789	0.745	0.790	0.745	0.789	0.743	0.782	0.728	0.633	0.591	-	-
		Bal	0.508	0.446	0.513	0.452	0.512	0.446	0.492	0.413	0.382	0.301	-	-
	92	Imb	0.653	0.575	0.653	0.575	0.653	0.575	0.652	0.571	0.651	0.567	0.652	0.573
		Bal	0.184	0.140	0.185	0.140	0.183	0.137	0.182	0.135	0.180	0.128	0.170	0.136
CFS	92	Imb	0.813	0.775	0.813	0.775	0.810	0.769	0.805	0.760	0.740	0.725	0.810	0.771
		Bal	0.585	0.526	0.585	0.527	0.578	0.529	0.572	0.512	0.521	0.467	0.576	0.540

As the number of samples that produced traces BEP and AEP is different we have also tested the performance of features from BEP on the normalized dataset, when we only take into account samples that produced traces AEP. These results are present in the Appendix Appendix A. We also combined features produced BEP and AEP and tested classification performance of the combined feature set. These results presented in the Appendix Appendix B.

5.2 Analysis

From the results presented in Tables 2 and 3 we can conclude that both Hypotheses 1 and 2 are supported: we can distinguish between malicious and benign behavior BEP and AEP. However, even if there is a visible decline in accuracy when switching from BEP behavior to AEP it is relatively low. Thus, we are not able to conclude that our approach allows to detect malware BEP better then AEP or vise versa. Thereby, we were not able to support or reject Hypothesis 3. This may be a reflection of property of our dataset or a limitation of our approach, and therefore needs further investigation in the future work.

By looking at the numbers of features selected by CFS we can see, that it selects more features for AEP data than for BEP data. And it's not surprising, since the behavior of executables become more diverse AEP: this is where their internal logic starts being executed. It is also confirmed by the amount of unique features produced by the samples BEP and AEP. Malicious samples

Table 5. 10 Malicious families vs Benign AEP classification performance.

Method	FSL		kNN ACC F1M	RF ACC F1M	J48 ACC F1M	SVM ACC F1M	NB ACC F1M	ANN ACC F1M
InfoGain	50K	Imb	0.890 0.883	0.902 0.890	0.897 0.888	- -	0.433 0.420	- -
		Bal	0.715 0.694	0.724 0.714	**0.749 0.737**	- -	0.503 0.418	- -
	30K	Imb	0.891 0.883	0.891 0.883	0.898 0.888	0.727 0.635	0.505 0.527	- -
		Bal	0.725 0.705	0.732 0.714	0.729 0.708	0.539 0.498	0.493 0.414	- -
	15K	Imb	0.889 0.881	0.900 0.891	0.898 0.887	0.780 0.712	0.508 0.530	- -
		Bal	0.724 0.704	0.731 0.714	0.723 0.702	0.625 0.589	0.499 0.420	- -
	10K	Imb	0.887 0.878	0.900 0.891	0.897 0.886	0.805 0.756	0.509 0.530	- -
		Bal	0.717 0.695	0.725 0.706	0.729 0.711	0.645 0.606	0.497 0.418	- -
	5K	Imb	0.866 0.851	0.872 0.854	0.865 0.848	0.747 0.669	0.384 0.384	- -
		Bal	0.660 0.618	0.661 0.619	0.653 0.605	0.504 0.442	0.433 0.342	- -
	40	Imb	0.694 0.615	0.694 0.616	0.693 0.613	0.688 0.604	0.670 0.597	0.693 0.617
		Bal	0.306 0.212	0.307 0.206	0.302 0.204	0.299 0.217	0.298 0.193	0.283 0.225
CFS	40	Imb	0.902 0.896	0.903 0.892	0.891 0.880	0.889 0.873	0.872 0.864	0.900 0.890
		Bal	0.725 0.701	0.726 0.704	0.717 0.695	0.706 0.667	0.695 0.653	0.722 0.692

produced more than 1M features BEP, and more than 7M features AEP. On the other hand, benign applications produced more than 4.5M of features BEP and almost 20.5M AEP. This resulted in more then 5M unique features to choose from for BEP classification, and 25M for AEP classification. This also shows, that benign applications are more diverse and produce more distinctive memory access patterns as a result of a more distinctive behavior. And it makes sense, since malware samples belong to 10 malware families, thus should share more common properties according to the definition of malware family from [7].

The results of multinomial classification (Tables 4 and 5) are more diverse then those for malicious against benign classification. This time, it is clearly easier to distinguish between 11 classes AEP than BEP. Even though multinomial classification accuracy BEP is not that impressive it is still significantly better than potential accuracy of 0.09 (09) that can be achieved by random guessing. Thus we can conclude, that Hypothesis 4 is supported. Multinomial classification accuracy AEP was significantly better. So we can conclude that Hypothesis 5 is also supported, thereby Hypothesis 6 as well.

This time CFS has chosen less features for the AEP classification than for the BEP classification. As we mentioned above, malware assigned to one of the families based on its particular functionality. And this functionality becomes revealed AEP. Thereby it is logical to say, that classification of 11 classes is more accurate based on the behavior generated AEP. Table 6 present combined results of the Hypotheses evaluation.

Table 6. Evaluation of Hypotheses after analyzing the results

	H1	H2	H3	H4	H5	H6
Supported	Yes	Yes	-	Yes	Yes	Yes

6 Discussion

In this section we present an attempt to interpret our findings. Earlier, we showed the possibility of malware detection based on the memory access patterns generated BEP. So, we wanted to find an explanation of why the BEP activity of malicious and benign executables is so different. More specifically we wanted to see which high-level activity is responsible for generating specific memory access patterns. As it was written in Subsect. 3.2, we recorded not only memory access operations, but also routine names for each executed opcode. Since BEP activity happens in the Windows libraries (Subsect. 3.1) we are always able to derive a name of a current routine. Thereby, a memory access pattern can be represented as a sequence of routine names. However, our memory access patterns are of a length 96, so having 96 routine names (many of which are repetitive) makes analysis harder and adds redundant information. Thus, we decided to represent each memory access pattern as a sequence of unique routine names. For example, if memory access pattern begins in a routine RTN_1, proceeds into the RTN_2 and finishes in the RTN_1 we store the following sequence: $\{RTN\_1, RTN\_2, RTN\_1\}$. After performing this search on the 9 features selected by CFS (Subsect. 5.1) we made a surprising discovery: most of these features originated in *RtlAllocateHeap* routine from the *ntdll.dll* Windows library. Some memory access patterns were completely generated by *RtlAllocateHeap*, while others involved other routines as well. The same memory access pattern can be found in different routine sequences. However, similar to [8], this is the result of our patterns structure and feature construction method (e.g. they can start and end with a sequence of repetitive W's or R's) that allow similar pattern to appear multiple times in a row. For example, one feature can be found in the following sequences: $\{RtlAllocateHeap\}$, $\{bsearch, RtlAllocateHeap\}$, $\{LdrGetProcedureAddressForCaller, RtlAllocateHeap\}$, $\{RtlEqualUnicodeString, RtlAllocateHeap\}$. The *RtlAllocateHeap* routine is responsible for allocating a memory block of a certain size from a heap. Thus, when the Final Process Initialization phase of process creating flow needs to allocate a memory block it produces a distinctive activity that allows to distinguish between malicious and benign processes on the stage of initialization. Unfortunately, we were not able to explain why this memory allocation activity can be so distinctive. Neither the official Microsoft documentation on *RtlAllocateHeap*, nor the Windows Internals book [28] gives enough details about memory allocation routines. To answer this question, one may need to revers engineer *ntdll.dll* library and perform a Kernel-level [25] debugging. And we leave it for the future work, as this is out of scope of this paper.

7 Conclusions

In this paper we presented a novel dynamical malware analysis approach, where we distinguish between activity produced before and after Entry Point. As we were able to show, it is possible to distinguish between malicious and benign executables BEP with accuracy of up to *0.999* with 10000 features, and up to *0.997* with just 9 features. It means, that it is possible to detect malicious executables on the stage of their launch: before they become malicious. We also found, that distinguishing between benign samples and samples from 10 malware families is also possible using BEP activity. We have also made an interesting discovery: many of the memory access patterns used for malware detection BEP are generated by the *RtlAllocateHeap* routine. This paper shows a need for further research of the low-level activity use in malware analysis. First of all, we need to make a complete explanation of why the BEP activity of malicious and benign executables are that different. Second, we have to check the robustness of this approach against the previously unknown malware. Lastly, to fully utilize the capabilities of BEP-AEP approach we need to study the possibility of building the real-time system that uses our approach. This will involve assessment of computational overhead and potential impact on the user experience.

Appendix A   Classification Results: Normalized Dataset

Here we present classification results for the normalized dataset using features from BEP (Tables 7 and 8).

Table 7. Malicious vs Benign BEP classification performance on the normalized dataset.

		kNN		RF		J48		SVM		NB		ANN	
Method	FSL	ACC	F1M	ACC	F1M	ACC	F1M	ACC	F1M	ACC	F1M	ACC	F1M
	50000	0.997	0.997	0.996	0.996	0.998	0.998	0.981	0.980	0.750	0.738	-	-
	30K	0.997	0.997	0.997	0.997	0.998	0.998	0.983	0.983	0.981	0.980	-	-
InfoGain	15K	0.997	0.997	**0.999**	**0.999**	0.998	0.998	0.990	0.990	0.981	0.980	-	-
	10K	0.997	0.997	**0.999**	**0.999**	0.998	0.998	0.990	0.990	0.981	0.980	-	-
	5K	0.995	0.994	0.996	0.996	0.997	0.997	0.988	0.988	0.981	0.981	-	-
	10	0.988	0.988	0.988	0.988	0.988	0.988	0.988	0.988	0.988	0.988	0.988	0.988
CFS	10	0.998	0.998	0.998	0.998	0.997	0.997	0.998	0.998	0.988	0.988	0.997	0.997

Table 8. 10 Malicious families vs Benign BEP classification performance on the normalized dataset.

Method	FSL		kNN ACC F1M	RF ACC F1M	J48 ACC F1M	SVM ACC F1M	NB ACC F1M	ANN ACC F1M
InfoGain	50K	Imb	0.819 0.779	0.818 0.776	0.817 0.774	- -	0.478 0.500	- -
		Bal	0.586 0.528	0.588 0.528	0.590 0.532	- -	0.386 0.292	- -
	30K	Imb	0.817 0.776	0.819 0.777	0.816 0.774	0.798 0.744	0.685 0.659	- -
		Bal	0.579 0.517	0.587 0.525	**0.591 0.536**	0.555 0.491	0.423 0.337	- -
	15K	Imb	0.815 0.774	0.821 0.779	0.815 0.770	0.799 0.747	0.686 0.662	- -
		Bal	0.574 0.511	0.587 0.525	0.584 0.522	0.587 0.525	0.428 0.345	- -
	10K	Imb	0.817 0.776	0.819 0.777	0.817 0.772	0.800 0.749	0.685 0.660	- -
		Bal	0.576 0.513	0.580 0.517	0.578 0.518	0.569 0.505	0.422 0.335	- -
	5K	Imb	0.812 0.769	0.815 0.771	0.814 0.770	0.803 0.750	0.631 0.572	- -
		Bal	0.571 0.505	0.570 0.505	0.570 0.509	0.564 0.502	0.419 0.313	- -
	52	Imb	0.663 0.579	0.663 0.579	0.663 0.579	0.661 0.575	0.661 0.575	0.661 0.575
		Bal	0.190 0.135	0.189 0.155	0.189 0.133	0.189 0.144	0.188 0.131	0.190 0.146
CFS	52	Imb	0.823 0.782	0.822 0.781	0.817 0.772	0.809 0.760	0.739 0.721	0.823 0.781
		Bal	0.588 0.531	0.584 0.525	0.584 0.525	0.571 0.510	0.507 0.444	0.567 0.529

Appendix B Classification Results: Combined Feature Set

Here we present classification results achieved with combined feature set (Tables 9 and 10).

Table 9. Malicious vs Benign classification performance on the normalized dataset using combined feature set

Method	FSL	kNN ACC F1M	RF ACC F1M	J48 ACC F1M	SVM ACC F1M	NB ACC F1M	ANN ACC F1M
InfoGain	50000	0.996 0.996	0.998 0.998	0.999 0.999	0.981 0.981	0.981 0.980	- -
	30K	0.996 0.996	**0.999 0.999**	0.998 0.998	0.982 0.982	0.981 0.980	- -
	15K	0.997 0.997	**0.999 0.999**	0.998 0.998	0.987 0.987	0.981 0.980	- -
	10K	0.998 0.998	**0.999 0.999**	0.998 0.998	0.989 0.989	0.981 0.980	- -
	5K	0.999 0.999	**0.999 0.999**	0.998 0.998	0.995 0.995	0.981 0.980	- -
	13	0.988 0.987	0.988 0.987	0.998 0.998	0.988 0.987	0.988 0.987	0.988 0.987
CFS	13	0.997 0.997	0.998 0.998	0.996 0.996	0.996 0.996	0.988 0.988	0.997 0.997

Table 10. 10 Malicious families vs Benign classification performance on the normalized dataset using combined feature set.

Method	FSL		kNN ACC F1M	RF ACC F1M	J48 ACC F1M	SVM ACC F1M	NB ACC F1M	ANN ACC F1M
InfoGain	50K	Imb	0.910 0.905	0.917 0.910	0.910 0.906	- -	0.802 0.771	- -
		Bal	0.740 0.718	**0.749** 0.726	0.746 **0.736**	- -	0.508 0.419	- -
	30K	Imb	0.906 0.900	0.918 0.910	0.910 0.904	0.787 0.750	0.795 0.761	- -
		Bal	0.744 0.744	0.743 0.722	0.734 0.718	0.518 0.465	0.495 0.403	- -
	15K	Imb	0.904 0.898	0.917 0.909	0.908 0.902	0.806 0.771	0.908 0.902	- -
		Bal	0.744 0.723	0.740 0.720	0.737 0.723	0.608 0.570	0.493 0.400	- -
	10K	Imb	0.903 0.896	0.909 0.901	0.908 0.898	0.799 0.765	0.790 0.753	- -
		Bal	0.735 0.708	0.729 0.705	0.728 0.707	0.593 0.550	0.486 0.388	- -
	5K	Imb	0.792 0.763	0.789 0.759	0.790 0.757	0.754 0.710	0.679 0.647	- -
		Bal	0.535 0.499	0.534 0.498	0.535 0.499	0.440 0.382	0.408 0.311	- -
	62	Imb	0.663 0.579	0.662 0.577	0.662 0.577	0.662 0.577	0.660 0.569	0.663 0.579
		Bal	0.190 0.134	0.191 0.156	0.190 0.134	0.189 0.133	0.181 0.418	0.185 0.140
CFS	62	Imb	0.915 0.909	0.916 0.909	0.909 0.903	0.896 0.879	0.876 0.862	0.908 0.903
		Bal	0.744 0.722	0.745 0.724	0.739 0.721	0.723 0.691	0.669 0.625	0.743 0.729

References

1. Virusshare.com. http://virusshare.com/. Accessed 09 Mar 2020
2. Weka: Data mining software in java (2019). http://www.cs.waikato.ac.nz/ml/weka/. Accessed Mar 2019
3. Aaraj, N., Raghunathan, A., Jha, N.K.: Dynamic binary instrumentation-based framework for malware defense. In: Zamboni, D. (ed.) DIMVA 2008. LNCS, vol. 5137, pp. 64–87. Springer, Heidelberg (2008). https://doi.org/10.1007/978-3-540-70542-0_4
4. AVTEST: The independent IT-Security Institute: Malware (2020). https://nvd.nist.gov/vuln/search/statistics?form_type=Basic&results_type=statistics&search_type=all
5. Bahador, M.B., Abadi, M., Tajoddin, A.: HPCMalHunter: behavioral malware detection using hardware performance counters and singular value decomposition. In: 2014 4th International eConference on Computer and Knowledge Engineering (ICCKE), pp. 703–708. IEEE (2014). https://doi.org/10.1109/iccke.2014.6993402
6. Bahador, M.B., Abadi, M., Tajoddin, A.: HLMD: a signature-based approach to hardware-level behavioral malware detection and classification. J. Supercomput. **75**(8), 5551–5582 (2019). https://doi.org/10.1007/s11227-019-02810-z
7. Banin, S., Dyrkolbotn, G.O.: Multinomial malware classification via low-level features. Digit. Investig. **26**, S107–S117 (2018). https://doi.org/10.1016/j.diin.2018.04.019
8. Banin, S., Dyrkolbotn, G.O.: Correlating high- and low-level features: In: Attrapadung, N., Yagi, T. (eds.) IWSEC 2019. LNCS, vol. 11689, pp. 149–167. Springer, Cham (2019). https://doi.org/10.1007/978-3-030-26834-3_9
9. Banin, S., Shalaginov, A., Franke, K.: Memory access patterns for malware detection. Norsk informasjonssikkerhetskonferanse (NISK), pp. 96–107 (2016)
10. Burnap, P., French, R., Turner, F., Jones, K.: Malware classification using self organising feature maps and machine activity data. Comput. Secur. **73**, 399–410 (2018). https://doi.org/10.1016/j.cose.2017.11.016

11. Hall, M.A.: Correlation-based feature subset selection for machine learning. Ph.D. thesis, University of Waikato, Hamilton, New Zealand (1998)
12. IntelPin: A dynamic binary instrumentation tool (2020)
13. Khasawneh, K.N., Ozsoy, M., Donovick, C., Abu-Ghazaleh, N., Ponomarev, D.: Ensemble learning for low-level hardware-supported malware detection. In: Bos, H., Monrose, F., Blanc, G. (eds.) RAID 2015. LNCS, vol. 9404, pp. 3–25. Springer, Cham (2015). https://doi.org/10.1007/978-3-319-26362-5_1
14. Khasawneh, K.N., Ozsoy, M., Donovick, C., Ghazaleh, N.A., Ponomarev, D.V.: EnsembleHMD: accurate hardware malware detectors with specialized ensemble classifiers. IEEE Trans. Dependable Secur. Comput. (2018). https://doi.org/10.1109/tdsc.2018.2801858
15. Kononenko, I., Kukar, M.: Machine Learning and Data Mining: Introduction to Principles and Algorithms. Horwood Publishing, Cambridge (2007)
16. NetMarkeshare: Operating system market share (2020). https://netmarketshare.com/operating-system-market-share.aspx
17. NIST: National vulnerability database (2020). https://nvd.nist.gov/vuln/search/statistics?form_type=Basic&results_type=statistics&search_type=all
18. NIST: National vulnerability database: windows (2020). https://nvd.nist.gov/vuln/search/statistics?form_type=Advanced&results_type=statistics&query=Windows&search_type=all
19. Ozsoy, M., Donovick, C., Gorelik, I., Abu-Ghazaleh, N., Ponomarev, D.: Malware-aware processors: a framework for efficient online malware detection. In: 2015 IEEE 21st International Symposium on High Performance Computer Architecture (HPCA), pp. 651–661. IEEE (2015). https://doi.org/10.1109/hpca.2015.7056070
20. Ozsoy, M., Khasawneh, K.N., Donovick, C., Gorelik, I., Abu-Ghazaleh, N., Ponomarev, D.: Hardware-based malware detection using low-level architectural features. IEEE Trans. Comput. 65(11), 3332–3344 (2016). https://doi.org/10.1109/tc.2016.2540634
21. Peng, H., Long, F., Ding, C.: Feature selection based on mutual information criteria of max-dependency, max-relevance, and min-redundancy. IEEE Trans. Pattern Anal. Mach. Intell. 27(8), 1226–1238 (2005)
22. PortableApps.com: Portableapps.com (2020). https://portableapps.com/apps
23. Reuters: Ukraine's power outage was a cyber attack: Ukrenergo (2017). https://www.reuters.com/article/us-ukraine-cyber-attack-energy/ukraines-power-outage-was-a-cyber-attack-ukrenergo-idUSKBN1521BA
24. Shalaginov, A., Banin, S., Dehghantanha, A., Franke, K.: Machine learning aided static malware analysis: a survey and tutorial. In: Dehghantanha, A., Conti, M., Dargahi, T. (eds.) Cyber Threat Intelligence. AIS, vol. 70, pp. 7–45. Springer, Cham (2018). https://doi.org/10.1007/978-3-319-73951-9_2
25. Sikorski, M., Honig, A.: Practical Malware Analysis: The Hands-on Guide to Dissecting Malicious Software. No Starch Press, San Francisco (2012)
26. The Verge: The Petya ransomware is starting to look like a cyberattack in disguise (2017). https://www.theverge.com/2017/6/28/15888632/petya-goldeneye-ransomware-cyberattack-ukraine-russia
27. VirusTotal: VirusTotal-free online virus, malware and URL scanner (2012). https://www.virustotal.com/en
28. Yosifovich, P.: Windows Internals, Part 1 (Developer Reference). Microsoft Press, Redmond (2017)

Multiparty Computation

Efficiency and Accuracy Improvements of Secure Floating-Point Addition over Secret Sharing

Kota Sasaki[1][(✉)] and Koji Nuida[1,2]

[1] Graduate School of Information Science and Technology,
The University of Tokyo, Tokyo, Japan
sakiut1053@g.ecc.u-tokyo.ac.jp, nuida@mist.i.u-tokyo.ac.jp
[2] National Institute of Advanced Industrial Science and Technology, Tokyo, Japan

Abstract. In secure multiparty computation (MPC), floating-point numbers should be handled in many potential applications, but these are basically expensive. In particular, for MPC based on secret sharing (SS), the floating-point addition takes many communication rounds though the addition is the most fundamental operation. In this paper, we propose an SS-based two-party protocol for floating-point addition with 13 rounds (for single/double precision numbers), which is much fewer than the milestone work of Aliasgari et al. in NDSS 2013 (34 and 36 rounds, respectively) and also fewer than the state of the art in the literature. Moreover, in contrast to the existing SS-based protocols which are all based on "roundTowardZero" rounding mode in the IEEE 754 standard, we propose another protocol with 15 rounds which is the first result realizing more accurate "roundTiesToEven" rounding mode. We also discuss possible applications of the latter protocol to secure Validated Numerics (a.k.a. Rigorous Computation) by implementing a simple example.

Keywords: Secure multiparty computation · Floating-point numbers · Secret sharing

1 Introduction

Secure multiparty computation (MPC) is a cryptographic technology enabling two or more parties to compute functions on their individual inputs in a way that each party's input is kept secret during the computation. Besides the interest from cryptology, MPC is also important in other areas as a core technology in privacy-preserving data mining, which is expected by the increasing social demands for both big-data utilization and sensitive data protection.

Major underlying cryptographic primitives in recent studies for MPC are *garbled circuit (GC)*, *homomorphic encryption (HE)*, and *secret sharing (SS)*. Each of them has its own advantages and disadvantages, and there are studies for developing general and efficient MPC protocols by combining these different primitives (e.g., [10,11]). On the other hand, studying MPC based on a single

© Springer Nature Switzerland AG 2020
K. Aoki and A. Kanaoka (Eds.): IWSEC 2020, LNCS 12231, pp. 77–94, 2020.
https://doi.org/10.1007/978-3-030-58208-1_5

primitive is still important by at least the following two reasons. First, such protocols can fully benefit from the advantages specific to the primitive. For example, SS (with ideally generated randomness) is the only primitive among those listed above that can achieve information-theoretic security. Secondly, improvements of building-block protocols based on each primitive can also potentially contribute to better performances of the mixed-primitive type MPC mentioned above. From such viewpoints, in this paper we focus on SS-based MPC.

In SS-based MPC, efficient constructions of three-party computation (3PC), i.e., with three computing parties, have been studied well (e.g., [4,5,25]). On the other hand, SS-based two-party computation (2PC) also has an advantage that it requires less hardware resources (e.g., fewer computing servers) than 3PC. This paper focuses on the latter, SS-based 2PC. In both 2PC and 3PC, a recent trend is to divide the whole computation into the input-independent offline (pre-computation) phase and the input-dependent online phase and to make the online phase more efficient. We also follow this strategy. Moreover, a major disadvantage of SS-based MPC is that it requires many communication rounds, which is frequently dominant among the whole running time due to the unavoidable network latency for each communication round, especially over Wide Area Network (WAN) with larger latency. Hence, reducing the number of communication rounds is particularly important in SS-based MPC.

1.1   Secure Computation for Floating-Point Numbers

There are studies of MPC for various kinds of applications where floating-point numbers are required (e.g., [2,12,16,23]). A milestone in SS-based MPC for floating-point numbers is the work by Aliasgari et al. [3], where 3PC protocols for basic arithmetic addition and multiplication (note that subtraction is immediately obtained from addition by flipping the sign of the second input) as well as for some advanced operations such as square root and logarithm are proposed. Their high-level protocol constructions are also applied to the 2PC case in [1] (but the underlying primitive in [1] is HE instead of SS).

However, there is a typical difficulty in SS-based MPC for floating-point numbers. For the cases of integers or fixed-point numbers, usually the addition is almost for free, i.e., executable locally at each party without communication. In contrast, for floating-point numbers, the addition requires complicated operations (e.g., alignment of the significands according to the difference of exponents) and therefore is much expensive (with more than 27 rounds in [3]), even more than the multiplication (11 rounds in [3]). As the addition is the most fundamental operation, it is undoubtedly important to improve the efficiency of the addition protocol. There are studies of improving MPC for floating-point arithmetic (including the addition) by combining SS with GC (e.g., [14,22]). In this paper, we focus on SS-based (without GC) 2PC for the floating-point addition; only few studies for this topic exist in the literature (see Sect. 1.2).

1.2   Our Contributions

In this paper, we propose an improvement of SS-based secure floating-point addition (and subtraction) with two computing parties in the semi-honest model. For the binary64 format in the IEEE 754 standard [15] (with 53-bit significand), our proposed 2PC protocol requires only 13 rounds in the online phase, which is approximately 36% of the number of communication rounds (36 rounds) in [3] (the latter takes $\log_2 l + \log_2 \log_2 l + 27$ rounds as shown in Table 1 of [3] and we have $\lceil \log_2 53 + \log_2 \log_2 53 + 27 \rceil = 36$). Some comparisons with the existing results are summarized in Table 1; see the text below for the details.

Table 1. Comparison of the SS-based floating-point addition protocols. (*) The encoding format is not compatible with [3]. (**) Changing probabilistically. (***) Depending on the signs of inputs (see the main text). (†) Assuming the trusted initializer model for pre-computation (see the main text).

Protocol	# of parties	Rounding direction	# of rounds binary32	binary64	Bit length of encoding	Security
[3]	3	Truncation	34	36	$2l + 1$	statistical
[7](*)	3	Truncation	15	15	$l + 1$	statistical
[8]	3	unstable(**)	19	19	$l + 2$	statistical
[9]	3	unstable(**)	16	16	$l + 2$	statistical
[17]	2(†)	unstable(***)	N/A	N/A	$l + 2$	perfect
Ours (trunc)	**2**(†)	**Truncation**	**13**	**13**	**$l + 2$**	**perfect**
Ours (even)	**2**(†)	**Round-to-Even**	**15**	**15**	**$l + 4$**	**perfect**

As mentioned in Sect. 1.1, the 3PC protocol in [3] can be converted into 2PC by replacing the subprotocols with those executable by 2PC. Instead of the aforementioned HE-based ones in [1], here we use the round-efficient SS-based 2PC protocols in a recent paper [20]. (The combination of our construction with other kinds of round-efficient protocols such as in [6] will be a future research topic.) However, we emphasize that our protocol is not just a straightforward combination of [20] with [3], as explained below.

In [3], each l-bit significand is encoded as a $(2l + 1)$-bit (or larger) integer and the alignment of significands is done by left-shift (toy example: treating $1.101 \times 2^3 + 1.010 \times 2^1$ as $(110.100 + 1.010) \times 2^1$). However, by this method, even a binary32 (resp. binary64) number with $l = 24$ (resp. 53) cannot be implemented by 32-bit (resp. 64-bit) integers. This is not only inconvenient in implementation, but also a source of inefficiency in a way that the efficiency of the subprotocols in [20] depends largely on the bit length of integers, therefore it is better to avoid unnecessarily large integers. Instead of the left-shift alignment, here we adopt the opposite, right-shift alignment for this purpose. However, we should also take care of the fact that a naive use of right-shift may make the direction of rounding unstable depending on the signs of inputs. We explain it by toy examples. When $1.110 \times 2^4 + 1.100 \times 2^1$ is treated as $(1.110 + 0.001\text{1̶0̶0̶}) \times 2^4$, the exact result 1.111100×2^4 is rounded *down* to 1.111×2^4. On the other hand, when $1.110 \times 2^4 - 1.100 \times 2^1$ is treated as $(1.110 - 0.001\text{1̶0̶0̶}) \times 2^4$, the exact result 1.100100×2^4 is rounded *up* to 1.101×2^4. (This kind of error in fact happens in the protocol of [17].) We avoid this issue by carefully combining the left-shift and the right-shift, obtaining a correct protocol with the significands encoded by just $(l + 2)$-bit integers. See Sect. 4.2 for details.

We note also that among the various rounding-direction attributes in the IEEE 754 standard, the existing SS-based floating-point addition protocols support *roundTowardZero* only (i.e., the absolute value of the precise result is rounded down). For simplicity, we call it *Truncation mode* in this paper. On the other hand, our protocol (with two additional communication rounds) also supports *roundTiesToEven*, which rounds the precise result to the nearest floating-point number; we call it *Round-to-Even mode* in this paper. In other words, *our protocol newly supports the most accurate mode for floating-point addition*. See Sect. 4.3 for details. This would be useful in potential applications of MPC where the accuracy is very important, e.g., secure numerical simulations using expensive experimental data held by private companies. As a toy example, based on our protocol with Round-to-Even mode, we implemented a 2PC protocol for error-free transformation for the sum of two floating-point numbers (see e.g., [24]), which is a simple kind of Validated Numerics (a.k.a. Rigorous Computation) in the area of numerical analysis. See Sect. 6 for details. Our future research topics include extension of our proposed protocol to other arithmetic operations for floating-point numbers (i.e., multiplication and division).

We summarize comparison results of our proposed protocols with the existing SS-based MPC for floating-point addition in Table 1 (we also note about other protocols in [16,21] where the number of communication rounds is not clear and the improvement relative to [3] seems not very large). We show the numbers of communication rounds in the online phase for binary32 and binary64 formats. The "Bit length of encoding" column shows the bit length of integers to which the l-bit significands are encoded during each protocol. The "Security" column shows whether each protocol (assuming ideally generated randomness) is perfectly secure or only statistically secure. In [7], the encoding format of floating-point numbers is slightly different from [3]; the *signed* significand is encoded as a single *signed* integer, while the sign bit and the unsigned significand are separated in [3], therefore the protocol in [7] does not have compatibility with those in [3]. In [8,9], some subprotocol inside the whole protocol performs rounding *probabilistically* towards one of the two directions. The protocols in [3,7–9] use imperfect random masking in some subprotocol and therefore have only statistical security. In [17], the number of communication rounds is not clear, and its rounding direction is not stable as mentioned above. By Table 1, our 2PC protocol (in Truncation mode) has round complexity even smaller than the best known (accurate) 3PC protocol [7]. We note that our protocols (as well as the protocols in [20]) require somewhat complicated correlated randomness and therefore the use of the so-called trusted initializer model, such as the client-aided model (e.g., [18,19]), in the offline phase suits well.

2 Preliminaries

2.1 Secure Multiparty Computation over Secret Sharing

This paper deals with two-party computation (2PC) based on the following standard 2-out-of-2 secret sharing (SS) scheme (Share, Reconst) over a ring of the form $\mathcal{M} = \mathbb{Z}/2^n\mathbb{Z}$. For a plaintext $m \in \mathcal{M}$, the algorithm Share(m) chooses $s_0 \leftarrow \mathcal{M}$ uniformly at random, sets $s_1 \leftarrow m - s_0$, and outputs $[\![m]\!] = ([\![m]\!]_0, [\![m]\!]_1) \leftarrow (s_0, s_1)$. Each $[\![m]\!]_i$ is called a *share* of m for i-th party, and by abusing the terminology, the pair $[\![m]\!]$ is also called a share of m. On the other hand, for a share $[\![m]\!] = ([\![m]\!]_0, [\![m]\!]_1)$, the algorithm Reconst($[\![m]\!]$) outputs a plaintext $[\![m]\!]_0 + [\![m]\!]_1$. We note that the reconstruction of the plaintext requires one communication round between the two parties to send each party's share to the other party. When $n = 1$ and a plaintext is regarded as a bit, each share is called a Boolean share and denoted by a symbol like $[\![m]\!]^{\mathsf{B}}$. Otherwise, each share is called an Arithmetic share and denoted by a symbol like $[\![m]\!]^{\mathsf{A}}$.

Given two Arithmetic shares $[\![m_1]\!]^{\mathsf{A}}$ and $[\![m_2]\!]^{\mathsf{A}}$ (with the same bit length n), addition of plaintexts is executable locally (without communication) by adding each party's shares; $[\![m_1 + m_2]\!]_i^{\mathsf{A}} \leftarrow [\![m_1]\!]_i^{\mathsf{A}} + [\![m_2]\!]_i^{\mathsf{A}}$ ($i = 0, 1$). We write this protocol simply as $[\![m_1]\!]^{\mathsf{A}} + [\![m_2]\!]^{\mathsf{A}}$. Subtraction $[\![m_1]\!]^{\mathsf{A}} - [\![m_2]\!]^{\mathsf{A}}$ and scalar multiplication $c \cdot [\![m]\!]^{\mathsf{A}}$ can be locally executed in a similar way. Addition by constant $[\![m]\!]^{\mathsf{A}} + c$ can be also done by using $[\![c]\!]^{\mathsf{A}} = (c, 0)$. By replacing $+$ with $\oplus$, exclusive OR (XOR) for Boolean shares $[\![b_1]\!]^{\mathsf{B}} \oplus [\![b_2]\!]^{\mathsf{B}}$ are obtained. Then NOT operation is given by $\overline{[\![b]\!]}^{\mathsf{B}} = \neg[\![b]\!]^{\mathsf{B}} = [\![b]\!]^{\mathsf{B}} \oplus 1$. On the other hand, multiplication of plaintexts $[\![m_1 \cdot m_2]\!]^{\mathsf{A}} = [\![m_1]\!]^{\mathsf{A}} \cdot [\![m_2]\!]^{\mathsf{A}}$ can be executed with one communication round sending one share to each other, by using auxiliary inputs $([\![a]\!]^{\mathsf{A}}, [\![b]\!]^{\mathsf{A}}, [\![c]\!]^{\mathsf{A}})$ called *Beaver Triple (BT)* where $a, b \in \mathcal{M}$ are uniformly random and not known by any party and we have $c = ab$. See e.g., [20] for the concrete protocol construction. Boolean AND $[\![b_1 \wedge b_2]\!]^{\mathsf{B}} = [\![b_1]\!]^{\mathsf{B}} \wedge [\![b_2]\!]^{\mathsf{B}}$ can be computed similarly (with one round sending one bit each), and Boolean OR $[\![b_1 \vee b_2]\!]^{\mathsf{B}} = [\![b_1]\!]^{\mathsf{B}} \vee [\![b_2]\!]^{\mathsf{B}}$ can be computed as well with the same communication complexity.

In this paper, we assume that any auxiliary input such as BT is ideally generated in the offline phase. For example, this may be realized by adopting *client-aided model* [18,19] for SS-based MPC where some trusted party other than the computing parties is supposed to be active only at the offline phase and to generate and send the necessary auxiliary inputs to the computing parties.

For the security of MPC, let $P_0, \ldots, P_{N-1}$ be parties computing functionality $f(x_0, \ldots, x_{N-1}) = (f_i(x_0, \ldots, x_{N-1}))_{i=0}^{N-1}$ with input x_i for P_i. Let the *view* $\mathsf{View}_i(x_0, \ldots, x_{N-1})$ for Party P_i during a protocol be the chronological list of all messages sent from other parties to P_i together with the local input x_i and the internal randomness for P_i used in the protocol. Let $\mathsf{Out}(x_0, \ldots, x_{N-1})$ denote the list of all parties' outputs at the end of the protocol. Then we say that a protocol is *secure (in the semi-honest model) against* P_i if there is a probabilistic polynomial-time algorithm $\mathcal{S}_i$ satisfying that the probability distribution of the pair $(\mathcal{S}_i(x_i, f_i(x_0, \ldots, x_{N-1})), f(x_0, \ldots, x_{N-1}))$ is indistinguishable from the probability distribution of $(\mathsf{View}_i(x_0, \ldots, x_{N-1}), \mathsf{Out}(x_0, \ldots, x_{N-1}))$; see e.g., Definition 7.5.1 of [13]. We note that we only consider a single (non-colluding) semi-honest adversary in this paper, which has simplified the definition above. When the two distributions above are identical (resp. statistically indistinguishable), the protocol is said to be perfectly (resp. statistically) secure.

The Composition Theorem (Theorem 7.5.7 of [13]) states, roughly speaking, that if a protocol $\Pi^{(g_1, \ldots, g_L)}$ using oracles computing functionalities $g_1, \ldots, g_L$ is secure and each g_j can be computed securely, then the protocol obtained by replacing each oracle call for g_j in $\Pi^{(g_1, \ldots, g_L)}$ with the secure protocol computing g_j is also secure. Now we note that, in any protocol proposed in this paper, the subprotocols used in the protocol are known to be secure, while the protocol assuming ideal subprotocols is trivially secure as the parties send data to each other only during some subprotocol; as a result, the whole protocol is proven secure due to the Composition Theorem. According to this fact, in the rest of this paper we omit discussions about the security of our proposed protocols.

2.2 Floating-Point Numbers

Floating-Point Representation. The floating-point numbers are the most common way of representing in computers an approximation to real numbers. Here, we explain the details of binary floating-point formats.

The set of all floating-point numbers consists of finite numbers (including normalized numbers, unnormalized numbers and zero), infinities, and NaN (not-a-number). For simplicity we only treat normalized numbers and zero.

Following the format in [3], a floating-point number x is defined as a tuple (f, e, s, z), where $f \in [2^{l-1}, 2^l - 1] \cup \{0\}$ is the unsigned, normalized significand, $e \in \mathbb{Z}/2^k\mathbb{Z}$ is the biased exponent, s is the sign bit which is set to 1 when the value is negative, and z is the zero-test bit which is set to 1 if and only if $x = 0$. The value of the number is $x = (1 - 2s) \cdot (1 - z) \cdot 2^{-l+1} f \cdot 2^{e - \mathsf{bias}}$, where $\mathsf{bias} = 2^{k-1} - 1$. We note that both f and e are set to 0 when x is zero.

The parameters l, k are not secret and determine the precision and range of the numbers, as well as the numbers of communication rounds and the computational complexity of the protocols. In this paper, we focus on $(l, k) = (24, 8)$, which corresponds to IEEE 754 single precision and $(l, k) = (53, 11)$, which corresponds to IEEE 754 double precision [15]. For example if $(l, k) = (24, 8)$, $x = 1.0$ is represented as

$$f = \underbrace{10 \cdots 0}_{24}, \quad e = 0 + (2^{8-1} - 1) = 127, \quad s = 0, \quad z = 0.$$

Floating-Point Addition/Subtraction and Rounding Mode. The floating-point addition/subtraction is executed as follows. Compare the absolute values of the two numbers. Shift the smaller number to the right until its exponent would match the larger exponent. Add or subtract the significands. Normalize the sum, either shifting right and incrementing the exponent or shifting left and decrementing the exponent. Round the significand to the appropriate number of bits. Check if the result is still normalized or not. If the result is not normalized, normalize the result again. In this paper, we assume for simplicity that no overflow or underflow occurs in addition/subtraction.

IEEE 754 standard defines five rounding rules; roundTiesToEven, roundTies-ToAway, roundTowardPositive, roundTowardNegative, and roundTowardZero. The first two rules round to a nearest value, the others are called directed roudings. In this paper, we use roundTiesToEven (we call it Round-to-Even mode) and roundTowardZero (we call it Truncation mode).

Round-to-Even mode rounds to the nearest value. With this mode, if two candidate values with equal distance exist, the number is rounded to the one with the least significant bit being 0. This mode is the most commonly used. Truncation mode is a direct rounding towards zero. Note that we have to check once that the intermediate result is normalized after rounding with Round-to-Even mode, but we do not need this check in Truncation mode.

Extra Bits to Obtain Accurate Result. To get the same result as if the intermediate result were calculated with infinite precision and then rounded, the following bits are defined for determining the magnitude lower than the units in the last place (ulp); *guard bit* has weight $1/2$ ulp, *round bit* has weight $1/4$ ulp, and *sticky bit* is the OR of all bits with weight $1/8$ ulp or lower. With these three extra bits, we can obtain accurate result with Round-to-Even mode. By almost the same idea, we can obtain accurate result with Truncation mode using one extra bit, which is set whenever there is some nonzero bit to the right of ulp.

3   The Previous Works

3.1   Secure Floating-Point Operations

In [3], SS-based protocols to compute fundamental arithmetic operations (including the addition) and some advanced functions for floating-point numbers are proposed. In their protocols, the two components f, e in the format described in Sect. 2.2 are treated as Arithmetic shares and the other two components s, z are treated as Boolean shares.

In the addition protocol of [3], first the two input numbers are sorted with respect to their significands (which requires secure comparison protocol) for the ease of the remaining steps. Then, in contrast to the addition algorithm for plain (non-secret) inputs explained in Sect. 2.2, the protocol in [3] aligns the significands by using left-shift instead of right-shift (see also an explanation in Sect. 1.2); this is convenient to ensure the accuracy of the resulting value, while this requires (almost) twice the bit length of integers to hold the intermediate significand. After that, the most significant non-zero bit of the intermediate significand is searched (which requires secure bit extraction protocol) and the intermediate significand is normalized by an appropriate shift. The protocol also includes procedures to handle some exceptional case (e.g., one of the two inputs is zero) and to maintain the bits s and z correctly. Here we omit the details of their protocol (see the original paper [3]), but we note that it is a three-party computation (3PC) protocol and it (with l-bit significands for inputs) takes $\log_2 l + \log_2 \log_2 l + 27$ rounds. This becomes 34 and 36 rounds for binary32 and binary 64 inputs with $l = 24$ and 53, respectively.

Table 2. Numbers of communication rounds for the subprotocols in [20] (upper part) and our subprotocols in Sect. 4.1 (lower part); here Arithmetic shares are n-bit integers. (*) $\beta_j = 1$ if and only if $b_j = 1$ and $b_k = 0$ for any $k > j$. (**) $b = 1$ if and only if $(\llbracket x \rrbracket_0^A \bmod 2^k) + (\llbracket x \rrbracket_1^A \bmod 2^k) \geq 2^k$. (***) Here $x = (x_{n-1} \cdots x_1 x_0)_2$ in binary.

Protocol	Functionality	# of communication rounds	
		$(n = 8)$	$(n \in \{16, 32, 64\})$
$\llbracket z \rrbracket \leftarrow N\text{-Mult}((\llbracket x_j \rrbracket)_{j=1}^N)$	$z = x_1 \cdots x_N$	1	1
$\llbracket b \rrbracket^B \leftarrow \text{Equality}(\llbracket x \rrbracket^A, \llbracket y \rrbracket^A)$	$b = (x \stackrel{?}{=} y)$	1	2
$(\llbracket \beta_j \rrbracket^B)_{j=0}^{N-1} \leftarrow \text{MSNZB}((\llbracket b_j \rrbracket^B)_{j=0}^{N-1})$	(*)	1	2
$\llbracket b \rrbracket^B \leftarrow \text{Overflow}(\llbracket x \rrbracket^A, k)$	(**)	1	2
$\llbracket b \rrbracket^B \leftarrow \text{Comparison}(\llbracket x \rrbracket^A, \llbracket y \rrbracket^A)$	$b = (x \stackrel{?}{<} y)$	2	3
$\llbracket z \rrbracket^A \leftarrow \text{B2A}(\llbracket b \rrbracket^B)$	$z = b$	1	1
$\llbracket z \rrbracket^A \leftarrow \llbracket b \rrbracket^B \times \llbracket x \rrbracket^A$	$z = b \cdot x$	1	1
$\llbracket z \rrbracket^A \leftarrow \llbracket b \rrbracket^B \times \llbracket c \rrbracket^B$	$z = b \cdot c$	1	1
$\llbracket z \rrbracket^A \leftarrow \llbracket b \rrbracket^B \times \llbracket c \rrbracket^B \times \llbracket x \rrbracket^A$	$z = b \cdot c \cdot x$	1	1
$\llbracket b \rrbracket^B \leftarrow \text{Modeq}(\llbracket x \rrbracket^A, k)$	$b = (x \bmod 2^k \stackrel{?}{=} 0)$	1	2
$\llbracket b \rrbracket^B \leftarrow \text{Extractbit}(\llbracket x \rrbracket^A, k)$	$b = x_k$ (***)	1	2
$(\llbracket b[j] \rrbracket^B)_{j=0}^{n-1} \leftarrow \text{Bitdec}(\llbracket x \rrbracket^A)$	$b[j] = x_j$ (***)	1	2

3.2 Round-Efficient Protocols over Secret Sharing

In our proposed protocols, we use the 2PC protocols in [20] as subprotocols. We omit their concrete constructions here and only refer to [20]. Their functionalities and numbers of communication rounds are listed in the upper part of Table 2.

We note that in [20], the N-fan-in multiplication (N-Mult) for $N > 2$ (and similarly, N-fan-in AND/OR) is realized with one round by introducing an extension of Beaver Triple (BT) called *Beaver Triple Extension* (*BTE*). The fan-in number N can in principle be arbitrary, but the computational and the communication costs grow exponentially in N, therefore the choice of N is limited as $N \leq 9$ in [20]. For the Equality protocol, roughly speaking, the computation is reduced to the computation of OR for at most n significant bits of the input; by using N-OR's for $N \leq 9$, it takes two rounds when $n \in \{16, 32, 64\}$ as described in [20], while it can be done simply with one round for $n = 8$. The situation is similar for the most significant non-zero bit search protocol MSNZB, the overflow detection protocol Overflow, and the less-than comparison protocol Comparison, where the number of rounds for $n = 8$ is fewer than those for $n \in \{16, 32, 64\}$ by one. On the other hand, the Boolean-to-Arithmetic conversion protocol B2A and the multiplication protocols for Boolean and Arithmetic inputs (regarded as Arithmetic values) are executable with one round for any $n \in \{8, 16, 32, 64\}$.

We note that, in our proposed protocols in this paper, we only need N-Mult for $N \leq 5$ (with at most $(2^5 - 1)n = 31n$ bits of BTE) and N-AND/OR for $N \leq 9$ (with at most $2^9 - 1 = 511$ bits of BTE), therefore the communication complexity of our protocol in the offline phase is not too large.

4   Our Proposed Protocols

4.1   Some More Subprotocols

Here we present some more subprotocols to be used in our proposed protocols. Their functionalities and numbers of communication rounds are listed in the lower part of Table 2.

Modeq. A protocol $\mathsf{Modeq}(\llbracket x \rrbracket^{\mathsf{A}}, k)$ outputs $\llbracket b \rrbracket^{\mathsf{B}}$, where $b = 1$ if and only if $(x \bmod 2^k) = 0$. By almost the same idea as Equality, we can construct this protocol with the same number of communication rounds as Equality owing to the relation $x \bmod 2^k = (\llbracket x \rrbracket_0^{\mathsf{A}} \bmod 2^k) + (\llbracket x \rrbracket_1^{\mathsf{A}} \bmod 2^k)$ in $\mathbb{Z}/2^k\mathbb{Z}$.

Extractbit. A protocol $\mathsf{Extractbit}(\llbracket x \rrbracket^{\mathsf{A}}, k)$ outputs $\llbracket b \rrbracket^{\mathsf{B}}$, where $b = x_k$ is the $(k+1)$-th least significant bit of (binary expanded) $x = (x_{n-1} \cdots x_1 x_0)_2$. Using Overflow, we can construct Extractbit with the same number of communication rounds as follows:

1. P_i ($i \in \{0, 1\}$) locally extend $\llbracket x \rrbracket_i^{\mathsf{A}}$ to binary and obtain a bit string $[\llbracket t[n-1] \rrbracket_i^{\mathsf{B}}, \cdots, \llbracket t[0] \rrbracket_i^{\mathsf{B}}]$, then set $\llbracket v \rrbracket_i^{\mathsf{B}} = \llbracket t[k] \rrbracket_i^{\mathsf{B}}$. P_i also compute $\llbracket w \rrbracket^{\mathsf{B}} \leftarrow \mathsf{Overflow}(\llbracket x \rrbracket^{\mathsf{A}}, k)$.
2. P_i compute $\llbracket z \rrbracket^{\mathsf{B}} = \llbracket v \rrbracket^{\mathsf{B}} \oplus \llbracket w \rrbracket^{\mathsf{B}}$.

Bitdec. A bit decomposition protocol $\mathsf{Bitdec}(\llbracket x \rrbracket^{\mathsf{A}})$ outputs a Boolean share vector $\llbracket b \rrbracket^{\mathsf{B}} = [\llbracket b[15] \rrbracket^{\mathsf{B}}, \cdots, \llbracket b[0] \rrbracket^{\mathsf{B}}]$, where $b[k] = x_k$ is the $(k+1)$-th least significant bit of (binary expanded) x. We can construct Bitdec by parallelly executing Extractbit n times.

4.2   Addition/Subtraction in Truncation Mode

Here we show our proposed floating-point addition protocol in Truncation mode (Algorithm 1). We abuse some notations; for example, we write $\llbracket b \rrbracket^{\mathsf{B}} \times \llbracket x \rrbracket^{\mathsf{A}}$ protocol simply as $\llbracket b \rrbracket^{\mathsf{B}} \llbracket x \rrbracket^{\mathsf{A}}$. In the algorithm, the numbers at the right side with symbols '▷' denote the numbers of communication rounds required for each step; for example, Step 1 takes three rounds where Comparison to compute $\llbracket c \rrbracket^{\mathsf{B}}$ is dominant among the parallel processes. We note that, for example, the formula to compute $[\![f'_{\min}]\!]^A$ in Step 4 seems to require two consecutive multiplications, but this description is just for clarifying the structure of the formula, and the actual computation is performed with its expanded form

$$\sum_{j=0}^{l} [\![t[j]]\!]^B [\![t'[j]]\!]^A - 2 \sum_{j=0}^{l} [\![s_2]\!]^B [\![t[j]]\!]^B [\![t'[j]]\!]^A$$

which requires only one round. Similar conventions for descriptions of functions are also adopted in several places. Summarizing, the total number of communication rounds is 13 for both binary32 and binary64 floating-point numbers.

Correctness of the Protocol. In Algorithm 1, we first swap the inputs (x_0, x_1) to $(x_{\max}, x_{\min})$ so that they are ordered by magnitude, and compute the corresponding significands and exponents, denoted by $f_{\max}, f_{\min}, e_{\max}, e_{\min}$, respectively (Step 1 and Step 2). In Step 2, we also compute both of the sign bit s and the zero-test bit z for the output of this protocol. We also compute $e_\Delta = e_{\max} - e_{\min}$ and $s_2 = s_0 \oplus s_1$. s_2 determines whether to perform addition or subtraction of the significands. If $s_2 = 0$ (the signs of inputs are the same), the values are being added; otherwise they are being subtracted. Then straightforward case-by-case analyses can verify the correctness of these steps.

In Step 3 and Step 4, we implement the addition/subtraction of the significands; we compute $f_2 = 2f_{\max} \pm (2f_{\min} \gg e_\Delta) + \delta$. In the addition/subtraction of the significands, we execute 1-bit left-shift for both of the significands (see below for the reason of the left-shift) and then execute right-shift alignment using e_Δ. δ is a correction term; $\delta = -1$ if subtraction is performed and there is any bit 1 in the least e_Δ bits of $2f_{\min}$ (in this case, $2f_{\max} - (2f_{\min} \gg e_\Delta)$ is the rounding up of the exact value and hence it should be further subtracted by one to be rounded down), and $\delta = 0$ otherwise. By this method, we can get the intermediate result f_2 needed for accurate rounding in Truncation mode. Note that f_2 is at most $(l + 2)$-bit integer.

Note for the left-shift: For addition, or subtraction with $e_\Delta = 0$, no accuracy loss occurs here. We consider subtraction with $e_\Delta > 0$. If $e_\Delta \geq 2$, then at most 1-bit loss of accuracy may happen, and the 1-bit left-shift is sufficient for preventing the accuracy loss. On the other hand, if $e_\Delta = 1$, then the 1-bit left-shift can keep all the bits of $f_{\min}$ even after the e_Δ ($= 1$)-bit right-shift, therefore no accuracy loss happens as well. Hence the accuracy is kept in any case.

In Step 5 and Step 6, we normalize the significand. We compute the most significant non-zero bit (MSNZB) of f_2 and rounds f_2 to l-bit integer by either right-shift (when MSNZB is at the l-th or $(l + 1)$-th least bit) or left-shift (otherwise). We also adjust the exponent of $x_{\max}$ to obtain the resulting exponent according to the position of MSNZB. This gives the correct output.

4.3   Addition/Subtraction in Round-to-Even Mode

Here we show our proposed floating-point addition protocol in Round-to-Even mode (Algorithm 2). The notations and conventions are the same as the case of

---

Algorithm 1. FLADDtrunc

Functionality: $[\![x]\!] \leftarrow$ FLADDtrunc($[\![x_0]\!], [\![x_1]\!]$)

Ensure: $[\![x]\!]$, where $x = x_0 + x_1$.

1: P_i ($i \in \{0,1\}$) parallelly compute ▷ 3
$$[\![a]\!]^B \leftarrow \text{Comparison}([\![e_0]\!]^A, [\![e_1]\!]^A),$$
$$[\![b]\!]^B \leftarrow \text{Equality}([\![e_0]\!]^A, [\![e_1]\!]^A),$$
$$[\![c]\!]^B \leftarrow \text{Comparison}([\![f_0]\!]^A, [\![f_1]\!]^A),$$
$$[\![b']\!]^B \leftarrow \text{Equality}([\![f_0]\!]^A, [\![f_1]\!]^A),$$
and then locally compute
$$[\![s_2]\!]^B \leftarrow [\![s_0]\!]^B \oplus [\![s_1]\!]^B.$$

2: P_i parallelly compute ▷ 1
$$[\![e_{\max}]\!]^A \leftarrow [\![a]\!]^B[\![e_1]\!]^A + \overline{[\![a]\!]}^B[\![e_0]\!]^A,$$
$$[\![e_{\min}]\!]^A \leftarrow [\![a]\!]^B[\![e_0]\!]^A + \overline{[\![a]\!]}^B[\![e_1]\!]^A,$$
$$[\![f_{\max}]\!]^A \leftarrow [\![a]\!]^B[\![f_1]\!]^A + [\![b]\!]^B[\![c]\!]^B[\![f_1]\!]^A + \overline{[\![a]\!]}^B\,\overline{[\![b]\!]}^B[\![f_0]\!]^A + [\![b]\!]^B\overline{[\![c]\!]}^B[\![f_0]\!]^A,$$
$$[\![f_{\min}]\!]^A \leftarrow [\![a]\!]^B[\![f_0]\!]^A + [\![b]\!]^B[\![c]\!]^B[\![f_0]\!]^A + \overline{[\![a]\!]}^B\,\overline{[\![b]\!]}^B[\![f_1]\!]^A + [\![b]\!]^B\overline{[\![c]\!]}^B[\![f_1]\!]^A,$$
$$[\![s]\!]^B \leftarrow [\![a]\!]^B[\![s_1]\!]^B \oplus [\![b]\!]^B[\![c]\!]^B[\![s_1]\!]^B \oplus \overline{[\![a]\!]}^B\,\overline{[\![b]\!]}^B[\![s_0]\!]^B$$
$$\oplus [\![b]\!]^B\overline{[\![c]\!]}^B\overline{[\![b']\!]}^B[\![s_0]\!]^B \oplus [\![b]\!]^B[\![b']\!]^B\overline{[\![s_2]\!]}^B[\![s_0]\!]^B,$$
$$[\![z]\!]^B \leftarrow [\![b]\!]^B[\![b']\!]^B[\![s_2]\!]^B \oplus [\![z_0]\!]^B[\![z_1]\!]^B,$$
and then locally compute
$$[\![e_\Delta]\!]^A \leftarrow [\![e_{\max}]\!]^A - [\![e_{\min}]\!]^A.$$

3: For $j = 0, 1, \cdots, l$, P_i parallelly compute ▷ 3
$$[\![t[j]]\!]^B \leftarrow \text{Equality}([\![e_\Delta]\!]^A, j),$$
$$[\![t'[j]]\!]^A \leftarrow \text{Rightshift}(2[\![f_{\min}]\!]^A, j),$$
$$[\![t''[j]]\!]^A \leftarrow \text{B2A}(\neg\text{Modeq}(2[\![f_{\min}]\!]^A, j)),$$
and then locally compute
$$[\![c_1]\!]^B \leftarrow \neg \bigoplus_{j=0}^l [\![t[j]]\!]^B.$$

4: P_i parallelly compute ▷ 1
$$[\![f'_{\min}]\!]^A \leftarrow (1 - 2[\![s_2]\!]^B)\sum_{j=0}^l [\![t[j]]\!]^B[\![t'[j]]\!]^A,$$
$$[\![\delta]\!]^A \leftarrow -[\![s_2]\!]^B\left([\![c_1]\!]^B + \sum_{j=0}^l [\![t[j]]\!]^B[\![t''[j]]\!]^A\right),$$
and then locally compute
$$[\![f_2]\!]^A \leftarrow 2[\![f_{\max}]\!]^A + [\![f'_{\min}]\!]^A + [\![\delta]\!]^A.$$

5: P_i compute ▷ 4
$$[\![d]\!]^B \leftarrow \text{Bitdec}([\![f_2]\!]^A),$$
and then compute
$$[\![d']\!]^B \leftarrow \text{MSNZB}([\![d]\!]^B).$$
Parallelly, P_i compute
$$[\![f[j]]\!]^A \leftarrow 2^{l-j-1}[\![f_2]\!]^A \text{ for } j \in \{0, \cdots, l-1\},$$
$$[\![f[j]]\!]^A \leftarrow \text{Rightshift}([\![f_2]\!]^A, j-l+1) \text{ for } j \in \{l, l+1\},$$
$$[\![z_2]\!]^B \leftarrow \overline{[\![z_0]\!]}^B\overline{[\![z_1]\!]}^B.$$
$$[\![z_3]\!]^B \leftarrow \overline{[\![z]\!]}^B\overline{[\![z_0]\!]}^B\overline{[\![z_1]\!]}^B.$$

6: P_i parallelly compute ▷ 1
$$[\![f]\!]^A \leftarrow [\![z_2]\!]^B\sum_{j=0}^{l+1}[\![d'[j]]\!]^B[\![f[j]]\!]^A + [\![z_1]\!]^B[\![f_0]\!]^A + [\![z_0]\!]^B[\![f_1]\!]^A,$$
$$[\![e]\!]^A \leftarrow [\![z_3]\!]^B\left([\![e_{\max}]\!]^A + \sum_{j=0}^{l+1}(j-l)[\![d'[j]]\!]^B\right) + [\![z_1]\!]^B[\![e_0]\!]^A + [\![z_0]\!]^B[\![e_1]\!]^A.$$

7: **return** $([\![f]\!]^A, [\![e]\!]^A, [\![s]\!]^B, [\![z]\!]^B)$.

Algorithm 2. FLADDeven

Functionality: $[\![x]\!] \leftarrow$ FLADDeven$([\![x_0]\!], [\![x_1]\!])$

Ensure: $[\![x]\!]$, where $x = x_0 + x_1$.

1: P_i $(i \in \{0,1\})$ parallelly compute $\quad\quad\quad\quad\quad\quad\quad\quad\quad\quad\quad\quad\quad\quad \triangleright\, 3$

$\quad [\![a]\!]^B \leftarrow$ Comparison$([\![e_0]\!]^A, [\![e_1]\!]^A), \quad [\![b]\!]^B \leftarrow$ Equality$([\![e_0]\!]^A, [\![e_1]\!]^A),$

$\quad [\![c]\!]^B \leftarrow$ Comparison$([\![f_0]\!]^A, [\![f_1]\!]^A), \quad [\![b']\!]^B \leftarrow$ Equality$([\![f_0]\!]^A, [\![f_1]\!]^A),$

and locally compute

$\quad [\![s_2]\!]^B \leftarrow [\![s_0]\!]^B \oplus [\![s_1]\!]^B.$

2: P_i parallelly compute $\quad\quad\quad\quad\quad\quad\quad\quad\quad\quad\quad\quad\quad\quad\quad\quad\quad\quad\quad \triangleright\, 1$

$\quad [\![e_{\max}]\!]^A \leftarrow [\![a]\!]^B [\![e_1]\!]^A + \overline{[\![a]\!]}^B [\![e_0]\!]^A, \quad [\![e_{\min}]\!]^A \leftarrow [\![a]\!]^B [\![e_0]\!]^A + \overline{[\![a]\!]}^B [\![e_1]\!]^A,$

$\quad [\![f_{\max}]\!]^A \leftarrow [\![a]\!]^B [\![f_1]\!]^A + [\![b]\!]^B [\![c]\!]^B [\![f_1]\!]^A + \overline{[\![a]\!]}^B\, \overline{[\![b]\!]}^B [\![f_0]\!]^A + [\![b]\!]^B \overline{[\![c]\!]}^B [\![f_0]\!]^A,$

$\quad [\![f_{\min}]\!]^A \leftarrow [\![a]\!]^B [\![f_0]\!]^A + [\![b]\!]^B [\![c]\!]^B [\![f_0]\!]^A + \overline{[\![a]\!]}^B\, \overline{[\![b]\!]}^B [\![f_1]\!]^A + [\![b]\!]^B \overline{[\![c]\!]}^B [\![f_1]\!]^A,$

$\quad [\![s]\!]^B \leftarrow [\![a]\!]^B [\![s_1]\!]^B \oplus [\![b]\!]^B [\![c]\!]^B [\![s_1]\!]^B \oplus \overline{[\![a]\!]}^B\, \overline{[\![b]\!]}^B [\![s_0]\!]^B$

$\quad\quad\quad \oplus [\![b]\!]^B \overline{[\![c]\!]}^B \overline{[\![b']\!]}^B [\![s_0]\!]^B \oplus [\![b]\!]^B [\![b']\!]^B \overline{[\![s_2]\!]}^B [\![s_0]\!]^B,$

$\quad [\![z]\!]^B \leftarrow [\![b]\!]^B [\![b']\!]^B [\![s_2]\!]^B \oplus [\![z_0]\!]^B [\![z_1]\!]^B,$

and then locally compute

$\quad [\![e_\Delta]\!]^A \leftarrow [\![e_{\max}]\!]^A - [\![e_{\min}]\!]^A.$

3: For $j = 0, 1, \cdots, l+1$, P_i parallelly compute $\quad\quad\quad\quad\quad\quad\quad\quad \triangleright\, 3$

$\quad [\![t[j]]\!]^B \leftarrow$ Equality$([\![e_\Delta]\!]^A, j),$

$\quad [\![t'[j]]\!]^A \leftarrow$ Rightshift$(4[\![f_{\min}]\!]^A, j),$

$\quad [\![t''[j]]\!]^A \leftarrow$ B2A$(\neg$Modeq$(4[\![f_{\min}]\!]^A, j)),$

and then locally compute

$\quad [\![c_1]\!]^B \leftarrow \neg \bigoplus_{j=0}^{l+1} [\![t[j]]\!]^B.$

4: P_i parallelly compute $\quad\quad\quad\quad\quad\quad\quad\quad\quad\quad\quad\quad\quad\quad\quad\quad\quad\quad\quad \triangleright\, 1$

$\quad [\![f'_{\min}]\!]^A \leftarrow (1 - 2[\![s_2]\!]^B) \sum_{j=0}^{l+1} [\![t[j]]\!]^B [\![t'[j]]\!]^A,$

$\quad [\![\delta]\!]^A \leftarrow (1 - 2[\![s_2]\!]^B)([\![c_1]\!]^B + \sum_{j=0}^{l+1} [\![t[j]]\!]^B [\![t''[j]]\!]^A),$

and then locally compute

$\quad [\![f_2]\!]^A \leftarrow 8[\![f_{\max}]\!]^A + 2[\![f'_{\min}]\!]^A + [\![\delta]\!]^A.$

5: P_i parallelly compute $\quad\quad\quad\quad\quad\quad\quad\quad\quad\quad\quad\quad\quad\quad\quad\quad\quad\quad\quad \triangleright\, 6$

$\quad [\![d]\!]^B \leftarrow$ Bitdec$([\![f_2]\!]^A), \quad [\![S]\!]^B \leftarrow \neg$Modeq$([\![f_2]\!]^A, 2),$

and then compute

$\quad [\![d']\!]^B \leftarrow$ MSNZB$([\![d]\!]^B),$

$\quad [\![r[l+3]]\!]^A \leftarrow [\![d[3]]\!]^B [\![d[2]]\!]^B \oplus [\![d[3]]\!]^B \overline{[\![d[2]]\!]}^B [\![S]\!]^B \oplus [\![d[4]]\!]^B [\![d[3]]\!]^B \overline{[\![d[2]]\!]}^B \overline{[\![S]\!]}^B,$

$\quad [\![r[l+2]]\!]^A \leftarrow [\![d[2]]\!]^B [\![d[1]]\!]^B \oplus [\![d[2]]\!]^B \overline{[\![d[1]]\!]}^B [\![d[0]]\!]^B \oplus [\![d[3]]\!]^B [\![d[2]]\!]^B \overline{[\![d[1]]\!]}^B \overline{[\![d[0]]\!]}^B,$

$\quad [\![r[l+1]]\!]^A \leftarrow [\![d[1]]\!]^B [\![d[0]]\!]^B \oplus [\![d[2]]\!]^B [\![d[1]]\!]^B \overline{[\![d[0]]\!]}^B.$

Parallelly, P_i compute

$\quad [\![f[j]]\!]^A \leftarrow 2^{l-j-1} [\![f_2]\!]^A$ for $j \in \{2, \cdots, l-1\},$

$\quad [\![f[j]]\!]^A \leftarrow$ Rightshift$([\![f_2]\!]^A, j-l+1)$ for $j \in \{l, \cdots, l+3\},$

then locally compute

$\quad [\![f[j]]\!]^A \leftarrow [\![f[j]]\!]^A + [\![r[j]]\!]^A$ for $j \in \{l+1, l+2, l+3\},$

then compute

$\quad [\![\mathrm{of}[j]]\!]^B \leftarrow$ Equality$([\![f[j]]\!]^A, 2^l)$ for $j \in \{l+1, l+2, l+3\}.$

6: P_i parallelly compute $\quad\quad\quad\quad\quad\quad\quad\quad\quad\quad\quad\quad\quad\quad\quad\quad\quad\quad\quad \triangleright\, 1$

$\quad [\![f]\!]^A \leftarrow \sum_{j=2}^{l} [\![d'[j]]\!]^B [\![f[j]]\!]^A + \sum_{j=l+1}^{l+3} [\![d'[j]]\!]^B (\overline{[\![\mathrm{of}[j]]\!]}^B [\![f[j]]\!]^A + [\![\mathrm{of}[j]]\!]^B 2^{l-1}),$

$\quad [\![e]\!]^A \leftarrow \overline{[\![z]\!]}^B [\![e_{\max}]\!]^A + \sum_{j=2}^{l} (j-l-2)[\![d'[j]]\!]^B + \sum_{j=l+1}^{l+3} (j-l-2+[\![\mathrm{of}[j]]\!]^B)[\![d'[j]]\!]^B.$

7: **return** $([\![f]\!]^A, [\![e]\!]^A, [\![s]\!]^B, [\![z]\!]^B).$

Truncation mode, and the total number of communication rounds is 15 for both binary32 and binary64 floating-point numbers.

Correctness of the Protocol. In the algorithm, the process until Step 4 is almost the same as Truncation mode, except that now we perform 3-bit (instead of 1-bit) left-shift to keep the information on the guard bit, the round bit, and the sticky bit (see the last paragraph of Sect. 2.2 for the terminology). More precisely, $f_{\min}$ is 2-bit left-shifted first to keep the guard bit and the round bit, and then 1-bit left-shifted later to reserve the space for the sticky bit. On the other hand, the correction bit δ now plays the role of the sticky bit for $f_{\min}$. Note that now the intermediate significand f_2 is at most $(l + 4)$-bit integer.

In Step 5, which is the main modification from the case of Truncation mode, we decide whether f_2 has to be rounded up or rounded down. We divide the argument into the following cases depending on the place of the MSNZB of f_2.

– When MSNZB is the $(l + 3)$-th least bit: now the guard bit G is $d[3]$, the round bit R is $d[2]$, and the sticky bit is $S = d[1] \vee d[0]$. If $G = 0$, then it should be rounded down, which is represented by setting $r[l + 3] = 0$. From now, we consider the other case $G = 1$. If $R = 1$ or $S = 1$, then it should be rounded up, which is represented by setting $r[l + 3] = 1$. In the other case where $R = S = 0$, it should be rounded up if and only if $d[4] = 1$ due to the rounding rule in Round-to-Even mode. This is correctly expressed by the formula of $r[l + 3]$ in the algorithm.
– When MSNZB is the $(l + 2)$-th or $(l + 1)$-th least bit: now the argument is similar to the previous case; in fact, the case of $(l + 1)$-th least bit is even simpler because now the sticky bit is always zero.
– Otherwise: by the same argument as the case of Truncation mode, such a large move of the place of MSNZB (which was originally at the $(l + 3)$-th least bit) can occur only when $e_\Delta \leq 1$. In such a case, the least two bits $d[1]$ and $d[0]$ are always zero due to the 3-bit left-shift, therefore all the necessary information is involved in the bits $d[l], d[l-1], \ldots, d[2]$ and only the normalization (without any rounding) is sufficient.

These arguments show that the direction of rounding is correctly chosen in the algorithm. However, we have another possibility to concern, which was not necessary in Truncation mode. That is, in the new case of rounding up, the bit length of the significand may be increased from l to $l + 1$. This happens only in the case $11 \cdots 1 \mapsto 100 \cdots 0$; in the algorithm, this possibility is checked by using the bits "of$[j]$", and the resulting output is adjusted according to the values of of$[j]$'s. This gives the correct output.

5 Experimental Results

We implemented our proposed protocols and performed experiments for the addition of two floating-point numbers. The results are summarized in Table 3.

Table 3. Experimental results on our proposed 2PC protocols for floating-point addition over simulated WAN with 10 MB/s bandwidth and 40 ms RTT latency

Batch size	Offline		Online				Total
	Comp. time (s)	Comm. size (bit)	Comp. time (s)	Comm. size (bit)	Data trans. time (ms)	Comm. latency (s)	time (s)
Truncation mode (binary32)							
1	0.163	352,565	0.065	74,373	0.930	0.520	0.586
10	1.538	3,525,650	0.079	743,730	9.297		0.608
100	13.697	35,256,500	0.175	7,437,300	92.966		0.788
1000	145.553	352,565,000	1.758	74,373,000	929.663		3.208
Truncation mode (binary64)							
1	1.075	2,506,416	0.131	324,617	4.058	0.520	0.655
10	15.739	25,064,160	0.223	3,246,170	40.577		0.784
100	160.971	250,641,600	1.405	32,461,700	405.771		2.331
Round-to-Even mode (binary32)							
1	0.185	298,923	0.077	64,095	0.801	0.600	0.678
10	1.639	2,989,230	0.089	640,950	8.012		0.697
100	14.408	29,892,300	0.177	6,409,500	80.119		0.857
1000	141.476	298,923,000	1.526	64,095,000	801.188		2.927
Round-to-Even mode (binary64)							
1	1.718	2,265,310	0.135	270,835	3.385	0.600	0.738
10	16.038	22,653,100	0.227	2,708,350	33.854		0.861
100	162.959	226,531,000	1.329	27,083,500	338.544		2.268

In our experiments, the computation (Comp.) times (sec) assuming the client-aided model and the communication (Comm.) sizes (bit) for each party were measured for the offline and the online phases separately; the offline communication means communication sending the pre-generated BTs/BTEs from the client to each computing party. The computation times shown in the table are averages of 10 trials for each parameter setting. To calculate the data transfer (trans.) time (msec) and the communication latency in total for the online phase, we did not use a real network and, instead, adopted the following simulated WAN environment setting which is the same as [20]: 10 MB/sec (= 80000 bit/msec) bandwidth and 40 msec round-trip time (RTT) latency. Our protocols were implemented on a single laptop computer with Intel Core i7-820 HQ 2.9 GHz and 16.0 GB RAM, and with Python3.7 and Numpy v1.16.3.

For inputs with binary32 formats, we performed the experiments for the cases of 1/10/100/1000 batches; the computation and the data transfer times grow as the batch numbers increase, while the communication latency depends only on the number of communication rounds (13 rounds) and is independent of the batch numbers. For the case of binary64 inputs (with 15 rounds), we performed the experiments similarly for the cases of 1/10/100 batches; the larger batches could not be performed due to memory error.

Algorithm 3. FastTwoSum

Functionality: $([\![x]\!], [\![y]\!]) \leftarrow \mathsf{FastTwoSum}([\![a]\!], [\![b]\!])$
Ensure: $x = \mathrm{fl}(a+b)$ and $x + y = a + b$.
1: P_i $(i \in \{0,1\})$ parallelly compute   ▷ 15
   $[\![x]\!] \leftarrow \mathsf{FLADDeven}([\![a]\!], [\![b]\!]), \quad ([\![a']\!], [\![b']\!]) \leftarrow \mathsf{swap}([\![a]\!], [\![b]\!]).$
2: P_i compute $[\![q]\!] \leftarrow \mathsf{FLADDeven}([\![x]\!], -[\![a']\!]).$ ▷ 15
3: P_i compute $[\![y]\!] \leftarrow \mathsf{FLADDeven}([\![b']\!], -[\![q]\!]).$ ▷ 15
4: **return** $([\![x]\!], [\![y]\!]).$

Algorithm 4. swap

Functionality: $([\![y_0]\!], [\![y_1]\!]) \leftarrow \mathsf{swap}([\![x_0]\!], [\![x_1]\!])$
Ensure: $\{y_0, y_1\} = \{x_0, x_1\}$ and $|y_0| \geq |y_1|$.
1: P_i $(i \in \{0,1\})$ parallelly compute   ▷ 3
   $[\![a]\!]^{\mathsf{B}} \leftarrow \mathsf{Comparison}([\![e_0]\!]^{\mathsf{A}}, [\![e_1]\!]^{\mathsf{A}}), \quad [\![b]\!]^{\mathsf{B}} \leftarrow \mathsf{Equality}([\![e_0]\!]^{\mathsf{A}}, [\![e_1]\!]^{\mathsf{A}}),$
   $[\![c]\!]^{\mathsf{B}} \leftarrow \mathsf{Comparison}([\![f_0]\!]^{\mathsf{A}}, [\![f_1]\!]^{\mathsf{A}}).$
2: P_i parallelly compute   ▷ 1
   $[\![e_{\max}]\!]^{\mathsf{A}} \leftarrow [\![a]\!]^{\mathsf{B}}[\![e_1]\!]^{\mathsf{A}} + \overline{[\![a]\!]}^{\mathsf{B}}[\![e_0]\!]^{\mathsf{A}}, \quad [\![e_{\min}]\!]^{\mathsf{A}} \leftarrow [\![a]\!]^{\mathsf{B}}[\![e_0]\!]^{\mathsf{A}} + \overline{[\![a]\!]}^{\mathsf{B}}[\![e_1]\!]^{\mathsf{A}},$
   $[\![f_{\max}]\!]^{\mathsf{A}} \leftarrow [\![a]\!]^{\mathsf{B}}[\![f_1]\!]^{\mathsf{A}} + [\![b]\!]^{\mathsf{B}}[\![c]\!]^{\mathsf{B}}[\![f_1]\!]^{\mathsf{A}} + \overline{[\![a]\!]}^{\mathsf{B}} \overline{[\![b]\!]}^{\mathsf{B}}[\![f_0]\!]^{\mathsf{A}} + [\![b]\!]^{\mathsf{B}}\overline{[\![c]\!]}^{\mathsf{B}}[\![f_0]\!]^{\mathsf{A}},$
   $[\![f_{\min}]\!]^{\mathsf{A}} \leftarrow [\![a]\!]^{\mathsf{B}}[\![f_0]\!]^{\mathsf{A}} + [\![b]\!]^{\mathsf{B}}[\![c]\!]^{\mathsf{B}}[\![f_0]\!]^{\mathsf{A}} + \overline{[\![a]\!]}^{\mathsf{B}} \overline{[\![b]\!]}^{\mathsf{B}}[\![f_1]\!]^{\mathsf{A}} + [\![b]\!]^{\mathsf{B}}\overline{[\![c]\!]}^{\mathsf{B}}[\![f_1]\!]^{\mathsf{A}},$
   $[\![s_{\max}]\!]^{\mathsf{B}} \leftarrow [\![a]\!]^{\mathsf{B}}[\![s_1]\!]^{\mathsf{B}} \oplus [\![b]\!]^{\mathsf{B}}[\![c]\!]^{\mathsf{B}}[\![s_1]\!]^{\mathsf{B}} \oplus \overline{[\![a]\!]}^{\mathsf{B}} \overline{[\![b]\!]}^{\mathsf{B}}[\![s_0]\!]^{\mathsf{B}} \oplus [\![b]\!]^{\mathsf{B}}\overline{[\![c]\!]}^{\mathsf{B}}[\![s_0]\!]^{\mathsf{B}},$
   $[\![s_{\min}]\!]^{\mathsf{B}} \leftarrow [\![a]\!]^{\mathsf{B}}[\![s_0]\!]^{\mathsf{B}} \oplus [\![b]\!]^{\mathsf{B}}[\![c]\!]^{\mathsf{B}}[\![s_0]\!]^{\mathsf{B}} \oplus \overline{[\![a]\!]}^{\mathsf{B}} \overline{[\![b]\!]}^{\mathsf{B}}[\![s_1]\!]^{\mathsf{B}} \oplus [\![b]\!]^{\mathsf{B}}\overline{[\![c]\!]}^{\mathsf{B}}[\![s_1]\!]^{\mathsf{B}},$
   $[\![z_{\max}]\!]^{\mathsf{B}} \leftarrow [\![a]\!]^{\mathsf{B}}[\![z_1]\!]^{\mathsf{B}} \oplus [\![b]\!]^{\mathsf{B}}[\![c]\!]^{\mathsf{B}}[\![z_1]\!]^{\mathsf{B}} \oplus \overline{[\![a]\!]}^{\mathsf{B}} \overline{[\![b]\!]}^{\mathsf{B}}[\![z_0]\!]^{\mathsf{B}} \oplus [\![b]\!]^{\mathsf{B}}\overline{[\![c]\!]}^{\mathsf{B}}[\![z_0]\!]^{\mathsf{B}},$
   $[\![z_{\min}]\!]^{\mathsf{B}} \leftarrow [\![a]\!]^{\mathsf{B}}[\![z_0]\!]^{\mathsf{B}} \oplus [\![b]\!]^{\mathsf{B}}[\![c]\!]^{\mathsf{B}}[\![z_0]\!]^{\mathsf{B}} \oplus \overline{[\![a]\!]}^{\mathsf{B}} [\![b]\!]^{\mathsf{B}}[\![z_1]\!]^{\mathsf{B}} \oplus [\![b]\!]^{\mathsf{B}}\overline{[\![c]\!]}^{\mathsf{B}}[\![z_1]\!]^{\mathsf{B}}.$
3: **return** $([\![f_{\max}]\!]^{\mathsf{A}}, [\![e_{\max}]\!]^{\mathsf{A}}, [\![s_{\max}]\!]^{\mathsf{B}}, [\![z_{\max}]\!]^{\mathsf{B}}), ([\![f_{\min}]\!]^{\mathsf{A}}, [\![e_{\min}]\!]^{\mathsf{A}}, [\![s_{\min}]\!]^{\mathsf{B}}, [\![z_{\min}]\!]^{\mathsf{B}}).$

Our experimental results show that in the online phase, the communication latency is dominant among the total execution time especially for small batches (e.g., ≤ 100 batches for binary32 and ≤ 10 batches for binary64). In such cases, our improvement in reducing the communication rounds in this paper has given significant effects to reduce the total online execution time. On the other hand, for the offline phase, the computation time might be reducible by just improving the implementation, while improvements of protocol designs are needed to reduce the communication size further, which is an important future research topic.

6 Application: Error-Free Transformation

Here we show a privacy-preserving error-free transformation protocol for the sum of two floating-point numbers; that is, we transform any pair of floating-point numbers (a, b) into a new pair (x, y) with $x = \mathrm{fl}(a+b)$ and $x+y = a+b$. Here $\mathrm{fl}(\cdot)$ denotes that the expression inside the parenthesis is calculated in floating-point. According to Dekker's algorithm in [24], we can construct privacy-preserving error-free transformation with 45 communication rounds as in Algorithm 3 using our protocol FLADDeven. In this algorithm, we use swap (Algorithm 4) as a sub-protocol so that the input is ordered by magnitude. We performed experiments for inputs with binary32 and binary64 where the computer and the (simulated) network environments are the same as Sect. 5. The experimental results are as in Table 4. Our protocol FLADDeven rounds the precise result to the nearest floating-point number, so we can obtain accurate result via Algorithm 3.

Table 4. Experimental results on our proposed 2PC protocols for error-free transformation over simulated WAN with 10 MB/s bandwidth and 40 ms RTT latency

| Batch size | Offline | | Online | | | | |
	Comp. time (s)	Comm. size (bit)	Comp. time (s)	Comm. size (bit)	Data trans. time (ms)	Comm. latency (s)	Total time (s)
binary32							
1	0.536	922, 170	0.233	199, 743	2.497	1.800	2.035
10	4.259	9, 221, 700	0.242	1, 997, 430	24.968		2.067
100	40.848	92, 217, 000	0.538	19, 974, 300	249.679		2.588
1000	427.950	922, 170, 000	4.498	199, 743, 000	2396.788		8.795
binary64							
1	4.916	6, 867, 189	0.426	823, 005	10.288	1.800	2.236
10	46.952	68, 671, 890	0.715	8, 230, 050	102.876		2.618
100	475.751	686, 718, 900	3.984	82, 300, 500	1028.756		6.813

Acknowledgements. This work was partly supported by the Ministry of Internal Affairs and Communications SCOPE Grant Number 182103105 and by JST CREST JPMJCR19F6. The authors thank Satsuya Ohata for his implemented library of basic protocols proposed in [20]. This work was done when the first author was an undergraduate student at Department of Mathematical Engineering and Information Physics, School of Engineering, The University of Tokyo.

References

1. Aliasgari, M., Blanton, M.: Secure computation of hidden markov models. Proc. SECRYPT **2013**, 242–253 (2013)
2. Aliasgari, M., Blanton, M., Bayatbabolghani, F.: Secure computation of hidden markov models and secure floating-point arithmetic in the malicious model. Int. J. Inf. Sec. **16**(6), 577–601 (2017)
3. Aliasgari, M., Blanton, M., Zhang, Y., Steele, A.: Secure computation on floating point numbers. In: NDSS 2013, San Diego, California, USA, 24–27 February 2013
4. Araki, T., et al.: Generalizing the SPDZ compiler for other protocols. Proc. ACM CCS **2018**, 880–895 (2018)
5. Araki, T., Furukawa, J., Lindell, Y., Nof, A., Ohara, K.: High-throughput semi-honest secure three-party computation with an honest majority. Proc. ACM CCS **2016**, 805–817 (2016)
6. Boyle, E., Gilboa, N., Ishai, Y.: Secure computation with preprocessing via function secret sharing. In: Hofheinz, D., Rosen, A. (eds.) TCC 2019. LNCS, vol. 11891, pp. 341–371. Springer, Cham (2019). https://doi.org/10.1007/978-3-030-36030-6_14

7. Catrina, O.: Towards practical secure computation with floating-point numbers. In: Proceedings Balkan CryptSec 2018 (2018)
8. Catrina, O.: Efficient secure floating-point arithmetic using shamir secret sharing. Proc. SECRYPT **2019**, 49–60 (2019)
9. Catrina, O.: Optimization and tradeoffs in secure floating point computation: products, powers, and polynomials. In: Proceedings of the 6th Conference on the Engineering of Computer Based Systems (ECBS 2019), pp. 7:1–7:10 (2019)
10. Demmler, D., Dessouky, G., Koushanfar, F., Sadeghi, A.-R., Schneider, T., Zeitouni, S.: Automated synthesis of optimized circuits for secure computation. Proc. ACM CCS **2015**, 1504–1517 (2015)
11. Demmler, D., Schneider, T., Zohner, M.: ABY – a framework for efficient mixed-protocol secure two-party computation. In: NDSS 2015, San Diego, California, USA, 8–11 February 2015
12. Eigner, F., Maffei, M., Pryvalov, I., Pampaloni, F., Kate, A.: Differentially private data aggregation with optimal utility. In: Proceedings ACSAC 2014, ACM, pp. 316–325 (2014)
13. Goldreich, O.: Foundations of Cryptography, vol. II. Cambridge University Press, Cambridge (2004)
14. Hemenway, B., Lu, S., Ostrovsky, R., Welser IV, W.: High-precision secure computation of satellite collision probabilities. In: Zikas, V., De Prisco, R. (eds.) SCN 2016. LNCS, vol. 9841, pp. 169–187. Springer, Cham (2016). https://doi.org/10.1007/978-3-319-44618-9_9
15. 754-2019 - IEEE Standard for Floating-Point Arithmetic (2019)
16. Kamm, L., Willemson, J.: Secure floating point arithmetic and private satellite collision analysis. Int. J. Inf. Sec. **14**(6), 531–548 (2015)
17. Liu, Y.-C., Chiang, Y.-T., Hsu, T.-S., Liau, C.-J., Wang, D.-W.: Floating point arithmetic protocols for constructing secure data analysis application. In: Proceedings KES 2013, Procedia Computer Science, vol. 22, pp. 152–161 (2013)
18. Mohassel, P., Zhang, Y.: SecureML: a system for scalable privacy-preserving machine learning. In: Proceedings of the IEEE S&P 2017, pp. 19–38 (2017)
19. Morita, H., Attrapadung, N., Teruya, T., Ohata, S., Nuida, K., Hanaoka, G.: Constant-round client-aided secure comparison protocol. In: Lopez, J., Zhou, J., Soriano, M. (eds.) ESORICS 2018. LNCS, vol. 11099, pp. 395–415. Springer, Cham (2018). https://doi.org/10.1007/978-3-319-98989-1_20
20. Ohata, S., Nuida, K.: Communication-Efficient (Client-Aided) secure two-party protocols and its application. In: Proceedings Financial Cryptography and Data Security(FC) 2020, to appear (https://arxiv.org/abs/1907.03415v2)
21. Omori, W., Kanaoka, A.: Efficient secure arithmetic on floating point numbers. In: Barolli, L., Enokido, T., Takizawa, M. (eds.) NBiS 2017. LNDECT, vol. 7, pp. 924–934. Springer, Cham (2018). https://doi.org/10.1007/978-3-319-65521-5_83
22. Pullonen, P., Siim, S.: Combining secret sharing and garbled circuits for efficient private IEEE 754 floating-point computations. In: Brenner, M., Christin, N., Johnson, B., Rohloff, K. (eds.) FC 2015. LNCS, vol. 8976, pp. 172–183. Springer, Heidelberg (2015). https://doi.org/10.1007/978-3-662-48051-9_13
23. Raeini, M.G., Nojoumian, M.: Secure trust evaluation using multipath and referral chain methods. In: Mauw, S., Conti, M. (eds.) STM 2019. LNCS, vol. 11738, pp. 124–139. Springer, Cham (2019). https://doi.org/10.1007/978-3-030-31511-5_8

24. Rump, S.M., Ogita, T., Oishi, S.: Accurate floating-point summation. Technical Report 05.12, Faculty for Information- and Communication Sciences, Hamburg University of Technology, 13 November 2005 (2005)
25. Zhang, Y., Steele, A., Blanton, M.: PICCO: a general-purpose compiler for private distributed computation. Proc. ACM CCS **2013**, 813–826 (2013)

Malicious Activity Detection 2

MKM: Multiple Kernel Memory for Protecting Page Table Switching Mechanism Against Memory Corruption

Hiroki Kuzuno[1,2]($\boxtimes$) and Toshihiro Yamauchi[1]

[1] Graduate School of Natural Science and Technology, Okayama University,
Okayama, Japan
kuzuno@s.okayama-u.ac.jp, yamauchi@cs.okayama-u.ac.jp
[2] Intelligent Systems Laboratory, SECOM CO., LTD., Mitaka, Japan

Abstract. Countermeasures against kernel vulnerability attacks on an operating system (OS) are highly important kernel features. Some kernels adopt several kernel protection methods such as mandatory access control, kernel address space layout randomization, control flow integrity, and kernel page table isolation; however, kernel vulnerabilities can still be exploited to execute attack codes and corrupt kernel memory. To accomplish this, adversaries subvert kernel protection methods and invoke these kernel codes to avoid administrator privileges restrictions and gain complete control of the target host. To prevent such subversion, we present Multiple Kernel Memory (MKM), which offers a novel security mechanism using an alternative design for kernel memory separation that was developed to reduce the kernel attack surface and mitigate the effects of illegal data manipulation in the kernel memory. The proposed MKM is capable of isolating kernel memory and dedicates the trampoline page table for a gateway of page table switching and the security page table for kernel protection methods. The MKM encloses the vulnerable kernel code in the kernel page table. The MKM mechanism achieves complete separation of the kernel code execution range of the virtual address space on each page table. It ensures that vulnerable kernel code does not interact with different page tables. Thus, the page table switching of the trampoline and the kernel protection methods of the security page tables are protected from vulnerable kernel code in other page tables. An evaluation of MKM indicates that it protects the kernel code and data on the trampoline and security page tables from an actual kernel vulnerabilities that lead to kernel memory corruption. In addition, the performance results show that the overhead is 0.020 μs to 0.5445 μs, in terms of the system call latency and the application overhead average is 196.27 μs to 6,685.73 μs , for each download access of 100,000 Hypertext Transfer Protocol sessions.

1 Introduction

Kernel vulnerability attacks are highly consequential and compromising processes in which an adversary takes control of the administrator account through

© Springer Nature Switzerland AG 2020
K. Aoki and A. Kanaoka (Eds.): IWSEC 2020, LNCS 12231, pp. 97–116, 2020.
https://doi.org/10.1007/978-3-030-58208-1_6

privilege escalation in the operating system (OS); to prevent this, the kernel must adopt protection methods.

Several kernel protection methods have been implemented, including stack monitoring of the kernel code [1], verification of kernel code control flow integration (CFI) to prevent the use of the return oriented programming (ROP) technique [2], system call isolation (SCI) for the creation of page table that contains necessity only kernel code at the system call invocation to prevent ROP attack selects an execution piece from the entire kernel code [3], kernel address space layout randomization (KASLR) to randomize the layout of the kernel code and data on the kernel memory [4], and the virtual address space separation method isolates the kernel memory to the kernel and the user page tables, to prevent meltdown side channel attacks from a user process (e.g., kernel page table isolation (KPTI) for Linux [5]). At the CPU layer, supervisor mode access prevention (SMAP) prevents access to the user memory region, whereas supervisor mode execution prevention (SMEP) prevents the execution of code in the user memory region of the virtual address space in the supervisor [6].

Privilege escalation leads to kernel vulnerability attacks; it employs an illegal memory corruption effect to overwrite privileged information variables on kernel memory. Although kernel protection methods restrict administrator privileges, the adversary also subverts kernel protection methods (e.g., achieving access control of SELinux [7]) to modify the kernel code and data on the kernel page table [8,9]. Moreover, kernel memory observer (KMO) involves the segregation of specific kernel codes as dedicated page tables [10]. Although, kernel protection methods calling kernel codes (e.g., the page table switching) need to be assigned to same virtual address space with vulnerable kernel code, the placement of kernel protection methods calling is the remaining of kernel attack surface.

This poses a threat to the kernel protection methods at the kernel layer. To mitigate this and protect specific kernel codes against kernel vulnerability attack targets, another perspective is necessary to ensure that the environment supports the limitations of kernel vulnerability attacks, thereby reducing the damage caused to the target kernel memory region.

In this study, we proposed a novel security mechanism called "Multiple Kernel Memory (MKM)", which enhances the resistance capabilities of the kernel using multiple page tables, thereby mitigating kernel vulnerability attacks that subvert kernel protection methods and these kernel code calling placement. An overview of the proposed security mechanism is presented below:

- MKM introduces an additional boundary of kernel code execution involving two page tables: trampoline and security. The gateway of page table switching feature is assigned and executed on the trampoline, then the kernel protection methods are dedicated and executed on the security page tables. A majority of the kernel code is confined to the kernel page table, and the remainder of the kernel code is stored in the user page table.
- To reduce the kernel attack surface and achieve isolation of the kernel code accessible range, a separation of the virtual address space is required. The MKM mechanism realizes that the potentiality of vulnerable kernel code is

enforced to execute to only the virtual address space of the kernel page table. Thus, it eliminates the risk of memory corruption of the gateway of page table switching and the kernel protection methods that are stored on the trampoline and security page tables.

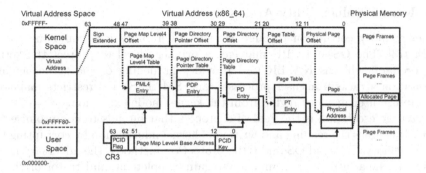

Fig. 1. Overview of page table structure (Linux x86_64) [11]

Here, the MKM was implemented on the Linux kernel using KPTI and SCI, and the kernel observation mechanism was executed. During evaluation, MKM mitigated the illegal modifications to the kernel code of the protection methods and page table switching function, and such instances were identified. The main contributions of the study are summarized below:

1. We present MKM, which is a novel kernel memory separation mechanism that is designed to specifically protect kernel protection methods at the kernel layer. We also discuss the threat model, capability, and limitation of MKM, which achieves resilience to kernel vulnerability attacks.
2. We evaluate the efficacy of the implementing MKM based on actual kernel vulnerability CVE-2017-16995 [12] Proof-of-Concepts (PoC) code attacks SELinux and the page table switching kernel code of the MKM. Both cases were identified via the kernel observation mechanism. The performance evaluation results indicate that the MKM overhead is from 0.020 μs to 0.5445 μs for each system call round time, and the application overhead average is from 196.27 μs to 6,685.73 μs for each HTTP download access.

2 Background

2.1 Virtual Address Space and Page Table

The design and implementation of the MKM was realized on a target architecture of is ×86_64 and the operating system used is Linux kernel. The page table structure manages multiple tables and pages for handling the virtual address space (Fig. 1). The length of the virtual address is 48 bits, the page size is 4 Kbytes, and CR3 register is the physical address of the page table in the Linux ×86_64 architecture. The page table maintains the page entry mechanism, which assigns the relationships between the physical and virtual addresses of each page on the page table.

2.2   Kernel Vulnerability Attack

Kernel memory corruption through kernel vulnerability is a common type of attack [13]. The OS and CPU manages a privilege level to protect the kernel code or data, whereas KASLR/CFI provides hardening of the kernel against exploitation attacks from user processes, and SMAP/SMEP restricts malicious codes in the user memory region from the kernel mode execution.

Privilege escalation is the goal of a process that intends to compromise the kernel. It enables the reading and writing of kernel information by corrupting the kernel memory. To avoid OS and CPU protection methods, the adversary needs to execute the arbitrary program code to gain complete administrator privileges at the kernel layer by exploiting kernel vulnerabilities in the kernel.

To achieve privilege escalation on Linux, the adversary force-calls the kernel functions `commit_creds` and `prepare_kernel_cred` to gain access to root privileges. Moreover, the adversary directory overwrites the `uid` variable of the `cred` structure on the kernel memory. To subvert the Linux kernel protection methods, the adversary directory overwrites the Linux security module (LSM) function pointer value of the `security_hook_list` that invokes different non-checking access control methods in the kernel code or changes the security context variable to escape a mandatory access control (MAC) mechanism (e.g., SELinux) restrictions [8,9].

2.3   Isolation of Virtual Address Space

The CPU and kernel protection mechanisms prohibit user processes from referring to the virtual address space of the kernel memory. The adversary has to escape these restrictions for the privilege escalation and the subversion of the kernel protection methods.

A meltdown side channel attack indicates that a user process can refer to virtual addresses of the kernel memory without the use of any kernel protection methods (e.g., KASLR). Therefore, an adversary uses this virtual address information to execute an arbitrary program for performing a kernel vulnerability attack, using the ROP technique. Moreover, the meltdown countermeasure method (e.g., Linux KPTI [5]) provides the page table to the user mode and kernel mode for virtual address space isolation.

Additionally, in the ROP countermeasure method (e.g., Linux SCI [3]), an independent page table for the kernel memory with minimum kernel codes is innovated from user process data to execute a system call. SCI limits the ROP technique and creates and executes a malicious code that concatenates code snippets from the complete kernel codes on kernel memory. Moreover, the KMO involves additional virtual address space isolation mechanism that provides security page table for the kernel mode. It is the dedicated memory region for the execution of the kernel protection method and segregation from the kernel page table [10].

2.4   Threat Model

Herein, we postulate that a threat model (i.e., an adversary) executing a kernel vulnerability attack corrupts the kernel memory only in the kernel mode. The adversary's goal is to execute any control of the OS kernel using administrator privileges. Although the adversary is a normal user, the adversary's user process changes the page table switching function on the kernel page table of the MKM, the LSM hook function pointer variable for disabling the MAC, and a credential variable through kernel vulnerability. It enables the adversary's user process to insert malicious code in the kernel memory. Consequently, the adversary gains complete administrator privileges on the OS kernel.

A limitation of a memory corruption is that the kernel vulnerability and the victim kernel code and data must be on the same virtual address space of the page table. This attack cannot overwrite other virtual address spaces of the page tables, which restricts access to the kernel and memory management unit.

3   Design and Implementation

3.1   Goal of Multiple Kernel Memory

The primary goal of the MKM is to prevent the subversion of kernel protection methods that keep to restrict access to complete administrator capabilities at the kernel layer.

– **Concept of protecting kernel protection methods**
   Kernel protection methods face threats on the kernel memory, because the adversary collapses kernel protection methods and bypasses accurate privilege-checking, which is performed for all user processes. To mitigate kernel memory corruption, it is essential to secure memory management and allocation for the execution of kernel code and for storing kernel data. It also necessary to segregate kernel protection methods and these kernel code invocation placement from vulnerable kernel code at the running kernel.

3.2   Challenge and Overview

To achieve the goal of MKM, which makes provision for the challenge of kernel resilience.

– **Securing of kernel protection methods**
   To automatically corresponds to the isolated processing of kernel features, kernel resilience is to manually assign the set of kernel protection methods

code, page table function code, and other kernel code are on different virtual address spaces. This mechanism ensures that the kernel code is forcefully accessed and executed. Thereafter, kernel code could only cause a pollution of memory corruption to their virtual address space.

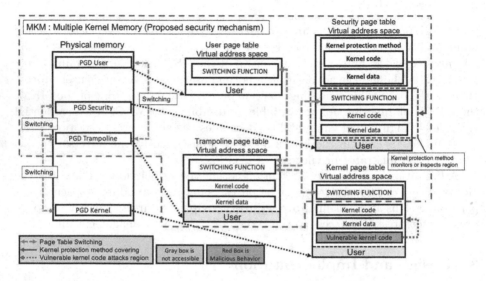

Fig. 2. Overview of multiple kernel memories.

To overcome this challenge, MKM (Fig. 2) comprises two dedicated page tables: the trampoline page table and the security page table. The MKM kernel automatically switches to the page table that is suitable for the processing of specific kernel code of the kernel protection method in the kernel mode. The kernel protection method covers the kernel memory region of the security page table to achieve feature responsibilities. These page tables were derived using different memory architectures from the latest kernels such as Linux with KPTI possesses kernel and user page tables.

An overview of the role of the proposed page tables is provided below:

Trampoline: The trampoline page table acts as the gateway of the transition between the user mode and the kernel mode. It causes an invariably switch from other page tables to the trampoline page table. Moreover, it facilitates page table switching functions.

Security: The security page table supports kernel code and kernel data that constructs the features of kernel protection methods. These kernel codes are only executed on virtual address spaces of the security page table, thereby forcing acceptance of the in and out transition with the trampoline page table.

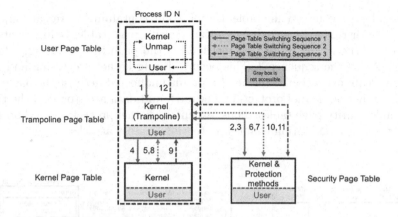

Fig. 3. Overview of page table switching sequences

3.3   Page Table Switching Sequence

MKM involves three switching sequences between multiple page tables for processing each kernel feature (Fig. 3). Additionally, MKM ensures that the trampoline page table is inserted to a middle position of each sequence, as described below:

Sequence 1: User $\xrightarrow{1}$ Trampoline $\xrightarrow{2}$ Security $\xrightarrow{3}$ Trampoline $\xrightarrow{4}$ Kernel
Sequence 1 is a system call invocation or exception request that triggers a transition from the user mode to the kernel mode. Simultaneously, it involves a change from the user to the kernel page tables, through the trampoline and security page tables. Thus, executing the kernel protection methods before the kernel feature deals with the request of user process.

Sequence 2: Kernel $\xrightarrow{5}$ Trampoline $\xrightarrow{6}$ Security $\xrightarrow{7}$ Trampoline $\xrightarrow{8}$ Kernel
Sequence 2 is the invocation of the kernel protection method invocation during kernel processing. It is the switch from the kernel page table to the security page table, through the trampoline page table.

Sequence 3: Kernel $\xrightarrow{9}$ Trampoline $\xrightarrow{10}$ Security $\xrightarrow{11}$ Trampoline $\xrightarrow{12}$ User
Sequence 3 is the return to the user mode from the kernel mode. It involves the switching from the kernel page table to the user page table, through the trampoline and security page tables. It executes kernel protection methods after the kernel features have completed the request of the user process.

3.4   Kernel Attack Surface

A kernel vulnerability attack can result in the corruption of the memory of other kernel code or data stored in the same virtual address space in the kernel mode.

The adversary uses vulnerable kernel code containing adversary-injected attack code disrupts the switching to the security page table. It intercepts the execution of the kernel protection method on the page table switching during sequence 2 and the sequence 3. This occurs during kernel processing and after the system call invocation. Sequence 1 remains unaffected because the page table switching function, kernel protection methods, and data are stored in the trampoline and security page tables. Thus, executing kernel protection method prior to the system call execution enables protection against attacks.

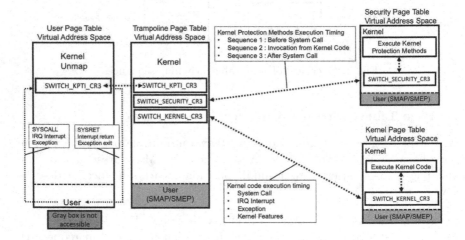

Fig. 4. Timing of switching page table

3.5   MKM Implementation

The proposed MKM was implemented on Linux using KPTI and SCI and the ×86_64 CPU architecture.

Page Table Management
The MKM adopts KPTI and SCI, which have pre-assigned virtual address spaces, and assigns them as the user and kernel page tables, respectively, for kernel feature processing. The MKM introduces the trampoline and the security page tables that support the gateway of page table switching and kernel protection methods. Each process shares the security page table. In this study, the proposed kernel memory monitoring feature was executed on the security page table.

MKM employs a variable `pgd` of the structure `init_mm` as the initial value of the trampoline page table. The security page table adopts a four page size OR physical address from the variable `pgd`. The user page table utilizes a one page size XOR (4 Kbytes on ×86_64) physical address from the variable `pgd`. MKM sets the kernel page table to the variable `kernel_pgd` of `mm_struct` of the `task_struct` structure.

Switching of Page Table

MKM selects a suitable page tables for the execution of kernel code for specific virtual address spaces (Fig. 4). The implementation of switching sequences is described below:

Sequence 1: User $\xrightarrow{1}$ Trampoline $\xrightarrow{2}$ Security $\xrightarrow{3}$ Trampoline $\xrightarrow{4}$ Kernel
To transition from the user mode to the kernel mode. MKM uses the SWITCH_KPTI_CR3 function, which writes the physical address of the trampoline page table to the CR3 register. MKM also employs SWITCH_SECURITY_CR3 to write the physical address of the security page table to the CR3 register, and then back to the trampoline page table after executing the kernel protection methods. Moreover, SWITCH_KERNEL_CR3 writes a physical address of the kernel page table on the trampoline page table

Sequence 2: Kernel $\xrightarrow{5}$ Trampoline $\xrightarrow{6}$ Security $\xrightarrow{7}$ Trampoline $\xrightarrow{8}$ Kernel
During kernel processing, MKM utilizes SWITCH_KERNEL_CR3 and SWITCH_SECURITY_CR3 to switch to the security page table through the trampoline page table, for the execution of kernel protection methods.

Sequence 3: Kernel $\xrightarrow{9}$ Trampoline $\xrightarrow{10}$ Security $\xrightarrow{11}$ Trampoline $\xrightarrow{12}$ User
For the transition from the kernel mode to the user mode, MKM uses SWITCH_KERNEL_CR3 to write the physical address of the trampoline page table to the CR3 register. Moreover, MKM also uses SWITCH_SECURITY_CR3 and SWITCH_KPTI_CR3 that to writes the user page table to the CR3 register through the security and trampoline page tables, for the execution of kernel protection methods.

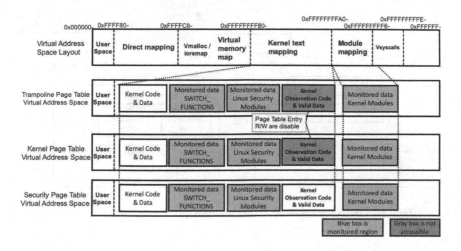

Fig. 5. Monitoring target of kernel code on the MKM

Monitoring of Virtual Address Space

The kernel observation mechanism monitors the kernel module, LSM variables, and page table switching functions for MKM (Fig. 5). To ensure accuracy of the monitoring data, the kernel observation mechanism identifies the virtual addresses of the target kernel code and data containing the `SWITCH_KERNEL_CR3` virtual address was specified on the kernel page table. Subsequently, it copies these monitoring data to the security page table as valid data, at the time of booting.

MKM enables timing the execution of the kernel protection method before and after the invocation of the system call and to interrupt kernel processing. The kernel observation mechanism involving MKM begins monitoring and compares the target data with the valid data on the security page table to determine if memory corruption has occurred.

Case Study of Page Table Switching Attack

The attack on the MKM kernel aims to completely disrupt the entire kernel protection method. In this study, the eBPF kernel vulnerability CVE-2017-16995 [12] PoC code that employs the `map_update_elem` function of `kernel/bpf/syscall.c` to exploit the kernel is considered. The adversary is able to write any restricted virtual address space of the kernel page table. It is considered that the attacking user process only succeeds in corrupting the `SWITCH_KERNEL_CR3` switching function of the kernel page table (Fig. 6). This indicates that the MKM kernel directory switches from the kernel page table to the user page table.

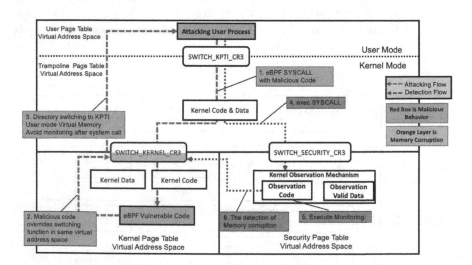

Fig. 6. Attack and detection flow of attacking user process using kernel vulnerability

4   Evaluation

4.1   Purpose and Environment of the Evaluation

The evaluation items and objectives are described as follows:

E1: Monitoring memory corruption of LSM with MKM
The identification and measurement times of the memory corruption over-writing the function pointer of LSM were evaluated. The kernel observation mechanism determined if the target memory region was valid, based on the security page table of MKM.

E2: Monitoring memory corruption of the page table switching feature
The identification and measurement times of the memory corruption of the page table switching function on the kernel page table were evaluated. The kernel observation mechanism preserves detection capability and then inspects whether the target memory region is valid after memory corruption.

E3: Measurement of system call invocation overhead
We measure the effect of kernel feasibility. A benchmark software is used to calculate the overhead of system call latency.

E4: Measurement of application overhead
We measure the performance overhead of a web application process using a benchmark software on MKM, which adopts several page tables switching.

The effectiveness of MKM was evaluated on the target implementation, Linux kernel 4.4.114 was used for monitoring and Linux kernel 5.0.0 was used for the performance evaluation. The Linux distribution used was Debian 9.0; the SCI was ported to kernel 4.4.114, and the CVE-2017-16995 PoC code was modified to handle any virtual addresses. The evaluation environment for stand alone and the server is a physical machine equipped with an Intel (R) Core (TM) i7-7700HQ (2.80 GHz, ×86_64) processor and 16 GB DDR4 memory. The client machine is an Intel(R) Core(TM) i5 4200U (1.6 GHz), with 8 GB of memory and running Windows 10. The network environment for the application benchmark uses 1 Gbps hub supporting different ports for server and client physical machines.

4.2   Monitoring Memory Corruption of LSM with MKM

The eBPF kernel attack uses CVE-2017-16995 [12] to disable the LSM feature on Linux, it modifies the LSM hook function pointer of `selinux_hooks` to the virtual address of the original kernel module function at the `sys_bpf` system call invocation. MKM allows the kernel observation mechanism stores the valid data at the kernel boot and runs an inspection scheme before and after the system call invocation. It compares the target virtual address with the valid virtual address on the security page table; thereafter, it outputs the result to log messages.

On identifying memory corruption, log messages are presented as "Invalid LSM function is detected" and "Virtual Address (Invalid)." The kernel observation mechanism employing MKM accurately identifies the invalid LSM function pointer (Fig. 7). The attack occurs on the virtual address space of the kernel page table; subsequently, MKM switches to the security page table through the trampoline page table, enabling the kernel protection method to detect and identify the actual attack within 0.0049 ms after the kernel executes the PoC kernel code.

```
1.  // Install LKM
2.  [  78.654425] lkm_address_module: module license 'unspecified' taints kernel.
3.  [  78.654853] Disabling lock debugging due to kernel taint
4.  [  78.718459] dummy_hook_function Address Value fffffffa0000000
5.  [  78.718427] selinux_hooks[56].hook.file_permission pointer Address ffffffff81e77c18
6.  [  78.718444] selinux_hooks[56].hook.file_permission pointer Address Value ffffffff812f3f20

7.  // Switching to trampoline, security page table, and monitoring
8.  [ 100.767961] Address ffffffff812f3f20 (Valid), ffffffff812f3f20 (Valid)
9.  // Switching to trampoline page table

10. // Switching to kernel page table
11. // CVE-2017-16995 attack overrides LSM function address via sys_bpf()
12. // Switching to trampoline page table

13. // Switching to security page table and monitoring after sys_bpf()
14. [ 100.772834] Invalid lsm function is detected
15. [ 100.772854] Address ffffffff812f3f20 (Valid), fffffffa0000000 (Invalid)
16. // Switching to trampoline page table
```

Fig. 7. Monitoring result for the memory corruption of LSM function pointer

4.3   Monitoring Memory Corruption of the Page Table Switching

The eBPF kernel attack also uses CVE-2017-16995 [12] to modify the page table switching function pointer SWITCH_KERNEL_CR3 to the virtual address of the kernel module function. It compromises sequence 3 of switching from the kernel to the trampoline page table. The kernel observation mechanism with MKM identifies the memory corruption by presenting the log messages of "Invalid vmem switching function is detected" and "Virtual Address (Invalid)."

The kernel observation mechanism with MKM also accurately identifies and shows that the attack overwrites the function pointer of SWITCH_KERNEL_CR3 to the kernel module function pointer on the kernel page table (Figure 8).

After the attack, the MKM was unable to switch to the security page table from the kernel page table through the trampoline page table. Moreover, the MKM directory is changed to the user page table from the kernel page table. Although the inspection was successfully prevented after the attack, the other inspections prior to system call invocation remain unaffected and detected it within 0.0039 ms after the kernel executed the attack system call.

4.4   Measurement of System Call Invocation Overhead

We measured the performance overhead that compares the Linux kernel using the MKM mechanism and a vanilla Linux kernel. We executed the lmbench software ten times to determine the system call overhead effect from the average

```
 1. // Install LKM
 2. [  105.738923] lkm_address_module: module license 'unspecified' taints kernel.
 3. [  105.739633] Disabling lock debugging due to kernel taint
 4. [  105.802694] dummy_hook_function Address Value ffffffffa0000000
 5. [  105.802637] vmem_switching_function pointer Address ffffffff821257e0
 6. [  105.802657] vmem_switching_function pointer Address Value ffffffff810593e0

 7. // Switching to trampoline, security page tables, and monitoring
 8. [  159.480809] Address ffffffff810593e0 (Valid), ffffffff810593e0 (Valid)
 9. // Switching to trampoline page table

10. // Switching to kernel page table
11. // CVE-2017-16995 attack overrides the virtual memory switching function address
    via sys_bpf
12. // Switching to trampoline page table

13. // Switching to security page table and monitoring at next system call
14. [  159.484758] Invalid vmem switching function is detected
15. [  159.484776] Address ffffffff810593e0 (Valid), ffffffffa0000000 (Invalid)
16. // Switching to trampoline page table
```

Fig. 8. Monitoring result for the memory corruption of page table switching function

score. The result is the switching cost of the page tables for each system call invocation (Table 1). The result of lmbench contains different counts of system calls invoked for each system call. fork+/bin/sh has 54; fork+execve has four; fork+exit and open/close have two invocations; and the others have one invocation. Table 1 demonstrates that the system calls with the highest overhead are fork+exit (0.5445 μs, 100.91%) and the lowest overheads are write (0.020 μs, 109.05%).

Table 1. Overhead of MKM mechanism on the Linux kernel (μs)

System call	Vanilla kernel	MKM kernel	Overhead
fork+/bin/sh	517.839	524.383	6.544 (101.26%)
fork+execve	133.954	134.823	0.869 (100.65%)
fork+exit	120.214	121.303	1.089 (100.91%)
open/close	3.070	3.226	0.156 (105.08%)
read	0.264	0.285	0.021 (107.95%)
write	0.221	0.241	0.020 (109.05%)
stat	1.095	1.128	0.033 (103.01%)
fstat	0.286	0.306	0.020 (106.99%)

Table 2. ApacheBench overhead of MKM mechanism on the Linux kernel (μs).

File size (KB)	Vanilla kernel	MKM kernel	Overhead
1	1,637.08	1,833.35	196.27 (111.99%)
10	1,868.17	2,542.07	673.9 (136.07%)
100	3,709.58	1,0395.31	6,685.73 (280.23%)

4.5   Measurement of Application Overhead

We compared the user process overhead between the vanilla kernel and MKM kernel. The user process used here is the Apache 2.4.25 web server. The benchmark software is ApacheBench 2.4. The ApacheBench calculates a download request average of 100,000 HTTP accesses to file sizes of 1 KB, 10 KB, and 100 KB in one connection. Table 2 demonstrates that MKM has an average overhead of 196.27 μs (111.99%) to 6685,73 μs (280.23%) for each file download access of 100,000 HTTP sessions. ApacheBench relies on the total count of system call invocations in the user process. The ApacheBench result shows that a small file requires a low overhead factor whereas large files increase the overhead factor.

We consider that the file transfer depends on the number of system call invocations. Numerous system call invocations increase the switching of page tables and cause additional processing time.

5   Discussion

5.1   Evaluation Consideration

During the evaluation, our kernel observation mechanism used the MKM security page table. Although the eBPF kernel vulnerability attack successfully modified the page table switching function on the kernel page table, thereby disabling one of the MKM mechanisms, it did not affect the rest of the MKM mechanisms. The MKM continued to run our kernel observation mechanism on the security page table from the trampoline page table before the system call invocation at the kernel layer. Moreover, it is difficult for the adversary to evade the inspection timing before the system call invocation of the kernel observation mechanism, after the adversary program has already compromised the host.

5.2   Limitations

When an actual kernel vulnerability PoC (e.g., CVE-2017-16995) attempts to defeat part of the MKM mechanism, MKM can not invoke kernel protection methods after the memory corruption caused by the system call invocation.

To enhance kernel resilience and protect specific kernel code and data, MKM provides two dedicated page tables at the kernel layer to restrict the attack to the entire kernel memory. The MKM supports the kernel protection method and the normal feature kernel code assigned on each individual page table. Therefore, the MKM complicates the access to the virtual address spaces of trampoline and security page tables when the vulnerable kernel code affects its virtual address space. The MKM relies on the accomplishing memory isolation through page tables. Thus, kernel protection methods or the kernel driver should satisfy the requirements for creating suitable isolation granularity on the MKM mechanism.

5.3 Performance Consideration

We consider the performance overhead resulting from the MKM handling multiple page tables for executing suitable processes on the running kernel. MKM enables tag-based TLBs, which reduces the performance overhead. The Linux KPTI mechanism, SCI, and MKM use the PCID of TLB. The cache on TLBs improves the physical memory access without a page table walk to identify the targeted page, which only requires the CR3 update.

The performance effect involves the switching of page tables, followed by the CR3 register access. MKM maintains the application process without overhead in the user mode. An overhead cost appears when the switching occurs in the kernel mode after the system call invocation from the user mode. In addition, the kernel typically only switches the user page table at the context switch of each process, whereas KPTI switches between the kernel and user page tables at each transition between the user mode and the kernel mode. The trampoline and security kernel page tables provided by MKM require additional overheads to switch page tables in the kernel mode.

5.4 Portability Consideration

We consider the capability of the MKM mechanism on other OSs. FreeBSD, which adopts page table isolation [14], is an accepted Linux implementation similar to the MKM approach. Therefore, additional CPU architectures can be realized in the future, to validate the use of multiple kernel page tables.

6 Related Work

Kernel Protection for Privilege Management. SELinux [7] and Capability [15] restrict the granularity of root privilege of user process, which reduces the harmful effects of a compromised host.

Kernel Protection for Running Kernel. Software based running kernel protection involves stack monitoring [1], randomization of kernel memory layout using KASLR [4], kernel control flow integrity [2], randomize the virtual address of the page table position [16], to mitigate a kernel attack with arbitrary program or ROP code snippets execution. In addition, kR^X are exclusive management methods that directly protect kernel code and kernel image data on the kernel memory [17]. Moreover, hardware based running kernel protection adopts trusted computing base (TCB) verifies the firmware and kernel validation at start up and protects them using tamper-proof features [18]. Sprobes uses the CPU security features and provides a trusted execution environment [19].

Kernel Monitoring. SecVisor and TrustVisor are hypervisors that monitor the kernel as the guest OS preserves the integrity of the kernel code and data [20, 21]. SIM inserts the monitoring mechanism into a guest OS memory space to achieve real-time kernel behavior inspection [22]. ED-Monitor is a kernel module that handles register management to enable hypervisor monitoring [23]. GRIM supports a kernel protection mechanism on the GPU device [24].

Kernel Vulnerability Suppression. The seL4 micro-kernel provides a small set of kernel-level functionality with formal verification of memory management to restrain memory invalidation and other vulnerability [25]. In addition, kernel memory fuzzing is the technique of discovering mis-implementations that result in vulnerabilities; kmemcheck [26] and KASAN [27] with syzbot and syzkaller [28] automatically inspect the memory handling processes on the kernel memory mechanism.

Reducing Kernel Memory Attack Surface. Separation of user and kernel memory using KPTI [5] and separation of the kernel memory using the extended page table are available on Intel CPUs [29]. KRAZOR reduces the visible kernel code list to the user process [30], KASR handles an execution permission at page granularity for user process [31], Additionally, PerspicuOS provides intra-kernel privilege separation to support isolation management at the kernel layer [32]. Multik prepares the minimum kernel code mapping of kernel memory for each application [33], and KMO provides the dedicated page table for executing specific kernel codes and data, to prevent failure of the kernel protection method [10]. Kernel multi-variant execution (kMVX) provides differential virtual address space and stack behaviors; anomalous process behavior is identified based on the success or failure of attacks in these environments [34].

The security features of MKM and previous research mechanisms were considered. Kernel protection for privilege management and running kernel provides effective kernel protection at each layer. Moreover, kernel monitoring using Hypervisor or a hardware layer (e.g., CPU) protection ensures integrity and enhances monitoring capability. By reducing the kernel memory attack surface, MKM provides an alternative attack mitigation method that separates or minimizes the kernel memory, to mitigate the attack code execution through kernel vulnerability and protect security features in the kernel memory mechanisms. Kernel vulnerability suppression automatically complements the additional kernel features. The fuzzing technique identifies mis-implementations of additional features and the formal verification approach subsequently ensures that anomalous control flow behavior is excluded. Kernel security capabilities are enhanced and restricted to realize multiple layer security quality using a combination of these research methods.

6.1   Comparison with Related Work

Based on a comparison of the security features of MKM and those of five reducing kernel attack mechanisms (Table 3) [10,30–33] , MKM satisfies a majority of the attack mitigation requirements for the running kernel.

KRAZOR [30] initially collects necessary kernel features for a targeted program and subsequently enforces the result at the deployment phase during user process execution. Moreover, KASR [31] builds up a kernel code database during the offline training of the targeted program; thereafter, the executable ker-

Table 3. Reducing kernel memory attack surface comparison (✓ is supported; △ is partially supported).

Feature	KRAZOR[30]	KASR [31]	PerspicuOS [32]	Multik [33]	KMO[10]	MKM
Page table switching protection						✓
Isolated kernel protection method			△	△	✓	✓
Memory corruption mitigation via system call	✓	✓	✓	✓	△	△
Reducing executable kernel code	✓	✓	✓			
Reducing kernel code from page table				✓	△	△

nel codes are employed for the execution of the user process from the hypervisor layer. Although KRAZOR forcibly minimizes callable kernel functions and KASR executes kernel functions at the running kernel to mitigate kernel attacks from user processes, these approach do not separate the kernel memory at each kernel feature.

PerspicuOS [32] supports isolation techniques of privilege for multiple kernel components. PerspicuOS ensures that nested kernel (trusted) contains a small part of kernel code and data, and the outer kernel (untrusted) contains the rest of the kernel with de-privileging. The nested kernel exclusively manages hardware privilege operations (e.g., MMU and CPU registers) for the protection of illegal memory corruption. Although MKM does not support hardware privilege deduction, MKM completely separates the virtual address space as a page table for the kernel code. We consider that MKM covers the entry gate of the Application Binary Interface (ABI) to a user process, and porting to other OSes at the kernel layer.

Multik [33] profiles the necessary kernel codes that are generated for a customized kernel image and then allocates a minimized kernel as the page table of each application. KMO [10] assigns specific portions of kernel codes to dedicated page tables for the isolation from complete kernel codes. Multik and KMO ensure that the independent page table is safeguarded from the effects of memory corruption. However, the invocation codes of the kernel protection method (e.g., page table switching function) are still assigned to the kernel page table with vulnerable kernel code.

These kernel memory layers attack mitigation approaches, similar to the capability of MKM. The MKM architecture focuses on strongly separating specific kernel codes at the earliest stage of the kernel protection method, through the invocation of system calls or kernel feature processing. Additionally, MKM does not support the kernel code reducing method for the user process; it needs to be combined with the MKM approach to achieve a more flexible adjustment of the page table assignment.

7   Conclusion

An OS kernel should be able to mitigate various attacks that exploit the kernel vulnerabilities. In general, kernels adopt stack monitoring, CFI, KASLR, KPTI, and KMO to minimize the attack surface and prevent the kernel vulnerabilities from being attacked. However, adversaries could utilize privilege escalation to subvert kernel protection methods and these kernel codes invocation by executing arbitrary code and exploiting the vulnerabilities at the kernel layer.

In this study, a novel security mechanism Multiple Kernel Memory (MKM) is proposed to provide two dedicated page tables: the trampoline and security page tables. MKM encapsulates the vulnerable kernel code in the kernel page table; thereafter, it assigns the page table switching function and kernel protection methods in the trampoline and security page tables to reduce the potential kernel attack surface. It ensures that kernel protection methods and vulnerable kernel code are executed on different virtual address spaces; this improves the resilient against memory corruption because kernel attacks can not target to the trampoline and security page tables. The evaluation of Linux using MKM could prevent the memory corruption of kernel protection methods. Additionally, our kernel observation mechanism works on the MKM implementation, which detects the memory corruption of the LSM hook function and page table switching function. Based on the performance evaluation, the overhead was 0.020 μs to 0.5445 μs for each system call invocation on the proposed kernel; moreover, the web client program overhead average for MKM was 196.27 μs to 6,685.73 μs, for each download access of 100,000 HTTP sessions.

Acknowledgment. This work was partially supported by JSPS KAKENHI Grant Number JP19H04109.

References

1. Kemerlis, P, V., Portokalidis, G. and Keromytis, D, A.: kGuard: lightweight kernel protection against return-to-user attacks. In: Proceedings of the 21st USENIX Conference on Security Symposium, USENIX (2012). https://doi.org/10.5555/2362793.2362832
2. Abadi, M., Budiu, M., Erlingsson, U., Ligatti, J.: Control-flow integrity principles, implementations. In: Proceedings of the 12th ACM Conference on Computer and Communications Security, pp. 340–353. ACM (2005). https://doi.org/10.1145/1609956.1609960
3. Rapoport, M.: ×86: introduce system calls address space isolation. https://lwn.net/Articles/786894/. Accessed 22 May 2019
4. Hund, R., Willems, C., Holz, T.: Practical timing side channel attacks against kernel space ASLR. In: Proceedings of the 2013 IEEE Symposium on Security and Privacy, pp. 191–205, IEEE (2013). https://doi.org/10.1109/SP.2013.23
5. Gruss, D., Lipp, M., Schwarz, M., Fellner, R., Maurice, C., Mangard, S.: KASLR is dead : long live KASLR, In: Bodden, E., Payer, M., Athanasopoulos, E. (eds.) ESSoS 2017. LNCS, vol. 10379, pp. 161–176, Springer, Cham (2017). https://doi.org/10.1007/978-3-319-62105-0_11

6. Mulnix D.: Intel® Xeon® Processor D Product Family Technical Overview, https://software.intel.com/en-us/articles/intel-xeon-processor-d-product-family-technical-overview. Accessed 10 Aug 2018
7. Security-enhanced Linux. http://www.nsa.gov/research/selinux/. Accessed 22 May 2019
8. Exploit Database, Nexus 5 Android 5.0 - Privilege Escalation. https://www.exploit-db.com/exploits/35711/. Accessed 21 May 2019
9. grsecurity: super fun 2.6.30+/RHEL5 2.6.18 local kernel exploit. https://grsecurity.net/~spender/exploits/exploit2.txt. Accessed 21 May 2019
10. Kuzuno, H., Yamauchi, T.: KMO: kernel memory observer to identify memory corruption by secret inspection mechanism. In: Heng, S,H., Lopez, J. (eds.) ISPEC 2019. LNCS, vol. 11879, pp. 75–94, Springer, Cham (2019). https://doi.org/10.1007/978-3-030-34339-2_5
11. Bovet, P.D., Cesati, M.: Understanding the Linux kernel, 3rd edition. O'Reilly Media (2005)
12. CVE-2017-16995. https://cve.mitre.org/cgi-bin/cvename.cgi?name=CVE-2017-16995. Accessed 10 June 2019
13. Chen, H., Mao, Y., Wang, X., Zhow, D., Zeldovich, N., Kaashoek, F, M.: Linux kernel vulnerabilities - state-of-the-art defenses and open problems. In: Proceedings of the Second Asia-Pacific Workshop on Systems, pp. 1–5, ACM (2011). https://doi.org/10.1145/2103799.2103805
14. Tetlow, G.: Response to Meltdown and Spectre. https://lists.freebsd.org/pipermail/freebsd-security/2018-January/009719.html. Accessed 21 May 2019
15. Linden, A. T.: Operating system structures to support security and reliable software. ACM Computing Surveys, vol. 8, no. 4, pp. 409–445. ACM (1976). https://doi.org/10.1145/356678.356682
16. Davi, L., Gens, D., Liebchen, C., Sadeghi, A.-R.: PT-Rand: practical mitigation of data-only attacks against page tables. In: Proceedings of the 23th Network and Distributed System Security Symposium, Internet Society (2016)
17. Pomonis, M., Petsios, T.: kR^X: comprehensive kernel protection against just-in-time code reuse. In: Protection of the Twelfth European Conference on Computer Systems, pp. 420–436, ACM (2017). https://doi.org/10.1145/3064176.3064216
18. Trusted computing group. tpm main specification. http://www.trustedcomputinggroup.org/resources/tpm_main_specification. Accessed 10 Aug 2018
19. Ge, X., Vijayakumar, H., Jaeger, T.: Sprobes: enforcing kernel code integrity on the trustzone architecture. In: Proceedings of the third Workshop on Mobile Security Technologies, ACM (2014)
20. Seshadri, A., Luk, M., Qu, N., Perrig, A.: SecVisor: a tiny hypervisor to provide lifetime kernel code integrity for commodity OSes. In: Proceedings of the 21st ACM SIGOPS Symposium on Operating Systems Principles, pp. 335–350, ACM (2007). https://doi.org/10.1145/1294261.1294294
21. McCune, M.J., Li, Y., Qu, Z., Zhou, A., Datta, V., Gligor, D., Perrig A.: TrustVisor: efficient TCB reduction and attestation. In: Proceedings of the 2010 IEEE Symposium on Security and Privacy, pp. 143–158, IEEE (2010). https://doi.org/10.1109/SP.2010.17
22. Sharif, I.M., Lee, W., Cui, W., Lanzi, A.: Secure in-VM monitoring using hardware virtualization. In: Proceedings of the 16th ACM Conference on Computer and Communications Security, pp. 477–487. ACM (2009). https://doi.org/10.1145/1653662.1653720

23. Deng, L., Liu, P., Xu, J., Chen, P., Zeng, Q.: Dancing with Wolves: towards practical event-driven VMM monitoring. In: Proceedings of the 13th ACM SIGPLAN / SIGOPS International Conference, pp. 83–96. ACM (2017). https://doi.org/10.1145/3050748.3050750

24. Koromilas, L., Vasiliadis, G., Athanasopoulos, E., Ioannidis, S.: GRIM: leveraging GPUs for kernel integrity monitoring. In: Monrose, F., Dacier, M., Blanc, G., Garcia-Alfaro, J. (eds.) RAID 2016. LNCS, vol. 9854, pp. 3–23. Springer, Cham (2016). https://doi.org/10.1007/978-3-319-45719-2_1

25. Klein, G., et al.: seL4: formal verification of an OS kernel. In: Proceedings of the 22nd ACM Symposium on Operating Systems Principles, pp. 207–220. ACM (2009). https://doi.org/10.1145/1629575.1629596

26. Getting started with kmemcheck. https://www.kernel.org/doc/dev-tools/kmemcheck.html. Accessed 21 May 2019

27. The Kernel Address Sanitizer (KASAN). https://www.kernel.org/doc/dev-tools/kasan.html Accessed 21 May 2019

28. syzkaller is an unsupervised, coverage-guided kernel fuzzer. https://github.com/google/syzkaller/. Accessed 22 May 2019

29. Hua. Z., Du, D., Xia, Y., Chen, H., Zang, B.: EPTI: efficient defence against meltdown attack for unpatched VMs. In: Proceedings of the 2018 USENIX Annual Technical Conference, pp. 255–266. USENIX (2018). https://doi.org/10.5555/3277355.3277380

30. Kurmus, A., Dechand, S., Kapitza, R.: Quantifiable run-time kernel attack surface reduction. In: Dietrich, S. (ed.) DIMVA 2014. LNCS, vol. 8550, pp. 212–234. Springer, Cham (2014). https://doi.org/10.1007/978-3-319-08509-8_12

31. Zhang, Z., Cheng, Y., Nepal, S., Liu, D., Shen, Q., Rabhi, F.: KASR: a reliable and practical approach to attack surface reduction of commodity OS kernels. In: Bailey, M., Holz, T., Stamatogiannakis, M., Ioannidis, S. (eds.) RAID 2018. LNCS, vol. 11050, pp. 691–710. Springer, Cham (2018). https://doi.org/10.1007/978-3-030-00470-5_32

32. Dautenhahn, N., Kasampalis, T., Dietz, W., Criswell, J., Adve, V.: Nested Kernel: an operating system architecture for intra-kernel privilege separation. In: Proceedings of the 20th International Conference on Architectural Support for Programming Languages and Operating Systems, pp. 191–206. ACM (2015). https://doi.org/10.1145/2694344.2694386

33. Kuo, H, C., Gunasekaran, A., Jang, Y., Mohan, S., Bobba, B, R., Lie, D., Walker, J.: MultiK: a framework for orchestrating multiple specialized kernels. https://arxiv.org/abs/1903.06889v1. Accessed 16 May 2019

34. Österlund, S., Koning, K., Olivier, P., Barbalace, A., Bos, H., Giuffrida, C.: kMVX: detecting kernel information leaks with multi-variant execution. In: Proceedings of the 24th International Conference on Architectural Support for Programming Languages and Operating Systems, pp. 559–572. ACM (2019). https://doi.org/10.1145/3297858.3304054

(Short Paper) Signal Injection Attack on Time-to-Digital Converter and Its Application to Physically Unclonable Function

Takeshi Sugawara[(⊠)], Tatsuya Onuma, and Yang Li

The University of Electro-Communications, Tokyo, Japan
{sugawara,liyang}@uec.ac.jp

Abstract. Physically unclonable function (PUF) is a technology to generate a device-unique identifier using process variation. PUF enables a cryptographic key that appears only when the chip is active, providing an efficient countermeasure against reverse-engineering attacks. In this paper, we explore the data conversion that digitizes a physical quantity representing PUF's uniqueness into a numerical value as a new attack surface. We focus on time-to-digital converter (TDC) that converts time duration into a numerical value. We show the first signal injection attack on a TDC by manipulating its clock, and verify it through experiments on an off-the-shelf TDC chip. Then, we show how to leverage the attack to reveal a secret key protected by a PUF that uses a TDC for digitization.

Keywords: Time-to-digital converter · Physically unclonable function · Fault injection attack · Signal injection attack

1 Introduction

Secure communication using cryptography is now the indispensable infrastructure of society. Secure key management is essential for cryptography, and can be challenging especially under a hostile environment in which a legitimate owner attacks the device with physical access, using techniques such as fault-injection attack. Industries have tackled the problem by encapsulating everything needed for cryptography in an independent cryptographic module that even a legitimate user cannot tamper. Designing secure cryptographic modules, however, is a challenging task, and researchers have studied new attacks and countermeasures for more than two decades.

Physically unclonable function (PUF) is a relatively new primitive for cryptographic modules that generate a device-unique identifier by using process variation in semiconductor chips [6]. By combining PUF with a secure error-correction technology, we can realize secure key storage that appears only after the chip

© Springer Nature Switzerland AG 2020
K. Aoki and A. Kanaoka (Eds.): IWSEC 2020, LNCS 12231, pp. 117–127, 2020.
https://doi.org/10.1007/978-3-030-58208-1_7

is turned on [2], which provides an additional layer of security against reverse-engineering attacks [12].

Another line of research, closely related to fault-injection attack, is signal-injection attack that breaches data integrity in the analog domain by using electromagnetic interference [4,14], out-of-band signal [13], and physical transduction [9]. Analog-to-digital converter (ADC) that converts electrical voltage into numerical values is a critical attack surface, and researchers have proposed attacks exploiting the ADC's nonideality: clipping and aliasing by Trippel et al. [13], rectification by Tu et al. [14], and unreliable voltage reference by Miki et al. [7].

Time-to-digital converter is yet another data converter that converts a time duration into a digital value [3]. Time measurement is essential in many applications, such as ranging and biomedical imaging. In addition to direct time measurement, TDC can measure other physical quantities with a transducer, and some PUFs use TDCs for converting a physical quantity representing PUF's uniqueness into a numerical value. Despite its important security applications, there is no security evaluation of TDC in the context of signal-injection attack as far as the authors are aware.

A question that naturally arises is the feasibility of signal-injection attack on TDC. We tackle the problem by setting the following particular questions: *can an attacker inject signal to TDC? If so, how can the attacker exploit such an injection to break systems' security under realistic conditions?*

Contributions. Key contributions of our work are summarized as follows:

(1) The first signal-injection attack of TDC (Sect. 3):   We propose the first signal injection attack of a particular type of TDC (counter-based TDC) by manipulating the TDC's clock during the measurement (i.e., clock glitching).

(2) Exploitation to PUF state-recovery attack (Sect. 4):   We propose an attack on a PUF that uses a TDC for digitization [16]. By attacking a TDC, an attacker can inject bias in the PUF's state, which enables a practical brute-forcing attack to reveal a key protected by the PUF.

(3) Experimental verification (Sects. 3 and 4):   We experimentally verify the proposed attack works on an off-the-shelf TDC chip.

(4) Analysis of attacker's capability for successful attack (Sect. 5):   We analyze how the attacker's capability of controlling the TDC's clock, in terms of the maximum frequency deviation and resolution, can affect the search space for the proposed PUF state-recovery attack.

2   Preliminary

2.1   Time-to-Digital Converter

What Is TDC? Time-to-digital converter converts the time duration into a digital value [3]. In addition to direct time measurement useful for applications such as ranging and biomedical imaging, TDC can measure other physical quantities with a transducer; we will see a resistance-to-time transducer in the latter part of this section. Moreover, there is a trend of replacing ADC with TDC because getting sufficient noise-margin in voltage-mode signals is more and more challenging by continuously lowering operation voltage as a result of technology shrink [15].

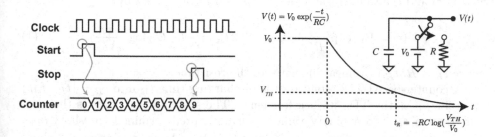

Fig. 1. (Left) Counter-based TDC. (Right) Resistance-to-time transducer [16].

Counter-Based TDC. Among many realizations of TDC, the counter-based TDC (also known as fully-digital TDC) is a common implementation of TDC. Figure 1-(left) shows the counter-based TDC's operation in which the circuit counts the number of clock edges in between the rising edges of the start and stop pulses. When the start and stop pulses are apart by τ seconds, and the TDC's clock frequency is f_{clk} Hz, the TDC outputs $\lfloor \tau \cdot f_{clk} \rfloor$. This realization is efficient in cost because all we need is a simple arithmetic counter.

2.2   ReRAM PUF and TDC

ReRAM and Its Application to PUF. Resistive random-access memory (ReRAM) is an emerging non-volatile memory technology that is much faster than conventional ones such as flash memory and EEPROM. A 1-bit ReRAM cell has a filament that can have either a high-resistance or a low-resistance state that represents a 1-bit value. The resistances of ReRAM cells have device-specific uniqueness, and researchers have exploited the property to construct a PUF [1,5,16].

The resistance of each ReRAM cell is (assumed to be) independently and identically distributed, and follows the log-normal distribution [16]. The system measures the resistivity of each cell independently, and combine them to form a longer PUF state $\vec{M}$. The PUF state is typically used to realize a secure key storage resistant against reverse-engineering attacks.

Measuring Resistance Using TDC [16]. TDC comes into play for precisely measuring resistance. In particular, Yoshimoto et al. use a counter-based TDC to measure the resistance, as shown in Fig. 1-(right) [16]. The idea is to use an RC circuit as a resistance-to-time transducer.

We first precharge the capacitor C with an initial voltage V_0, and then discharge it through the target resistor R while measuring the time duration until the voltage becomes smaller than a threshold V_{TH}. The voltage across the capacitor $V(t)$ and the time t_R satisfying $V(t_R) = T_{TH}$ are given by

$$V(t) = V_0 \cdot \exp(\frac{-t}{RC}), \qquad t_R = -R \cdot C \cdot \log(\frac{V_{TH}}{V_0}). \qquad (1)$$

Since $t_R \propto R$, t_R is a linear indicator of the resistance.

A counter-based TDC converts the discharging time t_R into $c_R = \lfloor t_R \cdot f_{clk} \rfloor$ wherein f_{clk} is the TDC's clock frequency. The system then converts the measured value c_R into a binary value by using a predetermined threshold c_{TH}. Finally, the system generates an N-bit PUF state $\vec{M}$ by repeating the above process for N different ReRAM cells and concatenating the bits together.

3   Attack on Time-to-Digital Converter

3.1   Target Description and Adversarial Model

We assume a counter-based TDC as a target. The attacker's goal is to control the output from a TDC. The attacker has physical access to the target chip and can change the clock frequency used for the TDC measurement.

3.2   Proposed Attack

We let f_{clk} denote the original clock frequency, and the attacker changes it to $f'_{clk} = (1 - \delta) \cdot f_{clk}$, wherein δ is a deviation factor. The injection changes the time duration τ into $\tau' = \tau \cdot \frac{f'_{clk}}{f_{clk}} = \tau \cdot (1 - \delta)$, and thus the attacker can linearly control the measured time duration through the deviation δ. Note that, hereafter, we ignore the floor function $\lfloor \cdot \rfloor$ for the sake of simplicity, and this simplification is justified considering that designers usually choose sufficiently fast clock frequency so that the quantization error is negligible.

3.3   Experiment

In this section, we verify the proposed attack on an off-the-shelf TDC chip to check if the idealized model in Sect. 3.2 still holds with a practical design.

We use Texas Instruments TDC7200 time-to-digital converter [10] mounted on the TDC7200EVM evaluation board [11] as an experimental platform. A microcontroller (MCU) receives the digitized data from TDC7200 via a serial interface (SPI), and transfer it to a GUI program running on a PC. The system repeats the measurement, and we can read the time series of the measured data in a graph.

Figure 2-(left) shows the setup composed of the evaluation board, PC, and two function generators, namely FG1 (Rigol DG1022Z) and FG2 (Tektronix AFG31152). FG1 generates the start and stop pulses. FG2 generates a clock signal for TDC7200. We use TDC7200 with its default setting that uses 8 MHz clock frequency.

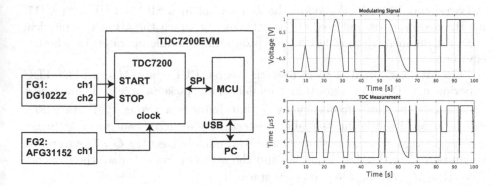

Fig. 2. (Left) Experimental setup. (Right) Injection of arbitrary waveform representing "WALNUT" [13].

We examine the TDC's output in reresponse to the same start and stop pulses while manipulating the clock signal. We first design a waveform representing a text "WALNUT", following the previous work [13], by using the waveform-editing functionality on FG2. Then, we generate the TDC's clock signal by modulating the frequency of a rectangular wave with the "WALNUT" waveform: the ± 1 V of the modulating signal is mapped to the frequency range 8 ± 4 MHz of a rectangular wave. Figure 2-(right) compares the source "WALNUT" waveform at FG2 and the corresponding TDC's output, which confirms successful manipulation of the TDC's measurement.

4   Application to ReRAM PUF

4.1   Target Description and Adversarial Model

Target. We consider Yoshimoto et al.'s ReRAM PUF [16] as the concrete target. We note, however, that the attack applies to other PUFs as far as they use a counter-based TDC for digitizing device-specific quantity. The target chip uses the PUF for realizing PUF-based key storage and provides a cryptographic service using the protected key.

Algorithm 1. TDCE: time-to-digital conversion experiment

Require: The clock deviation δ, and query Q.
Ensure: Response X
 1: Set the clock frequency $f'_{clk} = f_{clk} - \delta \cdot f_{clk}$
 2: Invoke PUF key generation   ▷ the PUF state becomes $\overrightarrow{M}_\delta$
 3: Get a response $X \leftarrow \mathsf{Dev}(\overrightarrow{M}_\delta, Q)$
 4: **return** X

Adversarial Model. We follow the Zeitouni et al.'s SRAM PUF attack [17] for the assumptions and goal of the attacker, in which the attacker's physical access is justified by considering a cryptographic module operated in a hostile environment.

The attacker's goal is to recover the secret PUF state $\overrightarrow{M}_{PUF}$. The TDC experiment (TDCE) in Algorithm 1 models the attacker's access. The attacker can change the clock frequency by δ that induces a wrong PUF state $\overrightarrow{M}_\delta$, yet the state itself is unobservable. Instead, the attacker can query Q to get a response that depends both on Q and $\overrightarrow{M}_\delta$, namely $\mathsf{Dev}(\overrightarrow{M}_\delta, Q)$. The response generation algorithm Dev is public, and the attacker can calculate the response $X \leftarrow \mathsf{Dev}(\overrightarrow{M_H}, Q)$ for a hypothetical state $\overrightarrow{M_H}$.

The target implementation can calibrate the threshold c_{TH} for optimization [16], which affects the prerequisite for changing the clock frequency in TDCE. When the calibration is infrequent (e.g., a factory calibration) and the c_{TH} stays the same during the attack, the attacker can change the frequency before powering on the target. When the calibration is frequent (e.g., power-on calibration), on the other hand, the attacker should change the clock frequency after the calibration has been finished, but the PUF operation has not yet started; the attacker needs prior knowledge about this timing. Interestingly, in the latter case, we can also attack the target in the other way round: manipulate c_{TH} by changing the clock frequency at the calibration phase, and feed a constant frequency for the PUF operation.

4.2 Manipulating PUF Digitization by Controlling TDC

We let R denote the resistance of the target ReRAM cell, and a resistance-to-time transducer converts it to a time duration t_R by Eq. (1). When a TDC counts t_R with a clock frequency f_{clk}, then it converts t_R into a counted value $c_R = t_R \cdot f_{clk}$. When the attacker manipulates the clock frequency to $f'_{clk} = (1 - \delta) \cdot f_{clk}$, the resulting output becomes

$$c'_R = c_R \cdot \frac{f'_{clk}}{f_{clk}} = c_R \cdot (1 - \delta). \tag{2}$$

The target system converts c'_R into a 1-bit value b_R using a threshold c_{TH}:

$$b_R = \begin{cases} 0 & (c'_R < c_{TH}) \Leftrightarrow (c_R < c_{TH}/(1 - \delta)) \\ 1 & \text{Otherwise} \end{cases}. \tag{3}$$

The attacker keeps the modified frequency f'_{clk} while the system is measuring N independent ReRAM cells for generating $\overrightarrow{M}_\delta$. The condition $c_R < c_{TH}/(1-\delta)$ in Eq. (3) suggests that the attacker virtually controls the threshold, which results in a bias in the population of 0 and 1 in the PUF state $\overrightarrow{M}_\delta$. Moreover, the attacker can control the magnitude of the bias through the deviation factor δ.

4.3   Recovering the Secret PUF State

The TDC experiment (TDCE) allows the attacker to parametrically bias the PUF state, in the same way as the Zeitouni et al.'s SRAM PUF attack [17]. Thus, a variant of the Zeitouni et al.'s state-recovery attack shown in Algorithm 2 is possible[1]. The attacker examines the frequency deviation $\delta_i = i \times \delta_{step}$ less than δ_{max}, where δ_{step} is the attacker's resolution in controlling the clock frequency. By calling TDCE, the attacker obtains X_i as a result of the PUF state denoted by $\overrightarrow{M}_{\delta_i}$.

Algorithm 2. State recovery attack using TDCE

Require: The maximum frequency deviation δ_{max}, and frequency resolution δ_{step}
Ensure: PUF state $\overrightarrow{M}_{PUF}$
1: Fix an arbitrary device query Q
2: Set $i \leftarrow 0$ and $\delta_0 \leftarrow 0$
3: **repeat**
4:     Record $X_i = \mathsf{TDCE}(\delta_i, Q)$
5:     Set $i \leftarrow i+1$
6:     Set $\delta_i \leftarrow \delta_{i-1} + \delta_{step}$
7: **until** $\delta_i < \delta_{max}$
8: Record $X_i = \mathsf{TDCE}(\delta_{max}, Q)$
9: $\overrightarrow{M}_{\delta_{i+1}} = \overrightarrow{0}$
10: **for** $j = i+1$ down to 1 **do**
11:     Compute $\overrightarrow{M}_{\delta(j-1)} = \mathsf{Finder}_*(\overrightarrow{M}_{\delta_j}, Q, X_{j-1})$
12: **end for**
13: **return** $\overrightarrow{M}_{\delta_0}$

The attacker recovers $\overrightarrow{M}_{\delta(j-1)}$ from $\overrightarrow{M}_{\delta_j}$ recursively in the descending order. $\mathsf{Finder}_*(\overrightarrow{M}_{\delta_j}, Q, X_j)$ models this process: for all candidates $\overrightarrow{M}_*$ near $\overrightarrow{M}_{\delta_j}$, the attacker simulates the target's response-generation algorithm to get the response X_* for the query Q. If the simulated response X_* is equal to X_{i-1}, the attacker finds $\overrightarrow{M}_* = \overrightarrow{M}_{\delta(j-1)}$. By repeating the process, starting from $\overrightarrow{M}_{\delta_i} = \overrightarrow{0}$, the attacker eventually reaches $\overrightarrow{M}_{\delta_0} = \overrightarrow{M}_{PUF}$, which is what the attacker wanted.

---

[1]   The attacker only increases the clock frequency in Algorithm 2, i.e., $\delta_i \geq 0$, to avoid a countermeasure monitoring overclocking. We note that the similar attack is possible with $\delta \leq 0$.

The feasibility of the attack depends on the attacker's capability to control the clock denoted by δ_{max} and δ_{step}. We discuss the conditions for a successful attack in Sect. 5.

4.4 Experiment

Setup. We built the resistance-to-time transducer in Fig. 1-(right) by wiring a 4.7 nF ceramic capacitor and a variable resistor on a breadboard, as shown in Fig. 3-(left). FG1 outputs the identical 3.3 V rectangular waves on both channels and charges the capacitor while its output voltage is high. TDC7200 starts counting by catching a falling edge of the rectangular wave. At the same time, the capacitor begins to release its charges through the variable resistor, as shown in Fig. 1-(right), and TDC7200 stops counting when the voltage reaches a certain threshold.

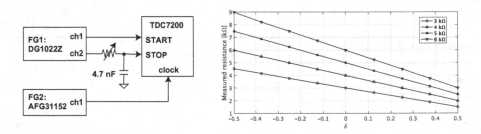

Fig. 3. (Left) Setup for emulating the TDC-based resistance measurement (Fig. 1-(right)). (Right) Resistance measured by TDC with different clock frequencies

Procedure. We first calibrate a scaling factor to convert a time duration to resistance by setting the resistance to 3 $k\Omega$, and measure the time duration at 8 MHz. Then, we repeated the same measurement with different clock frequencies (from 4 to 12 MHz at 1 MHz steps) and different resistance (4, 5, and 6 $k\Omega$).

Result. Figure 3-(right) shows the relationship between the measured resistances and the frequency deviation δ, which clearly shows linearity between them as predicted by Eq. (2). With this experiment, we confirm that the attacker can control the measured resistance by manipulating the clock frequency.

5 Discussion

Now we discuss how the attacker's capability, in terms of the maximum frequency deviation δ_{max} and the frequency resolution δ_{step}, affects the efficiency of the PUF state-recovery attack.

Distribution of Resistances: The resistance R of each ReRAM cell, as well as its digitization c_R, distributes independently and identically following the log-normal distribution [16]. Figure 4-(left) shows the concrete distribution of c_R, the log-normal distribution with the mean $\mu = 140$ and the standard deviation $\sigma = 31$ based on the Yoshimoto et al.'s work [16][2]. In this case, we assume the threshold to be its median, i.e., $c_{TH} = 136.7$.

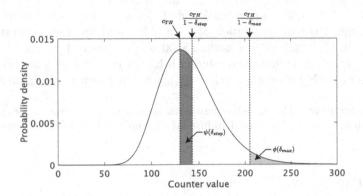

Fig. 4. Probability density function of log-normal distribution with μ=140, σ=31.

Maximum Frequency Deviation: The maximum frequency deviation δ_{max} in Algorithm 2 can be a security parameter because getting $\overrightarrow{M}_{\delta_i}$ from $\overrightarrow{M}_{\delta_{i+1}} = \overrightarrow{0}$ becomes impractical if δ_{max} is too small. We let $\phi(\delta_{max})$ denote the probability of observing ReRAM cells that generate '1' in Eq. (3) even with δ_{max}:

$$\phi(\delta_{max}) = \mathsf{Prob}[\frac{c_{TH}}{1 - \delta_{max}} \leq c_R], \tag{4}$$

as illustrated in Fig. 4-(left).

By evaluating ϕ for different δ_{max}, we observe that $\phi(\delta_{max}) < 0.001$ with $\delta_{max} = 0.5$, showing that reducing the clock frequency by half is sufficient to finish the attack in many cases. With an N-bit PUF state, the expected Hamming distance between $\overrightarrow{M}_{\delta_i}$ and $\overrightarrow{M}_{\delta_{i+1}}$ is $N \cdot \phi(\delta_{max})$, and it is less than 1 bit for $N = 512$ and $\delta = 0.5$.

Frequency Resolution: Another security parameter is the frequency resolution δ_{step} in Algorithm 2, which directly affects the distance between the intermediate states $\overrightarrow{M}_{\delta_i}$.

The probability of observing a bit flip for a PUF bit in between the consecutive states $\overrightarrow{M}_{\delta_j}$ and $\overrightarrow{M}_{\delta_{(j-1)}}$ is

$$\mathsf{Prob}[\frac{c_{TH}}{1 - \delta_i} < c_R \leq \frac{c_{TH}}{1 - \delta_i - \delta_{step}}]. \tag{5}$$

---

[2] The mean and standard deviation are obtained from Fig. 2-(b) of [16].

This probability is maximized at the center of the distribution, as shown in Fig. 4-(left), wherein $\delta_i = 0$. We let $\psi(\delta_{step})$ denote the probability to observe different bits between $\overrightarrow{M}_{\delta_0}$ and $\overrightarrow{M}_{\delta_1}$:

$$\psi(\delta_{step}) = \mathsf{Prob}[c_{TH} < c_R \leq \frac{c_{TH}}{1 - \delta_{step}}]. \tag{6}$$

By evaluating ψ with different δ_{step}, we observe that $\psi(\delta_{step}) \approx 0.001$ with $\delta_{step} = 0.5 \times 10^{-3}$. When $f_{clk} = 8$ MHz, $\delta \cdot f_{clk} = 0.5 \times 10^{-3} \times 8 = 4$ kHz, which is much larger than the resolution of even a low-end function generator: FG1 (Rigol DG1022Z), available at less than \$400 USD, achieves 1 μHz resolution [8]. Therefore, we conclude that the resolution is hardly the attacker's limitation, and the attacker can choose an appropriate δ_{step} achieving sufficiently small $\psi(\delta_{step})$.

Acknowledgement. This paper is based on results obtained from a project commissioned by the New Energy and Industrial Technology Development Organization (NEDO).

References

1. Chen, A.: Utilizing the variability of resistive random access memory to implement reconfigurable physical unclonable functions. IEEE Electron Dev. Lett. **36**(2), 138–140 (2015)
2. Guajardo, J., Kumar, S.S., Schrijen, G.-J., Tuyls, P.: FPGA intrinsic PUFs and their use for IP protection. In: Paillier, P., Verbauwhede, I. (eds.) CHES 2007. LNCS, vol. 4727, pp. 63–80. Springer, Heidelberg (2007). https://doi.org/10.1007/978-3-540-74735-2_5
3. Henzler, S. (ed.): Time-to-Digital Converters. Advanced Microelectronics. Springer, Netherland (2010). https://doi.org/10.1007/978-90-481-8628-0
4. Kune, D., et al.: Ghost talk: Mitigating EMI signal injection attacks against analog sensors. In: 2012 IEEE Symposium on Security and Privacy (2013)
5. Liu, R., Wu, H., Pang, Y., Qian, H., Yu, S.: A highly reliable and tamper-resistant RRAM PUF: design and experimental validation. In: 2016 IEEE International Symposium on Hardware Oriented Security and Trust (HOST) (2016)
6. Maes, R.: Physically Unclonable Functions. Springer, Heidelberg (2013). https://doi.org/10.1007/978-3-642-41395-7
7. Miki, T., Miura, N., Sonoda, H., Mizuta, K., Nagata, M.: A random interrupt dithering SAR technique for secure ADC against reference-charge side-channel attack. Express Briefs, IEEE Transactions on Circuits and Systems II (2020)
8. RIGOL Technologies, I.: User's guide: DG1000Z series function/arbitrary waveform generator (2013)
9. Sugawara, T., Cyr, B., Rampazzi, S., Genkin, D., Fu, K.: Light commands: Laser-based audio injection on voice-controllable systems (2019)
10. Texas Instruments: SNAS647D: TDC7200 time-to-digital converter for time-of-flight applications in lidar, magnetostrictive and flow meter. http://www.ti.com/lit/ds/symlink/tdc7200.pdf
11. Texas Instruments: SNAU177: TDC7200EVM user's guide. http://www.ti.com/lit/ug/snau177/snau177.pdf

12. Torrance, R., James, D.: The state-of-the-art in semiconductor reverse engineering. In: 2011 48th ACM/EDAC/IEEE Design Automation Conference (DAC), pp. 333–338 June 2011
13. Trippel, T., Weisse, O., Xu, W., Honeyman, P., Fu, K.: WALNUT: waging doubt on the integrity of mems accelerometers with acoustic injection attacks. In: 2017 IEEE European Symposium on Security and Privacy (EuroS&P) (2017)
14. Tu, Y., Rampazzi, S., Hao, B., Rodriguez, A., Fu, K., Hei, X.: Trick or heat?: Manipulating critical temperature-based control systems using rectification attacks. In: Proceedings of the 2019 ACM SIGSAC Conference on Computer and Communications Security, CCS 2019, pp. 2301–2315 (2019)
15. Turchetta, R.: Analog Electronics for Radiation Detection. CRC Press (2016)
16. Yoshimoto, Y., Katoh, Y., Ogasahara, S., Wei, Z., Kouno, K.: A ReRAM-based physically unclonable function with bit error rate $< 0.5\%$ after 10 years at 125 $^\circ$C for 40 nm embedded application. In: 2016 IEEE Symposium on VLSI Technology (2016)
17. Zeitouni, S., Oren, Y., Wachsmann, C., Koeberl, P., Sadeghi, A.: Remanence decay side-channel: the PUF case. IEEE Trans. Inf. Foren. Secur. **11**(6), 1106–1116 (2016)

Post Quantum Cryptography

On Collisions Related to an Ideal Class
of Order 3 in CSIDH

Hiroshi Onuki[✉] and Tsuyoshi Takagi

Department of Mathematical Informatics, The University of Tokyo, Tokyo, Japan
{onuki,takagi}@mist.i.u-tokyo.ac.jp

Abstract. CSIDH is an isogeny-based key exchange, which is a candidate for post quantum cryptography. It uses the action of an ideal class group on $\mathbb{F}_p$-isomorphism classes of supersingular elliptic curves. In CSIDH, the ideal classes are represented by vectors with integer coefficients. The number of ideal classes represented by these vectors determines the security level of CSIDH. Therefore, it is important to investigate the correspondence between the vectors and the ideal classes. Heuristics show that integer vectors in a certain range represent "almost" uniformly all of the ideal classes. However, the precise correspondence between the integer vectors and the ideal classes is still unclear. In this paper, we investigate the correspondence between the ideal classes and the integer vectors and show that the vector $(1,\dots,1)$ corresponds to an ideal class of order 3. Consequently, the integer vectors in CSIDH have collisions related to this ideal class. Here, we use the word "collision" in the sense of distinct vectors belonging to the same ideal class, i.e., distinct secret keys that correspond to the same public key in CSIDH. We further propose a new ideal representation in CSIDH that does not include these collisions and give formulae for efficiently computing the action of the new representation.

Keywords: CISDH · Post-quantum cryptography · Isogeny-based cryptography · Ideal class groups · Supersingular elliptic curve isogenies

1 Introduction

Once a large-scale quantum computer is built, many of the public-key cryptosystems currently in use will no longer be secure. For this reason, research on post-quantum cryptography (PQC) has been increasingly important. In 2017, the National Institute of Standards and Technology (NIST) started the process of PQC standardization [23]. Candidates for NIST's PQC standardization include supersingular isogeny key encapsulation (SIKE) [17], which is a cryptosystem based on isogenies between elliptic curves.

Isogeny-based cryptography was first proposed by Couveignes [9] in 1997 and independently rediscovered by Rostovtsev and Stolbunov [27,30]. Their proposed scheme is a Diffie-Hellman-style key exchange based on isogenies between ordinary elliptic curves over a finite field and typically called CRS. In 2011, Jao

K. Aoki and A. Kanaoka (Eds.): IWSEC 2020, LNCS 12231, pp. 131–148, 2020.
https://doi.org/10.1007/978-3-030-58208-1_8

and De Feo [16] proposed another isogeny-based key-exchange, supersingular isogeny Diffie-Hellman (SIDH). In 2018, Castryck, Lange, Martindale, Panny, and Renes [4] proposed commutative SIDH (CSIDH), which incorporates supersingular elliptic curves in the CRS scheme.

Diffie and Hellman [14] constructed their famous key-exchange scheme on the multiplicative group of a finite field. Koblitz [18] and Miller [21] proposed to use the group of points on an elliptic curve for the key-exchange scheme. The structures of these groups can be easily determined. Let G be a cyclic subgroup of one of these groups, g a generator of G, and N the order of G. Then, a secret key is an integer x, and the corresponding public key is the group element g^x. If one takes x from the interval $[0, N - 1]$, the correspondence $x \mapsto g^x$ is one-to-one. Buchmann and Williams [2] proposed a Diffie-Hellman-style key-exchange using the ideal class group of an imaginary quadratic field with a large discriminant. In their scheme, a secret key is an integer x, and the corresponding public key is the ideal class $\mathfrak{a}^x$, where $\mathfrak{a}$ is a public ideal class. Unlike the former two schemes, it is hard to determine the structure of the ideal class group, and thus, the correspondence between the integer x and the ideal class $\mathfrak{a}^x$ is unclear. However, Buchmann and Williams claimed that by using the heuristics of Cohen and Lenstra [6], a randomly chosen ideal class has a large order with high probability and it is unlikely that different integers generate the same ideal class. CSIDH uses the free and transitive action of the ideal class group $\mathrm{cl}(\mathcal{O})$ of an order $\mathcal{O}$ of an imaginary quadratic field on the set of $\mathbb{F}_p$-isomorphism classes of supersingular elliptic curves whose endomorphism ring is isomorphic to $\mathcal{O}$. An ideal class in CSIDH is represented by an ideal of the form $\mathfrak{l}_1^{e_1} \cdots \mathfrak{l}_n^{e_n}$, where $\mathfrak{l}_i$ are prime ideals whose action can be efficiently computed and e_i are integer. By using this correspondence, a secret key in CSIDH is represented by an integer vector (e_i). The corresponding public key is the elliptic curve $(\mathfrak{l}_1^{e_1} \cdots \mathfrak{l}_n^{e_n}) * E$, where E is a public elliptic curve. By using the heuristics of Cohen and Lenstra and the Gaussian heuristic, Castryck et al. claimed that if one takes e_i from a certain range, s/he can expect that all the ideal classes in $\mathrm{cl}(\mathcal{O})$ are uniformly represented by these vectors. However, the precise correspondence between these vectors and the ideal classes is still unclear. It is important to investigate the correspondence between integer vectors and ideal classes, because the number of ideal classes represented by the integer vectors determines the security level of CSIDH.

In this paper, we investigate this correspondence and show that the ideal representation in CSIDH has collisions related to an ideal class of order 3. In particular, the vectors $(e_1, e_2, \ldots, e_n)$ and $(e_1 + 3, e_2 + 3, \ldots, e_n + 3)$ represent the same ideal class. The order of the ideal class group $\mathrm{cl}(\mathcal{O})$ is three times the class number of $\mathbb{Q}(\sqrt{-p})$. Therefore, $\mathrm{cl}(\mathcal{O})$ always contains ideal classes of order 3. We show that the ideal class represented by $(1, \ldots, 1)$ has order 3; thus, the action of the ideal class represented by $(3, \ldots, 3)$ is trivial. Furthermore, we propose a new ideal representation in CSIDH that does not include these collisions and give formulae for computing the actions of the ideal classes represented by $(1, \ldots, 1)$ and $(-1, \ldots, -1)$. In particular, the actions of these ideal classes can be computed by isogenies of degree 4, and thus, they can be efficiently computed. By using these formulae, our representation can be computed more efficiently than the representation proposed by [4]. As an additional result, we give formulae for odd-degree isogenies between Montgomery curves using 4-torsion points. The computation of our formulae is faster than that of the previous formulae if the degree is less than 9.

Organization. The rest of this paper is organized as follows. In Sect. 2, we give preliminaries on isogenies, ideal class groups, and CSIDH. In Sect. 3, we describe our theoretical results. In particular, we show that the ideal class represented by the vector $(1, \ldots, 1)$ has order 3 and its action can be computed by using an isogeny of degree 4. Section 4 gives formulae for the action on Montgomery curves of this ideal class and its inverse. We conclude the paper in Sect. 5. The appendix gives new formulae for odd-degree isogenies between Montgomery curves.

Related Works. Beullens, Kleinjung, and Vercauteren [1] computed the ideal class group structure of CSIDH-512, which is a parameter set of CSIDH proposed in [4], and they proposed a method to uniformly sample ideal classes from this group. However, to obtain the structure of the ideal class group of CSIDH-512, they used an algorithm that has subexponential time in the ideal class group size. Therefore, their method may not be applicable to a larger CSIDH.

Recent work by Castryck, Panny and Vercauteren [5] contains the same results as this paper. In particular, Lemma 8 of [5] is essentially the same as Theorem 3 of this paper. They also claim the same statement as in Theorem 4 of this paper in the proof of Lemma 8 of [5]. Our work is independent of their work. The contents in Sect. 3.2 and 4 are only in this paper.

2 Preliminaries

We denote multiplication by $m \in \mathbb{Z}$ on an elliptic curve by $[m]$. For a group element g, we denote the group generated by g by $\langle g \rangle$.

In this section, we briefly introduce isogenies between elliptic curves, ideal class groups in number fields, the action of ideal classes on elliptic curves, and CSIDH. We refer the reader to the textbooks of Silverman [28,29] for an exposition on elliptic curves and Neukirch [24] for a description of ideal class groups. For details on CSIDH, the reader can consult Castryck et al. [4].

2.1 Isogenies

Since we use only elliptic curves defined over a finite prime field $\mathbb{F}_p$ with $p > 3$, we describe definitions and properties related to isogenies between these curves.

An *isogeny* is a rational map between elliptic curves that is a group homomorphism. Let E and E' be elliptic curves defined over $\mathbb{F}_p$, and $\varphi : E \to E'$ an isogeny defined over $\mathbb{F}_p$. If φ is a nonzero isogeny, then φ induces an injection between function fields $\varphi^* : \bar{\mathbb{F}}_p(E') \to \bar{\mathbb{F}}_p(E)$, where $\bar{\mathbb{F}}_p$ is an algebraic closure of $\mathbb{F}_p$. In this case, we define the *degree* of φ by the degree of a field extension $\bar{\mathbb{F}}_p(E)/\varphi^*(\bar{\mathbb{F}}_p(E'))$ and say that φ is *separable* or *inseparable* if this field extension has the corresponding property. If φ is the zero map, we define the degree of φ to be 0. We denote the degree of φ by $\deg \varphi$. For a nonzero separable isogeny $\varphi : E \to E'$, the degree of φ is finite and the cardinality of the kernel of φ is equal to $\deg \varphi$. Thus, a nonzero separable isogeny has a finite kernel. Conversely, a finite subgroup of an elliptic curve E determines a separable isogeny from E.

Proposition 1 (Lemma 6 of [4]). *Let E be an elliptic curve defined over $\mathbb{F}_p$ and Φ a finite subgroup of E that is stable under the action of the p-th power Frobenius map. Then there exists an elliptic curve E' defined over $\mathbb{F}_p$ and a separable isogeny $\varphi : E \to E'$ defined over $\mathbb{F}_p$ with kernel Φ. The codomain E' and the isogeny φ are unique up to $\mathbb{F}_p$-isomorphism.*

In the rest of this paper, we regard two elliptic curves as being the same if they are $\mathbb{F}_p$-isomorphic and denote the codomain of an isogeny $\varphi : E \to E'$ with kernel Φ by E/Φ.

For a nonzero separable isogeny $\varphi : E \to E'$, there exists a unique isogeny $\hat{\varphi} : E' \to E$ such that $\hat{\varphi} \circ \varphi = [\deg \varphi]$. We call the isogeny $\hat{\varphi}$ the *dual isogeny* of φ. We have $\deg \hat{\varphi} = \deg \varphi$. For a given elliptic curve E and subgroup Φ, one can explicitly calculate the curve E' and isogeny $\varphi : E \to E'$ by using Vélu's formula [31].

2.2 Ideal Class Groups

Let K be a number field of degree n. An *order* in K is a subring of K whose rank as a $\mathbb{Z}$-module is n. It is known that the integral closure of $\mathbb{Z}$ in K is the unique maximal order in K. We denote the maximal order by $\mathcal{O}_K$. Let $\mathcal{O}$ be an order of K. A *fractional ideal* of $\mathcal{O}$ is a finitely generated $\mathcal{O}$-submodule of K. A fractional ideal $\mathfrak{a}$ is *invertible* if there exists a fractional ideal $\mathfrak{b}$ such that $\mathfrak{ab} = \mathcal{O}$, *integral* if $\mathfrak{a} \subseteq \mathcal{O}$, and *principal* if there exists $\alpha \in K$ such that $\mathfrak{a} = \alpha\mathcal{O}$. The set of invertible ideals of $\mathcal{O}$ forms an abelian group. We denote this group by $I(\mathcal{O})$. The subgroup of $I(\mathcal{O})$ consisting of principal ideals is denoted by $P(\mathcal{O})$. The *ideal class group* of $\mathcal{O}$ is the quotient group

$$\mathrm{cl}(\mathcal{O}) = I(\mathcal{O})/P(\mathcal{O}).$$

We denote the equivalence class of $\mathfrak{a}$ by $\{\mathfrak{a}\}$. It is known that $\mathrm{cl}(\mathcal{O})$ is a finite group. The order of $\mathrm{cl}(\mathcal{O}_K)$ is called the *class number* of K and denoted by h_K.

The *conductor* of $\mathcal{O}$ is the set $\{\alpha \in \mathcal{O}_K \mid \alpha\mathcal{O}_K \subseteq \mathcal{O}\}$. Note that the conductor of $\mathcal{O}$ is contained in $\mathcal{O}$ and can be regarded as an integral ideal of both $\mathcal{O}_K$ and $\mathcal{O}$. We need the following theorem, which provides a relation between the ideal class group of the maximal order and of an order.

Theorem 1. *Let K be a number field, $\mathcal{O}$ an order of K, and $\mathfrak{f}$ the conductor of $\mathcal{O}$. Then there is an exact sequence*

$$1 \to \mathcal{O}_K^\times/\mathcal{O}^\times \to (\mathcal{O}_K/\mathfrak{f})^\times/(\mathcal{O}/\mathfrak{f})^\times \to \mathrm{cl}(\mathcal{O}) \to \mathrm{cl}(\mathcal{O}_K) \to 1. \qquad (1)$$

Proof. See [24, Theorem 12.12 in Chapter 1].

2.3   The Class Group Action

Let $p > 3$ be a prime number and E an elliptic curve defined over $\mathbb{F}_p$. We denote the $\mathbb{F}_p$-rational endomorphism ring of E by $\mathrm{End}_{\mathbb{F}_p}(E)$. The ring $\mathrm{End}_{\mathbb{F}_p}(E)$ contains the p-th power Frobenius endomorphism ϕ, which satisfies the characteristic equation

$$\phi^2 - t\phi + p = 0, \tag{2}$$

where $t \in \mathbb{Z}$ is called the *trace of Frobenius*. The curve E is *supersingular* if and only if $t = 0$. The $\mathbb{F}_p$-rational endomorphism ring $\mathrm{End}_{\mathbb{F}_p}(E)$ is isomorphic to an order in an imaginary quadratic field. For an order $\mathcal{O}$ in an imaginary quadratic field and $\pi \in \mathcal{O}$, we define $\mathcal{E}\ell\ell_p(\mathcal{O}, \pi)$ to be the set of $\mathbb{F}_p$-isomorphism classes of elliptic curves E defined over $\mathbb{F}_p$ such that there is an isomorphism $\mathcal{O} \to \mathrm{End}_{\mathbb{F}_p}(E)$, $\alpha \mapsto [\alpha]$ that maps π to the Frobenius endomorphism.

Let $E \in \mathcal{E}\ell\ell_p(\mathcal{O}, \pi)$ and $\mathfrak{a}$ be an integral ideal of $\mathcal{O}$. We define the $\mathfrak{a}$-torsion subgroup $E[\mathfrak{a}]$ of E by

$$E[\mathfrak{a}] := \{P \in E \mid [\alpha]P = \infty, \text{ for all } \alpha \in \mathfrak{a}\}.$$

The subgroup $E[\mathfrak{a}]$ is finite, since $E[\mathfrak{a}] \subseteq E[\mathrm{N}(\mathfrak{a})]$, where N is the absolute norm. Therefore, by Proposition 1, there exists a unique elliptic curve $E/E[\mathfrak{a}]$ and an isogeny $\varphi_{\mathfrak{a}} : E \to E/E[\mathfrak{a}]$ with kernel $E[\mathfrak{a}]$. We denote the elliptic curve $E/E[\mathfrak{a}]$ by $\mathfrak{a} * E$. If $\mathfrak{a}$ is a principal ideal generated by $\alpha \in \mathcal{O}$, then $\varphi_{\mathfrak{a}}$ is a composition of the endomorphism $[\alpha]$ and an $\mathbb{F}_p$-automorphism of E, and $\mathfrak{a} * E = E$. This correspondence induces an action of $\mathrm{cl}(\mathcal{O})$ on $\mathcal{E}\ell\ell_p(\mathcal{O}, \pi)$. The following theorem describes the details.

Theorem 2 (Theorem 7 of [4]). *Let $\mathcal{O}$ be an order in an imaginary quadratic field and $\pi \in \mathcal{O}$ such that $\mathcal{E}\ell\ell_p(\mathcal{O}, \pi)$ is non-empty. Then the ideal class group $\mathrm{cl}(\mathcal{O})$ acts freely and transitively on the set $\mathcal{E}\ell\ell_p(\mathcal{O}, \pi)$ via the map*

$$\mathrm{cl}(\mathcal{O}) \times \mathcal{E}\ell\ell_p(\mathcal{O}, \pi) \to \mathcal{E}\ell\ell_p(\mathcal{O}, \pi)$$
$$(\{\mathfrak{a}\}, E) \mapsto \mathfrak{a} * E,$$

in which $\mathfrak{a}$ is chosen as an integral representative.

2.4   CSIDH

Let $p > 3$ be a prime of the form $4\ell_1 \cdots \ell_n - 1$, where $\ell_1, \ldots, \ell_n$ are distinct odd primes. Let $\pi = \sqrt{-p}$ and $\mathcal{O} = \mathbb{Z}[\pi]$. The primes ℓ_i split in $\mathcal{O}$ as $\ell_i\mathcal{O} = \mathfrak{l}_i\bar{\mathfrak{l}}_i$, where $\mathfrak{l}_i = \ell_i\mathcal{O} + (\pi - 1)\mathcal{O}$ and $\bar{\mathfrak{l}}_i = \ell_i\mathcal{O} + (\pi + 1)\mathcal{O}$. The isogeny defined by $\mathfrak{l}_i$ has degree ℓ_i, and its dual isogeny is the isogeny defined by $\bar{\mathfrak{l}}_i$. The action of $\mathrm{cl}(\mathcal{O})$ on $\mathcal{E}\ell\ell_p(\mathcal{O}, \pi)$ is used in CSIDH. Note that $\mathcal{E}\ell\ell_p(\mathcal{O}, \pi)$ is not empty, since the elliptic curve defined by $y^2 = x^3 + x$ is contained in this set (see §4 in [4] for details). Therefore, by Theorem 2, the cardinality of $\mathcal{E}\ell\ell_p(\mathcal{O}, \pi)$ is equal to that of $\mathrm{cl}(\mathcal{O})$.

For an elliptic curve $E \in \mathcal{E}\ell\ell_p(\mathcal{O}, \pi)$, the torsion subgroups of the above ideals can be written as

$$E[\mathfrak{l}_i] = E[\ell_i] \cap E(\mathbb{F}_p), \tag{3}$$
$$E[\bar{\mathfrak{l}}_i] = E[\ell_i] \cap \{Q \in E \mid [\pi]Q = -Q\}. \tag{4}$$

Since the actions of $\mathfrak{l}_i$ and $\bar{\mathfrak{l}}_i$ on $\mathcal{E}\ell\ell_p(\mathcal{O}, \pi)$ can be efficiently computed (see §8 in [4]), Castryck et al. [4] represented an ideal class in $\mathrm{cl}(\mathcal{O})$ by the product of these ideals; i.e., they represented it by an ideal of the form

$$\mathfrak{l}_1^{e_1} \cdots \mathfrak{l}_n^{e_n} \quad \text{for} \quad -m \le e_i \le m, \tag{5}$$

where m is an integer such that $(2m + 1)^n \ge \sqrt{p}$. This representation induces a correspondence between integer vectors and ideal classes. Castryck et al. [4] showed that one can expect that this correspondence is "almost" surjective and uniform. (See §7.1 in [4] for details). A secret key in CSIDH is expressed by an integer vector $(e_1, \ldots, e_n)$, and we call this vector "secret exponents." A public key in CSIDH is an elliptic curve in $\mathcal{E}\ell\ell_p(\mathcal{O}, \pi)$. By Theorem 2, there is a one-to-one correspondence between $\mathrm{cl}(\mathcal{O})$ and $\mathcal{E}\ell\ell_p(\mathcal{O}, \pi)$. Figure 1 illustrates this situation. In this paper, we say that there is a *collision* in an ideal representation if there are two distinct secret exponents which represent the same ideal class.

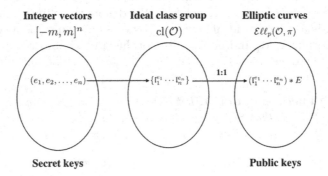

Fig. 1. Correspondence of keys in CSIDH

The protocol of CSIDH is as follows: Alice and Bob share an elliptic curve $E \in \mathcal{E}\ell\ell_p(\mathcal{O}, \pi)$ as a public parameter. Alice chooses her secret exponents $(e_1, \ldots, e_n)$ and computes the curve $\mathfrak{a} * E$, where $\mathfrak{a} = \prod_i \mathfrak{l}_i^{e_i}$. She sends the curve to Bob as her public key. Bob proceeds in the same way by choosing his secret ideal $\mathfrak{b} = \prod_i \mathfrak{l}_i^{e_i'}$. Then, both parties can compute the shared secret $\mathfrak{a}\mathfrak{b} * E = \mathfrak{b}\mathfrak{a} * E$. Note that $\mathrm{cl}(\mathcal{O})$ is commutative.

3   Collisions Related to an Ideal Class of Order 3

First, we describe the notation that will be used in the rest of this paper. We will consider a slightly more general setting than that of CSIDH. Let $p > 3$ be a prime such that $p \equiv 3 \pmod 8$. Then $(p + 1)/4$ is an odd integer, so it can be factorized as $\ell_1^{r_1} \cdots \ell_n^{r_n}$, where ℓ_i are distinct odd primes and r_i are positive integers. Let $\pi = \sqrt{-p}$, $K = \mathbb{Q}(\pi)$, and $\mathcal{O} = \mathbb{Z}[\pi]$. As in CSIDH, the primes ℓ_i split in $\mathcal{O}$ as $\ell_i \mathcal{O} = \mathfrak{l}_i \bar{\mathfrak{l}}_i$, where $\mathfrak{l}_i = \ell_i \mathcal{O} + (\pi - 1)\mathcal{O}$, $\bar{\mathfrak{l}}_i = \ell_i \mathcal{O} + (\pi + 1)\mathcal{O}$.

3.1   An Ideal Class of Order 3

We prove two main theorems of this paper. The first theorem implies that there are two distinct secret exponents that represent the same ideal class.

Theorem 3. *The ideal classes* $\{\mathfrak{l}_1^{r_1} \cdots \mathfrak{l}_n^{r_n}\}$ *has order 3 in* $\mathrm{cl}(\mathcal{O})$.

Proof. The unit groups $\mathcal{O}_K^\times$ and $\mathcal{O}^\times$ are $\{\pm 1\}$. Therefore, by Theorem 1, we obtain the exact sequence

$$1 \to (\mathcal{O}_K/\mathfrak{f})^\times/(\mathcal{O}/\mathfrak{f})^\times \to \mathrm{cl}(\mathcal{O}) \to \mathrm{cl}(\mathcal{O}_K) \to 1, \tag{6}$$

where $\mathfrak{f}$ is the conductor $\mathfrak{f}$ of $\mathcal{O}$. Note that the maximal order $\mathcal{O}_K = \mathbb{Z}[\frac{1+\pi}{2}]$. Since $\mathfrak{f} = 2\mathcal{O}_K = 2\mathcal{O} + (\pi - 1)\mathcal{O}$, it can be easily checked that $\mathcal{O}_K/\mathfrak{f} \cong \mathbb{F}_4$ and $\mathcal{O}/\mathfrak{f} \cong \mathbb{F}_2$. Therefore, the group $(\mathcal{O}_K/\mathfrak{f})^\times/(\mathcal{O}/\mathfrak{f})^\times$ is of order 3. The ideal $\mathfrak{l}_1^{r_1} \cdots \mathfrak{l}_n^{r_n} \mathcal{O}_K$ is a principal ideal of $\mathcal{O}_K$ because $\frac{\pi - 1}{2}$ generates this ideal in $\mathcal{O}_K$. Therefore, the exact sequence (6) indicates that the ideal class $\{\mathfrak{l}_1^{r_1} \cdots \mathfrak{l}_n^{r_n}\}$ comes from $(\mathcal{O}_K/\mathfrak{f})^\times/(\mathcal{O}/\mathfrak{f})^\times$, so its order divides 3. We assume that the order of $\{\mathfrak{l}_1^{r_1} \cdots \mathfrak{l}_n^{r_n}\}$ is 1; i.e., $\mathfrak{l}_1^{r_1} \cdots \mathfrak{l}_n^{r_n}$ is principal in $\mathcal{O}$. Then, there exist $\alpha \in \mathcal{O}$ such that $\mathfrak{l}_1^{r_1} \cdots \mathfrak{l}_n^{r_n} = \alpha \mathcal{O}$. As we stated above, $\mathfrak{l}_1^{r_1} \cdots \mathfrak{l}_n^{r_n} \mathcal{O}_K = \frac{\pi - 1}{2}\mathcal{O}_K$, so we have $\alpha = \pm\frac{\pi - 1}{2}$. This contradicts $\alpha \in \mathcal{O}$. Consequently, the ideal class $\{\mathfrak{l}_1^{r_1} \cdots \mathfrak{l}_n^{r_n}\}$ has order 3 in $\mathrm{cl}(\mathcal{O})$.
□

The following corollary directly follows from this theorem and shows that there are collisions in the ideal representation in CSIDH if $m \geq 2$. Figure 2 illustrates the assertion in the corollary.

Corollary 1. *In CSIDH, the secret exponents*

$$(e_1, e_2 \ldots, e_n) \quad and \quad (e_1 + 3, e_2 + 3, \ldots, e_n + 3)$$

represent the same ideal class.

The second main theorem claims that the ideal class of $\mathfrak{l}_1^{r_1} \cdots \mathfrak{l}_n^{r_n}$ has a simple representative. We define the ideals of $\mathcal{O}$ as follows:

$$\mathfrak{c} = 4\mathcal{O} + (\pi - 1)\mathcal{O}, \tag{7}$$
$$\bar{\mathfrak{c}} = 4\mathcal{O} + (\pi + 1)\mathcal{O}. \tag{8}$$

It can be easily checked that $\mathfrak{c}\bar{\mathfrak{c}} = 4\mathcal{O}$.

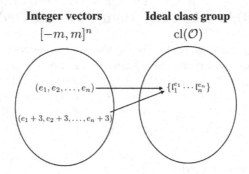

Fig. 2. Collision in the ideal representation

Theorem 4. *The ideals $\mathfrak{c}$ and $\bar{\mathfrak{c}}$ are invertible and*

$$\mathfrak{c}\mathfrak{l}_1^{r_1} \cdots \mathfrak{l}_n^{r_n} = (\pi - 1)\mathcal{O}, \tag{9}$$
$$\bar{\mathfrak{c}}\bar{\mathfrak{l}}_1^{r_1} \cdots \bar{\mathfrak{l}}_n^{r_n} = (\pi + 1)\mathcal{O}. \tag{10}$$

Proof. It can be easily shown that

$$\mathfrak{c}\left(\mathcal{O} + \frac{\pi + 1}{4}\mathcal{O}\right) = \mathcal{O}, \quad \bar{\mathfrak{c}}\left(\mathcal{O} + \frac{\pi - 1}{4}\mathcal{O}\right) = \mathcal{O}. \tag{11}$$

Therefore, $\mathfrak{c}$ and $\bar{\mathfrak{c}}$ are invertible.

By definition, the ideal $\mathfrak{c}\mathfrak{l}_1^{r_1} \cdots \mathfrak{l}_n^{r_n}$ is generated by $4\prod_i \ell_i^{r_i}$ and multiples of $\pi - 1$. Since $4\prod_i \ell_i^{r_i} = p + 1 = -(\pi - 1)(\pi + 1)$, the ideal $(\pi - 1)\mathcal{O}$ contains $\mathfrak{c}\mathfrak{l}_1^{r_1} \cdots \mathfrak{l}_n^{r_n}$.

Next, we show the inclusion $\mathfrak{c}\mathfrak{l}_1^{r_1} \cdots \mathfrak{l}_n^{r_n} \supseteq (\pi - 1)\mathcal{O}$. There exists an integer $N > 0$ such that $(\pi - 1)^N \in \mathfrak{c}\mathfrak{l}_1^{r_1} \cdots \mathfrak{l}_n^{r_n}$, since the ideals $\mathfrak{c}$ and $\mathfrak{l}_i$ contain $\pi - 1$. By the congruence

$$(\pi - 1)^N \equiv (-2)^N \pmod{\pi + 1}, \tag{12}$$

there exists $\alpha \in \mathcal{O}$ such that $(\pi - 1)^N - \alpha(\pi + 1) = (-2)^N$. Since $(\pi - 1)^N$ and $-(\pi - 1)(\pi + 1) = 4\prod_i \ell_i^{r_i}$ are contained in $\mathfrak{c}\mathfrak{l}_1^{r_1} \cdots \mathfrak{l}_n^{r_n}$, we have

$$(-2)^N(\pi - 1) = (\pi - 1)^{N+1} - \alpha(\pi - 1)(\pi + 1) \in \mathfrak{c}\mathfrak{l}_1^{r_1} \cdots \mathfrak{l}_n^{r_n}.$$

On the other hand, we have $(\prod_i \ell_i^{r_i})(\pi - 1) \in \mathfrak{c}\mathfrak{l}_1^{r_1} \cdots \mathfrak{l}_n^{r_n}$. Since 2 and $\prod_i \ell_i^{r_i}$ are relatively prime, it follows that $\pi - 1 \in \mathfrak{c}\mathfrak{l}_1^{r_1} \cdots \mathfrak{l}_n^{r_n}$. This proves Eq. (9). The second equation is the complex conjugate of the first. □

In terms of the ideal class group, Theorem 4 says that

$$\{\mathfrak{l}_1^{r_1} \cdots \mathfrak{l}_n^{r_n}\} = \{\bar{\mathfrak{c}}\}, \tag{13}$$
$$\{\bar{\mathfrak{l}}_1^{r_1} \cdots \bar{\mathfrak{l}}_n^{r_n}\} = \{\mathfrak{c}\}. \tag{14}$$

Note that $\{\mathfrak{l}_1^{r_1} \cdots \mathfrak{l}_n^{r_n}\}^{-1} = \{\bar{\mathfrak{l}}_1^{r_1} \cdots \bar{\mathfrak{l}}_n^{r_n}\}$ and $\{\mathfrak{c}\}^{-1} = \{\bar{\mathfrak{c}}\}$. An application of this theorem to CSIDH is that the action of $\{\mathfrak{l}_1^{r_1} \cdots \mathfrak{l}_n^{r_n}\}$ on $\mathcal{E}\ell\ell_p(\mathcal{O}, \pi)$ can be computed via an isogeny of degree 4.

Corollary 2. *Let $E \in \mathcal{E}\ell\ell_p(\mathcal{O}, \pi)$. Then, the torsion subgroups $E[\mathfrak{c}]$ and $E[\bar{\mathfrak{c}}]$ are cyclic groups of order 4 and*

$$(\mathfrak{l}_1^{r_1} \cdots \mathfrak{l}_n^{r_n}) * E = \bar{\mathfrak{c}} * E, \tag{15}$$

$$(\bar{\mathfrak{l}}_1^{r_1} \cdots \bar{\mathfrak{l}}_n^{r_n}) * E = \mathfrak{c} * E. \tag{16}$$

Proof. Since $E[\mathfrak{c}] = E[4] \cap E[\pi - 1] = E[4] \cap E(\mathbb{F}_p)$ and $\#E(\mathbb{F}_p) = p + 1 = 4 \prod_i \ell_i^{r_i}$, we have $\#E[\mathfrak{c}] = 4$. Therefore, the isogeny defined by $\mathfrak{c}$ has degree 4. It can be easily checked that $\mathfrak{c}\bar{\mathfrak{c}} = 4\mathcal{O}$; i.e., the composition of isogenies defined by $\mathfrak{c}$ and $\bar{\mathfrak{c}}$ is multiplication by 4. Therefore, the isogeny defined by $\bar{\mathfrak{c}}$ is the dual isogeny of the isogeny defined by $\mathfrak{c}$, so it has degree 4. Thus, we have $\#E[\bar{\mathfrak{c}}] = 4$.

Consequently, we have that $E[\mathfrak{c}]$ and $E[\bar{\mathfrak{c}}]$ are cyclic of order 4 or isomorphic to $\mathbb{Z}/2\mathbb{Z} \oplus \mathbb{Z}/2\mathbb{Z}$. We assume $E[\mathfrak{c}] \cong \mathbb{Z}/2\mathbb{Z} \oplus \mathbb{Z}/2\mathbb{Z}$. This means that $E[\mathfrak{c}] = E[2]$; i.e., the action of the ideal class of $\mathfrak{c}$ on $\mathcal{E}\ell\ell_p(\mathcal{O}, \pi)$ is trivial. Therefore, by Theorem 2, $\mathfrak{c}$ is principal. Furthermore, by Theorem 4, $\mathfrak{l}_1^{r_1} \cdots \mathfrak{l}_n^{r_n}$ is also principal. This contradicts Theorem 3 that says the order of $\{\mathfrak{l}_1^{r_1} \cdots \mathfrak{l}_n^{r_n}\}$ is 3. Thus, $E[\mathfrak{c}]$ is cyclic of order 4. The statement for $E[\bar{\mathfrak{c}}]$ can be proven similarly.

Equations (15) and (16) directly follow from Eqs. (13) and (14). $\square$

3.2 Ideal Representation Without the Collisions Stated in Section 3.1

For simplicity, we use the setting in CSIDH in this subsection; i.e., we assume $r_1 = \cdots = r_n = 1$.

Corollary 1 says that if one uses the secret exponents $(e_1, \ldots, e_n)$ in the intervals $[-m, m]^n$ with $m \geq 2$ in CSIDH, then there are collisions in the ideal representation. For example, CSIDH-512, which is a parameter set of CSIDH with a prime p about 512 bits proposed by Castryck et al. [4], uses the intervals $[-5, 5]^{74}$, so it contains collisions.

On the other hand, for CSIDH-512, Beullens, Kleinjung, and Vercauteren [1] proposed a method to choose ideal classes uniformly. However, their method relies on knowledge of the structure of the ideal class group; in particular, it needs a list of secret exponents which represent the identity element of the ideal class group. To obtain the structure of the ideal class group, they used the algorithm due to Hafner and McCurley [15]. Since that algorithm is subexponential time in the discriminant of the target number field, their method can not be applied to a CSIDH when a large base field is used. Therefore, the ideal representation proposed in Castryck et al. [4] is still important.

For the general case, one way to avoid the collisions stated in Sect. 3.1 is to use different intervals for each e_i in which there is at least one interval of the form $[-1, 1]$. De Feo, Kieffer, and Smith [11] and Meyer, Campos, and Reith [19] proposed using different intervals for each e_i for speeding up the computation of the action of the ideal classes. One can expect that this representation is "almost" surjective and uniform, from a similar argument to the one in §7.1 in [4] (for the case of using different intervals, see §5.4 in [25]).

We propose another representation that is more efficiently computable than the method described in the above paragraph. Our representation uses $\mathfrak{c}$ instead of $\mathfrak{l}_n$ and is of the form

$$\mathfrak{l}_1^{e_1} \cdots \mathfrak{l}_{n-1}^{e_{n-1}} \mathfrak{c}^f \quad \text{for} \quad -m_i \le e_i \le m_i, \ f \in \{-1, 0, 1\}, \tag{17}$$

where $m_1, \ldots, m_{n-1}$ are positive integers such that $\prod_i (2m_i + 1) \ge \sqrt{p}$. By Corollary 2, the action of $\mathfrak{c}$ can be efficiently computed by an isogeny of degree 4. We give the formulae for computing this isogeny between Montgomery curves in Sect. 4.2. The reason for choosing $\mathfrak{l}_n$ as a replacement is that the cost of the isogeny associated with $\mathfrak{l}_n$ is the highest in the prime ideals $\mathfrak{l}_1, \ldots, \mathfrak{l}_n$ (for the cost of the isogeny, see [7,20]).

To show the validity of our representation, recall the exact sequence (6)

$$1 \to (\mathcal{O}_K/\mathfrak{f})^\times / (\mathcal{O}/\mathfrak{f})^\times \to \mathrm{cl}(\mathcal{O}) \to \mathrm{cl}(\mathcal{O}_K) \to 1.$$

We denote the image of $(\mathcal{O}_K/\mathfrak{f})^\times / (\mathcal{O}/\mathfrak{f})^\times$ in $\mathrm{cl}(\mathcal{O})$ by G. As we stated in the proof of the Theorem 3, G is a group of order 3 generated by $\{\bar{\mathfrak{l}}_1^{r_1} \cdots \bar{\mathfrak{l}}_n^{r_n}\} = \{\mathfrak{c}\}$. We define a set

$$M = \bigoplus_{i=1}^{n-1} ([-m_i, m_i] \cap \mathbb{Z}). \tag{18}$$

Then, we want to show the map

$$M \to \mathrm{cl}(\mathcal{O})/G, \quad (e_i) \mapsto \text{the image of } \mathfrak{l}_1^{e_1} \ldots \mathfrak{l}_{n-1}^{e_{n-1}} \tag{19}$$

is "almost" uniform and surjective. We can do so by using the same discussion as in §7.1 in [4]. Therefore, the map

$$M \times \{-1, 0, 1\} \to \mathrm{cl}(\mathcal{O}), \quad (e_1, \ldots, e_{n-1}; f) \mapsto \{\mathfrak{l}_1^{e_1} \ldots \mathfrak{l}_{n-1}^{e_{n-1}} \mathfrak{c}^f\} \tag{20}$$

is also "almost" uniform and surjective.

Remark 1. The ideal class of $\mathfrak{l}_1^{e_1} \cdots \mathfrak{l}_{n-1}^{e_{n-1}} \mathfrak{c}^f$ in $\mathrm{cl}(\mathcal{O}_K)$ does not depend on the factor $\mathfrak{c}^f$. Therefore, if an adversary against the protocol works on the isogeny problem on elliptic curves whose endomorphism ring is isomorphic to $\mathcal{O}_K$ [1], the factor $\mathfrak{c}^f$ does not increase the difficulty of the attack. However, in the last part of this attack, the adversary should determine an ideal class in $\mathrm{cl}(\mathcal{O})$ from one in $\mathrm{cl}(\mathcal{O}_K)$. There are three choices in $\mathrm{cl}(\mathcal{O})$. Therefore, if the adversary uses the meet-in-the-middle attack for finding an ideal class [4], the attack on $\mathrm{cl}(\mathcal{O}_K)$ is less effective than that on $\mathrm{cl}(\mathcal{O})$, since the complexity of the attack is $O(\sqrt{N})$, where N is the order of the target group. Therefore, we conclude that the factor $\mathfrak{c}^f$ increases the difficulty of attacks, since it increases the number of ideal classes which are represented by (17).

Remark 2. Recently, variants of CSIDH using the ideal class group of the maximal order $\mathcal{O}_K$ was proposed in [3,12]. Using these variants is another solution of avoiding the collisions in Sect. 3, since the collisions come from using the ideal class group of a non-maximal order.

---

[1] This can be done by taking 2-isogeny from an elliptic curve whose endomorphism ring is isomorphic to $\mathcal{O}$. See [13].

4   Formulae for Montgomery Curves

In this section, we give formulae for computing the action of our new representation on Montgomery curves [22]. A Montgomery curve defined over $\mathbb{F}_p$ is an elliptic curve defined by

$$By^2 = x^3 + Ax^2 + x, \tag{21}$$

where $A, B \in \mathbb{F}_p$. We denote this curve by $E_{A,B}$ or E_A if $B = 1$. Castryck et al. [4] showed that all curves in $\mathcal{E}\ell\ell_p(\mathcal{O}, \pi)$ can be defined as unique Montgomery curves and proposed an implementation of CSIDH on Montgomery curves.

4.1   Existing Formulae

First, let us recall the formulae for computing an isogeny between Montgomery curves presented by De Feo, Jao, and Plût [10] and Costello and Hisil [7]. We will use these formulae for proving our new formulae.

Theorem 5. *Let $E_{A,B}$ be a Montgomery curve over $\mathbb{F}_p$. Let $P_+, P_- \in E_{A,B}$ such that the x-coordinate of P_+ is 1 and the x-coordinate of P_- is -1. Then the points P_+ and P_- have order 4, the elliptic curve $E_{A,B}/\langle P_+ \rangle$ is defined by*

$$\frac{B}{2-A}y^2 = x^3 + 2\frac{A+6}{A-2}x^2 + x, \tag{22}$$

and the elliptic curve $E_{A,B}/\langle P_- \rangle$ is defined by

$$\frac{B}{2+A}y^2 = x^3 - 2\frac{A-6}{A+2}x^2 + x. \tag{23}$$

Proof. The first assertion can be easily checked by using the duplication formula for Montgomery curves [22]. For the second, see Eq. (20) in [10].

For the third, we use an isomorphism between a Montgomery curve and its twist. Let i be a square root of -1 in $\bar{\mathbb{F}}_p$. For $a, b \in \mathbb{F}_p$, we define the isomorphism

$$t_{a,b} : E_{a,b} \to E_{-a,b}, \quad (x,y) \mapsto (-x, iy). \tag{24}$$

Then, $t_{A,B}(P_-)$ is a point of $E_{-A,B}$ whose x-coordinate is 1. Let φ be the isogeny $E_{-A,B} \to E_{-A,B}/\langle t_{A,B}(P_-) \rangle$. By the second assertion of this theorem, we have $E_{-A,B}/\langle t_{A,B}(P_-) \rangle = E_{A',B'}$, where

$$A' = 2\frac{A-6}{A+2}, \quad B' = \frac{B}{2+A}. \tag{25}$$

Then the composition

$$t_{A',B'} \circ \varphi \circ t_{A,B} : E_{A,B} \to E_{-A',B'} \tag{26}$$

is the isogeny defined over $\mathbb{F}_p$ with kernel $\langle P_- \rangle$. This proves the third assertion. $\qquad\square$

Theorem 6. *Let $E_{A,B}$ be a Montgomery curve defined over $\mathbb{F}_p$, $P \in E_{A,B}$ a point of order $\ell = 2d + 1$, and φ the isogeny from $E_{A,B}$ with kernel $\langle P \rangle$. For $i \in \mathbb{N}$, we denote the x-coordinate of $[i]P$ by x_i. Then, the codomain of φ is $E_{A',B'}$, where*

$$A' = \left(6 \sum_{i=1}^{d} \frac{1}{x_i} - 6 \sum_{i=1}^{d} x_i + A \right) \left(\prod_{i=1}^{d} x_i \right)^2 \quad and \quad B' = B \left(\prod_{i=1}^{d} x_i \right)^2, \quad (27)$$

and φ maps

$$(x, y) \mapsto (f(x), y f'(x)), \quad (28)$$

where

$$f(x) = x \prod_{i=1}^{d} \left(\frac{x x_i - 1}{x - x_i} \right)^2, \quad (29)$$

and $f'(x)$ is its derivative.

Proof. This is the case of a field $K = \mathbb{F}_p$ in Theorem 1 of [7]. $\qquad\square$

4.2   New Formulae

We give formulae for isogenies corresponding to the ideals $\mathfrak{l}_1^{r_1} \cdots \mathfrak{l}_n^{r_n}$ and $\bar{\mathfrak{l}}_1^{r_1} \cdots \bar{\mathfrak{l}}_n^{r_n}$ between Montgomery curves. By Corollary 2, these isogenies can be computed by the actions of the ideals $\mathfrak{c}$ and $\bar{\mathfrak{c}}$. First, we give generators of the torsion subgroups $E[\mathfrak{c}]$ and $E[\bar{\mathfrak{c}}]$.

Lemma 1. *Let $A \in \mathbb{F}_p$ such that $E_A \in \mathcal{E}\ell\ell_p(\mathcal{O}, \pi)$, P_+ be a point of E_A of x-coordinate 1, and P_- be a point of E_A of x-coordinate -1. Then*

$$E_A[\mathfrak{c}] = \langle P_- \rangle, \quad (30)$$
$$E_A[\bar{\mathfrak{c}}] = \langle P_+ \rangle. \quad (31)$$

Proof. By definition, we have

$$E_A[\mathfrak{c}] = E_A[4] \cap E_A(\mathbb{F}_p), \quad (32)$$
$$E_A[\bar{\mathfrak{c}}] = E_A[4] \cap \{Q \in E_A \mid [\pi]Q = -Q\}. \quad (33)$$

Furthermore, by Theorem 5, the points P_- and P_+ have order 4. Therefore, it suffices to show that $P_- \in \mathbb{F}_p$ and $[\pi]P_+ = -P_+$.

By Corollary 2, $E_A[\mathfrak{c}]$ is cyclic of order 4. Therefore, the 2-torsion subgroup $E_A[2]$ is not contained in $E_A(\mathbb{F}_p)$. This means the equation

$$x^3 + Ax^2 + x = 0 \quad (34)$$

has only one solution $x = 0$ in $\mathbb{F}_p$. Thus, the discriminant $A^2 - 4$ of $x^2 + Ax + 1$ is not a square in $\mathbb{F}_p$. Therefore, one of $A - 2$ or $A + 2$ is a square in $\mathbb{F}_p$, and the other is not. Since the y-coordinate of P_- is a square root of $A - 2$, while that of P_+ is a square root of $A + 2$, one of P_- or P_+ is in $E_A(\mathbb{F}_p)$ and the other is not. Since the x-coordinate of P_+ is in $\mathbb{F}_p$, if $P_+ \notin E_A(\mathbb{F}_p)$, then $[\pi]P_+ = -P_+$. Therefore, it suffices to prove $P_- \in E_A(\mathbb{F}_p)$.

Since $p \equiv 3 \pmod 8$, -2 is a square in $\mathbb{F}_p$. Therefore, the lemma holds in the case $A = 0$. For the general case, we consider an isogeny from E_0 to E_A. Let P'_- be a point of E_0 whose x-coordinate is -1. By Theorem 2, there exists an integral invertible ideal $\mathfrak{a}$ such that $E_A = \mathfrak{a} * E_0$. By changing a representative of the ideal class if necessary, we may assume that the absolute norm of $\mathfrak{a}$ is odd; i.e., the isogeny defined by $\mathfrak{a}$ has an odd degree. By substituting $x = -1$ into Eq. (29) in Theorem 6, it follows that this isogeny maps P'_- to P_-. (Note that for $b \in \mathbb{F}_p^\times$, E_{A,b^2} is isomorphic over $\mathbb{F}_p$ to E_A by $(x, y) \mapsto (x, by)$.) Since P'_- is defined over $\mathbb{F}_p$, P_- is also defined over $\mathbb{F}_p$. □

Next, we give formulae for the isogenies corresponding to the ideals $\mathfrak{l}_1^{r_1} \cdots \mathfrak{l}_n^{r_n}$ and $\bar{\mathfrak{l}}_1^{r_1} \cdots \bar{\mathfrak{l}}_n^{r_n}$.

Theorem 7. *Let $A \in \mathbb{F}_p$ such that $E_A \in \mathcal{Ell}_p(\mathcal{O}, \pi)$. We define*

$$A' = -2\frac{A+6}{A-2}, \quad A'' = 2\frac{A-6}{A+2}. \tag{35}$$

Then

$$(\mathfrak{l}_1^{r_1} \cdots \mathfrak{l}_n^{r_n}) * E_A = E_{A'}, \quad (\bar{\mathfrak{l}}_1^{r_1} \cdots \bar{\mathfrak{l}}_n^{r_n}) * E_A = E_{A''}. \tag{36}$$

Proof. By Corollary 2, we have $\mathfrak{l}_1^{r_1} \cdots \mathfrak{l}_n^{r_n} * E_A = \bar{\mathfrak{c}} * E_A$. The above lemma says that $\mathfrak{c} * E_A = E_A / \langle P_+ \rangle$. Therefore, by Theorem 5, $\mathfrak{l}_1^{r_1} \cdots \mathfrak{l}_n^{r_n} * E_A$ can be defined by

$$\frac{1}{2-A}y^2 = x^3 + 2\frac{A+6}{A-2}x^2 + x. \tag{37}$$

For $a, b \in \mathbb{F}_p$, the Montgomery curve $E_{a,-b^2}$ is $\mathbb{F}_p$-isomorphic to E_{-a} by $(x, y) \mapsto (-x, by)$. Since $P_- \in E_A(\mathbb{F}_p)$, the element $A - 2$ is a square in $\mathbb{F}_p$. Therefore, the curve defined by Eq. (37) is $\mathbb{F}_p$-isomorphic to the curve defined by

$$y^2 = x^3 - 2\frac{A+6}{A-2}x^2 + x. \tag{38}$$

This proves the first assertion of the theorem. One can prove the second similarly. □

By using Corollary 2 and Theorem 7, we can compute the action of the ideal representation proposed in Sect. 3.2. The action of $\mathfrak{l}_1^{e_1} \cdots \mathfrak{l}_{n-1}^{e_{n-1}} \mathfrak{c}^f$ on a Montgomery curve $E_A \in \mathcal{Ell}_p(\mathcal{O}, \pi)$ can be computed as follows:

(i) Set $A' = 2\frac{A-6}{A+2}$ if $f = 1$, $A' = A$ if $f = 0$, and $A' = -2\frac{A+6}{A-2}$ if $f = -1$.

(ii) Compute $(\mathfrak{l}_1^{e_1} \cdots \mathfrak{l}_{n-1}^{e_{n-1}}) * E_{A'}$ by using Algorithm 2 in [4].

5   Conclusion

We showed that the ideal class of $\mathfrak{l}_1^{r_1} \cdots \mathfrak{l}_n^{r_n}$ has order 3 in the ideal class group and the same class of the ideal $\bar{\mathfrak{c}}$. In CSIDH, the former means that the secret exponents $(e_1, e_2 \ldots, e_n)$ and $(e_1 + 3, e_2 + 3, \ldots, e_n + 3)$ generate the same public key. The latter means that the action of the secret exponents $(1, \ldots, 1)$ can be computed by an isogeny of degree 4. We gave formulae for computing this action on Montgomery curves. Furthermore, we proposed a new ideal representation for CSIDH that does not contain the collisions we found. Our new ideal representation can be computed efficiently by using the formula for computing the action of the secret exponents $(1, \ldots, 1)$.

Acknowledgment. This work was supported by JST CREST Grand Number JPMJ CR14D6, Japan.

Appendix A   Odd-degree Isogenies Using 4-Torsion Points

We give new formulae for computing odd-degree isogenies between Montgomery curves by calculating the images of P_+ and P_-. We denote the degree of the isogeny we compute by $\ell = 2d + 1$ as in Theorem 6.

Theorem 8. *We use the same notation as in Theorem 6 and assume $B = 1$. Further, we assume that the group $\langle P \rangle$ is stable under the action of the p-th power Frobenius endomorphism. Then, there exists $A' \in \mathbb{F}_p$ such that $E_{A'} = E_A/\langle P \rangle$. Furthermore, A' satisfies the equations*

$$A' + 2 = (A + 2) \left(\left(1 + 2 \sum_{i=1}^{d} \frac{x_i + 1}{x_i - 1} \right) \prod_{i=1}^{d} x_i \right)^2, \tag{39}$$

$$A' - 2 = (A - 2) \left(\left(1 + 2 \sum_{i=1}^{d} \frac{x_i - 1}{x_i + 1} \right) \prod_{i=1}^{d} x_i \right)^2. \tag{40}$$

Proof. Let $b = \prod_{i=1}^{d} x_i$. Then we have $b \in \mathbb{F}_p$, because the group $\langle P \rangle$ is stable under the action of the p-th power Frobenius map. Theorem 6 says that the isogeny with kernel $\langle P \rangle$ is given by

$$E_A \to E_{A', b^2}, \quad (x, y) \mapsto (f(x), y f'(x)), \tag{41}$$

where A' is defined in Theorem 6. We have $E_{A', b^2} = E_{A'}$ because $E_{A', b^2} \to E_{A'}$, $(x, y) \mapsto (x, by)$ is a $\mathbb{F}_p$-isomorphism. This proves the first assertion.

Let $P_+, P_- \in E_A$ be the same as in Lemma 1. We denote the y-coordinate of P_+ by y_+. Note that $y_+^2 = A + 2$. The image of P_+ under the isogeny $E_A \to E_{A'}$ is $(1, by_+ f'(1))$. One can easily check that

$$f'(1) = 1 + 2 \sum_{i=1}^{d} \frac{x_i + 1}{x_i - 1}. \tag{42}$$

Substituting $(1, by_+ f'(1))$ into the equation of $E_{A'}$ yields Eq. (39). By considering the image of P_-, we obtain Eq. (40). □

As with the other formulae for isogenies between Montgomery curves [7, 8, 10, 20, 26], our formulae can avoid inversions by using a projective coordinate of A. For $x \in \mathbb{F}_p$, we call a pair $X, Z \in \mathbb{F}_p$ such that $x = X/Z$ a projective coordinate of x and denote it by $(X : Z)$. The following corollary gives a projectivized variant of Eq. (40) in the above theorem. Note that a projectivized variant of Eq. (39) can be obtained in the same way.

Corollary 3. *We use the same notation as in Theorem 8. Let $(a : c)$ be a projective coordinate of A and $(X_i : Z_i)$ a projective coordinate of x_i. We define*

$$c' = c(\prod_{i=1}^{d} S_i \prod_{i=1}^{d} Z_i)^2), \tag{43}$$

$$a' = (a - 2c)((\prod_{i=1}^{d} S_i + 2\sum_{i=0}^{d} D_i \prod_{j\neq i} S_j) \prod_{i=1}^{d} X_i)^2 + 2c', \tag{44}$$

where $S_i = X_i + Z_i$, $D_i = X_i - Z_i$. Then $(a' : c')$ is a projective coordinate of A'.

Proof. This follows immediately from equation (40). □

By Corollary 2, we obtain an algorithm (Algorithm 1) for computing the coefficient of the codomain of an odd-degree isogeny. We assume that the elements X_i, Z_i, S_i and D_i are precomputed. These elements are used in the computation of the image of a point under an isogeny. In CSIDH, one needs to compute not only the coefficient of the codomain of an isogeny, but also the image of a point under that isogeny. Therefore, it is natural to separate the computation of these elements from that of an isogeny.

Algorithm 1. Odd-degree isogeny

Require: A projective coordinate $(a : c)$ of the coefficient of a Montgomery curve, projective coordinates $(X_i : Z_i)$ of the x-coordinate of $[i]P$, where $P \in E_{a/c}$ has odd order $\ell = 2d + 1$, $S_i = X_i + Z_i$, and $D_i = X_i - Z_i$ for $i = 1, \ldots, d$.
Ensure: a projective coordinate $(a' : c')$ such that $E_{a'/c'} = E_{a/c}/\langle P \rangle$.
1: $X \leftarrow X_1, Z \leftarrow Z_i, F \leftarrow D_1, G \leftarrow S_1$
2: **for** $i = 2$ to d **do**
3:     $X \leftarrow XX_i$.
4:     $Z \leftarrow ZZ_i$.
5:     $F \leftarrow FS_i + GD_i$.
6:     $G \leftarrow GS_i$.
7: **end for**
8: $c' \leftarrow c(GZ)^2$.
9: **return** $((a - 2c)((G + 2F)X)^2 + 2c' : c')$.

The cost of Algorithm 1 is

$$(5d-1)\mathbf{M} + 2\mathbf{S} + (d+5)\mathbf{a}, \tag{45}$$

where $\mathbf{M}$, $\mathbf{S}$, and $\mathbf{a}$ mean multiplication, squaring, and addition or subtraction on the field $\mathbb{F}_p$, respectively.

On the other hand, the costs of the similar algorithms in the previous studies are as follows. Castryck et al. [4] used the formula from Costello and Hisil [7] and Renes [26]. The cost is

$$(6d-2)\mathbf{M} + 3\mathbf{S} + 4\mathbf{a}. \tag{46}$$

Meyer and Reith [20] proposed an algorithm that exploits the correspondence between Montgomery curves and twisted Edwards curves. The cost is

$$2d\mathbf{M} + 6\mathbf{S} + 6\mathbf{a} + 2w(\ell), \tag{47}$$

where $w(\ell)$ is the cost of the ℓ-th power on $\mathbb{F}_p$. If we use the binary algorithm for exponentiation, we obtain $w(\ell) = (h-1)\mathbf{M} + (t-1)\mathbf{S}$, where h and t are the Hamming weight and the bit length of ℓ, respectively.

For comparing the above costs, we assume that $\mathbf{S} = 0.8\,\mathbf{M}$ and $\mathbf{a} = 0.05\,\mathbf{M}$ as in [20]. We conclude that Algorithm 1 is the fastest if $\ell \leq 7$ and the algorithm in [20] is the fastest if $\ell > 7$. Table 1 shows the costs of these algorithms for small degrees.

Table 1. Costs of odd-degree isogeny computations

Degree	Algorithm 1	Algorithm in [4]	Algorithm in [20]
3	5.90 M	6.70 M	10.70 M
5	10.95 M	12.80 M	14.30 M
7	16.00 M	18.90 M	18.30 M
9	21.05 M	25.00 M	19.90 M
11	26.10 M	31.00 M	23.90 M

References

1. Beullens, W., Kleinjung, T., Vercauteren, F.: CSI-FiSh: efficient isogeny based signatures through class group computations. In: Galbraith, S.D., Moriai, S. (eds.) ASIACRYPT 2019. LNCS, vol. 11921, pp. 227–247. Springer, Cham (2019). https://doi.org/10.1007/978-3-030-34578-5_9
2. Buchmann, J., Williams, H.C.: A key-exchange system based on imaginary quadratic fields. J. Cryptology 1, 107–118 (1988)
3. Castryck, W., Decru, T.: CSIDH on the surface. In: Ding, J., Tillich, J.-P. (eds.) PQCrypto 2020. LNCS, vol. 12100, pp. 111–129. Springer, Cham (2020). https://doi.org/10.1007/978-3-030-44223-1_7

4. Castryck, W., Lange, T., Martindale, C., Panny, L., Renes, J.: CSIDH: an efficient post-quantum commutative group action. In: Peyrin, T., Galbraith, S. (eds.) ASIACRYPT 2018. LNCS, vol. 11274, pp. 395–427. Springer, Cham (2018). https://doi.org/10.1007/978-3-030-03332-3_15

5. Castryck, W., Panny, L., Vercauteren, F.: Rational isogenies from irrational endomorphisms. In: Canteaut, A., Ishai, Y. (eds.) EUROCRYPT 2020. LNCS, vol. 12106, pp. 523–548. Springer, Cham (2020). https://doi.org/10.1007/978-3-030-45724-2_18

6. Cohen, H., Lenstra Jr., H.W.: Heuristics on class groups of number fields. Number Theory, Noordwijkerhout **1983**, 33–62 (1984)

7. Costello, C., Hisil, H.: A simple and compact algorithm for SIDH with arbitrary degree isogenies. In: Takagi, T., Peyrin, T. (eds.) ASIACRYPT 2017. LNCS, vol. 10625, pp. 303–329. Springer, Cham (2017). https://doi.org/10.1007/978-3-319-70697-9_11

8. Costello, C., Longa, P., Naehrig, M.: Efficient algorithms for supersingular isogeny Diffie-Hellman. In: Robshaw, M., Katz, J. (eds.) CRYPTO 2016. LNCS, vol. 9814, pp. 572–601. Springer, Heidelberg (2016). https://doi.org/10.1007/978-3-662-53018-4_21

9. Couveignes, J.M.: Hard homogeneous spaces. IACR Cryptology ePrint Archive 2006/291. https://eprint.iacr.org/2006/291

10. De Feo, L., Jao, D., Plût, J.: Towards quantum-resistant cryptosystems from supersingular elliptic curve isogenies. J. Math. Cryptology **8**(3), 209–247 (2014)

11. De Feo, L., Kieffer, J., Smith, B.: Towards practical key exchange from ordinary isogeny graphs. In: Peyrin, T., Galbraith, S. (eds.) ASIACRYPT 2018. LNCS, vol. 11274, pp. 365–394. Springer, Cham (2018). https://doi.org/10.1007/978-3-030-03332-3_14

12. Fan, X., Tian, S., Li, B., Xu, X.: CSIDH on other form of elliptic curves. IACR Cryptology ePrint Archive 2019/1417. https://eprint.iacr.org/2019/1417

13. Delfs, C., Galbraith, S.D.: Computing isogenies between supersingular elliptic curves over $\mathbb{F}_p$. Des. Codes Crypt. **78**(2), 425–440 (2016)

14. Diffie, W., Hellman, M.: New directions in cryptography. IEEE Trans. Inf. Theor. **22**(6), 644–654 (1976)

15. Hafner, J.L., McCurley, K.S.: A rigorous subexponential algorithm for computation of class groups. J. Am. Math. Soc. **2**, 837–850 (1989)

16. Jao, D., De Feo, L.: Towards quantum-resistant cryptosystems from supersingular elliptic curve isogenies. In: Yang, B.-Y. (ed.) PQCrypto 2011. LNCS, vol. 7071, pp. 19–34. Springer, Heidelberg (2011). https://doi.org/10.1007/978-3-642-25405-5_2

17. Jao, D., et al.: Supersingular isogeny key encapsulation. Submission to the NIST Post-Quantum Cryptography Standardization project (2017). https://sike.org

18. Koblitz, N.: Elliptic curve cryptosystems. Math. Comput. **48**(177), 203–209 (1987)

19. Meyer, M., Campos, F., Reith, S.: On lions and elligators: an efficient constant-time implementation of CSIDH. In: Ding, J., Steinwandt, R. (eds.) PQCrypto 2019. LNCS, vol. 11505, pp. 307–325. Springer, Cham (2019). https://doi.org/10.1007/978-3-030-25510-7_17

20. Meyer, M., Reith, S.: A faster way to the CSIDH. In: Chakraborty, D., Iwata, T. (eds.) INDOCRYPT 2018. LNCS, vol. 11356, pp. 137–152. Springer, Cham (2018). https://doi.org/10.1007/978-3-030-05378-9_8

21. Miller, V.S.: Use of elliptic curves in cryptography. In: Williams, H.C. (ed.) CRYPTO 1985. LNCS, vol. 218, pp. 417–426. Springer, Heidelberg (1986). https://doi.org/10.1007/3-540-39799-X_31

22. Montgomery, P.L.: Speeding the Pollard and elliptic curve methods of factorization. Math. Comput. **48**(177), 24–264 (1987)

23. National Institute of Standards and Technology (NIST): NIST post-quantum cryptography standardization (2016). https://csrc.nist.gov/Projects/Post-Quantum-Cryptography

24. Neukirch, J.: Algebraic Number Theory. Springer, Heidelberg (1999). https://doi.org/10.1007/978-3-662-03983-0

25. Onuki, H., Aikawa, Y., Yamazaki, T., Takagi, T.: A faster constant-time algorithm of CSIDH keeping two points IACR cryptology ePrint Archive 2019/353. https://eprint.iacr.org/2019/353

26. Renes, J.: Computing isogenies between Montgomery curves using the action of (0, 0). In: Lange, T., Steinwandt, R. (eds.) PQCrypto 2018. LNCS, vol. 10786, pp. 229–247. Springer, Cham (2018). https://doi.org/10.1007/978-3-319-79063-3_11

27. Rostovtsev, A., Stolbunov, A.,: Public-key cryptosystem based on isogenies. IACR Cryptology ePrint Archive 2006/14. https://eprint.iacr.org/2006/145

28. Silverman, J.H.: Advanced Topics in the Arithmetic of Elliptic Curves. GTM, vol. 151. Springer, New York (1994). https://doi.org/10.1007/978-1-4612-0851-8

29. Silverman, J.H.: The Arithmetic of Elliptic Curves. GTM, vol. 106, 2nd edn. Springer, New York (2009). https://doi.org/10.1007/978-0-387-09494-6

30. Stolbunov, A.: Constructing public-key cryptographic schemes based on class group action on a set of isogenous elliptic curves. Adv. Math. Commun. **4**(2), 215–235 (2010)

31. Vélu, J.: Isogénies entre courbes elliptiques. C. R. Acad. Sci. **273**, 238–241 (1971)

Optimization of Search Space for Finding Very Short Lattice Vectors

Yoshitatsu Matsuda[✉]

Department of Computer and Information Science, Seikei University, 3-3-1,
Kichijojikitamachi, Musashino-shi, Tokyo 180-8633, Japan
matsuda@st.seikei.ac.jp

Abstract. Shortest vector problem on lattices (SVP) is a well-known algorithmic combinatorial problem. The hardness of SVP is a foundation for the security of Lattice-based cryptography, which is a promising candidate of the post-quantum cryptographic algorithms. Therefore, many works have focused on the estimation of the hardness of SVP and the construction of efficient algorithms. Recently, a probabilistic approach has been proposed for estimating the hardness, which is based on the randomness assumption. The approach can estimate quite accurately the distribution of very short lattice vectors in a search space. In this paper, a new method is proposed for optimizing a box-type search space in random sampling by this probabilistic approach. It has been known empirically that the tail part of the search space should be more intensively explored for finding very short lattice vectors efficiently. However, it was difficult to adjust the search space quantitatively. On the other hand, our proposed method can find the best search space approximately. Experimental results show that our method is useful when the lattice basis is small or already reduced in advance.

1 Introduction

Shortest vector problem (SVP) on lattices is a combinatorial problem of finding the shortest non-zero lattice vector in a given lattice. SVP is known as one of the most promising candidates in post-quantum cryptography [10]. As the hardness of SVP gives a foundation to the security of the cryptographic system, it has become more important to estimate the hardness. The computational complexity for solving SVP is theoretically estimated in many algorithms such as enumeration [11], sieving [1], the Lenstra-Lenstra-Lovász algorithm (LLL) [12], the block Korkine-Zolotarev algorithm (BKZ) [17], random sampling reduction (RSR) [18], and so on. However, the complexity deeply depends on each specific algorithm so that it is different from the general hardness of SVP. Actually, there are several much more efficient algorithm in practice, for example, [7,20] and [2]. In order to estimate the general hardness irrespective of the algorithms, it is useful to estimate the number of very short vectors in a search space of a given lattice. The widely-used approach is called the Gaussian heuristic (GH) [6], which assumes that the number of very short vectors in a search space is proportional

© Springer Nature Switzerland AG 2020
K. Aoki and A. Kanaoka (Eds.): IWSEC 2020, LNCS 12231, pp. 149–161, 2020.
https://doi.org/10.1007/978-3-030-58208-1_9

to the volume of the intersection between a ball with the short diameter and the search space [3,8]. GH is theoretically based on the theorem by Goldstein and Mayer [9]. However, the GH-based approach is not so efficient in practice because of its complicated estimation. On the other hand, the probabilistic approach has been proposed recently for estimating the number of short vectors [7,14,15], which is based on the Schnorr's randomness assumption (RA) [18]. RA assumes that the residuals in the Gram-Schmidt orthogonalized basis of a given lattice are independently and uniformly distributed. The probabilistic approach can estimate the distribution of the lengths of lattice vectors over the search space. It has been experimentally shown in [14] that the probabilistic approach using the Gram-Charlier A series can estimate the distribution of the lengths of very short lattice vectors over a search space both accurately and quite efficiently.

In this paper, a method is proposed for finding approximately the best search space under the same size by utilizing the probabilistic approach. Such best search space is expected to be useful for both estimating the theoretical complexity and constructing efficient algorithms. The essential assumption is that the mean of the distribution should be minimized in the best search space. This assumption can enable us to calculate the best search space concretely and to estimate the theoretical bound of this optimization.

This paper is organized as follows. Section 2 gives the preliminaries of this work. Section 3 gives a method for finding the best search space under a given lattice basis and a given size of search space. In Sect. 4, the experimental results of the proposed optimization method are described. Lastly, this paper is concluded in Sect. 5.

2   Preliminaries

2.1   Lattices and Shortest Vector Problem

A lattice basis is given as a full-rank $n \times n$ integral matrix $B = \{b_1, \ldots, b_n\}$, where each $b_i = (b_{ij}) \in \mathbb{Z}^n$ is called a basis vector. The lattice $L(B)$ is defined as an additive group consisting of $\sum_{i=1}^{n} a_i b_i$ for $a_i \in \mathbb{Z}$. The Euclidean inner product of x and y is denoted by $\langle x, y \rangle = x^T y$. The Euclidean norm (namely, the length) of x is defined as $\|x\| = \sqrt{\langle x, x \rangle}$. The exact SVP is defined as the problem of finding a non-zero integer vector $a = (a_i)$ so that the length $\ell = \|a^T b\|$ is minimized. The approximate version of SVP is also widely used, where we search a very short vector with a sufficiently small length. In other words, we search a non-zero integer vector a satisfying $\|a^T b\| < \hat{\ell}$, where $\hat{\ell}$ is a threshold. The approximate SVP is denoted by SVP hereafter.

The determinant of B (denoted by $\det(B)$) is constant even if the current lattice basis is changed. By using $\det(B)$, the length of the shortest lattice vector can be estimated as

$$\ell_{\mathrm{GH}} = \frac{\left(\Gamma\left(\frac{n}{2}+1\right)\det(B)\right)^{\frac{1}{n}}}{\sqrt{\pi}}, \tag{1}$$

where Γ is the gamma function occurring in the calculation of the volume of an n-dimensional ball [10]. This approximation is called the Gaussian heuristic.

Though this heuristic does not hold for any lattice, it holds at least for a random lattice. The threshold $\hat{\ell}$ in SVP can be given as $(1 + \epsilon)\ell_{GH}$ where ϵ is a small positive constant ($\epsilon = 0.05$ in TU Darmstadt SVP challenge [16]).

2.2 Gram-Schmidt Orthogonalization and Search Space

$\boldsymbol{b}_i$ can be orthogonalized to $\boldsymbol{b}_i^* = (b_{ij}^*)$ by the Gram-Schmidt orthogonalization:

$$\boldsymbol{b}_i^* = \boldsymbol{b}_i - \sum_{j=1}^{i-1} \eta_{ji}\boldsymbol{b}_j^* \text{ and } \eta_{ji} = \frac{\langle \boldsymbol{b}_j^*, \boldsymbol{b}_i \rangle}{\|\boldsymbol{b}_j^*\|^2}, \tag{2}$$

where $\langle \boldsymbol{b}_i^*, \boldsymbol{b}_j^* \rangle = 0$ holds for $i \neq j$. Note that $\|\boldsymbol{b}_i^*\|$ is not constrained to be 1. $\boldsymbol{B}^* = (\boldsymbol{b}_1^*, \ldots, \boldsymbol{b}_n^*)$ is called an orthogonalized lattice basis. $\boldsymbol{B}^*$ can be characterized by a vector $\boldsymbol{\rho} = (\rho_i)$, where ρ_i is defined as

$$\rho_i = \|\boldsymbol{b}_i^*\|^2 = \sum_{j=1}^{n} \left(b_{ij}^*\right)^2. \tag{3}$$

$\boldsymbol{\rho}$ is called the shape of $\boldsymbol{B}^*$. Any lattice vector $\sum_{i=1}^{n} a_i \boldsymbol{b}_i$ ($a_i \in \mathbb{Z}$) can be given as $\sum_{i=1}^{n} \zeta_i \boldsymbol{b}_i^*$. The squared length of this lattice vector is given as

$$\ell^2 = \sum_{i=1}^{n} \rho_i \zeta_i^2. \tag{4}$$

Because each $\zeta_i \in \mathbb{R}$ is given as the sum of $\bar{\zeta}_i$ ($-\frac{1}{2} \leq \bar{\zeta}_i < \frac{1}{2}$) and an integer, ζ_i is uniquely determined by a natural number d_i satisfying

$$-\frac{d_i + 1}{2} \leq \zeta_i < -\frac{d_i - 1}{2} \text{ or } \frac{d_i - 1}{2} \leq \zeta_i < \frac{d_i}{2}. \tag{5}$$

Here, the natural numbers begin with 1. A vector $\boldsymbol{d} = (d_1, \ldots, d_n)$ is called a tag in the same way as in [3]. $\bar{\zeta}_i$ is called the residual of ζ_i.

It was proved in [7] that any lattice vector is uniquely determined by $\boldsymbol{d}$, and vice versa. Therefore, a search space of the lattice vectors can be defined as a set of tags (denoted by Υ). In this paper, Υ is constrained to be an n-ary Cartesian product in the same way as in random sampling [4,13,18]: $\Upsilon = v_1 \times v_2 \times \cdots \times v_n$. Here, each v_i is a set of natural numbers under a maximum T_i: $\{1, \ldots, T_i\}$. It is called a box-type search space characterized by a natural number vector $\boldsymbol{T} = (T_i) \in \mathbb{N}^n$. The size of a search space is defined as $V(\boldsymbol{T}) = \prod_{i=1}^{n} T_i$.

2.3 Randomness Assumption and Gram-Charlier a Series

The probabilistic approach is based on the following assumption asserted in [18].

Assumption 1 (Randomness Assumption (RA)). *Each residual $\bar{\zeta}_i$ is uniformly distributed in $[-\frac{1}{2}, \frac{1}{2})$ and is statistically independent of $\bar{\zeta}_j$ for $j \neq i$.*

Though there are some different definitions of RA, the above one is employed here. Though RA cannot hold rigorously [3], it empirically holds if the index i is not near to n [19]. Regarding a box-type search space, RA can be extended to the assumption that each ζ_i is independently and uniformly distributed in the range $\left[-\frac{T_i}{2}, \frac{T_i}{2}\right)$. Therefore, the distribution of the squared lengths $\ell^2 = \sum \rho_i \zeta_i$ of the lattice vectors over a box-type search space is uniquely determined by T and ρ.

The distribution of ℓ^2 can be approximated by the Gram-Charlier A series [5,22]. The details of this technique are described in [14,15]. Here, only the necessary parts for the proposed method are explained. Generally, the cumulative distribution function $\bar{F}(x)$ of a normalized random variable x (the mean and the variance are 0 and 1, respectively) can be approximated by the following Gram-Charlier A series:

$$\bar{F}_Q(x) = \int_{-\infty}^{x} \frac{e^{-\frac{w^2}{2}}}{\sqrt{2\pi}} dw - \left(\sum_{r=3}^{Q} c_r He_{r-1}(x)\right) \frac{e^{-\frac{x^2}{2}}}{\sqrt{2\pi}}, \tag{6}$$

where $He_r(x)$ is the r-th degree Hermite polynomial and c_r is a coefficient depending on from the 3rd to the r-th order cumulants of x. It is guaranteed to converge to the true distribution for $Q \to \infty$ if x is bounded [22]. A general cumulative distribution function $F(z)$ with non-normalized z (with the mean μ and the variance σ^2) is given as

$$F_Q(z) = \bar{F}_Q\left(\frac{z-\mu}{\sigma}\right). \tag{7}$$

Now, let ℓ^2 be the random variable z. Then, the r-th order cumulant of ℓ^2 (denoted by $\kappa_r(\ell^2)$) is given as

$$\kappa_r(\ell^2) = \sum_{i=1}^{n} \rho_i^r \kappa_r(T_i) \tag{8}$$

due to the homogeneity and the additivity of cumulants. Here, $\kappa_r(T_i)$ denotes the r-th order cumulant of ζ^2, where ζ is uniformly distributed over $\left[-\frac{T_i}{2}, \frac{T_i}{2}\right)$. $\kappa_r(T_i)$ is determined by only T_i. μ and σ^2 correspond to $\kappa_1(\ell^2)$ and $\kappa_2(\ell^2)$, respectively. The normalized cumulants of $\bar{F}\left(\frac{z-\mu}{\sigma}\right)$ are given as

$$\bar{\kappa}_r = \frac{\kappa_r(\ell^2)}{\sqrt{\kappa_2(\ell^2)}^r} \tag{9}$$

for $r \geq 3$. Consequently, we can estimate $F_Q(\ell^2; T, \rho)$ by T and ρ. In addition, it is guaranteed in [14] that $F_Q(\ell^2)$ monotonically converges to the true distribution as Q becomes larger.

Note that we can easily calculate $F_Q(\ell)$ (the cumulative distribution of Euclidean lengths of the lattice vectors) from $F_Q(\ell^2)$ (*squared* Euclidean) and vice versa. $F_Q(\ell^2)$ is employed in this paper.

3   Method and Algorithm

3.1   Purpose

Our purpose is to find the search space including as many very short lattice vectors as possible under the same size K. In the original random sampling [18], the search space T is given as

$$T_i = \begin{cases} 1 & i \leq n - u, \\ 2 & \text{otherwise}, \end{cases} \tag{10}$$

where the size of the space is 2^u. In other words, d_i can be switched between 1 and 2 in only the tail u indices (otherwise, d_i is fixed to 1). However, it is still unclear whether the employment of the only two choices (1 or 2) is sufficiently efficient or not. In [4,13], the choices are generalized into $d_i \in \{1, 2, \ldots, T_i\}$. Nevertheless, it has not been known what search space is best.

3.2   Principle and Assumption

In the principle of the probabilistic approach under RA, the best search space $\hat{T}$ has the highest probability of generating very short lattice vectors for a current lattice basis (whose shape is ρ), where the size of the search space $V\left(\hat{T}\right)$ is constrained to be a constant K. By utilizing $F_Q\left(\ell^2; T, \rho\right)$, it is formalized as follows:

$$\hat{T} = \text{argmax}_T \, F_Q\left(\ell^2; T, \rho\right) \text{ subject to } V\left(T\right) = K. \tag{11}$$

Unfortunately, it is intractable to estimate F_Q over all the possible T. Therefore, the following assumption is introduced.

Assumption 2 (Best Search Assumption (BSA)). *When the mean μ of the distribution $F_Q\left(\ell^2; T, \rho\right)$ is the lowest, the probability of generating very short lattice vector is the highest. In other words, T minimizing μ is the best search space.*

This assumption utilizes only the first order cumulant (namely, the mean) and neglects the other cumulants. Thus, the form of the distribution is assumed to be unchanged except for its mean. Therefore, the lowest mean maximizes the expected number of very short vectors. This assumption can be justified at least if $T_i \geq 2$ holds for only relatively small ρ_i. It is because the effects of large T_i on the r-th order cumulants are decreased in proportion to ρ_i^r.

3.3   Problem and Algorithm

The mean of ζ_i^2 over the uniform distributed ζ_i in $\left[-\frac{T_i}{2}, \frac{T_i}{2}\right)$ is given as

$$\mu_i = \int_{-\frac{T_i}{2}}^{\frac{T_i}{2}} \frac{x^2}{T_i} \mathrm{d}x = \frac{T_i^2}{12} \tag{12}$$

Then, the mean of $F_Q\left(\ell^2; \boldsymbol{T}, \boldsymbol{\rho}\right)$ is given as

$$\mu = \frac{\sum_{i=1}^{n} \rho_i T_i^2}{12}. \tag{13}$$

Under BSA, the best search space $\hat{\boldsymbol{T}}$ can be estimated by solving the following optimization problem:

$$\hat{\boldsymbol{T}} = \mathrm{argmin}_{\boldsymbol{T} \in \mathbb{N}^n} \sum_{i=1}^{n} \rho_i T_i^2 \text{ subject to } \prod_{i=1}^{n} T_i \geq 2^u. \tag{14}$$

Here, the size of the search space is limited to 2^u for simplicity. In addition, the constraint is changed to the lower bound because the equality constraint hardly can be satisfied. This is a sort of combinatorial integer problem. This problem is solved by using the two stages.

At the bound stage, the search space of $\boldsymbol{T}$ is bounded. First, ρ_i is sorted in descending order. Then, $\boldsymbol{T}$ is constrained to be monotonically increasing along the index i. Second, $T_i = 2$ is allocated to the smallest u elements of the shape $\boldsymbol{\rho}$ (otherwise, $T_i = 1$) in the similar way as in the original random sampling. This allocation is utilized as the baseline. Under the monotonically increasing constraint, the upper bound U_i for each T_i is given so that the objective function for the candidate $\boldsymbol{T}$ does not exceed the baseline. Third, the lower bound L_i for each T_i is given so that the current upper bounds can satisfy $\prod_{i=1}^{n} T_i \geq 2^u$. Lastly, the upper bounds and the lower bounds are updated alternately until the convergence. The algorithm is described in Algorithm 1. It can be carried out instantly.

At the minimization stage, the minimum of $\sum_{i=1}^{n} \rho_i T_i^2$ is searched within the above bounded space. It can be implemented by a recursive function, which finds the best tail part $\tilde{\boldsymbol{T}}_p = (T_p, T_{p+1}, \ldots, T_n)$ minimizing $E = \sum_{i=p}^{n} \rho_i T_i^2$ for the head index p of the current tail part, the preceding T_{p-1}, the current lower bound of the size K_{cur}. The details are described in Algorithm 2. This can be regarded as a sort of breadth first search. Though its complexity is exponential, it is not so time consuming in practice.

3.4   Theoretical Lower Bound

Though the best search space can be found by the above algorithm, the theoretical analysis is difficult. Here, a simple lower bound of the effects of the best search space is introduced. By neglecting the integer constraint, the optimization problem is relaxed into

$$\hat{\boldsymbol{T}} = \mathrm{argmin}_{\boldsymbol{T}} \sum_{i=n-u+1}^{n} \rho_i T_i^2 \text{ subject to } \sum_{i=n-u+1}^{n} \log_2\left(T_i\right) = u, \tag{15}$$

where $T_i = 1$ for every $i \leq n - u$. This problem can be solved easily by the method of Lagrange multiplier, where the optimum $\hat{T}_i(i > n - u + 1)$ is given as

$$\hat{T}_i = \frac{2\left(\prod_{k=n-u+1}^{n} \rho_k\right)^{\frac{1}{2u}}}{\sqrt{\rho_i}}. \tag{16}$$

Algorithm 1. Calculation of Lower and Upper Bounds of T.

Require: ρ (the shape of a lattice basis) and u (the exponent of 2^u search space).
Ensure: $U = (U_i)$ and $L = (L_i)$.
 1: Sort ρ_i in descending order.
 2: **for all** i **do**
 3:     $U_i \leftarrow 1$, $L_i \leftarrow 1$.
 4: **end for**
 5: **repeat**
 6:     $E_{\text{base}} \leftarrow \sum_{i=1}^{n-u} \rho_i + \sum_{i=n-u+1}^{n} 4\rho_i$.
 7:     **for** $j \leftarrow n$ to $n - u + 1$ **do**
 8:         $U_j \leftarrow \left\lfloor \sqrt{\dfrac{E_{\text{base}} - \sum_{i=1}^{j-1} L_i^2 \rho_i}{\sum_{i=j}^{n} \rho_i}} \right\rfloor$.
 9:     **end for**
10:     **for** $j \leftarrow n$ to $n - u + 1$ **do**
11:         **if** $\prod_{i=j+1}^{n} U_i < 2^u$ **then**
12:             $L_j \leftarrow 2$.
13:         **end if**
14:     **end for**
15: **until** every U_i and L_i does not change.
16: **return** U, L.

This solution gives a lower bound of the best search space.

4   Experimental Results

Here, it is experimentally investigated whether the best search space in our proposed method is useful in practice or not for the following four lattice bases:

- **B100** was originally generated in TU Darmstadt SVP challenge [16] ($n = 100$, seed $= 0$) and was roughly reduced by the BKZ algorithm of the fplll package [21] with block size 20.
- **B128** was generated in the same way as B100 except for $n = 128$.
- **B150** was generated in the same way as B100 except for $n = 150$.
- **B128reduced** was a reduced basis from B128 (ranked in [16] with the Euclidean norm 2984).

The best search space is compared with the baseline 2^u. The baseline allocates $T_i = 2$ to the smallest u elements of the shape ρ in the similar way as in the original random sampling [18].

Figure 1 shows the results for B100, where the baseline was set to 2^{28} (namely, $u = 28$). The actual number of short lattice vectors is displayed by the (cumulative) histograms for the baseline and the best search space. Note that the trivial zeros vector ($d_i = 1$ for every i) is removed. Note also that $10^0 = 1$ in vertical axis is the minimum of the actual number. The estimated number using the Gram-Charier approximation ($V(T) F_Q$) is also displayed by the curves for each space ($Q = 150$). Figure 1 shows that the estimated number over the best search

---

Algorithm 2. Search of $\hat{T}$ minimizing $\sum_i T_i^2 \rho_i$.

Require: U, L, ρ, and u.
Ensure: $\hat{E}$ and $\hat{T}$.
 1: **function** SEARCHBESTPART(p, T_{p-1}, K_{cur})
 2:     **if** $p = n + 1$ **then**
 3:         **if** $K_{\text{cur}} = 1$ **then**
 4:             **return** 0, [].
 5:         **else**
 6:             **return** ∞, [].
 7:         **end if**
 8:     **end if**
 9:     $L_{\text{cur}} \leftarrow \max(T_{p-1}, L_p)$.
10:     **if** $L_{\text{cur}} > U_p$ **then**
11:         **return** ∞, []
12:     **end if**
13:     $E_{\min} \leftarrow \infty$.
14:     **for** $T \leftarrow L_{\text{cur}}$ to U_p **do**
15:         $E_{\text{next}}, \tilde{T}_{p+1} \leftarrow$ SEARCHBESTPART($p+1$, T, $\lceil \frac{K_{\text{cur}}}{T} \rceil$).
16:         $E \leftarrow E_{\text{next}} + T^2 \rho_p$.
17:         **if** $E_{\min} > E$ **then**
18:             $E_{\min} \leftarrow E$.
19:             $\tilde{T}_p \leftarrow \left[T, \tilde{T}_{p+1} \right]$.
20:         **end if**
21:     **end for**
22:     **return** $E_{\min}$, $\tilde{T}_p$.
23: **end function**
24: $\hat{E}, \hat{T} \leftarrow$ SEARCHBESTPART($1, 1, 2^u$).
25: **return** $\hat{E}, \hat{T}$.

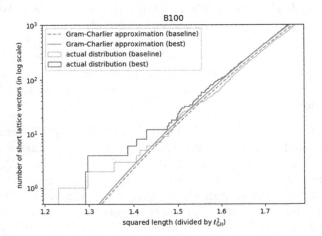

Fig. 1. Actual numbers and Gram-Charlier approximation of short lattice vectors from B100 (the bases with $n = 100$) over the baseline (2^{28}) and the best search space.

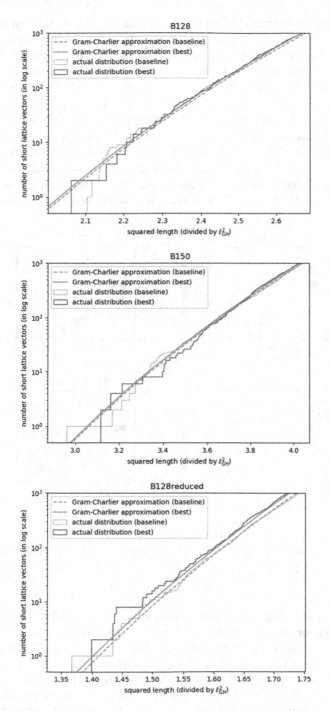

Fig. 2. Actual numbers and Gram-Charlier approximation of short lattice vectors from B128, B150, and B128reduced over the baseline (2^{28}) and the best search space.

space is always larger than that over the baseline. It suggests the validity of BSA. Figure 1 also shows the best search space tends to find more very short lattice vectors actually. The actual number of quite short lattice vectors is fluctuating because it is determined probabilistically. Actually, the shortest lattice vector of the baseline is shorter than that of the best search space. Nevertheless, the actual number over the best space is larger than that over the baseline in almost all lengths. Figure 2 shows the results for B128, B150, and B128reduced. It shows that there is not much difference between the best search space and the baseline for B128 and B150. The actual number seems to be fluctuating irrespective of the search space. On the other hand, the best search space seems to be superior to the baseline for B128reduced. Those results suggest that the best search space is useful for a relatively small lattice basis and a reduced lattice basis.

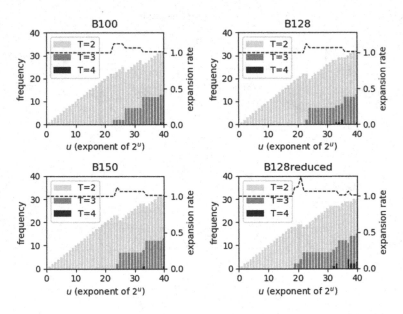

Fig. 3. Cumulative bar chart of the frequency of T_i in the best search space of the four bases for various u (from 1 to 40): The curves (scaled by the right axis) show the expansion rate $V\left(\hat{T}\right)/2^u$.

In order to investigate the best search space furthermore, its behavior was observed for changing u from 1 to 40. Figure 3 shows the frequency of each value of T_i in the best search space for various u. The results are similar in all the four bases. It shows that the best search space is completely equivalent to the baseline for relatively small u (around $u < 20$). As u is larger, the number of relatively large T_i is larger. The maximum of T_i was 4. Figure 3 also shows the expansion rate of the size of the best search space in proportion to the baseline 2^u. It shows that the expansion rate is always near to 1. It verifies that the relaxation of the size constraint is useful. Figure 4 shows the mean of the distribution for the best

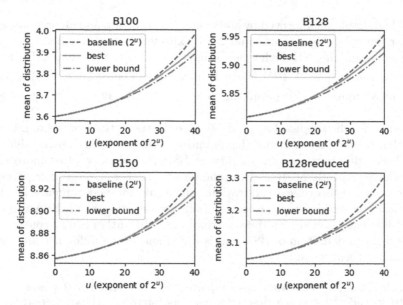

Fig. 4. Mean of the distribution of the squared lengths over the best search space and the baseline for various u (from 1 to 40): The theoretical lower bound without the integer constraint is also shown. The left axis is divided by ℓ_{GH}^2.

search space and the baseline. Under BSA, as the mean is lower, the number of very short lattice vector is larger. The qualitative results are similar in the four bases. If u is relatively small (around $u < 20$), the mean for the best search space is approximately equal to that for the baseline and the theoretical lower bound. As u is larger, the theoretical lower bound is lower than the baseline. In addition, the mean for the search space is nearer to the theoretical bound for relatively large u (around $u = 40$). These results are consistent with Fig. 3. On the other hand, the quantitative results are different among the four bases. The scale of the left axis (regularized by ℓ_{GH}^2) is relatively large in B100 and B128reduced. It is small in B128 and B150. These results are consistent with the relatively large fluctuations in B128 and B150 as shown in Fig. 2.

5   Conclusion

In this paper, a new method is proposed, which finds approximately the best search space in the random sampling. This method is based on the probabilistic approach for SVP under RA. The experimental results show that the proposed method is effective for a small lattice basis and a reduced one.

The proposed method is not so time consuming and can be easily implemented in any algorithm including the random sampling. Therefore, the author is planning to utilize this method for accelerating the sampling reduction algorithms such as [20] and solving high-dimensional SVP in [16]. For this purpose, the method should be improved by additional experimental and algorithmic analysis. For example, Algorithms 1 and 2 are expected to be simplified as a linear integer programming with higher performance. For another example, though the size of the search space $V\left(\hat{T}\right)$ is constrained to be a constant K in this paper, the adaptive tuning of K is promising to accelerate the sampling reduction algorithms.

In addition, the proposed method can give the theoretical lower bound. Now, the author is planning to utilize this bound for estimating the general difficulty of SVP. For this purpose, the validity of BSA should be verified more rigorously. The asymptotic analysis using the Gram-Charlier A series is expected to be crucial to the theoretical verification. The asymptotic convergence has been theoretically proved for a single distribution. On the other hand, BSA is related to the "difference" among multiple distributions. The author is now constructing a more rigorous definition of BSA and is investigating the difference among the distributions theoretically.

Acknowledgments. This work was supported by JSPS KAKENHI Grant Number JP20H04190 and "Joint Usage/Research Center for Interdisciplinary Large-scale Information Infrastructures" in Japan (Project ID: jh200005). The author is grateful to Dr. Tadanori Teruya for valuable comments.

References

1. Ajtai, M., Kumar, R., Sivakumar, D.: A sieve algorithm for the shortest lattice vector problem. In: Proceedings of the Thirty-third Annual ACM Symposium on Theory of Computing, STOC 2001, pp. 601–610. ACM, New York (2001). https://doi.org/10.1145/380752.380857
2. Albrecht, M.R., Ducas, L., Herold, G., Kirshanova, E., Postlethwaite, E.W., Stevens, M.: The general sieve kernel and new records in lattice reduction. Cryptology ePrint Archive, Report 2019/089 (2019). https://eprint.iacr.org/2019/089
3. Aono, Y., Nguyen, P.Q.: Random sampling revisited: lattice enumeration with discrete pruning. In: Coron, J.-S., Nielsen, J.B. (eds.) EUROCRYPT 2017. LNCS, vol. 10211, pp. 65–102. Springer, Cham (2017). https://doi.org/10.1007/978-3-319-56614-6_3
4. Buchmann, J., Ludwig, C.: Practical lattice basis sampling reduction. In: Hess, F., Pauli, S., Pohst, M. (eds.) ANTS 2006. LNCS, vol. 4076, pp. 222–237. Springer, Heidelberg (2006). https://doi.org/10.1007/11792086_17
5. Cramér, H.: Mathematical Methods of Statistics. Princeton Mathematical Series. Princeton University Press, Princeton (1946)
6. Fincke, U., Pohst, M.: Improved methods for calculating vectors of short length in a lattice, including a complexity analysis. Math. Comput. **44**(170), 463–471 (1985)
7. Fukase, M., Kashiwabara, K.: An accelerated algorithm for solving SVP based on statistical analysis. JIP **23**, 67–80 (2015)
8. Gama, N., Nguyen, P.Q., Regev, O.: Lattice enumeration using extreme pruning. In: Gilbert, H. (ed.) EUROCRYPT 2010. LNCS, vol. 6110, pp. 257–278. Springer, Heidelberg (2010). https://doi.org/10.1007/978-3-642-13190-5_13
9. Goldstein, D., Mayer, A.: On the equidistribution of hecke points. Forum Mathematicum **15**, 165–189 (2006)

10. Hoffstein, J.: Additional topics in cryptography. An Introduction to Mathematical Cryptography. UTM, pp. 1–23. Springer, New York (2008). https://doi.org/10.1007/978-0-387-77993-5_8
11. Kannan, R.: Improved algorithms for integer programming and related lattice problems. In: Proceedings of the Fifteenth Annual ACM Symposium on Theory of Computing, STOC 1983, pp. 193–206. ACM, New York (1983). https://doi.org/10.1145/800061.808749
12. Lenstra, A., Lenstra, H., Lovász, L.: Factoring polynomials with rational coefficients. Math. Ann. **261**(4), 515–534 (1982)
13. Ludwig, C.: Practical lattice basis sampling reduction. Ph.D. thesis, Technische Universität Darmstadt (2006)
14. Matsuda, Y., Teruya, T., Kashiwabara, K.: Efficient estimation of number of short lattice vectors in search space under randomness assumption. In: Proceedings of the 6th on ASIA Public-Key Cryptography Workshop. APKC 2019, pp. 13–22. Association for Computing Machinery, New York (2019). https://doi.org/10.1145/3327958.3329543
15. Matsuda, Y., Teruya, T., Kasiwabara, K.: Estimation of the success probability of random sampling by the gram-charlier approximation. Cryptology ePrint Archive, Report 2018/815 (2018). https://eprint.iacr.org/2018/815
16. Schneider, M., Gama, N.: SVP challenge. https://www.latticechallenge.org/svp-challenge/
17. Schnorr, C.P., Euchner, M.: Lattice basis reduction: improved practical algorithms and solving subset sum problems. Math. Program. **66**(2), 181–199 (1994). https://doi.org/10.1007/BF01581144
18. Schnorr, C.P.: Lattice reduction by random sampling and birthday methods. In: Alt, H., Habib, M. (eds.) STACS 2003. LNCS, vol. 2607, pp. 145–156. Springer, Heidelberg (2003). https://doi.org/10.1007/3-540-36494-3_14
19. Teruya, T.: An observation on the randomness assumption over lattices. In: 2018 International Symposium on Information Theory and Its Applications (ISITA), pp. 311–315 (2018)
20. Teruya, T., Kashiwabara, K., Hanaoka, G.: Fast lattice basis reduction suitable for massive parallelization and its application to the shortest vector problem. In: Public-Key Cryptography - PKC 2018–21st IACR International Conference on Practice and Theory of Public-Key Cryptography, Rio de Janeiro, Brazil, March 25–29, 2018, Proceedings, Part I, pp. 437–460 (2018)
21. The FPLLL development team: fplll, a lattice reduction library (2016). https://github.com/fplll/fplll
22. Wallace, D.L.: Asymptotic approximations to distributions. Ann. Math. Statist. **29**(3), 635–654 (1958). https://doi.org/10.1214/aoms/1177706528

Symmetric-Key Cryptography 2

Sublinear Bounds on the Distinguishing Advantage for Multiple Samples

Serge Fehr[1,2] and Serge Vaudenay[3]([✉])

[1] CWI, Amsterdam, The Netherlands
serge.fehr@cwi.nl
[2] Mathematical Institute, Leiden University, Leiden, The Netherlands
[3] EPFL, Lausanne, Switzerland
serge.vaudenay@epfl.ch

Abstract. The maximal achievable advantage of a (computationally unbounded) distinguisher to determine whether a source Z is distributed according to distribution P_0 or P_1, when given access to *one* sample of Z, is characterized by the statistical distance $d(P_0, P_1)$. Here, we study the distinguishing advantage when given access to *several i.i.d. samples* of Z. For n samples, the advantage is then naturally given by $d(P_0^{\otimes n}, P_1^{\otimes n})$, which can be bounded as $d(P_0^{\otimes n}, P_1^{\otimes n}) \leq n \cdot d(P_0, P_1)$. This bound is tight for some choices of P_0 and P_1; thus, *in general*, a linear increase in the distinguishing advantage is unavoidable.

In this work, we show new and improved bounds on $d(P_0^{\otimes n}, P_1^{\otimes n})$ that circumvent the above pessimistic observation. Our bounds assume, necessarily, certain additional information on P_0 and/or P_1 beyond, or instead of, a bound on $d(P_0, P_1)$; in return, the bounds grow as $\sqrt{n}$, rather than linearly in n. Thus, whenever applicable, our bounds show that the number of samples necessary to distinguish the two distributions is substantially larger than what the standard bound would suggest.

Such bounds have already been suggested in previous literature, but our new bounds are more general and (partly) stronger, and thus applicable to a larger class of instances.

In a second part, we extend our results to a modified setting, where the distinguisher only has *indirect* access to the source Z. By this we mean that instead of obtaining samples of Z, the distinguisher now obtains i.i.d. samples that are chosen according to a probability distribution that depends on the (one) value produced by the source Z.

Finally, we offer applications of our bounds to the area of cryptography. We show on a few examples from the cryptographic literature how our bounds give rise to improved results. For instance, importing our bounds into the analyses of Blondeau et al. for the security of block ciphers against multidimensional linear and truncated differential attacks, we obtain immediate improvements to their results.

© Springer Nature Switzerland AG 2020
K. Aoki and A. Kanaoka (Eds.): IWSEC 2020, LNCS 12231, pp. 165–183, 2020.
https://doi.org/10.1007/978-3-030-58208-1_10

1   Introduction

1.1   Motivation and Background

(In)distinguishability of probability distributions is a concept that is of fundamental importance in cryptography, for instance in the context of defining and
analyzing security of cryptographic schemes. It is well known that for a computationally unbounded distinguisher, given access to *one* sample of the source
(i.e. random variable) Z in question, the maximal achievable advantage in distinguishing whether Z is distributed according to distribution P_0 or P_1, is given
by the statistical distance

$$d(P_0, P_1) = \frac{1}{2} \sum_z |P_0(z) - P_1(z)| \,.$$

If the distinguisher has access to *multiple* samples $Z_1, \ldots, Z_n$ instead, each Z_i
being *identically and independently distributed* (i.i.d) according to P_0 or P_1, the
best distinguishing advantage is then given by the statistical distance of the
respective product distributions $P_b^{\otimes n}(z_1, \ldots, z_n) := P_b(z_1) \cdots P_b(z_n)$. Unfortunately, in general it is not easy to estimate $d(P_0^{\otimes n}, P_1^{\otimes n})$; a simple and commonly
used bound is

$$d(P_0^{\otimes n}, P_1^{\otimes n}) \leq n \cdot d(P_0, P_1) \,. \tag{1}$$

This bound is very useful in that it is universally applicable, and in case no
more information on P_0 and P_1 is available, it is the best one can hope for.
E.g., if P_0 and P_1 are Boolean distributions with $P_0(1) = \epsilon$ and $P_1(1) = 0$, then
$d(P_0, P_1) = \epsilon$ and $d(P_0^{\otimes n}, P_1^{\otimes n}) = 1 - (1 - \epsilon)^n \approx n\epsilon$ when $\epsilon \ll \frac{1}{n}$. Thus, the
bound (1) is tight *in general*, if one has no additional information on P_0 and P_1.

However, in typical examples, one would expect to have some more information available on P_0 and P_1. In such cases, one may then hope for a better
bound on the distinguishing advantage. Indeed, a few examples are known. For
instance, Vaudenay [10] showed that for Boolean distributions and P_1 being the
uniform distribution U, the bound

$$d(P_0^{\otimes n}, U^{\otimes n}) \leq 4\sqrt{n} \cdot d(P_0, U) \tag{2}$$

holds. A somewhat generalized variant of this is by Renner [8], which states that
for any pair of (not necessarily Boolean) distributions, it holds that

$$d(P_0^{\otimes n}, P_1^{\otimes n}) \leq \sqrt{\frac{n}{2\bar{p}}} \cdot d(P_0, P_1) \tag{3}$$

where $\bar{p} := \min_z \min\{P_0(z), P_1(z)\}$ and the outer min is over all z with $P_0(z) \neq P_1(z)$. Finally, one can also obtain a bound that grows with $\sqrt{n}$ by means of
the *Rényi divergence* D_α. Indeed, using basic properties of D_α, and applying
Gilardoni's inequality [3,5] if $0 < \alpha < 1$, and *Pinsker's inequality* if $\alpha = 1$, one
immediately obtains the bound

$$d(P_0^{\otimes n}, P_1^{\otimes n}) \leq \sqrt{n} \cdot \sqrt{\frac{1}{2\alpha} D_\alpha(P_0 \| P_1)}$$

for α in the range $0 < \alpha \leq 1$. The case $\alpha = 1$, where the Rényi divergence is referred to as *Kullback-Leibler Divergence* (or KL divergence), was for instance used by Pöppelmann, Ducas, and Güneysu [6,7, Lemma 1].

In our work here, we give new support to this general hypothesis: we show new, non-trivial bounds on $d(P_0^{\otimes n}, P_1^{\otimes n})$ that apply if one has some more control over P_0 and P_1, beyond—or instead of—a bound on $d(P_0, P_1)$. Our bounds can be appreciated as generalizations and unification of (2) and (3) above.

Like the above examples, all our bounds, when applicable, show that the distinguishing advantage grows as $\sqrt{n}$ only, compared to the linear growth implied by (1). This means that in those cases, the number of samples necessary to distinguish the two distributions is substantially larger than what the bound (1) would suggest, i.e. quadratically more samples are actually needed. We discuss this on several concrete examples from the cryptographic literature, and we show how our new bounds give immediate rise to improved results.

Next to the concrete technical results and the applications discussed below, the goal of this work is to showcase the usefulness in the area of cryptography of the various notions of distance measures and their relations as studied in pure information theory (see e.g. [9] and the reference therein).

1.2   Our Technical Results

New Bounds on the Distinguishing Advantage. We show new bounds on the distinguishing advantage when given access to n i.i.d. samples. Our first bound is a generalization (and slight improvement) of (2) that applies also for a non-uniform P_1; it shows that for any two Boolean distributions

$$d(P_0^{\otimes n}, P_1^{\otimes n}) \leq \sqrt{\frac{n}{2q(1-q)}}\, d(P_0, P_1) \tag{4}$$

where $q := P_1(0)$.

Our second bound removes the condition on the distributions being Boolean and is in terms of the 2-distance of P_0 and P_1. It states that

$$d(P_0^{\otimes n}, P_1^{\otimes n}) \leq \sqrt{\frac{n}{2\min_{z \in \Delta} P_1(z)}} \cdot \|P_0 - P_1\|_2\,, \tag{5}$$

where $\Delta = \{z \in \mathcal{Z} \; : \; P_0(z) \neq P_1(z)\}$. This improves upon Renner's bound (3) in that it requires control over the small probabilities of *one* of the two distributions only, and in that the 2-distance may be substantially smaller than the statistical distance. Also, compared to Renner's proof of (3), which relies on a cumbersome derivative estimation [8, Lemma 2.2] that goes over two pages, our proof is significantly simpler.

Using that $\|P_0 - P_1\|_2 \leq 2d(P_0, P_1)$, we thus obtain the bound

$$d(P_0^{\otimes n}, P_1^{\otimes n}) \leq \sqrt{\frac{2n}{\min_{z \in \Delta} P_1(z)}} \cdot d(P_0, P_1)\,, \tag{6}$$

which still requires control over the small probabilities of one of the two distributions only, but it is slightly worse in the constant factor than (3).

Finally, applying (5) to $P_1 = U$, the uniform distribution over $\mathcal{Z}$, and setting $N = \#\mathcal{Z}$, we obtain the bound

$$d(P_0^{\otimes n}, U^{\otimes n}) \leq \sqrt{\frac{nN}{2}} \cdot \|P_0 - U\|_2 \leq \sqrt{2nN} \cdot d(P_0, U), \tag{7}$$

which again can be appreciated as a generalization (and slight improvement) of Vaudenay's bound (2), now to non-Boolean distributions.

Sources with Indirect Access. We also study a variation of the setting discussed so far, where we considered a distinguisher with *direct access* to the source. Here, we show extensions of our results, i.e., bounds on the distinguishing advantage that grow as $\sqrt{n}$, when the distinguisher has *indirect* access only to the source.

Here, the distinguisher's goal is still to decide if a source Z is distributed according to one or another distribution, which we now refer to as Q_0 and Q_1, but now he needs to do so by means of samples $W_1, \ldots, W_n$ that are obtained as follows: conditioned on that $Z = z$, which happens with probability either $Q_0(z)$ or $Q_1(z)$, the samples W_i are i.i.d. according to a distribution P_z that *depends on z*. Formally, given that Z has distribution Q_b, the joint distribution of $W_1, \ldots, W_n$ is given by $\bar{P}_b^n := \sum_z Q_b(z) P_z^{\otimes n}$.

This setting naturally occurs in cryptography. E.g., let Z be the key of a cipher following either a distribution Q_0 or a distribution Q_1. If we assume that the adversary obtains random plaintext/ciphertext pairs W_i for that key, and lets say that the adversary wants to determine one bit of the secret (namely, whether it followed Q_0 or Q_1), then $d(\bar{P}_0^n, \bar{P}_1^n)$ offers a bound on the adversary's advantage.

Based on our bounds above, we show two bounds on $d(\bar{P}_0^n, \bar{P}_1^n)$, which both grow as $\sqrt{n}$. Like (4), (7) and (6) above, they differ in what kind of additional information is needed on the distributions Q_0 and Q_1, and on $\{P_z\}_{z \in \mathcal{Z}}$, for the bound to be meaningful. For the details, we refer to Sect. 4.

1.3   Applications

We show three immediate applications of our new bounds in the area of cryptography. The first two applications improve on the results of Blondeau et al. [1]. The first one is an improvement on the security bound for *multidimensional linear cryptanalysis* derived in [1], and the second application is an improvement on the security bound for *truncated differential cryptanalysis* derived in [1]. In both cases, our techniques apply very directly and enable to improve both bounds by a factor $\sqrt{n}$. Interestingly, such improvements were actually anticipated by Blondeau et al., but proving them was outside the scope of their techniques. We thus solve the open problems mentioned in [1].

The third application is to *decorrelation theory*, as introduced by Vaudenay [10]. By means of our bounds, we can improve the bound in [10] by a factor $\Theta(n^{1/6})$. This enables to prove the security of ciphers against iterated attacks for a larger number of iterations than was known before.

2 Preliminaries

2.1 The p-Norm and the Statistical Distance

Throughout the document, $\mathcal{Z}$ is a finite, non-empty set. We recall that for parameter $1 \leq p \leq \infty$, the p-norm of a function $f : \mathcal{Z} \to \mathbb{R}$ is defined as

$$\|f\|_p := \left(\sum_{z \in \mathcal{Z}} |f(z)|^p \right)^{1/p},$$

with the natural understanding that $\|f\|_\infty = \max_z |f(z)|$.

The definition of the p-norm obviously applies to *distributions* as well, i.e., to functions $P : \mathcal{Z} \to [0,1]$ with $\sum_z P(z) = \|P\|_1 = 1$. In particular, the *statistical distance* of two distributions $P_0, P_1 : \mathcal{Z} \to [0,1]$ is defined as

$$d(P_0, P_1) := \frac{1}{2}\|P_0 - P_1\|_1 = \frac{1}{2}\sum_z |P_0(z) - P_1(z)|.$$

We recall some basic properties of the statistical distance that are relevant for us. From the well-known fact that the statistical distance equals the *total variation distance*, i.e., $d(P_0, P_1) = \max_{E \subseteq \mathcal{Z}} |P_0(E) - P_1(E)|$, it follows that the statistical distance measures the maximal distinguishing advantage for (computationally unbounded) distinguishers that obtain one sample.

The statistical distance is *jointly convex*: if P_0^i and P_1^i are distributions that depend on some parameter $i \in \mathcal{I}$, and $\bar{P}_0 := \sum_i Q(i) P_0^i$ and $\bar{P}_1 := \sum_i Q(i) P_1^i$ are the corresponding mixtures with respect to distribution $Q : \mathcal{I} \to [0,1]$, then

$$d(\bar{P}_0, \bar{P}_1) \leq \sum_i Q(i) \, d(P_0^i, P_1^i). \tag{8}$$

This follows immediately from basic properties of the 1-norm.

Finally, it is easy to see that $d(P_0 \otimes P', P_1 \otimes P') = d(P_0, P_1)$, where a *product distribution* $P \otimes P'$ is defined by $P \otimes P' : \mathcal{Z} \times \mathcal{Z}' \to [0,1]$, $(z, z') \mapsto P(z)P'(z')$. Together with the triangular inequality, this implies *subadditivity* for product distributions, i.e., $d(P_0 \otimes P_0', P_1 \otimes P_1') \leq d(P_0, P_1) + d(P_0', P_1')$. Thus, in particular, writing $P^{\otimes n}$ for $P \otimes \cdots \otimes P$ (n times), we get inequality (1).

2.2 The Kullback-Leibler and the Rényi Divergence

The *Kullback-Leibler divergence* (or KL divergence) between two distributions $P_0, P_1 : \mathcal{Z} \to [0,1]$ is defined by

$$D_{\mathsf{KL}}(P_0\|P_1) = \sum_{\substack{z \in \mathcal{Z} \\ P_0(z)>0}} P_0(z) \ln \frac{P_0(z)}{P_1(z)},$$

with the convention that $D_{KL}(P_0\|P_1) = \infty$ if the support of P_0 is not included in the support of P_1.

The Kullback-Leibler divergence is additive in the sense that

$$D_{KL}(P_0 \otimes Q_0 \| P_1 \otimes Q_1) = D_{KL}(P_0\|P_1) + D_{KL}(Q_0\|Q_1).$$

Consequently, we have

$$D_{KL}(P_0^{\otimes n} \| P_1^{\otimes n}) = n \cdot D_{KL}(P_0\|P_1).$$

It relates to the statistical distance as follows.

Theorem 1 (Pinsker inequality). *For any two distributions P_0 and P_1, we have*

$$d(P_0, P_1) \leq \sqrt{\frac{1}{2}D_{KL}(P_0\|P_1)}.$$

The Kullback-Leibler divergence is a special case of the *Rényi divergence*

$$D_\alpha(P_0\|P_1) = \frac{1}{\alpha - 1} \ln \sum_{\substack{z \in \mathcal{Z} \\ P_0(z)>0}} P_0(z)^\alpha P_1(z)^{1-\alpha},$$

defined for any $0 < \alpha \neq 1$, where the Kullback-Leibler divergence is recovered in the limit $\alpha \to 1$. Like the Kullback-Leibler divergence, the Rényi divergence is additive, and the Pinsker inequality generalizes as follows.

Theorem 2 (Gilardoni inequality [3,5]). *For any two distributions P_0 and P_1 and $0 < \alpha < 1$, we have*

$$d(P_0, P_1) \leq \sqrt{\frac{1}{2\alpha}D_\alpha(P_0\|P_1)}.$$

2.3   The Neyman Divergence

We also make use of the *Neyman χ^2 divergence*, which we denote by D_N. For distributions $P_0, P_1 : \mathcal{Z} \to [0,1]$, it is defined as

$$D_N(P_0\|P_1) = \sum_{\substack{z \in \mathcal{Z} \\ P_1(z)>0}} \frac{\left(P_0(z) - P_1(z)\right)^2}{P_1(z)},$$

with the convention that $D_N(P_0\|P_1) = \infty$ if the support of P_0 is not included in the support of P_1.

Theorem 3. *For any two distributions P_0 and P_1, we have*

$$D_{KL}(P_0\|P_1) \leq D_N(P_0\|P_1).$$

This was proven by Dai et al. [2] but has been known in the information-theory community for longer (see e.g. [9]); we recall here the proof for completeness.

Proof. Multiplying out the square in the enumerator, we obtain

$$D_N(P_0\|P_1) = \sum_z \frac{P_0(z)^2}{P_1(z)} - 1 = e^{\ln\left(\sum_z \frac{P_0(z)^2}{P_1(z)}\right)} - 1$$

$$\geq \ln\left(\sum_z \frac{P_0(z)^2}{P_1(z)}\right) \geq \sum_z P_0(z) \ln \frac{P_0(z)}{P_1(z)} = D_{KL}(P_0\|P_1),$$

where the first inequality uses $e^x - 1 \geq x$, which is verified by having equality for $x = 0$ and comparing derivatives, and the second inequality is Jensen's inequality, exploiting concavity of ln. □

2.4   Warm-Up Observation

We discuss yet another distance measure for distributions $P_0, P_1 : \mathcal{Z} \to [0, 1]$. The *fidelity* of P_0 and P_1 (aka. *Bhattacharyya distance*) is defined as

$$F(P_0, P_1) := \sum_{z \in \mathcal{Z}} \sqrt{P_0(z)P_1(z)}.$$

Like the statistical distance, the fidelity of two distributions is always in the range 0 to 1; this follows immediately from the Chauchy-Schwarz inequality. We emphasize though that the fidelity is *not* a metric in the mathematical sense. In particular, $F(P_0, P_1)$ is *small* when P_0 and P_1 are *far apart*, and it is *large*, i.e. close to 1, when P_0 and P_1 are *close*. As a matter of fact, it turns out that $H(P_0, P_1) := \sqrt{1 - F(P_0, P_1)}$ is a metric, known as *Hellinger distance*. Nevertheless, it is useful to consider the fidelity directly as a measure of distance. Fidelity is related to the Rényi divergence of order $\frac{1}{2}$ by

$$D_{1/2}(P_0\|P_1) = -2\ln(F(P_0, P_1)).$$

Sometimes referred to as the *Fuchs – van de Graaf inequalities*, the following relates the fidelity to the statistical distance.

Theorem 4. *For distributions P_0 and P_1,*

$$1 - F(P_0, P_1) \leq d(P_0, P_1) \leq \sqrt{1 - F(P_0, P_1)^2}.$$

We conclude this brief introduction to the fidelity by pointing out that the fidelity is *multiplicative* for product distributions, and thus in particular

$$F(P_0^{\otimes n}, P_1^{\otimes n}) = F(P_0, P_1)^n. \tag{9}$$

We show here a simple standard application of the fidelity and its properties. A typical question is to wonder how many samples n are needed to distinguish two known distributions P_0 and P_1 with constant advantage t. Motivated by this question, let n_t be such that $n \geq n_t \iff d(P_0^{\otimes n}, P_1^{\otimes n}) \geq t$ hold for all n. Using (1), we only get the relatively crude bound $n_t \geq t/d(P_0, P_1)$. However, if we actually control the fidelity $F(P_0, P_1)$ and set[1] $\epsilon := -2\log_2(F(P_0, P_1))$ then we obtain from Theorem 4 and property (9) that

$$-\frac{1}{\epsilon}\log_2(1 - t^2) \leq n_t \leq -\frac{2}{\epsilon}\log_2(1 - t),$$

which is a much more precise estimate of the threshold number n_t. For instance, $n_{0.5}$ is in the range $0.41/\epsilon \leq n_{0.5} \leq 2/\epsilon$. In Appendix A, we work out a concrete application of this in the context of side-channel attacks.

3   Sublinear Bounds on the Statistical Distance

We present here our new bounds on the statistical distance of i.i.d. samples. At the core of the bounds is the following lemma.[2]

Lemma 5. *For any two distributions $P_0, P_1 : \{0, 1\} \to [0, 1]$ and any integer n,*

$$d(P_0^{\otimes n}, P_1^{\otimes n}) \leq \sqrt{\frac{n}{2}D_\mathsf{N}(P_0\|P_1)}.$$

Proof. We have

$$d(P_0^{\otimes n}, P_1^{\otimes n}) \leq \sqrt{\frac{1}{2}D_\mathsf{KL}(P_0^{\otimes n}\|P_1^{\otimes n})} = \sqrt{\frac{n}{2}D_\mathsf{KL}(P_0\|P_1)} \leq \sqrt{\frac{n}{2}D_\mathsf{N}(P_0\|P_1)},$$

where the first inequality is Pinsker's inequality, the equality is by the additivity of the Kullback-Leibler divergence, and the final inequality is by Theorem 3. $\square$

3.1   A Bound for Boolean Distributions

We first consider Boolean distributions.

Theorem 6. *Let $P_0, P_1 : \{0, 1\} \to [0, 1]$ be two Boolean distributions. Then*

$$d(P_0^{\otimes n}, P_1^{\otimes n}) \leq \sqrt{\frac{n}{2q(1 - q)}}\, d(P_0, P_1),$$

where $q := P_1(0)$.

We observe that in the special case of $P_1 = U$, the uniform distribution on $\{0, 1\}$, we recover a slightly improved version of the bound (2) from [10].

Proof. Setting $p := P_0(0)$ and $q := P_1(0)$, we have

$$D_\mathsf{N}(P_0\|P_1) = \frac{(p - q)^2}{q} + \frac{(q - p)^2}{1 - q} = \frac{(p - q)^2}{q(1 - q)} = \frac{d(P_0, P_1)^2}{q(1 - q)}.$$

The claim thus holds by Lemma 5. $\square$

---

[1] As a matter of fact, ϵ is the Rényi divergence measured in bits.
[2] This lemma was hinted at by an anonymous reviewer. It improves and simplifies on an earlier version of this paper.

3.2   Bounds for Non-Boolean Distributions

Here, we drop the assumption on the distributions P_0 and P_1 being Boolean but instead assume that we have control over the small probabilities of one of the two distributions. Concretely, we assume control over

$$\min{}_\Delta(P_1) := \min_{z \in \Delta} P_1(z)$$

where $\Delta := \Delta(P_0, P_1) := \{z \in \mathcal{Z} : P_0(z) \neq P_1(z)\}$. This is well defined for $P_0 \neq P_1$.

Theorem 7. *For different distributions* $P_0, P_1 : \mathcal{Z} \to [0,1]$ *and* $\min_\Delta(P_1)$ *as above,*

$$d(P_0^{\otimes n}, P_1^{\otimes n}) \leq \sqrt{\frac{n}{2 \min_\Delta(P_1)}} \cdot \|P_0 - P_1\|_2 .$$

Proof. If there exists $z \in \mathcal{Z}$ with $P_0(z) \neq 0 = P_1(z)$ then $\min_\Delta(P_1) = 0$ and the claim holds trivially, with the right hand side being ∞ then. If no such $z \in \mathcal{Z}$ exists then $D_{\mathsf{N}}(P_0 \| P_1)$ is finite and equal to

$$D_{\mathsf{N}}(P_0 \| P_1) = \sum_{\substack{z \in \mathcal{Z} \\ P_1(z) > 0}} \frac{(P_0(z) - P_1(z))^2}{P_1(z)} = \sum_{\substack{z \in \mathcal{Z} \\ P_0(z) \neq P_1(z) > 0}} \frac{(P_0(z) - P_1(z))^2}{P_1(z)}$$

$$\leq \sum_{z \in \mathcal{Z}} \frac{(P_0(z) - P_1(z))^2}{\min_\Delta(P_1)} = \frac{\|P_0 - P_1\|_2^2}{\min_\Delta(P_1)} .$$

The claimed bound then holds by Lemma 5. $\qquad\qquad\qquad\qquad\qquad\qquad\square$

Recalling that $\|P_0 - P_1\|_2 \leq 2d(P_0, P_1)$, we obtain the following.

Corollary 8. *For different distributions* $P_0, P_1 : \mathcal{Z} \to [0,1]$ *and* $\min_\Delta(P_1)$ *as above,*

$$d(P_0^{\otimes n}, P_1^{\otimes n}) \leq \sqrt{\frac{2n}{\min_\Delta(P_1)}} \cdot d(P_0, P_1) .$$

This bound can be appreciated as a variant of Renner's bound (3), which we rephrase here as

$$d(P_0^{\otimes n}, P_1^{\otimes n}) \leq \sqrt{\frac{n}{2 \min_\Delta(P_0 \cup P_1)}} \cdot d(P_0, P_1)$$

for

$$\min{}_\Delta(P_0 \cup P_1) := \min_{z \in \Delta} \min\{P_0(z), P_1(z)\} ,$$

where Δ is as above. Our new bound improves on this in that it requires control over the small probabilities of *one* of the two distributions only (but is slightly worse in the constant factor). Additionally, compared to Renner's result [8], we also have a substantially simpler proof.

Applying Theorem 7 to P_1 being the uniform distribution with $U(z) = 1/|\mathcal{Z}|$ for all $z \in \mathcal{Z}$, we obtain the following.

Corollary 9. *Let P_0 be a distribution over a set $\mathcal{Z}$ with cardinality $N := |\mathcal{Z}|$, and let U be the uniform distribution over the same set $\mathcal{Z}$. Then, we have*

$$d(P_0^{\otimes n}, U^{\otimes n}) \leq \sqrt{\frac{nN}{2}} \cdot \|P_0 - U\|_2 \leq \sqrt{2nN} \cdot d(P_0, U).$$

This as well can be appreciated as a generalization (and slight improvement) of the bound (2), now to non-Boolean distributions.

4   Indistinguishability for Sources with Indirect Access

The above bounds—on distinguishing whether a source Z is distributed according to P_0 or P_1—apply when the distinguisher has access to independently generated samples of Z. Here, we consider a variation of this problem where the distinguisher does not have direct access to the source Z, distributed according to Q_0 or Q_1; instead, the distinguisher obtains independent samples $W_1, \ldots, W_n$ of a source W that depends on Z. Formally, conditioned on the event $Z = z$, which happens with probability $Q_0(z)$ or $Q_1(z)$, the joint distribution of $W_1, \ldots, W_n$ is given by $P_z^{\otimes n}$, where $\{P_z\}_{z \in \mathcal{Z}}$ is a given family of distributions over a set $\mathcal{W}$. Algorithmically, for a fixed guessing function f, the task of distinguishing Q_0 from Q_1 in this setting can be captured as illustrated in Fig. 1, and the maximal distinguishing advantage is given by $d(\bar{P}_0^n, \bar{P}_1^n)$, where $\bar{P}_b^n := \sum_z Q_b(z) P_z^{\otimes n}$.

Distinguisher:
1: pick z following Q_b
2: **for** $i = 1$ to n **do**
3:     pick w_i following P_z
4: **end for**
5: output $f(w_1, \ldots, w_n)$

Fig. 1. Distinguisher with indirect access to Z.

Below and for the remainder, we use the following notation. Assuming the range $\mathcal{Z}$ of Z to be in $\mathbb{R}$, and given that Z is distributed according to Q (which will either be Q_0 or Q_1), we let $E(Z)$ be the *expectation*, i.e., $E(Z) := \sum_z Q(z) \, z$, and correspondingly $E(g(Z)) := \sum_z Q(z) \, g(z)$ for any function g on $\mathbb{R}$. Similarly, $V(Z)$ denotes the *variance* $V(Z) := E\big((Z - E(Z))^2\big) = E(Z^2) - E(Z)^2$. If we want to make Q explicit, we write $E_Q(Z)$, $E_Q(g(Z))$ and $V_Q(Z)$ instead. This notation generalizes to Z with range $\mathcal{Z}$ in an arbitrary vector space (with a given 2-norm): E is obvious, and V then becomes $V(Z) := E\big(\|Z - E(Z)\|_2^2\big)$.

4.1   The Boolean Case

We first consider the case of Boolean samples, i.e., where the W_i's have values in $\{0,1\}$. Since P_z is fully defined by $P_z(1)$ then, we may assume without loss of generality that $\mathcal{Z} \subset [0,1] \subset \mathbb{R}$ and $P_z(1) = z$ for any $z \in \mathcal{Z}$. In other words, the output of the source not only determines but *equals* the probability of each sample to be 1.

For $n = 1$ and guessing function $f(w_1) = w_1$, the distinguishing advantage is given by $E_{Q_0}(Z) - E_{Q_1}(Z)$. For $n = 2$ and $f(w_1, w_2) = w_1 w_2$, the advantage is

$$E_{Q_0}(Z^2) - E_{Q_1}(Z^2) = V_{Q_0}(Z) - V_{Q_1}(Z) + E_{Q_0}(Z)^2 - E_{Q_1}(Z)^2.$$

Therefore, to keep the advantage low for arbitrary distinguishers, we obviously need $E_{Q_0}(Z) \approx E_{Q_1}(Z)$ (due to the $n = 1$ case) and $V_{Q_0}(Z) \approx V_{Q_1}(Z)$ (due to the $n = 2$ case). These two conditions are necessary. We show below that these conditions, and the assumption that the two variances are small, are also *sufficient* for indistinguishability.

Theorem 10. *Let Q_0 and Q_1 be two distributions for Z, and let $\{P_z\}_{z \in \mathcal{Z}}$ be a family of Boolean distributions. Then, for any n and for $\bar{P}_0^n$ and $\bar{P}_1^n$ defined as above,*

$$d(\bar{P}_0^n, \bar{P}_1^n) \leq \sqrt{\frac{n}{2}} \cdot \frac{\sqrt{V_{Q_0}(Z) + (E_{Q_0}(Z) - E_{Q_1}(Z))^2} + \sqrt{V_{Q_1}(Z)}}{\sqrt{E_{Q_1}(Z)(1 - E_{Q_1}(Z))}}$$

We will show in Section 5.3 a direct application of this to [10].

Proof. Recall that the source Z takes values $0 \leq z \leq 1$, and for any such z, P_z is a Boolean distribution with $P_z(1) = z$. For an arbitrary but fixed $0 \leq \mu \leq 1$, we also consider the Boolean distribution P_μ with $P_\mu(1) = \mu$. Applying Theorem 6, we obtain

$$d(P_z^{\otimes n}, P_\mu^{\otimes n}) \leq \sqrt{\frac{n}{2\mu(1 - \mu)}}\, d(P_z, P_\mu) = \sqrt{n \frac{(z - \mu)^2}{2\mu(1 - \mu)}}.$$

By convexity (8) of the statistical distance, and applying Jensen inequality with $\sqrt{\cdot}$ and using that $E((Z - \mu)^2) = V(Z) + (E(Z) - \mu)^2$, we obtain

$$d(\bar{P}_b^n, P_\mu^{\otimes n}) \leq E_{Q_b}(d(P_Z^{\otimes n}, P_\mu^{\otimes n})) \leq \sqrt{n \frac{V_{Q_b}(Z) + (E_{Q_b}(Z) - \mu)^2}{2\mu(1 - \mu)}}$$

for $b \in \{0,1\}$. Hence, by triangular inequality,

$$d(\bar{P}_0^n, \bar{P}_1^n) \leq \sqrt{n \frac{V_{Q_0}(Z) + (E_{Q_0}(Z) - \mu)^2}{2\mu(1 - \mu)}} + \sqrt{n \frac{V_{Q_1}(Z) + (E_{Q_1}(Z) - \mu)^2}{2\mu(1 - \mu)}}.$$

This holds for any μ. We can apply it to $\mu = E_{Q_1}(Z)$ and obtain the result. $\square$

4.2   The Non-Boolean Case

Here, we consider the non-Boolean case where the samples W_i have range $\mathcal{W}$ of arbitrary size N. Our result gives a meaningful bound if the distributions P_z are close to uniform on average.

Theorem 11. *Let Q_0 and Q_1 be two distributions for Z, and let $\{P_z\}_{z \in \mathcal{Z}}$ be a family of distributions over a set of size N. Then, for any n and for $\bar{P}_0^n$ and $\bar{P}_1^n$ defined as above,*

$$d(\bar{P}_0^n, \bar{P}_1^n) \leq \sqrt{\frac{nN}{2}} \cdot \left(E_{Q_0}(\|P_Z - U\|_2) + E_{Q_1}(\|P_Z - U\|_2) \right).$$

For clarification, given that Z is a random variable, we recall that P_Z is a random variable as well; its range being $\{P_z : z \in \mathcal{Z}\}$, a subset of the distributions over $\mathcal{W}$. As such, $\|P_Z - U\|_2$ is then a real-valued random variable, and so its expectation is well defined.

Proof. Applying Corollary 9, we have $d(P_z^{\otimes n}, U^{\otimes n}) \leq \sqrt{\frac{nN}{2}} \cdot \|P_z - U\|_2$, and by convexity (8) of the statistical distance, we then obtain

$$d(\bar{P}_b^n, U^{\otimes n}) \leq E_{Q_b}(d(P_Z^{\otimes n}, U^{\otimes n})) \leq \sqrt{\frac{nN}{2}} \cdot E_{Q_b}(\|P_Z - U\|_2).$$

The claim then follows from triangular inequality. □

5   Applications

We discuss three direct applications of our new bounds in the context of block-cipher security, giving rise to immediate improvements to results in [1] and [10].

5.1   Resistance to Multidimensional Linear Cryptanalysis

As a first application, we improve the security bound from Blondeau et al. [1] against *multidimensional linear* (ML) cryptanalysis. As considered in [1], for a block cipher Enc over ℓ-bit blocks and a vector subspace V of $\{0,1\}^\ell \times \{0,1\}^\ell$ spanned by a basis $(\alpha_1, \beta_1), \ldots, (\alpha_k, \beta_k)$, the so-called *linear masks*, an *ML distinguisher* works as described in Fig. 2. We refer to [1] for the motivation and for additional explanations.

Adopting the notation from Blondeau et al. [1], we write $p_{\mathsf{Enc}}^{\mathsf{ML}}$ for the probability that the distinguisher outputs 1 using Enc with an arbitrary but *fixed* key, and we write $p_{C_K}^{\mathsf{ML}}$ for the same probability but now considered as a random variable with the randomness stemming from the random choice of the key. We note that for Enc with a fixed key, the b_i's are i.i.d. over $\{0,1\}^k$, and we denote the distribution of one b_i by D_{Enc} then.

Distinguisher ML with oracle Enc:

1: **for** $i = 1$ to n **do**
2:    pick a random $x \in \{0,1\}^{\ell}$
3:    set $y = \mathsf{Enc}(x)$
4:    **for** $j = 1$ to k **do**
5:       set $b_{i,j} = (\alpha_j \cdot x) \oplus (\beta_j \cdot y)$
6:    **end for**
7:    set $b_i = (b_{i,1}, \ldots, b_{i,k})$
8: **end for**
9: output $f(b_1, \ldots, b_n)$

Fig. 2. ML distinguisher

In [1, Thm. 19], it is shown that[3]

$$\left| E(p_{C_K}^{\mathsf{ML}}) - E(p_{C^*}^{\mathsf{ML}}) \right| \leq n\sqrt{2^k} \sqrt{2^{-\ell} + \frac{1}{4} \left\| [C_K]^2 - [C^*]^2 \right\|_{\infty}} \tag{10}$$

where $\left\| [C_K]^2 - [C^*]^2 \right\|_{\infty}$ denotes the *decorrelation of order 2*, i.e., twice the best non-adaptive advantage to distinguish the cipher C_K from a uniformly random permutation C^* using two queries. Our results allow us to improve this bound by a factor $\sqrt{2n}$.

At the core of the proof in [1] is the observation that for any two fixed encryption functions Enc and Enc*(with fixed keys), by [1, Lemma 14] and triangular inequality,

$$\left| p_{\mathsf{Enc}}^{\mathsf{ML}} - p_{\mathsf{Enc}^*}^{\mathsf{ML}} \right| \leq \frac{n}{2} \sqrt{2^k} \| D_{\mathsf{Enc}} - D_{\mathsf{Enc}^*} \|_2 \leq \frac{n}{2} \sqrt{2^k} \left(\| D_{\mathsf{Enc}} - U \|_2 + \| D_{\mathsf{Enc}^*} - U \|_2 \right),$$

and then these 2-norms are further worked out, using [1, Lemma 12] etc. How exactly the bound (10) is then derived in [1] is not so important here; what is important is that the factor n from above directly carries into (10).

Our improvement is now to apply triangular inequality to $d(D_{\mathsf{Enc}}, D_{\mathsf{Enc}^*})$ and then invoke Corollary 9 to show that

$$\left| p_{\mathsf{Enc}}^{\mathsf{ML}} - p_{\mathsf{Enc}^*}^{\mathsf{ML}} \right| \leq \sqrt{n 2^{k-1}} \left(\| D_{\mathsf{Enc}} - U \|_2 + \| D_{\mathsf{Enc}^*} - U \|_2 \right)$$

instead. Then, we can argue exactly as in [1] to conclude the following, which in particular solves one of the open questions posed in [1].

---

[3] We point out that in the derivation of their bound, [1] uses $\sqrt{a+b} + \sqrt{a} \leq 2\sqrt{a+b}$. If, instead, we use $\sqrt{a+b} + \sqrt{a} \leq 2\sqrt{a+b/2}$, which hold by Jensen's inequality, we obtain the slightly improved version stated here in (10), with a factor $1/4$ instead $1/2$.

Theorem 12. *For every cipher* C_K *over* ℓ*-bit blocks, the ML-advantage for* k*-linear masks, i.e., the advantage of an ML distinguisher as in Fig. 2, is bounded by*

$$\left|E(p_{C_K}^{\mathsf{ML}}) - E(p_{C^*}^{\mathsf{ML}})\right| \leq \sqrt{n2^{k+1}}\sqrt{2^{-\ell} + \frac{1}{4}\left\|[C_K]^2 - [C^*]^2\right\|_\infty}.$$

Alternatively, and slightly more directly, we can use Theorem 11 to argue that

$$\left|E(p_{C_K}^{\mathsf{ML}}) - E(p_{C^*}^{\mathsf{ML}})\right| \leq \sqrt{n2^{k-1}} \cdot \left(E_{Q_0}(\|P_Z - U\|_2) + E_{Q_1}(\|P_Z - U\|_2)\right),$$

and then apply Lemma 12, Theorem 1 and Lemma 17 and 18 from [1] to obtain the above bound.

5.2   Resistance to Truncated Differential Attacks

Here, we revisit and improve the security bound from Blondeau et al. [1] against what is knows as *truncated differential* (TD) attacks. Following the definition given in [1], for a block cipher Enc over ℓ-bit blocks and for a vector space $V^\perp = V_{\mathsf{in}}^\perp \times V_{\mathsf{out}}^\perp$ with $V_{\mathsf{in}}^\perp$ having dimension $\ell - s > 0$, a TD distinguisher works as described in Fig. 3 to the right.

Distinguisher TD with oracle Enc:
1: **for** $i = 1$ to n **do**
2:     pick $(x, x') \in (\{0,1\}^\ell)^2$ uniformly such that $x \oplus x' \in V_{\mathsf{in}}^\perp$
3:     set $y = \mathsf{Enc}(x)$ and $y' = \mathsf{Enc}(x')$
4:     set $b_i = 1_{((x,y)\oplus(x',y'))\in V^\perp}$
5: **end for**
6: output $f(b_1, \ldots, b_n)$

Fig. 3. TD distinguisher

Using notation similar to as above, [1, Thm. 21] shows that

$$\left|E(p_{C_K}^{\mathsf{TD}}) - E(p_{C^*}^{\mathsf{TD}})\right| \leq n2^s\left(2 \cdot 2^{-\ell} + \frac{1}{2}\left\|[C_K]^2 - [C^*]^2\right\|_\infty\right). \tag{11}$$

At the core of the proof of (11) is the bound

$$\begin{aligned}
\left|p_{\mathsf{Enc}}^{\mathsf{TD}} - p_{\mathsf{Enc}^*}^{\mathsf{TD}}\right| &\leq n\, d(D_{\mathsf{Enc}}, D_{\mathsf{Enc}^*}) \\
&= n2^s\left|p_{\mathsf{Enc}}^{\mathsf{STD}} - p_{\mathsf{Enc}^*}^{\mathsf{STD}}\right| \\
&\leq n2^s\left(\left|p_{\mathsf{Enc}}^{\mathsf{STD}} - 2^{-\ell}\right| + \left|p_{\mathsf{Enc}^*}^{\mathsf{STD}} - 2^{-\ell}\right|\right)
\end{aligned}$$

where $p_{\mathsf{Enc}}^{\mathsf{STD}}$ is defined in [1] and happens to coincide with $2^{-s}D_{\mathsf{Enc}}(1)$. Again, it is not relevant here how (11) is then derived from this; important for us is that the factor $n2^s$ carries into the bound.

Our improvement is obtained by applying Corollary 8 to the Boolean distributions D_{Enc} and D_{ref}, with the latter defined as $D_{\mathsf{ref}}(1) = 2^{s-\ell}$. This gives

$$d(D_{\mathsf{Enc}}^{\otimes}, D_{\mathsf{ref}}^{\otimes}) \le \sqrt{\frac{n}{2\min(2^{s-\ell}, 1 - 2^{s-\ell})}}\, d(D_{\mathsf{Enc}}, D_{\mathsf{ref}})$$

$$= \sqrt{\frac{n}{2^{s-\ell+1}}}\, \left|2^s p_{\mathsf{Enc}}^{\mathsf{STD}} - 2^{s-\ell}\right|$$

$$= \sqrt{n2^{s+\ell-1}}\left|p_{\mathsf{Enc}}^{\mathsf{STD}} - 2^{-\ell}\right|.$$

Therefore, by triangular inequality, we obtain

$$\left|p_{\mathsf{Enc}}^{\mathsf{TD}} - p_{\mathsf{Enc}^*}^{\mathsf{TD}}\right| \le d(D_{\mathsf{Enc}}^{\otimes}, D_{\mathsf{Enc}^*}^{\otimes}) \le \sqrt{n2^{s+\ell-1}}\left(\left|p_{\mathsf{Enc}}^{\mathsf{STD}} - 2^{-\ell}\right| + \left|p_{\mathsf{Enc}^*}^{\mathsf{STD}} - 2^{-k}\right|\right).$$

By the techniques of [1], this then result in the following bound, which improves (11) by a factor $\sqrt{n}\,2^{(s-\ell+1)/2}$ and solves the second open problem from [1].

Theorem 13. *For every cipher C_K over ℓ-bit blocks, the TD-advantage for $V_{\mathsf{in}}^{\perp}$ of dimension $\ell - s$, i.e., the advantage of a TD distinguisher as in Fig. 3, is bounded by*

$$\left|E(p_{C_K}^{\mathsf{TD}}) - E(p_{C^*}^{\mathsf{TD}})\right| \le \sqrt{n2^{s+\ell-1}}\left(2 \cdot 2^{-\ell} + \frac{1}{2}\left\|[C_K]^2 - [C^*]^2\right\|_{\infty}\right).$$

5.3   Decorrelation

As a last application, we now move to decorrelation theory, as introduced by Vaudenay [10]. Again, we consider a block cipher Enc over ℓ-bit blocks.[4] As considered and studied in [10], an iterated distinguisher of order q is a distinguisher as described in Fig. 4 to the right, where n is a positive integer, D is a probability distribution over $(\{0,1\}^{\ell})^q$, and T and f are functions $T : (\{0,1\}^{\ell})^{2q} \to \{0,1\}$ and $f : \{0,1\}^n \to \{0,1\}$.

Expressed in terms of notation similar to as above, it was shown in [10, Th. 18] that the advantage of any such distinguisher with Boolean T is bounded by

$$\left|E(p_{C_K}^{\mathsf{Iter}}) - E(p_{C^*}^{\mathsf{Iter}})\right| \le 5\sqrt[3]{n^2\left(2\delta + \frac{5q^2}{2 \cdot 2^{\ell}} + \frac{3}{2}\epsilon,\right)} + n\epsilon \qquad (12)$$

where $\epsilon := \|[C_K]^{2q} - [C^*]^{2q}\|_{\infty}$, i.e., twice the best advantage of a distinguisher making $2q$ non-adaptive queries, and δ is the probability that two given iterations (say for $i = 1$ and $i = 2$) would select at least one x_j in common (not necessarily for the same index j). We let Z be the probability that $b_i = 1$ in the probability

---

[4] As a matter of fact, here Enc may also be a pseudorandom functions (PRF), but we ignore this here and keep the notation consistent with above.

Distinguisher Iter with oracle Enc:
1: **for** $i = 1$ to n **do**
2:    pick $(x_1, \ldots, x_q) \in (\{0,1\}^\ell)^q$ following distribution D
3:    set $y_j = \mathsf{Enc}(x_j)$ for $j = 1, \ldots, q$
4:    set $b_i = T(x_1, \ldots, x_q, y_1, \ldots, y_q) \in \{0,1\}$
5: **end for**
6: output $f(b_1, \ldots, b_n)$

Fig. 4. Iterated distinguisher

space induced by D with a fixed Enc and write $E(Z)$ for the expected value of Z with respect to the corresponding distribution of a random Enc. By definition, it holds that

$$|E_{C_K}(Z) - E_{C^*}(Z)| \leq \frac{1}{2}\left\|[C_K]^q - [C^*]^q\right\|_\infty \leq \frac{\epsilon}{2}.$$

Furthermore, by considering a distinguisher that samples b_i and b_i' and returns $b_i b_i'$, which is 1 with probability Z^2, we see that

$$|E_{C_K}(Z^2) - E_{C^*}(Z^2)| \leq \frac{1}{2}\left\|[C_K]^{2q} - [C^*]^{2q}\right\|_\infty = \frac{\epsilon}{2}.$$

Given that $E_{C^*}(Z)^2 - E_{C_K}(Z)^2 = \big(E_{C^*}(Z) - E_{C_K}(Z)\big)\big(E_{C^*}(Z) + E_{C_K}(Z)\big) \leq \epsilon$, it is then easy to see that

$$V_{C_K}(Z) - V_{C^*}(Z) = E_{C_K}(Z^2) - E_{C^*}(Z^2) + E_{C^*}(Z)^2 - E_{C_K}(Z)^2 \leq \frac{3}{2}\epsilon.$$

Finally, it was shown in [10] that

$$V_{C^*}(Z) \leq \delta + \frac{q^2}{4 \cdot 2^\ell} + \frac{q^2}{2 \cdot (2^\ell - q)}.$$

So, applying Theorem 10 we obtain the bound

$$\left|E(p_{C_K}^{\mathsf{Iter}}) - E(p_{C^*}^{\mathsf{Iter}})\right| \leq \sqrt{\frac{n}{2}} \cdot \frac{\sqrt{V_{C_K}(Z) + (E_{C_K}(Z) - E_{C^*}(Z))^2} + \sqrt{V_{C^*}(Z)}}{\sqrt{E_{C^*}(Z)(1 - E_{C^*}(Z))}}$$

$$\leq \sqrt{\frac{n}{2E_{C^*}(Z)(1 - E_{C^*}(Z))}}\left(\sqrt{\frac{3}{2}\epsilon + V_{C^*}(Z) + \epsilon^2} + \sqrt{V_{C^*}(Z)}\right)$$

$$\leq \sqrt{\frac{2n}{E_{C^*}(Z)(1 - E_{C^*}(Z))}}\sqrt{\delta + \frac{q^2}{4 \cdot 2^\ell} + \frac{q^2}{2 \cdot (2^\ell - q)} + \frac{5}{2}\epsilon}.$$

Thus, in summary, and using the notation from above, we obtain the following improved version of (12).

Theorem 14. *Let C_K be a cipher over ℓ-bit blocks. Then, for any positive integers q and n, any distribution D over $(\{0,1\}^\ell)^q$, and any functions $T : (\{0,1\}^\ell)^{2q} \to \{0,1\}$ and $f : \{0,1\}^n \to \{0,1\}$, the iterated distinguisher of order q from Fig. 4 has an advantage*

$$\left| E(p_{C_K}^{\mathsf{Iter}}) - E(p_{C^*}^{\mathsf{Iter}}) \right| \leq \sqrt{\frac{2n}{p(1-p)}} \sqrt{\delta + \frac{q^2}{4 \cdot 2^\ell} + \frac{q^2}{2 \cdot (2^\ell - q)} + \frac{5}{2}\epsilon},$$

where $p := E_{C^*}(Z)$ is the probability that $b_i = 1$ in case of a random permutation, and ϵ and δ are as in [10], i.e., $\epsilon = \|[C_K]^{2q} - [C^*]^{2q}\|_\infty$ and δ is the probability that two given iterations have one x_j in common (not necessarily for the same index j).

This is better than (12) by a ratio which is asymptotically $\Theta(n^{1/6})$, but requires that we know $E_{C^*}(Z)$. This is normally the case though. We can further see that for $E_{C^*}(Z)$ close to $1/2$, we obtain security for $n \ll 1/\epsilon$ while the previous result (12) offers security only for $n \ll 1/\sqrt{\epsilon}$. We thus obtain security for significantly larger n.

6   Conclusion

We derived new bounds on the statistical distance $d(P_0^{\otimes n}, P_1^{\otimes n})$ of i.i.d. samples of a source Z that is distributed according to distribution P_0 or P_1, as well as on the statistical distance of i.i.d. samples that are chosen according a distribution that depends on Z. All the bounds grow as $\sqrt{n}$ in the number n of samples, and they are applicable if some additional information on the distributions is known.

We expect these new bounds to become useful tools in cryptography. Indeed, we demonstrated the usefulness on several applications in the context of block-cipher analysis. In all these examples, our bounds lead to an immediate improvement over the prior results.

A   Computing the Threshold Number in Power-Analysis Attacks

At the core of a power-analysis attack is the task to distinguish whether a source X over a finite set $\mathcal{X}$ is distributed according to P_0 or P_1 when given i.i.d. samples of the form $X + N$, where N is noise that follows a normal distribution with expected value 0 and standard deviation σ. Formally, given that X is distributed according to P_b, the random variable $X + N$ has density

$$f_{Q_b}(t) = \sum_{x \in \mathcal{Z}} P_b(x) \frac{1}{\sigma\sqrt{2\pi}} e^{-\frac{(t-x)^2}{2\sigma^2}}.$$

Hence, not worrying that we are now dealing with continuous random variables, we have

$$F(Q_0\|Q_1) = \int_{-\infty}^{+\infty} \sqrt{f_{Q_0}(t) f_{Q_1}(t)} \, dt$$

$$= \frac{1}{\sigma\sqrt{2\pi}} \int_{-\infty}^{+\infty} \sqrt{\sum_{x,y\in\mathcal{X}} P_0(x) P_1(y) e^{-\frac{(t-x)^2+(t-y)^2}{2\sigma^2}}} \, dt \, .$$

Thus, the threshold number of samples is given by

$$n_{1/2} = \frac{\theta}{-2\log_2\left(\frac{1}{\sigma\sqrt{2\pi}} \int_{-\infty}^{+\infty} \sqrt{\sum_{x,y\in\mathcal{X}} P_0(x) P_1(y) e^{-\frac{(t-x)^2+(t-y)^2}{2\sigma^2}}} \, dt\right)}$$

for some $0.41 \leq \theta \leq 2$.

As a concrete example, if P_0 and P_1 are such that $P_0(x) = 1 = P_1(y)$ for some fixed values $x, y \in \mathcal{X}$, then we get

$$F(Q_0\|Q_1) = \frac{1}{\sigma\sqrt{2\pi}} \int_{-\infty}^{+\infty} \sqrt{e^{-\frac{(t-x)^2+(t-y)^2}{2\sigma^2}}} \, dt$$

$$= \frac{1}{\sigma\sqrt{2\pi}} \int_{-\infty}^{+\infty} e^{-\frac{(t-\frac{x+y}{2})^2+(\frac{x-y}{2})^2}{2\sigma^2}} \, dt$$

$$= e^{-\frac{(x-y)^2}{8\sigma^2}}$$

and thus

$$-2\log F(Q_0\|Q_1) = \frac{(x-y)^2}{(4\ln 2)\cdot\sigma^2} \, .$$

Thus, the number of samples needed to have a distinguishing advantage $1/2$ (i.e., guess correctly with probability $3/4$) is

$$n_{1/2} = \theta\frac{(4\ln 2)\cdot\sigma^2}{(x-y)^2}$$

with $0.41 \leq \theta \leq 2$.

References

1. Blondeau, C., Bay, A., Vaudenay, S.: Protecting against multidimensional linear and truncated differential cryptanalysis by decorrelation. In: Leander, G. (ed.) FSE 2015. LNCS, vol. 9054, pp. 73–91. Springer, Heidelberg (2015). https://doi.org/10.1007/978-3-662-48116-5_4. Eprint 2015/380. http://eprint.iacr.org/2015/380.pdf
2. Dai, W., Hoang, V.T., Tessaro, S.: Information-theoretic indistinguishability via the chi-squared method. In: Katz, J., Shacham, H. (eds.) CRYPTO 2017. LNCS, vol. 10403, pp. 497–523. Springer, Cham (2017). https://doi.org/10.1007/978-3-319-63697-9_17

3. van Erven, T., Harremoës, P.: Rényi divergence and Kullback-Leibler divergence. IEEE Trans. Inf. Theory **IT–60**(7), 3797–3820 (2014). http://arxiv.org/abs/1206.2459

4. Fuchs, C.A., van de Graaf, J.: Cryptographic distinguishability measures for quantum mechanical states. IEEE Trans. Inf. Theory **IT–45**(4), 1216–1227 (1999). https://arxiv.org/abs/quant-ph/9712042

5. Gilardoni, G.L.: On Pinsker's and Vajda's type inequalities for Csiszár's f-Divergences. IEEE Trans. Inf. Theory **5IT–5**(11), 5377–5386 (2010)

6. Pöppelmann, T., Ducas, L., Güneysu, T.: Enhanced lattice-based signatures on reconfigurable hardware. In: Batina, L., Robshaw, M. (eds.) CHES 2014. LNCS, vol. 8731, pp. 353–370. Springer, Heidelberg (2014). https://doi.org/10.1007/978-3-662-44709-3_20

7. Pöppelmann, T., Ducas, L., Güneysu, T.: Enhanced lattice-based signatures on reconfigurable hardware. IACR Eprint 2014/254 report (2014). http://eprint.iacr.org/2014/254.pdf

8. Renner, R.: On the variational distance of independently repeated experiments. CoRR abs/cs/0509013 (2005). http://arxiv.org/abs/cs/0509013

9. Sason, I., Verdú, S.: f-Divergence Inequalities. arXiv:1508.00335 [cs.IT] (2016). https://arxiv.org/abs/1508.00335

10. Vaudenay, S.: Decorrelation: a theory for block cipher security. J. Cryptol. **16**, 249–286 (2003)

Symmetric Asynchronous Ratcheted Communication with Associated Data

Hailun Yan$^{(\boxtimes)}$ and Serge Vaudenay

École Polytechnique Fédérale de Lausanne (EPFL), Lausanne, Switzerland
{hailun.yan,serge.vaudenay}@epfl.ch

Abstract. Following up mass surveillance and privacy issues, modern secure communication protocols now seek strong security, such as forward secrecy and post-compromise security, in the face of state exposures. To address this problem, ratcheting was thereby introduced, widely used in real-world messaging protocols like Signal. However, ratcheting comes with a high cost. Recently, Caforio et al. proposed pragmatic constructions which compose a weakly secure "light" protocol and a strongly secure "heavy" protocol, in order to achieve the so-called ratcheting on demand. The light protocol they proposed has still a high complexity.

In this paper, we prove the security of the lightest possible protocol we could imagine, which essentially encrypts then hashes the secret key. We prove it without any random oracle by introducing a new security notion in the standard model. Our protocol composes well with the generic transformation techniques by Caforio et al. to offer high security and performance at the same time.

1 Introduction

A classic communication model usually assumes that the endpoints are secure while the adversary is on the communication channel. However, protocols in recent messaging applications are secured with end-to-end encryption due to the prevalence of malware and system vulnerabilities. They attempt to enable secure communication services by regularly updating (ratcheting) the encryption key. One notable example of ratcheting is the Signal protocol [14] by Open Whisper Systems with its double-ratchet algorithm. It is also widely used in WhatsApp, Skype and many other secure messaging systems.

The term ratcheting on its own does not mean too much, instead, it is an umbrella term for a number of different security guarantees. One security guarantee which is easiest to provide is *forward secrecy*, which, in case of an exposure, prevents the adversary from decrypting messages exchanged in the past. Typically, it is achieved by deleting old states and generating new ones through one-way functions. Moreover, to prevent the adversary from decrypting messages in the future, some source of randomness is added when updating every state to obtain the so-called *future secrecy*, or *backward secrecy*, or *post-compromise security*, or even *self-healing*. The ratcheting technique is mainly related to how keys are used and updated, rather than how they are obtained. We thereby will

© Springer Nature Switzerland AG 2020
K. Aoki and A. Kanaoka (Eds.): IWSEC 2020, LNCS 12231, pp. 184–204, 2020.
https://doi.org/10.1007/978-3-030-58208-1_11

not be concerned with the method of key distribution, regarding the initial keys as created and distributed in a trusted way.

Besides security, there are many other characteristics of communication systems. In a bidirectional two-party secure communication, participants alternate their role as senders and receivers. The modern instant messaging protocols are substantially *asynchronous*. In other words, for a two-party communication, the messages should be transmitted even though the counterpart is not online. Moreover, the moment when a participant wants to send a message is undefined. The participants can use *random roles* (sender or receiver) arbitrarily.

Previous Work. The ratcheting technique was first deployed in real life protocols, such as the off-the-record (OTR) [5] messaging protocol and the Signal protocol [14]. The Signal protocol especially, gained a lot of interest and adopted by a number of other secure messaging apps. A clean description of Signal was posted by the inventors Marlinspike and Perrin [12]. Cohn-Gordon et al. [7] later gave the first academic analysis of Signal security. Recently, Blazy et al. [4] revisited the Signal protocol. They showed some attacks on the original design and proposed SAID, which reshapes Signal into an identity-based asynchronous messaging protocol with authenticated ratcheting.

The first formal definitions of ratcheting security is given by Bellare et al. [3] at CRYPTO 2017. Following their work, a line of studies about ratcheting protocols have been made with different security levels and primitives [1,6,8–10,13]. Some of these results study secure messaging while others are about key-exchange. These works can be considered as equivalent since secure ratcheted communication can reduce to regularly secure key-exchange. At CRYPTO 2018, Poettering and Rösler [13] designed a protocol with "optimal" security (in the sense that we know no better security so far), but using a random oracle, and heavy algorithms such as hierarchical identity-based encryption (HIBE). Jaeger and Stepanovs [9] proposed a similar protocol with security against compromised random coins: with random coin leakage before usage, which also requires HIBE and a random oracle. Durak and Vaudenay [8] proposed a protocol with slightly lower security but relying on neither HIBE nor random oracle. They also prove that public-key encryption is necessary to construct post-compromise secure messaging. At EUROCRYPT 2019, Jost et al. [10] proposed a protocol with security between optimal security and the security of the Durak-Vaudenay protocol. In the same conference, Alwen et al. [1] proposed two other ratcheting protocols with security against adversarially chosen random coins and immediate decryption. Caforio et al. [6] proposed a generic construction of a messaging protocol offering *on-demand ratcheting*, by composing a strongly secure protocol (to be used infrequently) and a weakly secure one. Their construction further generically strengthen protocols by adding the notion of *security awareness*. Recently, Jost et al. [11] modeled the ratcheting components in a unified and composable framework, allowing for their reuse in a modular fashion. Balli et al. [2] modeled optimally secure ratcheted key exchange (RKE) under randomness manipulation and showed that key-update encryption (which is only constructed from HIBE so far) is necessary and sufficient.

In this paper, we are mostly interested in the work by Caforio et al. [6]. They considered message encryption and adapted Durak-Vaudenay protocol to define asynchronous ratcheted communication with associated data (ARCAD). They designed a weakly secure protocol called liteARCAD which is solely based on symmetric cryptography. It achieves provable forward secrecy and excellent software performances. Moreover, they defined a bidirectional secure communication messaging protocol with hybrid on-demand ratcheting. By integrating two ratcheting protocols with different security levels — a strongly secure protocol (such as Durak-Vaudenay protocol) and a weaker but lighter protocol (such as liteARCAD), the hybrid system allows the sender to select which security level he wants to use. When the ratcheting becomes infrequent, the communication system enjoys satisfactory implementation performance thanks to the high efficiency of liteARCAD. Although already quite efficient, liteARCAD has send/receive complexities which can grow linearly with the number of messages. For instance, a participant who sends n messages without receiving any response accumulates n secret keys in his secret state. When he finally receives a message, he must go through all accumulated keys and clean up his state. Furthermore, the typical number of cryptographic operation per message is still high: sending a message requires one hash and $n + 1$ symmetric encryptions. Receiving a message is similar.

Contribution. In this paper we study the simplest protocol we can imagine: we encrypt a message with a secret key then update the key with a hash function. This guarantees one hash and encryption per message. We call this protocol *Encrypt-then-Hash* (EtH). We introduce a new security notion which relates symmetric encryption with key update by hashing. Essentially, we say that the hash of the encryption key is indistinguishable from random. With this notion, we prove the security of EtH in the standard model. We prove that EtH enforces confidentiality and authentication. We deduce that we can use EtH in the generic constructions by Caforio et al. [6].

Organization. In Section 2, we revisit the preliminary notions from Caforio-Durak-Vaudenay [6], all of which are very relevant to our work. In Section 3, we construct a correct and secure symmetric-cryptography-based ARCAD protocol. Meanwhile, we define a new security notion with respect to one-time authenticated encryption and hash function family. Finally, in Section 4, we formally prove that our scheme is secure.

2   Primitives

In this section, we recall some definitions from Caforio et al. [6]. We mark some of the definitions with the reference [6], indicating that these definitions are unchanged except for possible necessary notation changes. Especially, we slightly adapt the definition of asynchronous ratcheted communication with associated data (ARCAD) for symmetric-cryptography-based ARCAD (SARCAD).

Notations and General Definitions. In the following, we will use these notations. We have two participants Alice (A) and Bob (B). Whenever we talk about either one of the participants, we represent it as P, then $\overline{P}$ refers to P's counterpart. We have two roles send and rec for sender and receiver respectively. We define send = $\overline{rec}$ and rec = $\overline{send}$. When participants A and B have exclusive roles (like in unidirectional cases), we call them *sender S* and *receiver R*.

Definition 1 (SARCAD). *A symmetric-cryptography-based asynchronous ratcheted communication with associated data (SARCAD) consists of the following PPT algorithms:*

- Setup(1^λ) $\xrightarrow{\$}$ pp: *This defines the common public parameters* pp.
- Initall(1^λ, pp) $\rightarrow$ (st_A, st_B): *This returns the initial state of* A *and* B.
- Send(st_P, ad, pt) $\xrightarrow{\$}$ (st'_P, ct): *It takes as input a plaintext* pt *and some associated data* ad *and produces a ciphertext* ct *together with an updated state* st'_P.
- Receive(st_P, ad, ct) $\xrightarrow{\$}$ (acc, st'_P, pt): *It takes as input a ciphertext* ct *and some associated data* ad *and produces a plaintext* pt *together with an updated state* st'_P *and a flag* acc.

We consider bidirectional asynchronous communications. Sending/receiving is then refined by the RATCH[P, role, ·, ·] call as depicted in Fig. 1. To formally capture the communication status and the trivial cases during the communication, Caforio et al. [6] gave a set of definitions (originally defined in [8] and adapted to ARCAD). We do not want to overload this section by redefining the already existing terminology, so we put these less essential definitions in Appendix A for completeness.

Moreover, we will need a symmetric one-time authenticated encryption (OTAE) scheme in our protocol, which consists of a key space OTAE.$\mathcal{K}(\lambda)$ and the OTAE.Enc and OTAE.Dec algorithms. We will also need a hash function family H consisting of a key space H.$\mathcal{K}(\lambda)$, a domain H.$\mathcal{D}(\lambda)$, and the H.Eval(hk, sk) algorithm which maps hk $\in$ H.$\mathcal{K}(\lambda)$ and sk $\in$ H.$\mathcal{D}(\lambda)$ to an element of H.$\mathcal{D}(\lambda)$. We also put the definitions of the above primitives in Appendix A.

Correctness of SARCAD. We say that a symmetric ratcheted communication protocol functions correctly if the receiver performs a right decryption and gets exactly the same plaintext as sent by its counterpart. Correctness implies that participant P has received messages in the same order as those sent by participant $\overline{P}$.

We formally define the CORRECTNESS game given in Fig. 5 in Appendix B, in which we initialize two participants. Meanwhile, we define variables $sent^P_{pt}$ (resp. received$^P_{pt}$) which keeps a list of messages sent (resp. received) by participant P when running Sent (resp. Receive). For each variable v such as $sent^P_{pt}$ or st_P relative to participant P, we denote by $v(t)$ the value of v at time t. The scheduling[1] is defined by a sequence sched of tuples of the form either (P, send, ·, ·) or

---

[1] Scheduling communication is under the control of the adversary except in the CORRECTNESS game, in which there is no adversary.

Oracle RATCH (P, "send", ad, pt)	Oracle RATCH (P, "rec", ad, ct)
1: $pt_P \leftarrow pt$	1: $ct_P \leftarrow ct$
2: $ad_P \leftarrow ad$	2: $ad_P \leftarrow ad$
3: $(st'_P, ct_P) \leftarrow Send(st_P, ad_P, pt_P)$	3: $(acc, st'_P, pt_P) \leftarrow Receive(st_P, ad_P, ct_P)$
4: $st_P \leftarrow st'_P$	4: **if** acc **then**
5: append (ad_P, pt_P) to $sent^P_{pt}$	5: $\quad st_P \leftarrow st'_P$
6: append (ad_P, ct_P) to $sent^P_{ct}$	6: $\quad$ append (ad_P, pt_P) to $received^P_{pt}$
7: **return** ct_P	7: $\quad$ append (ad_P, ct_P) to $received^P_{ct}$
	8: **return** acc

Oracle $EXP_{st}(P)$	Oracle $EXP_{pt}(P)$
1: **return** st_P	1: **return** pt_P

Oracle CHALLENGE(P, ad, ct)	
1: **if** $t_{test} \neq \perp$ **then return** $\perp$	3: $ct \leftarrow RATCH(P, "send", ad, pt)$
2: **if** $b = 0$ **then** replace pt by a random	4: $(t, P, ad, pt, ct)_{test} \leftarrow (time, P, ad, pt, ct)$
string of the same length	5: **return** ct

Fig. 1. Oracles

$(P, rec, \cdot, \cdot)$. In this game, the communication between participants uses a waiting queue for messages in each direction. Each participant has a queue of incoming messages and is pulling them in the order they have been pushed in. Sent messages from P are buffered in the queue of $\overline{P}$.

Definition 2 (Correctness [6]). *We say that a* SARCAD *protocol is* correct *if for all sequence* sched *of tuples of the form* (P, "send", ad, pt) *or* (P, "rec", ad, ct), *the game never returns* 1. *Namely,*

- *at each stage, for each* P, $received^P_{pt}$ *is prefix²* *of* $sent^{\overline{P}}_{pt}$, *and*
- *each* RATCH(P, "rec", ad, ct) *call returns* acc=true.

Security of SARCAD. We define the security of SARCAD with IND-CCA notion resp. FORGE notion, which is captured by using the advantage of an adversary playing the IND-CCA resp. FORGE game.

In addition to the RATCH oracles, the adversary can access several other oracles called EXP_{st}, EXP_{pt} and CHALLENGE, see Fig. 1.

- RATCH. This oracle is used to ratchet (either to send or to receive), which is essentially the message exchange procedure.
- EXP_{st}. This oracle is used to obtain the state of a participant, which implies that the adversary can expose the state of Alice or Bob.
- EXP_{pt}. This oracle is used to obtain the last received message of a participant.

---

² By saying that $received^P_{pt}$ is prefix of $sent^{\overline{P}}_{pt}$, we mean that $sent^{\overline{P}}_{pt}$ is the concatenation of $received^P_{pt}$ with a (possible empty) list of (ad, pt) pairs.

- CHALLENGE. This oracle is used (only in the IND-CCA game) to send either the plaintext or a random string.

Following previous work [6,8], we introduce a *cleanness* predicate when defining the security of a SARCAD scheme. The cleanness predicate identifies and captures all trivial ways of attacking. The adversary is not allowed to make a trivial attack when playing games, as defined by the cleanness predicate C_{clean} appearing on Step 6 in the games in Fig. 2. Note that identifying the appropriate cleanness predicate C_{clean} is not easy. The difficulty is perhaps to clearly forbid all trivial attacks while allowing efficient protocols. For more details and discussions, we refer our readers to [6,8].

Definition 3 (C_{clean}-IND-CCA Security [6]). *Let C_{clean} be a cleanness predicate. We consider the IND-CCA$_{b,C_{clean}}^{A}$ game in Fig. 2. We say that SARCAD is C_{clean}-IND-CCA-secure if for any PPT adversary A, the advantage*

$$\mathsf{Adv}(A) = | \Pr\left[\mathsf{IND\text{-}CCA}_{0,C_{clean}}^{A}(1^\lambda) \to 1\right] - \Pr\left[\mathsf{IND\text{-}CCA}_{1,C_{clean}}^{A}(1^\lambda) \to 1\right] |$$

of A in IND-CCA$_{b,C_{clean}}^{A}$ game is negligible.

Definition 4 (C_{clean}-FORGE Security [6]). *Let C_{clean} be a cleanness predicate. Consider FORGE$_{C_{clean}}^{A}$ game in Fig. 2. We say that SARCAD is C_{clean}-FORGE-secure if for any PPT adversary A, the advantage $\Pr\left[\mathsf{FORGE}_{C_{clean}}^{A}(1^\lambda) \to 1\right]$ of A in FORGE$_{C_{clean}}^{A}$ is bounded by ϵ.*

Game IND-CCA$_{b,C_{clean}}^{A}(1^\lambda)$	Game FORGE$_{C_{clean}}^{A}(1^\lambda)$
1: Setup$(1^\lambda) \xrightarrow{\$}$ pp	1: Setup$(1^\lambda) \xrightarrow{\$}$ pp
2: Initall$(1^\lambda,$ pp$) \xrightarrow{\$} (st_A, st_B)$	2: Initall$(1^\lambda,$ pp$) \xrightarrow{\$} (st_A, st_B)$
3: set all sent$_*^*$ and received$_*^*$ variables to $\emptyset$	3: set all sent$_*^*$ and received$_*^*$ variables to $\emptyset$
4: Set t_{test} to $\bot$	4: $(P,$ ad, ct$) \leftarrow A^{RATCH,EXP_{st},EXP_{pt}}(pp)$
5: $b' \leftarrow A^{RATCH,EXP_{st},EXP_{pt},CHALLENGE}(pp)$	5: RATCH$(P,$"rec"$,$ad,ct$) \to$ acc
6: **if** $\neg C_{clean}$ **then return** $\bot$	6: **if** $\neg C_{clean}$ **then return** 0
7: **return** b'	7: **if** acc $=$ false **then return** 0
	8: **if** (ad, ct) is not a forgery (Def. 9) for P
	then return 0
	9: **return** 1

Fig. 2. IND-CCA, FORGE Games

Setup(1^λ)	Initall(1^λ, hk)
1: hk $\xleftarrow{\$}$ H.$\mathcal{K}(\lambda)$ 2: **return** hk	1: k, k' $\xleftarrow{\$}$ OTAE.$\mathcal{K}(\lambda)$ 2: $st_A \leftarrow (1^\lambda, hk, k, k')$ 3: $st_B \leftarrow (1^\lambda, hk, k', k)$ 4: **return** (st_A, st_B)
Send(st, ad, pt)	Receive(st, ad, ct)
1: parse st $= (1^\lambda, hk, sk, rk)$ 2: ct $\leftarrow$ OTAE.Enc(sk, ad, pt) 3: sk' $\leftarrow$ H.Eval(hk, sk) 4: st' $\leftarrow (1^\lambda, hk, sk', rk)$ 5: **return** (st', ct)	1: parse st $= (1^\lambda, hk, sk, rk)$ 2: pt $\leftarrow$ OTAE.Dec(rk, ad, ct) 3: **if** pt $=\perp$ **then** 4: **return** (false, $\perp, \perp$) 5: rk' $\leftarrow$ H.Eval(hk, rk) 6: st' $\leftarrow (1^\lambda, hk, sk, rk')$ 7: **return** (true, st', pt)

Fig. 3. EtH: our SARCAD scheme

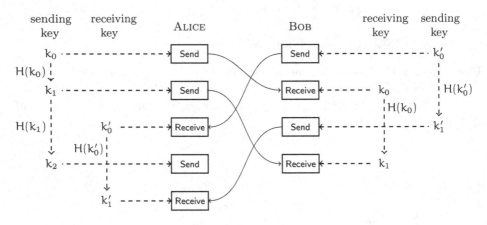

Fig. 4. Message exchanges between Alice and Bob.

3   Construction of a SARCAD Scheme

In this section, we propose a SARCAD scheme, as depicted in Fig. 3. We call it *Encrypt-then-Hash* (EtH), as we encrypt the message with OTAE then update the secret key with H. In this construction, we assume that OTAE.$\mathcal{K}(\lambda) =$ H.$\mathcal{D}(\lambda)$. An example of a flow of messages is depicted on Fig. 4. Our scheme guarantees most of the security properties, which can be a perfect alternative to liteARCAD [6]. Note that we do not expect full security (especially the postcompromise security) from this symmetric-only protocol. As pointed by Durak and Vaudenay in [8], a secure and a correct unidirectional ARCAD always implies public-key encryption. We formalize below the security that we achieve for Theorem 2.

In our SARCAD scheme, the participants share two secret symmetric keys as the initial keys, one for encrypting (sending) messages and one for (decrypting) receiving messages. The two communication directions are independent channels in our scheme. Communications are protected by a symmetric one-time authenticated encryption (OTAE) scheme. Moreover, the key states are updated after each communication by a hash function family.

Theorem 1 (Correctness). *Suppose that* OTAE *is correct.* EtH *is a correct* SARCAD.

Proof. In the EtH protocol, the two directions of communication are quite independent. Therefore, the correctness of both directions will separately imply the correctness of the whole protocol.

The correctness of the unidirectional case is trivial, which can be easily deduced from the correctness of the OTAE scheme and the deterministic property of the hash function family H. At the beginning, the sender S and the receiver R share the same initial secret key k, and clearly the communication functions correctly at the first step of the loop in the CORRECTNESS game. Suppose that it functions correctly before the i-th step. Let $\mathsf{send}_{\mathsf{pt}}^{\mathsf{S}} = (\mathsf{seq}_1, (\mathsf{ad}, \mathsf{pt}), \mathsf{seq}_2)$ and $\mathsf{received}_{\mathsf{pt}}^{\mathsf{R}} = \mathsf{seq}_1$ at the $(i\text{-}1)$-th step, and let the key used for encrypting/decrypting the last message in seq_1 be k'. Now consider a RATCH(R, "rec") call at the i-th step of the loop, namely $\mathsf{sched}_i = (\mathsf{R}, \text{"rec"}, \mathsf{ad}, \mathsf{ct})$. Let $\mathsf{received}_{\mathsf{pt}}^{\mathsf{R}} = (\mathsf{seq}_1, (\mathsf{ad}', \mathsf{pt}'))$. Note that the key states are updated after each communication by H. Due to the deterministic property of H, the key used by S for encrypting $(\mathsf{ad}, \mathsf{pt})$ (to $(\mathsf{ad}, \mathsf{ct})$) and the key used by R for decrypting $(\mathsf{ad}, \mathsf{ct})$ (to $(\mathsf{ad}', \mathsf{pt}')$) are the same, which is $H(k')$. Further, due to the correctness of the OTAE scheme, there must be $(\mathsf{ad}', \mathsf{pt}') = (\mathsf{ad}, \mathsf{pt})$ and RATCH(R, "rec", ad, ct) = acc. □

The SARCAD scheme uses a hash function family with an ad-hoc *pseudorandom* (PR) property.

Definition 5 (PR-Security). *Let* H *be a hash function family and* OTAE *be a one-time authenticated encryption scheme. We say that* H *is pseudorandom for* OTAE *(PR) if for any PPT adversary* $\mathcal{A}$ *playing the following game, the advantage*

$$\Pr\left[\mathrm{PR}_0^{\mathcal{A}} \to 1\right] - \Pr\left[\mathrm{PR}_1^{\mathcal{A}} \to 1\right]$$

is negligible.

Game $\mathrm{PR}_b^{\mathcal{A}}$:	Oracle ENC(ad, pt)
1: $\mathsf{query}_{\mathsf{enc}} = \bot$	1: **if** $\mathsf{query}_{\mathsf{enc}} \neq \bot$ **then** abort
2: $\mathsf{hk} \xleftarrow{\$} H.\mathcal{K}(\lambda)$	2: $\mathsf{ct} \leftarrow$ OTAE.Enc(k, ad, pt)
3: $k \xleftarrow{\$}$ OTAE.$\mathcal{K}(\lambda)$	3: $\mathsf{query}_{\mathsf{enc}} \leftarrow \mathsf{ct}$
4: $k' \leftarrow$ H.Eval(hk, k)	4: **return** ct
5: **if** b = 0 **then** replace k' by a ran-	
dom value with the same length	Oracle DEC(ad, ct)
6: $\mathcal{A}^{\mathsf{ENC,DEC}}(\mathsf{hk}, k') \to z$	1: **return** OTAE.Dec(k, ad, ct)

The PR security allows us to prove forward secrecy without using the random oracle model. In practice, we can use e.g. AES-GCM and SHA-256 truncated to the required length. However, having an extra hashing may be unnecessary as we could build an integrated primitive. We give further discussions on the PR security in a full version of this paper.

When there is a state exposure, it allows simulating every subsequent reception of messages. Therefore, there is no possible healing after a state exposure. To formalize our IND-CCA-security, we prune out post-compromise security but leave forward secrecy by using the following C_{sym} predicates from Caforio et al. [6]. Similarly, the notion of trivial forgery changes as the exposure of the state of P now allows to forge for P as well, due to the symmetric key. Thus, a forgery becomes trivial when an EXP_{st} occurs. Hence, the FORGE game cannot allow any state exposure at all. We formalize the security by using the C_{noexp} cleanness [6] predicate in FORGE-security.

C_{noexp}: neither A nor B has an EXP_{st} before seeing (ad_{test}, ct_{test}).

C_{sym}: the following conditions are all satisfied:

- there is no $EXP_{pt}(P_{test})$ after time t_{test} until there is a $RATCH(P_{test}, \cdot, \cdot, \cdot)$;
- if the CHALLENGE call makes the i-th $RATCH(P_{test}, \text{"send"}, \cdot, \cdot)$ call and the i-th accepting $RATCH(\overline{P}_{test}, \text{"rec"}, \cdot, \cdot)$ call occurs in a matching status (Def. 8) at some time $\overline{t}$, then there is no $EXP_{pt}(\overline{P}_{test})$ after time $\overline{t}$ until there is another $RATCH(\overline{P}_{test}, \cdot, \cdot, \cdot)$ call;
- (C_{noexp}) neither A nor B has an EXP_{st} before seeing (ad_{test}, ct_{test}).

Theorem 2. *Consider the SARCAD scheme EtH in Fig. 3. If OTAE is IND-OTCCA-secure and SEF-OTCMA-secure, and H is PR-secure for OTAE, then the scheme is C_{sym}-IND-CCA-secure and C_{noexp}-FORGE-secure.*

Proof. We will give the proof in Sect. 4.   □

Theorem 1 and Theorem 2 show that EtH satisfies the conditions of the theorems from Caforio et al. [6]. Hence, EtH can play the role of the weakly secure ARCAD in their hybrid "on-demand ratcheting" construction. EtH can also be generically strengthened by the block strengthening [6] to offer security awareness. For instance, if an adversary releases a trivial forgery after a state exposure, the participants can notice it by seeing they can no longer talk with each other. Furthermore, they can see which messages have been received by their counterparts.

4   Security Proof for Our SARCAD Scheme

In this section, we will prove that our scheme is secure (corresponding to Theorem 2).

IND-CCA-Security. We first consider the IND-CCA-security. We define Γ_b the initial C_{sym}-IND-CCA game which has a challenge message (ad_{test}, ct_{test}). We consider the event C_{noexp} that no participant P has an $EXP_{st}(P)$ query before having seen (ad_{test}, ct_{test}). The game Γ_b has the property that whenever C_{sym} does not occur, it never returns 1 due to the C_{sym} cleanness condition.

We define below for each (Q, m, n) the hybrids $\Gamma^b_{Q,m,n}$ (refer to Fig. 6) which essentially assumes that the challenge message is the n-th message sent by Q. The game maintains two counters: one counter cnt^{send}_Q for the number of messages sent by Q and one counter $cnt^{rec}_{\overline{Q}}$ for the number of messages received and accepted by $\overline{Q}$. For the unidirectional communication from Q to $\overline{Q}$, the m first session keys are picked randomly, while the following session keys are just updated by hashing the previous one as usual. This is implemented by (1) preparing m randomly-chosen keys $k_1, \ldots, k_m$ in the Initall phase, and (2) modifying the RATCH $(Q, \text{"send"}, \cdot, \cdot)$ oracle (Line 6–10) and the RATCH $(\overline{Q}, \text{"rec"}, \cdot, \cdot)$ oracle (Line 8–12). When the challenge message is released, the values of Q and n are verified. If it is incorrect, the game aborts. This is enforced by modifying the CHALLENGE oracle (Line 5–6). Clearly, we have that

$$\Pr[\Gamma_b \to 1] = \sum_{Q,n} \Pr[\Gamma^b_{Q,1,n} \to 1]. \tag{1}$$

In the following, we will prove that for $1 \leqslant m \leqslant n$, the difference between $\Pr[\Gamma^b_{Q,m,n} \to 1]$ and $\Pr[\Gamma^b_{Q,m+1,n} \to 1]$ is negligible. Recall that the $(m+1)$-th session key k_{m+1} in $\Gamma^b_{Q,m,n}$ is generated by hashing k_m while in $\Gamma^b_{Q,m+1,n}$ it is picked at random. This is the only difference. For any distinguisher A playing game which is either $\Gamma^b_{Q,m,n}$ or $\Gamma^b_{Q,m+1,n}$, define an adversary B (refer to Fig. 7) playing game $PR^B_{b'}$:

Game $PR^B_{b'}$:
1: $query_{enc} = \perp$
2: $hk \xleftarrow{\$} H.\mathcal{K}(\lambda)$
3: $k_m \xleftarrow{\$} OTAE.\mathcal{K}(\lambda)$
4: $k' \leftarrow H.Eval(hk, k_m)$
5: **if** $b' = 0$ **then** replace k' by a random value with the same length
6: $B^{ENC,DEC}(hk, k') \to z$

Oracle $ENC(ad, pt)$
1: **if** $query_{enc} \neq \perp$ **then** abort
2: $ct \leftarrow OTAE.Enc(k, ad, pt)$
3: $query_{enc} \leftarrow ct$
4: **return** ct

Oracle $DEC(ad, ct)$
1: **return** $OTAE.Dec(k, ad, ct)$

The adversary $\mathcal{B}$ can simulate the difference between $\Gamma^b_{Q,m,n}$ and $\Gamma^b_{Q,m+1,n}$ by using k' he received in game $PR^{\mathcal{B}}_{b'}$, which is either a hash value or a random value, as the $(m+1)$-th session key k_{m+1}. Finally, $\mathcal{B}$ outputs what $\mathcal{A}$ outputs. We can see that the advantage of $\mathcal{B}$ is

$$\left| \Pr\left[\Gamma^b_{Q,m,n} \to 1\right] - \Pr\left[\Gamma^b_{Q,m+1,n} \to 1\right] \right|,$$

which is negligible due to PR-security (recall Definition. 5). Note that

$$\left| \Pr\left[\Gamma^b_{Q,1,n} \to 1\right] - \Pr\left[\Gamma^b_{Q,n+1,n} \to 1\right] \right|$$

is upper bounded by $\sum_{m=1}^{n} \left| \Pr\left[\Gamma^b_{Q,m,n} \to 1\right] - \Pr\left[\Gamma^b_{Q,m+1,n} \to 1\right] \right|$, thereby also negligible. Combined with Eq. (1), we can then deduce that

$$\left| \Pr\left[\Gamma_b \to 1\right] - \sum_{Q,n} \Pr\left[\Gamma^b_{Q,n+1,n} \to 1\right] \right| \text{ is negligible.} \tag{2}$$

Until now, we have reduced the game $\Gamma^b_{Q,1,n}$ to an ideal case $\Gamma^b_{Q,n+1,n}$. In game $\Gamma^b_{Q,n+1,n}$, $k_1,\ldots,k_{n+1}$ are randomly picked. When sending the challenge message, each session key is only used to encrypt/decrypt one message. Moreover, according to C_{sym}-cleanness, no participant has an EXP_{st} before seeing (ad_{test}, ct_{test}), and the plaintext pt_{test} corresponding to (ad_{test}, ct_{test}) has no direct or indirect leakage. We can deduce that the difference

$$\left| \Pr\left[\Gamma^0_{Q,n+1,n} \to 1\right] - \Pr\left[\Gamma^1_{Q,n+1,n} \to 1\right] \right|$$

is negligible by the IND-OTCCA security of OTAE. More specifically, for any distinguisher $\mathcal{A}$ playing game which is either $\Gamma^0_{Q,n+1,n}$ or $\Gamma^1_{Q,n+1,n}$, define an adversary $\mathcal{D}$ (refer to Fig. 8) playing game IND-OTCCA$^{\mathcal{D}}_b$:

Game IND-OTCCA$^{\mathcal{D}}_b$
1: challenge $= \perp$
2: $k_n \xleftarrow{\$} OTAE.\mathcal{K}_\lambda$
3: $\mathcal{D}^{CH,DEC}() \to b'$
4: **return** b'

Oracle DEC(ad, ct)
1: **if** (ad, ct) = challenge **then** abort
2: **return** OTAE.Dec(k_n, ad, ct)

Oracle CH(ad, pt)
1: **if** challenge $\neq \perp$ **then** abort
2: **if** $b = 0$ **then**
3:     replace pt by a random message of the same length
4: OTAE.Enc(k_n, ad, pt) $\to$ ct
5: challenge $\leftarrow$ (ad, ct)
6: **return** (ct)

The adversary $\mathcal{D}$ can simulate the difference between $\Gamma^0_{Q,n+1,n}$ and $\Gamma^1_{Q,n+1,n}$ by using the challenge message he received in game $\mathsf{IND\text{-}OTCCA}^{\mathcal{D}}_b$ (where pt is replaced by some random value for $b = 0$) as the challenge message in game $\Gamma^b_{Q,n+1,n}$. Finally, $\mathcal{D}$ outputs what $\mathcal{A}$ outputs. The advantage of $\mathcal{D}$ is

$$\left| \Pr\left[\Gamma^0_{Q,n+1,n} \to 1 \right] - \Pr\left[\Gamma^1_{Q,n+1,n} \to 1 \right] \right|,$$

which is negligible due to the $\mathsf{IND\text{-}OTCCA}$ security of OTAE.

Finally, we can deduce that the difference $|\Pr[\Gamma_0 \to 1] - \Pr[\Gamma_1 \to 1]|$ is negligible combined with (2).

FORGE-security. We then consider the FORGE-security. We now define Γ as the initial C_{noexp}-FORGE game which has a special message $(\mathsf{ad}^*, \mathsf{ct}^*)$. This special message is the forgery sent by the adversary to participant P, where $\mathsf{P} = \overline{\mathsf{Q}}$. The game Γ returns 1 if the special message is a forgery. We also consider the event C_{noexp} that no participant P has an $\mathsf{EXP}_{st}(\mathsf{P})$ query before having seen $(\mathsf{ad}^*, \mathsf{ct}^*)$. The game Γ has the property that whenever C_{noexp} does not occur, it never returns 1 due to the C_{noexp} cleanness condition.

Similarly with the IND-CCA-security proof, we define below for each (Q, m, n) the hybrids $\Gamma_{\mathsf{Q},m,n}$ (refer to Fig. 9) which essentially assumes that the forgery message is the n-th message sent by Q. We have that

$$\Pr[\Gamma \to 1] = \sum_{Q,n} \Pr[\Gamma_{Q,1,n} \to 1]. \tag{3}$$

Moreover, we have that $|\Pr[\Gamma_{Q,m,n} \to 1] - \Pr[\Gamma_{Q,m+1,n} \to 1]|$ is negligible due to PR-security (Fig. 7 reduction). Therefore,

$$|\Pr[\Gamma_{Q,1,n} \to 1] - \Pr[\Gamma_{Q,n+1,n} \to 1]| \leqslant \sum_{m=1}^{n} |\Pr[\Gamma_{Q,m,n} \to 1] - \Pr[\Gamma_{Q,m+1,n} \to 1]|$$

is negligible. Combined with Eq. (3), we can then deduce that

$$\left| \Pr[\Gamma \to 1] - \sum_{Q,n} \Pr[\Gamma_{Q,n+1,n} \to 1] \right| \text{ is negligible.} \tag{4}$$

The probability that $\Pr[\Gamma_{Q,n+1,n} \to 1]$ is negligible due to the SEF-OTCMA-security of OTAE. Again, for any distinguisher $\mathcal{A}$ playing game $\Gamma_{Q,n+1,n}$, we define an adversary $\mathcal{E}$ (refer to Fig. 10) playing game $\mathsf{SEF\text{-}OTCMA}^{\mathcal{E}}$:

Game SEF-OTCMA$^\mathcal{E}$

1: $k_n \xleftarrow{\$} \text{OTAE}.\mathcal{K}_\lambda$

2: $\mathcal{E}(\lambda) \xrightarrow{\$} \text{sent}^Q_{pt}[n]$ ($:= \text{ad}, \text{pt}$)

3: $\text{OTAE.Enc}(k_n, \text{ad}, \text{pt}) \to \text{ct}$

4: $\mathcal{E}(\text{ad}, \text{pt}, \text{ct}) \to (\text{ad}^*, \text{ct}^*)$

5: **if** $(\text{ad}^*, \text{ct}^*) = (\text{ad}, \text{ct})$ **then** abort

6: **if** $\text{OTAE.Dec}(k_n, \text{ad}^*, \text{ct}^*) = \perp$ **then** abort

7: **return** 1

Meanwhile, $\mathcal{E}$ makes a forgery by using the forgery given by $\mathcal{A}$ in game $\Gamma_{Q,n+1,n}$. The advantage of $\mathcal{A}$, which is

$$\Pr\left[\Gamma_{Q,n+1,n} \to 1\right],$$

is upper bounded by the advantage of $\mathcal{E}$, thereby negligible. Finally, we deduce that the probability $\Pr[\Gamma \to 1]$ is negligible combine with (4).

5   Conclusion

We have shown that the simplest Encrypt-then-Hash protocol EtH provides confidentiality and authentication is a very strong sense. Namely, it provides forward secrecy and unforgeability, except for trivial attacks. It can be used as a replacement of liteARCAD in the hybrid ratchet-on-demand protocol with security awareness by Caforio et al. [6]. It provides good complexity advantages. Furthermore, we avoided the use of a random oracle by expliciting a combined security assumption of encryption and hashing (PR security).

A   Used Definitions

Function Families. A function family H defines a key space $\text{H}.\mathcal{K}(\lambda)$, a domain $\text{H}.\mathcal{D}(\lambda)$, and a polynomially bounded deterministic algorithm $\text{H.Eval}(hk, x)$ which takes a key hk in $\text{H}.\mathcal{K}(\lambda)$ and a message x in $\text{H}.\mathcal{D}(\lambda)$ to produce a digest in $\text{H}.\mathcal{D}(\lambda)$.

One-Time Authenticated Encryption (OTAE). An OTAE scheme defines a key space $\text{OTAE}.\mathcal{K}(\lambda)$ and two polynomially bounded deterministic algorithms OTAE.Enc and OTAE.Dec, associated with a message domain $\text{OTAE}.\mathcal{D}(\lambda)$. OTAE.Enc takes a key k in $\mathcal{K}(\lambda)$, an associated data ad and a message pt in $\text{OTAE}.\mathcal{D}(\lambda)$ and returns a string $\text{ct} = \text{OTAE.Enc}(k, \text{ad}, \text{pt})$. OTAE.Dec takes k, ad and ct and returns a string in $\text{OTAE}.\mathcal{D}(\lambda)$ or else the distinguished symbol $\perp$. It satisfies that

$$\text{OTAE.Dec}(k, \text{ad}, \text{OTAE.Enc}(k, \text{ad}, \text{pt})) = \text{pt}$$

for all $k \in \mathcal{K}(\lambda)$, and $\text{ad}, \text{pt} \in \text{OTAE}.\mathcal{D}(\lambda)$. Moreover, we require that it satisfy the one-time IND-CCA security and SEF-CMA security.

Definition 6 (IND-OTCCA [6]). *An OTAE scheme is* IND-OTCCA-*secure, if for any PPT adversary $\mathcal{A}$ playing the following game, the advantage*

$$\Pr\left[\text{IND-OTCCA}_0^{\mathcal{A}} \to 1]\right] - \Pr\left[\text{IND-OTCCA}_1^{\mathcal{A}} \to 1\right]$$

is negligible.

Game IND-OTCCA$_b^{\mathcal{A}}(1^\lambda)$
1: *challenge* $= \perp$
2: $k \xleftarrow{\$} \text{OTAE}.\mathcal{K}(\lambda)$
3: $\mathcal{A}^{\text{CH,DEC}}(1^\lambda) \to b'$
4: *return* b'

Oracle DEC(ad, ct)
1: *if* (ad, ct) = *challenge* *then abort*
2: *return* OTAE.Dec(k, ad, ct)

Oracle CH(ad, pt)
1: *if challenge* $\neq \perp$ *then abort*
2: *if* $b = 0$ *then*
3:    replace pt *by a random message of the same length*
4: OTAE.Enc(k, ad, pt) $\to$ ct
5: *challenge* $\leftarrow$ (ad, ct)
6: *return* ct

Definition 7 (SEF-OTCMA [6]). *An OTAE scheme resists to strong existential forgeries under one-time chosen message attacks (SEF-OTCMA), if for any PPT adversary $\mathcal{A}$ playing the following game, the advantage* $\Pr\left[\text{SEF-OTCMA}^{\mathcal{A}} \to 1\right]$ *is negligible.*

Game SEF-OTCMA$^{\mathcal{A}}(1^\lambda)$
1: $k \xleftarrow{\$} \text{OTAE}.\mathcal{K}_\lambda$
2: $\mathcal{A}(1^\lambda) \xrightarrow{\$} (\text{st}, \text{ad}, \text{pt})$
3: OTAE.Enc(k, ad, pt) $\to$ ct
4: $\mathcal{A}(\text{st}, \text{ad}, \text{pt}, \text{ct}) \to (\text{ad}', \text{ct}')$
5: *if* (ad', ct') = (ad, ct) *then abort*
6: *if* OTAE.Dec(k, ad', ct') $= \perp$ *then abort*
7: *return 1*

We further append some necessary definitions in ARCAD [6] (adapted from Durak-Vaudenay protocol [8]). For more details, please refer to [6] and [8].

Definition 8 (Matching status [6]). *We say that P is in a matching status at time* t *if*

- *at any moment of the game before time* t *for* P, received$_{\text{ct}}^{\text{P}}$ *is a prefix of* sent$_{\text{ct}}^{\overline{\text{P}}}$ — *this defines this defines the time* $\overline{\text{t}}$ *for* $\overline{\text{P}}$ *when* $\overline{\text{P}}$ *sent the last message in* received$_{\text{ct}}^{\text{P}}(\text{t})$.
- *and at any moment of the game before time* $\overline{\text{t}}$ *for* $\overline{\text{P}}$, received$_{\text{ct}}^{\overline{\text{P}}}$ *is a prefix of* sent$_{\text{ct}}^{\text{P}}$.

Definition 9 (Forgery [6]**).** *Given a participant* P *in a game, we say that* $(\mathsf{ad}, \mathsf{ct}) \in \mathsf{received}^{\mathsf{P}}_{\mathsf{ct}}$ *is a forgery if at the moment of the game just before* P *received* $(\mathsf{ad}, \mathsf{ct})$, P *was in a matching status, but no longer after receiving* $(\mathsf{ad}, \mathsf{ct})$.

B   Correctness Game

We formally define the CORRECTNESS game in Fig. 5.

C   Hybrids and Adversaries in Security Proof

We define hybrids $\Gamma^{\mathsf{b}}_{\mathsf{Q},\mathsf{m},\mathsf{n}}$ in Fig. 6, adversary $\mathcal{B}$ in Fig. 7, adversary $\mathcal{D}$ in Fig. 8, hybrids $\Gamma_{\mathsf{Q},\mathsf{m},\mathsf{n}}$ in Fig. 9 and adversary $\mathcal{E}$ in Fig. 10.

Game CORRECTNESS(sched)

1: set all sent^*_* and $\mathsf{received}^*_*$ to $\emptyset$
2: $\mathsf{Setup}(1^\lambda) \xrightarrow{\$} \mathsf{pp}$
3: $\mathsf{Initall}(1^\lambda, \mathsf{pp}) \xrightarrow{\$} (\mathsf{st}_A, \mathsf{st}_B)$
4: initialize two FIFO lists $\mathsf{incoming}_A, \mathsf{incoming}_B \leftarrow \emptyset$
5: $i \leftarrow 0$
6: **loop**
7:     $i \leftarrow i + 1$
8:     **if** sched_i of form (P, "rec", ad, ct) **then**
9:         **if** $\mathsf{incoming}_P$ is empty **then**
10:             **return** 0
11:         pull (ad, ct) from $\mathsf{incoming}_P$
12:         $\mathsf{acc} \leftarrow \mathsf{RATCH}(\mathsf{P}, \text{"rec"}, \mathsf{ad}, \mathsf{ct})$
13:         **if** $\mathsf{acc} = \mathsf{false}$ **then return** 1
14:     **else**
15:         parse $\mathsf{sched}_i = (\mathsf{P}, \text{"send"}, \mathsf{ad}, \mathsf{pt})$
16:         $\mathsf{ct} \leftarrow \mathsf{RATCH}(\mathsf{P}, \text{"send"}, \mathsf{ad}, \mathsf{pt})$
17:         push (ad, ct) to $\mathsf{incoming}_{\bar{\mathsf{P}}}$
18:     **if** $\mathsf{received}^A_{\mathsf{pt}}$ not prefix of $\mathsf{sent}^B_{\mathsf{pt}}$ **then return** 1
19:     **if** $\mathsf{received}^B_{\mathsf{pt}}$ not prefix of $\mathsf{sent}^A_{\mathsf{pt}}$ **then return** 1

Fig. 5. The CORRECTNESS Game of the SARCAD Protocol

Game $\Gamma^b_{Q,m,n}$

1: $hk \xleftarrow{\$} H.\mathcal{K}(\lambda)$
2: $cnt^{send}_Q, cnt^{rec}_{\overline{Q}} \leftarrow 0$
3: pick $k_1, \ldots, k_m, k \xleftarrow{\$} \mathcal{K}_\lambda$
4: $st_Q \leftarrow (1^\lambda, hk, k_1, k)$

5: $st_{\overline{Q}} \leftarrow (1^\lambda, hk, k, k_1)$
6: set sent$^*_*$ and received$^*_*$ variables to $\emptyset$
7: Set t_{test} to $\perp$
8: $z \leftarrow \mathcal{A}^{RATCH,EXP_{st},EXP_{pt},CHALLENGE}(hk)$
9: if $\neg C_{clean}$ then return $\perp$
10: return z

Oracle RATCH $(P, \text{"send"}, ad, pt)$

1: $pt_P \leftarrow pt$
2: $ad_P \leftarrow ad$
3: parse $st_P = (1^\lambda, hk, sk, rk)$
4: $ct_P \leftarrow OTAE.Enc(sk, ad_P, pt_P)$
5: $sk' \leftarrow H.Eval(hk, sk)$
6: if $P = Q$ then
7:     $cnt^{send}_Q \leftarrow cnt^{send}_Q + 1$
8:     if $cnt^{send}_Q \leqslant m - 1$ then
9:         $cnt \leftarrow cnt^{send}_Q + 1$
10:        $sk' \leftarrow k_{cnt}$
11: $st_P \leftarrow (1^\lambda, hk, sk', rk)$
12: append (ad_P, pt_P) to sent$^P_{pt}$
13: append (ad_P, ct_P) to sent$^P_{ct}$
14: return ct_P

Oracle RATCH $(P, \text{"rec"}, ad, ct)$

1: $ct_P \leftarrow ct$
2: $ad_P \leftarrow ad$
3: parse $st_P = (1^\lambda, hk, sk, rk)$
4: $pt_P \leftarrow OTAE.Dec(rk, ad, ct)$
5: if $pt_P = \perp$ then
6:     return false
7: $rk' \leftarrow H.Eval(hk, rk)$
8: if $P = \overline{Q}$ then
9:     $cnt^{rec}_{\overline{Q}} \leftarrow cnt^{rec}_{\overline{Q}} + 1$
10:    if $cnt^{rec}_{\overline{Q}} \leqslant m - 1$ then
11:        $cnt \leftarrow cnt^{rec}_{\overline{Q}} + 1$
12:        $rk' \leftarrow k_{cnt}$
13: $st_{\overline{P}} \leftarrow (1^\lambda, hk, sk, rk')$
14: append (ad_P, pt_P) to received$^P_{pt}$
15: append (ad_P, ct_P) to received$^P_{ct}$
16: return true

Oracle $EXP_{st}(P)$

1: if $(P = Q$ and $cnt^{send}_Q \leqslant n)$ or $(P = \overline{Q}$ and $cnt^{rec}_{\overline{Q}} \leqslant n)$ then abort
2: return st_P

Oracle $EXP_{pt}(P)$

1: return pt_P

Oracle CHALLENGE(P, ad, pt)

1: if $t_{test} \neq \perp$ then return $\perp$
2: if $b = 0$ then
3:     replace pt by a random string of the same length

4: $ct \leftarrow RATCH(P, \text{"send"}, ad, pt)$
5: if $cnt^{send}_Q \neq n$ or $P \neq Q$ then
6:     abort
7: $(t, P, ad, pt, ct)_{test} \leftarrow (time, P, ad, pt, ct)$
8: return ct

Fig. 6. IND-CCA-Security: Hybrids $\Gamma^b_{Q,m,n}$

$\mathcal{B}^{\mathsf{ENC},\mathsf{DEC}}(\mathsf{hk},\mathsf{k}')$:

1: $\mathsf{hk} \xleftarrow{\$} \mathsf{H}.\mathcal{K}(\lambda)$
2: $\mathsf{cnt}_Q^{\mathsf{send}}, \mathsf{cnt}_{\overline{Q}}^{\mathsf{rec}} \leftarrow 0$
3: pick $\mathsf{k}_1, \ldots, \mathsf{k}_{m-1}, \mathsf{k} \xleftarrow{\$} \mathcal{K}_\lambda, \mathsf{k}_m \leftarrow \bot$
4: $\mathsf{st}_Q \leftarrow (1^\lambda, \mathsf{hk}, \mathsf{k}_1, \mathsf{k})$
5: $\mathsf{st}_{\overline{Q}} \leftarrow (1^\lambda, \mathsf{hk}, \mathsf{k}, \mathsf{k}_1)$
6: set sent_*^* and $\mathsf{received}_*^*$ variables to $\emptyset$
7: set $\mathsf{t}_{\mathsf{test}}$ to $\bot$
8: $z \leftarrow \mathcal{A}^{\mathsf{RATCH},\mathsf{EXP}_{\mathsf{st}},\mathsf{EXP}_{\mathsf{pt}},\mathsf{CHALLENGE}}(\mathsf{hk})$
9: if $\neg C_{\mathsf{clean}}$ then return $\bot$
10: return z

Subroutine RATCH (P, "send", ad, pt)

1: $\mathsf{pt}_P \leftarrow \mathsf{pt}$
2: $\mathsf{ad}_P \leftarrow \mathsf{ad}$
3: parse $\mathsf{st}_P = (1^\lambda, \mathsf{hk}, \mathsf{sk}, \mathsf{rk})$
4: if $P = Q$ and $\mathsf{cnt}^{\mathsf{send}} = m - 1$ then
5:      $\mathsf{ct}_P \leftarrow \mathsf{ENC}(\mathsf{ad}_P, \mathsf{pt}_P)$
6:      $\mathsf{cnt}_Q^{\mathsf{send}} = \mathsf{cnt}_Q^{\mathsf{send}} + 1$
7:      $\mathsf{sk}' \leftarrow \mathsf{k}'$
8: else
9:      $\mathsf{ct}_P \leftarrow \mathsf{OTAE}.\mathsf{Enc}(\mathsf{sk}, \mathsf{ad}_P, \mathsf{pt}_P)$
10:      $\mathsf{sk}' \leftarrow \mathsf{H}.\mathsf{Eval}(\mathsf{hk}, \mathsf{sk})$
11:      if $P = Q$ then
12:          $\mathsf{cnt}_Q^{\mathsf{send}} = \mathsf{cnt}_Q^{\mathsf{send}} + 1$
13:          if $\mathsf{cnt}_Q^{\mathsf{send}} \leqslant m - 1$ then
14:              $\mathsf{cnt} \leftarrow \mathsf{cnt}_Q^{\mathsf{send}} + 1$
15:              $\mathsf{sk}' \leftarrow \mathsf{k}_{\mathsf{cnt}}$
16: $\mathsf{st}_P \leftarrow (1^\lambda, \mathsf{hk}, \mathsf{sk}', \mathsf{rk})$
17: append $(\mathsf{ad}_P, \mathsf{pt}_P)$ to $\mathsf{sent}_{\mathsf{pt}}^P$
18: append $(\mathsf{ad}_P, \mathsf{ct}_P)$ to $\mathsf{sent}_{\mathsf{ct}}^P$
19: return ct_P

Subroutine RATCH (P, "rec", ad, ct)

1: $\mathsf{ct}_P \leftarrow \mathsf{ct}$
2: $\mathsf{ad}_P \leftarrow \mathsf{ad}$
3: parse $\mathsf{st}_P = (1^\lambda, \mathsf{hk}, \mathsf{sk}, \mathsf{rk})$
4: if $P = \overline{Q}$ and $\mathsf{cnt}^{\mathsf{rec}} = m - 1$ then
5:      $\mathsf{pt}_P \leftarrow \mathsf{DEC}(\mathsf{ad}_P, \mathsf{pt}_P)$
6:      if $\mathsf{pt}_P = \bot$ then
7:          return false
8:      $\mathsf{rk}' \leftarrow \mathsf{k}'$
9:      $\mathsf{cnt}_{\overline{Q}}^{\mathsf{rec}} \leftarrow \mathsf{cnt}_{\overline{Q}}^{\mathsf{rec}} + 1$
10: else
11:      $\mathsf{pt}_P \leftarrow \mathsf{OTAE}.\mathsf{Dec}(\mathsf{rk}, \mathsf{ad}, \mathsf{ct})$
12:      if $\mathsf{pt}_P = \bot$ then
13:          return false
14:      $\mathsf{rk}' \leftarrow \mathsf{H}.\mathsf{Eval}(\mathsf{hk}, \mathsf{rk})$
15:      if $P = \overline{Q}$ then
16:          $\mathsf{cnt}_{\overline{Q}}^{\mathsf{rec}} \leftarrow \mathsf{cnt}_{\overline{Q}}^{\mathsf{rec}} + 1$
17:          if $\mathsf{cnt}_{\overline{Q}}^{\mathsf{rec}} \leqslant m - 1$ then
18:              $\mathsf{cnt} \leftarrow \mathsf{cnt}_{\overline{Q}}^{\mathsf{rec}} + 1$
19:              $\mathsf{rk}' \leftarrow \mathsf{k}_{\mathsf{cnt}}$
20: $\mathsf{st}_P \leftarrow (1^\lambda, \mathsf{hk}, \mathsf{sk}, \mathsf{rk}')$
21: append $(\mathsf{ad}_P, \mathsf{pt}_P)$ to $\mathsf{received}_{\mathsf{pt}}^P$
22: append $(\mathsf{ad}_P, \mathsf{ct}_P)$ to $\mathsf{received}_{\mathsf{ct}}^P$
23: return true

Subroutine EXP$_{\mathsf{st}}$(P)

1: if ($P = Q$ and $\mathsf{cnt}_Q^{\mathsf{send}} \leqslant n$) or ($P = \overline{Q}$ and $\mathsf{cnt}_{\overline{Q}}^{\mathsf{rec}} \leqslant n$) then abort
2: return st_P

Subroutine EXP$_{\mathsf{pt}}$(P)

1: return pt_P

Subroutine CHALLENGE(P, ad, pt)

1: if $\mathsf{t}_{\mathsf{test}} \neq \bot$ then return $\bot$
2: if $b = 0$ then
3:      replace pt by a random string of the same length
4: $\mathsf{ct} \leftarrow \mathsf{RATCH}(P, \text{"send"}, \mathsf{ad}, \mathsf{pt})$
5: if $\mathsf{cnt}_Q^{\mathsf{send}} \neq n$ or $P \neq Q$ then
6:      abort
7: $(\mathsf{t}, P, \mathsf{ad}, \mathsf{pt}, \mathsf{ct})_{\mathsf{test}} \leftarrow (\mathsf{time}, P, \mathsf{ad}, \mathsf{pt}, \mathsf{ct})$
8: return ct

Fig. 7. Adversary $\mathcal{B}$: Simulating $\Gamma_{Q,m,n}$ and $\Gamma_{Q,m+1,n}$

$\mathcal{D}^{\mathsf{DEC,CH}}()$:

1: $\mathsf{hk} \xleftarrow{\$} \mathsf{H.\mathcal{K}}(\lambda)$
2: $\mathsf{cnt}_Q^{\mathsf{send}}, \mathsf{cnt}_{\overline{Q}}^{\mathsf{rec}} \leftarrow 0$

3: pick $k_1, \ldots, k_{n-1}, k_{n+1}, k \xleftarrow{\$} \mathcal{K}_\lambda$
4: set $k_n \leftarrow \bot$
5: $\mathsf{st}_Q \leftarrow (1^\lambda, \mathsf{hk}, k_1, k)$

6: $\mathsf{st}_{\overline{Q}} \leftarrow (1^\lambda, \mathsf{hk}, k, k_1)$
7: set sent_*^* and $\mathsf{received}_*^*$ variables to $\emptyset$
8: set t_{test} to $\bot$
9: $b' \leftarrow \mathcal{A}^{\mathsf{RATCH,EXP_{st},EXP_{pt},CHALLENGE}}(\mathsf{hk})$
10: if $\neg C_{\mathsf{clean}}$ then return $\bot$
11: return b'

Subroutine RATCH (P, "send", ad, pt)

1: $\mathsf{pt}_P \leftarrow \mathsf{pt}$
2: $\mathsf{ad}_P \leftarrow \mathsf{ad}$
3: parse $\mathsf{st}_P = (1^\lambda, \mathsf{hk}, \mathsf{sk}, \mathsf{rk})$
4: $\mathsf{ct}_P \leftarrow \mathsf{OTAE.Enc}(\mathsf{sk}, \mathsf{ad}_P, \mathsf{pt}_P)$
5: $\mathsf{sk}' \leftarrow \mathsf{H.Eval}(\mathsf{hk}, \mathsf{sk})$
6: if $P = Q$ and $\mathsf{cnt}_Q^{\mathsf{send}} = n$ then
7:     $\mathsf{ct}_P \leftarrow \mathsf{CH}(\mathsf{ad}_P, \mathsf{pt}_P)$
8:     $\mathsf{cnt}_Q^{\mathsf{send}} \leftarrow \mathsf{cnt}_Q^{\mathsf{send}} + 1$
9:     $\mathsf{sk}' \leftarrow k_{n+1}$
10: else if $P = Q$ then
11:     $\mathsf{cnt}_Q^{\mathsf{send}} \leftarrow \mathsf{cnt}_Q^{\mathsf{send}} + 1$
12:     if $\mathsf{cnt}_Q^{\mathsf{send}} \leqslant n - 1$ then
13:         $\mathsf{cnt} \leftarrow \mathsf{cnt}_Q^{\mathsf{send}} + 1$
14:         $\mathsf{sk}' \leftarrow k_{\mathsf{cnt}}$
15: $\mathsf{st}_P \leftarrow (1^\lambda, \mathsf{hk}, \mathsf{sk}', \mathsf{rk})$
16: append $(\mathsf{ad}_P, \mathsf{pt}_P)$ to $\mathsf{sent}_{\mathsf{pt}}^P$
17: append $(\mathsf{ad}_P, \mathsf{ct}_P)$ to $\mathsf{sent}_{\mathsf{ct}}^P$
18: return ct_P

Subroutine RATCH (P, "rec", ad, ct)

1: $\mathsf{ct}_P \leftarrow \mathsf{ct}$
2: $\mathsf{ad}_P \leftarrow \mathsf{ad}$
3: parse $\mathsf{st}_P = (1^\lambda, \mathsf{hk}, \mathsf{sk}, \mathsf{rk})$
4: if $P = \overline{Q}$ and $\mathsf{cnt}_{\overline{Q}}^{\mathsf{rec}} = n - 1$ then
5:     if $\mathsf{ad} = \mathsf{ad}_{\mathsf{test}}$ and $\mathsf{ct} = \mathsf{ct}_{\mathsf{test}}$ then
6:         $\mathsf{pt}_P \leftarrow \mathsf{pt}_{\mathsf{test}}$
7:     else
8:         $\mathsf{pt}_P \leftarrow \mathsf{DEC}(\mathsf{ad}, \mathsf{ct})$
9:     if $\mathsf{pt}_P = \bot$ then
10:        return false
11: else
12:     $\mathsf{pt}_P \leftarrow \mathsf{OTAE.Dec}(\mathsf{rk}, \mathsf{ad}, \mathsf{ct})$
13:     if $\mathsf{pt}_P = \bot$ then
14:        return false
15:     $\mathsf{rk}' \leftarrow \mathsf{H.Eval}(\mathsf{hk}, \mathsf{rk})$
16:     if $P = \overline{Q}$ then
17:        $\mathsf{cnt}_{\overline{Q}}^{\mathsf{rec}} \leftarrow \mathsf{cnt}_{\overline{Q}}^{\mathsf{rec}} + 1$
18:        if $\mathsf{cnt}_{\overline{Q}}^{\mathsf{rec}} \leqslant n - 1$ then
19:            $\mathsf{cnt} \leftarrow \mathsf{cnt}_{\overline{Q}}^{\mathsf{rec}} + 1$
20:            $\mathsf{rk}' \leftarrow k_{\mathsf{cnt}}$
21:     $\mathsf{st}_P \leftarrow (1^\lambda, \mathsf{hk}, \mathsf{sk}, \mathsf{rk}')$
22:     append $(\mathsf{ad}_P, \mathsf{pt}_P)$ to $\mathsf{received}_{\mathsf{pt}}^P$
23:     append $(\mathsf{ad}_P, \mathsf{ct}_P)$ to $\mathsf{received}_{\mathsf{ct}}^P$
24:     return true

Subroutine $\mathsf{EXP_{st}}(P)$

1: if $(P = Q$ and $\mathsf{cnt}_Q^{\mathsf{send}} \leqslant n)$ or $(P = \overline{Q}$ and $\mathsf{cnt}_{\overline{Q}}^{\mathsf{rec}} \leqslant n)$ then abort
2: return st_P

Subroutine $\mathsf{EXP_{pt}}(P)$

1: return pt_P

Subroutine CHALLENGE(P, ad, pt)

1: if $t_{\mathsf{test}} \neq \bot$ then return $\bot$
2: $\mathsf{ct} \leftarrow \mathsf{RATCH}(P, \text{"send"}, \mathsf{ad}, \mathsf{pt})$
3: if $\mathsf{cnt}_Q^{\mathsf{send}} \neq n$ or $P \neq Q$ then abort
4: $(t, P, \mathsf{ad}, \mathsf{pt}, \mathsf{ct})_{\mathsf{test}} \leftarrow (\mathsf{time}, P, \mathsf{ad}, \mathsf{pt}, \mathsf{ct})$
5: return ct

Fig. 8. Adversary $\mathcal{D}$: Simulating $\Gamma_{Q,n+1,n}^0$ and $\Gamma_{Q,n+1,n}^1$

Game $\Gamma_{Q,m,n}$

1: $hk \xleftarrow{\$} H.\mathcal{K}(\lambda)$
2: $cnt_Q^{send}, cnt_Q^{rec} \leftarrow 0$
3: pick $k_1, \ldots, k_m, k \xleftarrow{\$} \mathcal{K}_\lambda$
4: $st_Q \leftarrow (1^\lambda, hk, k_1, k)$
5: $st_{\overline{Q}} \leftarrow (1^\lambda, hk, k, k_1)$
6: set all $sent_*^*$ and $received_*^*$ variables to $\emptyset$
7: $(P, ad^*, ct^*) \leftarrow \mathcal{A}^{RATCH, EXP_{st}, EXP_{pt}}(hk)$
8: if $P \neq \overline{Q}$ or $cnt_Q^{send} \neq n$ then abort
9: $RATCH(P, \text{"rec"}, ad^*, ct^*) \rightarrow acc$
10: if $\neg C_{clean}$ then return 0
11: if $acc = false$ then return 0
12: if (ad^*, ct^*) is not a forgery for P then return 0
13: return 1

Oracle RATCH (P, "send", ad, pt)

1: $pt_P \leftarrow pt$
2: $ad_P \leftarrow ad$
3: parse $st_P = (1^\lambda, hk, sk, rk)$
4: $ct_P \leftarrow OTAE.Enc(sk, ad_P, pt_P)$
5: $sk' \leftarrow H.Eval(hk, sk)$
6: if $P = Q$ then
7:     $cnt_Q^{send} \leftarrow cnt_Q^{send} + 1$
8:     if $cnt_Q^{send} \leqslant m - 1$ then
9:         $cnt \leftarrow cnt_Q^{send} + 1$
10:        $sk' \leftarrow k_{cnt}$
11: $st_P \leftarrow (1^\lambda, hk, sk', rk)$
12: append (ad_P, pt_P) to $sent_{pt}^P$
13: append (ad_P, ct_P) to $sent_{ct}^P$
14: return ct_P

Oracle RATCH (P, "rec", ad, ct)

1: $ct_P \leftarrow ct$
2: $ad_P \leftarrow ad$
3: parse $st_P = (1^\lambda, hk, sk, rk)$
4: $pt_P \leftarrow OTAE.Dec(rk, ad, ct)$
5: if $pt_P = \perp$ then
6:     return false
7: $rk' \leftarrow H.Eval(hk, rk)$
8: if $P = Q$ then
9:     $cnt_{\overline{Q}}^{rec} \leftarrow cnt_{\overline{Q}}^{rec} + 1$
10:    if $cnt_{\overline{Q}}^{rec} \leqslant m - 1$ then
11:        $cnt \leftarrow cnt_{\overline{Q}}^{rec} + 1$
12:        $rk' \leftarrow k_{cnt}$
13: $st_{\overline{P}} \leftarrow (1^\lambda, hk, sk, rk')$
14: append (ad_P, pt_P) to $received_{pt}^P$
15: append (ad_P, ct_P) to $received_{ct}^P$
16: return true

Oracle $EXP_{st}(P)$

1: if $(P = Q$ and $cnt_Q^{send} \leqslant n)$ or $(P = \overline{Q}$ and $cnt_{\overline{Q}}^{rec} \leqslant n)$ then abort
2: return st_P

Oracle $EXP_{pt}(P)$

1: return pt_P

Fig. 9. FORGE-Security: Hybrids $\Gamma_{Q,m,n}$

$\mathcal{E}^{\mathsf{ENC},\mathsf{DEC}}()$:

1: $hk \xleftarrow{\$} H.\mathcal{K}(\lambda)$
2: $cnt_Q^{send}, cnt_{\overline{Q}}^{rec} \leftarrow 0$

3: pick $k_1, \ldots, k_{n-1}, k_{n+1}, k \xleftarrow{\$} \mathcal{K}_\lambda, k_n \leftarrow \perp$
4: $st_Q \leftarrow (1^\lambda, hk, k_1, k)$
5: $st_{\overline{Q}} \leftarrow (1^\lambda, hk, k, k_1)$
6: set all $sent_*^*$ and $received_*^*$ variables to $\emptyset$
7: $(P, ad^*, ct^*) \leftarrow \mathcal{A}^{\mathsf{RATCH},\mathsf{EXP}_{st},\mathsf{EXP}_{pt}}(hk)$
8: if $P \neq \overline{Q}$ or $cnt_Q^{send} \neq n$ then abort
9: return (ad^*, ct^*)

Subroutine RATCH (P, "send", ad, pt)	Subroutine RATCH (P, "rec", ad, ct)
1: $pt_P \leftarrow pt$	1: $ct_P \leftarrow ct$
2: $ad_P \leftarrow ad$	2: $ad_P \leftarrow ad$
3: parse $st_P = (1^\lambda, hk, sk, rk)$	3: parse $st_P = (1^\lambda, hk, sk, rk)$
4: if $P = Q$ and $cnt_Q^{send} = n - 1$ then	4: if $P = \overline{Q}$ and $cnt_{\overline{Q}}^{rec} = n - 1$ then
5: $ct_P \leftarrow \mathsf{ENC}(ad_P, pt_P)$	5: abort
6: $cnt_Q^{send} = cnt_Q^{send} + 1$	6: else
7: $sk' \leftarrow k_{n+1}$	7: $pt_P \leftarrow \mathsf{OTAE.Dec}(rk, ad, ct)$
8: else	8: if $pt_P = \perp$ then
9: $ct_P \leftarrow \mathsf{OTAE.Enc}(sk, ad_P, pt_P)$	9: return false
10: $sk' \leftarrow H.\mathsf{Eval}(hk, sk)$	10: $rk' \leftarrow H.\mathsf{Eval}(hk, rk)$
11: if $P = Q$ then	11: if $P = \overline{Q}$ then
12: $cnt_Q^{send} = cnt_Q^{send} + 1$	12: $cnt_{\overline{Q}}^{rec} \leftarrow cnt_{\overline{Q}}^{rec} + 1$
13: if $cnt_Q^{send} \leqslant n - 1$ then	13: if $cnt_{\overline{Q}}^{rec} \leqslant n - 1$ then
14: $cnt \leftarrow cnt_1^{send} + 1$	14: $cnt \leftarrow cnt_{\overline{Q}}^{rec} + 1$
15: $sk' \leftarrow k_{cnt}$	15: $rk' \leftarrow k_{cnt}$
16: $st_P \leftarrow (1^\lambda, hk, sk', rk)$	16: $st_{\overline{P}} \leftarrow (1^\lambda, hk, sk, rk')$
17: append (ad_P, pt_P) to $sent_{pt}^P$	17: append (ad_P, pt_P) to $received_{pt}^P$
18: append (ad_P, ct_P) to $sent_{ct}^P$	18: append (ad_P, ct_P) to $received_{ct}^P$
19: return ct_P	19: return true

Subroutine $\mathsf{EXP}_{st}(P)$
1: if $(P = Q$ and $cnt_Q^{send} \leqslant n)$ or $(P = \overline{Q}$ and $cnt_{\overline{Q}}^{rec} \leqslant n)$ then abort

2: return st_P

Subroutine $\mathsf{EXP}_{pt}(P)$
1: return pt_P

Fig. 10. Adversary $\mathcal{E}$: Simulating $\Gamma_{Q,n+1,n}$

References

1. Alwen, J., Coretti, S., Dodis, Y.: The double ratchet: security notions, proofs, and modularization for the signal protocol. In: Ishai, Y., Rijmen, V. (eds.) EURO-CRYPT 2019. LNCS, vol. 11476, pp. 129–158. Springer, Cham (2019). https://doi.org/10.1007/978-3-030-17653-2_5
2. Balli, F., Rösler, P., Vaudenay, S.: Determining the core primitive for optimally secure ratcheting. IACR Cryptology ePrint Archive 2020/148 (2020)
3. Bellare, M., Singh, A.C., Jaeger, J., Nyayapati, M., Stepanovs, I.: Ratcheted encryption and key exchange: the security of messaging. In: Katz, J., Shacham, H. (eds.) CRYPTO 2017. LNCS, vol. 10403, pp. 619–650. Springer, Cham (2017). https://doi.org/10.1007/978-3-319-63697-9_21
4. Blazy, O., Bossuat, A., Bultel, X., Fouque, P., Onete, C., Pagnin, E.: SAID: reshaping signal into an identity-based asynchronous messaging protocol with authenticated ratcheting. In: EuroS&P, pp. 294–309. IEEE (2019)
5. Borisov, N., Goldberg, I., Brewer, E.A.: Off-the-record communication, or, why not to use PGP. In: WPES, pp. 77–84. ACM (2004)
6. Caforio, A., Durak, F.B., Vaudenay, S.: On-demand ratcheting with security awareness. IACR Cryptology ePrint Archive 2019/965 (2019). https://eprint.iacr.org/2019/965
7. Cohn-Gordon, K., Cremers, C.J.F., Dowling, B., Garratt, L., Stebila, D.: A formal security analysis of the signal messaging protocol. In: EuroS&P, pp. 451–466. IEEE (2017)
8. Durak, F.B., Vaudenay, S.: Bidirectional asynchronous ratcheted key agreement with linear complexity. In: Attrapadung, N., Yagi, T. (eds.) IWSEC 2019. LNCS, vol. 11689, pp. 343–362. Springer, Cham (2019). https://doi.org/10.1007/978-3-030-26834-3_20
9. Jaeger, J., Stepanovs, I.: Optimal channel security against fine-grained state compromise: the safety of messaging. In: Shacham, H., Boldyreva, A. (eds.) CRYPTO 2018. LNCS, vol. 10991, pp. 33–62. Springer, Cham (2018). https://doi.org/10.1007/978-3-319-96884-1_2
10. Jost, D., Maurer, U., Mularczyk, M.: Efficient ratcheting: almost-optimal guarantees for secure messaging. In: Ishai, Y., Rijmen, V. (eds.) EUROCRYPT 2019. LNCS, vol. 11476, pp. 159–188. Springer, Cham (2019). https://doi.org/10.1007/978-3-030-17653-2_6
11. Jost, D., Maurer, U., Mularczyk, M.: A unified and composable take on ratcheting. In: Hofheinz, D., Rosen, A. (eds.) TCC 2019. LNCS, vol. 11892, pp. 180–210. Springer, Cham (2019). https://doi.org/10.1007/978-3-030-36033-7_7
12. Perrin, T., Marlinspike, M.: The double ratchet algorithm. GitHub wiki (2016)
13. Poettering, B., Rösler, P.: Towards bidirectional ratcheted key exchange. In: Shacham, H., Boldyreva, A. (eds.) CRYPTO 2018. LNCS, vol. 10991, pp. 3–32. Springer, Cham (2018). https://doi.org/10.1007/978-3-319-96884-1_1
14. Systems, O.W.: Signal protocol library for Java/Android. GitHub repository (2017). https://github.com/WhisperSystems/libsignal-protocol-java

Privacy

On Limitation of Plausible Deniability

Atsushi Waseda[1(✉)] and Ryo Nojima[2]

[1] Tokyo University of Information Sciences,
4-1 Onaridai, Wakaba-ku, Chiba, Japan
aw207189@rsch.tuis.ac.jp
[2] National Institute of Information and Communications Technology,
4-2-1, Nukui-Kitamachi, Koganei, Tokyo, Japan
ryo-no@nict.go.jp

Abstract. Recently, a new security definition, named plausible deniability, for synthetic records has been proposed by Bindschaedler et al. Intuitively, the synthetic record r is said to satisfy plausible deniability if there are multiple "original" records that may become r. In this paper, we show that even if each synthetic record satisfies the plausible deniability, there is a possibility that the collection of these records will not have the plausible deniability, i.e., some of these records are re-identifiable.

Keywords: Privacy · Plausible deniability · Re-identifiable

1 Introduction

BACKGROUND: Recently, many companies have been focusing on the research and development of machine learning and big data. When researchers and engineers analyze data using a machine learning algorithm, they often encounter a *privacy* problem. To overcome this, many anonymization or privacy-preserving algorithms such as k-anonymity [9], l-diversity [7], t-closeness [5], and differential privacy [3] have been proposed. In 2017, a new security definition, named *plausible deniability*, for data synthesis, one of the data anonymization methods [6], was proposed [1]. Let D be a dataset and let Anon be an anonymization algorithm. Then, each $d_1 \in D$ is anonymized by Anon to obtain the anonymized record $r = \mathsf{Anon}(d_1)$.[1] This anonymized record r is said to satisfy (thres, γ)-plausible deniability if there are at least or equal to thres $- 1$ distinct records $d_2, \ldots, d_{\mathsf{thres}} \in D$, that may become r,

$$r = \mathsf{Anon}(d_i),$$

with similar probability, where the similarity is parameterized by γ. Moreover, the authors proved that adding some Laplace noise results in differential privacy being satisfied. Hence, this definition is strongly related to the well-accepted definition of differential privacy. Although plausible deniability itself is attractive,

---

[1] In fact, there is another input, par, which will be explained later.

© Springer Nature Switzerland AG 2020
K. Aoki and A. Kanaoka (Eds.): IWSEC 2020, LNCS 12231, pp. 207–217, 2020.
https://doi.org/10.1007/978-3-030-58208-1_12

there is some difficulty in handling it, as we will explain in this paper. That is, the security of plausible deniability only focuses on a *single* record and not on a *collection* of records.

CONTRIBUTION: In this paper, we show that even if each record satisfies plausible deniability, the collection of records will not have plausible deniability, i.e., some of them can be re-identified. This is demonstrated by our new attack, named a *greedy elimination* attack. To demonstrate the effectiveness of our attack, we first anonymize the Online Retail dataset [2] by the anonymization algorithm introduced in [4] to satisfy plausible deniability and then apply our proposed, greedy elimination attack. The result of the attack indicates us that our algorithm is sufficiently powerful even for practical use.

The greedy elimination attack is different from other re-identification algorithms such as that in [8]. That is, if the algorithm generates the output then the output is always correct, i.e., there is no deniability. This property is important. To see this, let us consider the following simple and natural algorithm. Let `distance` be some distance function between an anonymized record and an original record. Then, the algorithm predicts the original record of r to be d if the following is satisfied:

$$\min_{d' \in D} \texttt{distace}(d', r) = \texttt{distance}(d, r).$$

Although this approach is natural, the output of the algorithm is a predication, i.e., it may be incorrect. On the other hand, the algorithm proposed in this paper has the property that its output is always correct.

ORGANIZATION: The organization of this paper is as follows: In Sect. 3, the definition of plausible deniability is given. Next, we show the weakness of the definition and introduce the greedy elimination attack. Finally, in Sect. 5, the usefulness of the greedy elimination attack is shown through experiments.

2   Definition

In this section, security definition for the synthetic dataset generation proposed by Bindschaedler et al. is introduced [1].

Let D be a dataset to be anonymized. We consider the anonymization algorithm Anon, which takes a *record* $d \in D$ and some parameter `par` as the input and outputs an anonymized record $r = \textsf{Anon}(\textsf{par}, d)$. We say that d is a *seed* of r if $r = \textsf{Anon}(\textsf{par}, d)$.

Definition 1 (Plausible deniability [1]). *Let* `thres` *be a natural number, let* D *be a dataset such that* $|D| \geq$ `thres` *and let* Anon *be a probabilistic algorithm. Then, we say that*

$$r = \textsf{Anon}(\textsf{par}, d_1)$$

is releasable *under* (`thres`, γ) *plausible deniability (or* (`thres`, γ)*-PD for short) if there are distinct* $d_2, \ldots, d_{\texttt{thres}} \in D \setminus \{d_1\}$ *such that*

$$\forall i, j \in \{1, \ldots, \texttt{thres}\} : \gamma^{-1} \leq \frac{\Pr[r = \textsf{Anon}(\textsf{par}, d_i)]}{\Pr[r = \textsf{Anon}(\textsf{par}, d_j)]} \leq \gamma.$$

Intuitively, plausible deniability ensures that there are at least `thres` $- 1$ seeds, which produce r with similar probability.

Definition 2 (Testability of plausible deniability [1]). *We say that the anonymization algorithm* Anon *is testable if there exists an algorithm*

$$\mathsf{Test}(r, d, \gamma, \mathsf{par}, \mathsf{thres}, D)$$

that outputs True *if r (with d a seed) satisfies* (thres, γ)*-PD and outputs* False *otherwise.*

3   Limitation of Plausible Deniability

We show that the collections of records can be re-identified, even if each record satisfies plausible deniability. Then, we define "re-identifiability" and consider the toy example for limitation of Plausible Deniability in Sect. 3.1. In Sect. 3.2, we propose the Greedy Elimination attack, generalized the attack algorithm for the toy example.

3.1   Meaning of Re-identification

The key observation of Definition 1 is that the definition only considers the security of a single anonymized record r. However, for practical use, a *collection* of anonymized records should be considered. In this paper, as we have mentioned, we show that there exists an anonymized record that can be re-identified. The meaning of re-identifiability in this paper is as follows:

Definition 3 (Re-identifiability of an anonymized record). *Let D be an original dataset, let* Anon *be an anonymization algorithm, and let $R \subseteq R^\circ$, where*

$$R^\circ = \{r = \mathsf{Anon}(\mathsf{par}, d) \mid d \in D\}.$$

We say that the anonymized record $r = \mathsf{Anon}(\mathsf{par}, d)$, with $r \in R$ and $d \in D$, is re-identifiable or does not have deniability if

$$\mathbf{H}(d \mid r, D, R, \mathsf{par}) = 0, \tag{1}$$

where $\mathbf{H}$ is an entropy function and we regard r, d, D, R and par *as random variables.*

Intuitively, the above definition states that the entropy of a seed, i.e., an original record, d is zero given r, par, D and R. Note that the entropy is measured under D, R, which we regard the adversary has *perfect knowledge* of the original dataset D and the parameter par.

Toy Example: To point out the *limitation* of Definition 1, we consider the following toy dataset D composed of three non-anonymized records:

$$D = \{d_1, d_2, d_3\}.$$

Next, let us consider the anonymized records generated from the following probability distributions:
$$\Pr[\mathsf{Anon}(\mathbf{par}, d_i) = r_j] = 1/2,$$

where

- if $i = 1$, $j = 1, 2$
- if $i = 2$, $j = 2, 3$
- if $i = 3$, $j = 1, 3$.

Hence, the resulting anonymized datasets may become as follows:

Original Dataset	d_1	d_2	d_3
Anonymized Dataset 1	r_1	r_3	r_3
Anonymized Dataset 2	r_2	r_2	r_1
Anonymized Dataset 3	r_1	r_2	r_3

Clearly, the anonymized records satisfy $(2, 1)$-plausible deniability since for any i, there are j_1 and j_2 such that

$$\Pr[\mathsf{Anon}(\mathbf{par}, d_i) = r_{j_1}] = 1/2, \text{ and } \Pr[\mathsf{Anon}(\mathbf{par}, d_i) = r_{j_2}] = 1/2.$$

However, if we release the three records at the same time, then the plausible deniability of some records becomes questionable.

To see this, let us assume that the records (d_1, d_2, d_3) are anonymized as (r_2, r_2, r_1). Since

$$\Pr[\mathsf{Anon}(\mathbf{par}, d_1) = r_2] = 1/2,$$
$$\Pr[\mathsf{Anon}(\mathbf{par}, d_2) = r_2] = 1/2,$$
$$\Pr[\mathsf{Anon}(\mathbf{par}, d_3) = r_2] = 0,$$

and there are two r_2's, the adversary can find that the seed of r_3 is d_3. Hence, r_3 does not have deniability in the sense of Definition 2. Moreover, the probability of losing the deniability in the above case is

$$1/2 \times 1/2 \times 1/2 = 1/8,$$

and is not small.

3.2 Greedy Elimination Attack

Let us generalize the algorithm introduced in Sect. 3.1. We define

$$\mathsf{range}(\mathbf{par}, D) = \{r \mid \Pr[r = \mathsf{Anon}(\mathbf{par}, d)] > 0 \wedge d \in D\}.$$

That is, the set $\mathsf{range}(\mathbf{par}, D)$ is all *possible* anonymized records.

Definition 4 (Predicate algorithm). *A predicate* $algorithm$ Pred *is defined as* Pred : PAR $\times$ D $\times$ range(par, D) $\rightarrow$ {True, False}, *where* Pred(par, d, r) = True *if*

$$\Pr[\mathsf{Anon}(\mathsf{par}, d) = r] > 0,$$

and False *otherwise, where* PAR *is the set of all possible parameters.*

Table 1. The Format of the dataset

ID	Date
12321	2015/10/01, 2015/11/03, ..., 2016/03/04
22321	2015/12/04
21999	2014/01/11, 2015/02/22
08892	2016/03/11, 2017/06/21, ..., 2018/01/11

GREEDY ELIMINATION ATTACK: Given an original dataset D, a parameter par, and an anonymized dataset

$$R \subseteq R^{\circ} = \{\mathsf{Anon}(\mathsf{par}, d) \mid d \in D\},$$

defined as a multiset,[2] our algorithm re-identifies records as follows:

- (Step 1) $G \leftarrow \emptyset$, $D' \leftarrow D$, $R' \leftarrow R$
- (Step 2) While there exists $r \in R'$ such that

$$n_{R'}(r) = |D'_{\mathrm{coll}}(r)|$$

do the following, where $n_{R'}(r)$ is the number of r in the multiset R' and $D'_{\mathrm{coll}}(r) = \{d \in D' \mid \mathsf{Pred}(\mathsf{par}, d, r) = \mathtt{True}\}$:
  1. if $n_{R'}(r) = 1$, $G \leftarrow G \cup \{(d^*, r)\}$, where $\mathsf{Pred}(\mathsf{par}, d^*, r) = \mathtt{True}$.
  2. $R' \leftarrow R' \setminus \{r\}$ and $D' \leftarrow D' \setminus D'_{\mathrm{coll}}(r)$.
- (Step 3) Output G

4   Experiments

4.1   Dataset

Now, we demonstrate the limitation through experiments. In our experiments, the anonymized dataset is obtained by anonymizing the Online Retail dataset [2]. This dataset is a transactional dataset where each record has a customer ID, dates and so on as attributes. The dataset starts on December 1st, 2010 and ends on December 9th, 2011. There are about 4,300 customers after data cleansing. The format of the dataset we used for the experiments is depicted in Table 1.

---

[2] We assume that an original dataset is a set, and an anonymized dataset is a multiset.

4.2   Algorithms

Anonymization Algorithm. As a concrete anonymization algorithm, we chose that from [4]. The algorithm anonymizes the (non-anonymized) dataset of the form shown in Table 1.

Let Perm be a random permutation on a set of IDs. The operation $s \xleftarrow{R} S$ indicates choosing an element s uniformly at random from a set S. Similarly, $A \leftarrow b$ implies assigning b to variable A. Let Date be a date. Then, $\text{Date} + s$ is s days after Date. Similarly, $\text{Date} - s$ is s days before Date.

ALGORITHM Anon (Based on [4]): For input a *rate* x, every record

$$(\text{ID}, \text{Date}_1, \ldots, \text{Date}_m)$$

is anonymized as follows:

- (Step 1) $\text{AID} \leftarrow \text{Perm}(\text{ID})$
- (Step 2) $s_1, \ldots, s_m \xleftarrow{R} \{-x, -(x-1), \cdots, x-1, x\}$, and $\text{ADate}_i \leftarrow \text{Date}_i + s_i$ for every $1 \leq i \leq m$
- (Step 3) Output

$$(\text{AID}, \text{ADate}_1, \ldots, \text{ADate}_m)$$

Design of Pred. The concrete algorithm Pred used in our greedy elimination attack is designed as follows:

- The input is (x, d, r), where

$$d = (\text{ID}, \text{Date}_1, \text{Date}_2, \ldots \text{Date}_m)$$
$$r = (\text{AID}, \text{ADate}_1, \text{ADate}_2, \ldots, \text{ADate}_n),$$

such that $\text{Date}_i \leq \text{Date}_j$, $\text{ADate}_i \leq \text{ADate}_j$ if $i \leq j$.
- The algorithm Pred is as follows:
  - (Step 1) if $m \neq n$, then output 0 and terminate
  - (Step 2) if $|\text{Date}_i - \text{ADate}_i| \leq x$ for every $1 \leq i \leq m$ then output True, and otherwise output False.

Design of Test. Given a dataset D, every record $d \in D$ is anonymized in accordance with Anon introduced in Sect. 4.2. To obtain plausible deniability, each anonymized record $\text{Anon}(\text{par}, d)$ is released if it satisfies (thres, γ)-plausible deniability. This is checked by the algorithm Test as defined in Definition 2.

The design of Test depends on the anonymization algorithm. The algorithm introduced here works when $\gamma = 1$ and hence we omit γ from the input. Given par, r, d, D, and thres, our Test is as follows:

- If there exists $D_{\text{sub}} \subseteq D$ such that

$$D_{\text{sub}} = \{d' \in D \setminus \{d\} | \text{Pred}(\text{par}, r, d') = \text{True}\}| \text{ and } |D_{\text{sub}}| \geq \text{thres} - 1$$

then output True, meaning releasable, and output False otherwise.

Lemma 1. *Let* Anon *be the algorithm introduced in Sect. 4.2. Then,*

$$\text{True} = \text{Test}(\text{par}, r, d)$$

implies that r *satisfies* (**thres**, 1)-*plausible deniability.*

Proof. The construction of the algorithm ensures that if

$$\text{Anon}(\text{par}, d_i) = \text{Anon}(\text{par}, d_j),$$

then

$$\Pr[\text{Anon}(\text{par}, d_i)] = \Pr[\text{Anon}(\text{par}, d_j)].$$

This implies r satisfies (**thres**, 1) plausible deniability.

4.3 Demonstrating the Limitation of Plausible Deniability

We now analyze plausible deniability with the greedy elimination attack. Each record in the dataset is first anonymized by the algorithm Anon and then tested by Test. If the anonymized record passes the test, then it is released. Finally, all passed anonymized records are attacked by the greedy elimination attack. That is, we consider the following experiment.

Experiment(D, par(= rate), thres)

- (Step 1) Generate the anonymized dataset $R^\circ = \{r = \text{Anon}(\text{par}, d) \mid d \in D\}$. If r is generated from d, then we denote $r^{-1} = d$.
- (Step 2) Generate the plausible deniable anonymized dataset

$$R = \{r \in R^\circ \mid \text{Test}(r^{-1}, r, D, \text{par}, \text{thres}) = \text{True}\}$$

- (Step 3) Run the greedy elimination attack on input (D, R, par). Then output $|G|$, where G is the set of re-identified records.

Our experiment Experiment(D, par(= rate), thres) is performed with the following parameters:

- D is Online Retail dataset,
- rate $= 1, 2, \ldots, 20$, and
- thres $= 2, 3, 4$.

Hence, there are 60 patterns.

Figure 1 and Table 2 show the result when thres $= 2$ and rate $= 1, \ldots, 20$, and Fig. 2 and Table 3 show the result when thres $= 3$ and rate $= 1, \ldots, 20$. For both cases, when rate is not so large there are re-identified customers by our algorithm. Note that each number is averaged over 50 trials. When thres ≥ 4, our algorithm does not re-identify any customers. This is not so surprising since if thres is large enough (for example thres is the number of customers) then the re-identification becomes impossible. At this moment, the problem of choosing correct thres, in the sense of re-identification, remains unsolved. This implies that we should be careful in using the plausible deniability.

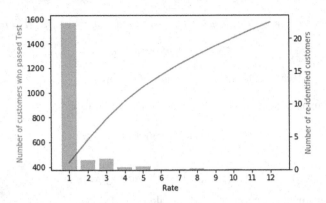

Fig. 1. The number of re-identified customers when **thres** = 2

Table 2. The number of re-identified customers when **thres** = 2

Rate	Num. of customers remained (out of 3069)	Re-identified
1	432.92	22.46
2	617.78	1.5
3	785.56	1.66
4	928.1	0.46
5	1046.12	0.48
6	1140.32	0.12
7	1227.66	0.12
8	1304.22	0.24
9	1376.56	0.02
10	1445.18	0.04
11	1512.32	0.0
12	1573.5	0.0

4.4 Power of Greedy Elimination Attack

Even if the plausible deniability has the limitation, it prevents many anonymized records from re-identification. This is shown by releasing the anonymized records *without* applying Test and then attacking with the greedy elimination attack. Hence, this demonstrates the usefulness of Test from another view point. The experiment can be written as follows:

Experiment(D, par)

- (Step 1) Generate the anonymized dataset $R = \{\text{Anon}(\text{par}, d) \mid d \in D\}$
- (Step 2) Run greedy elimination attack to obtain $|G|$ on input (par, D, R).

Our experiment is performed with the Online Retail dataset, and par = $1, 2, \ldots, 20$. Hence, there are 20 patterns.

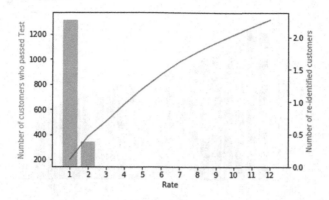

Fig. 2. The number of re-identified customers when **thres** = 3

Table 3. The number of re-identified customers when **thres** = 3

Rate	Num. of customers remaining (out of 3069)	Re-identified
1	201.18	2.26
2	384.54	0.38
3	503.52	0.0
4	636.82	0.0
5	764.98	0.0
6	876.94	0.0
7	977.34	0.0
8	1057.86	0.0
9	1129.96	0.0
10	1195.56	0.0
11	1255.64	0.0
12	1316.14	0.0

Figure 3 shows the result of this experiment. Our algorithm succeeds in re-identifying more than half the customers even if the rate is as large as 20. This demonstrates the power of our proposed attack and also the impact of applying the algorithm Test to remove non-plausible deniable records.

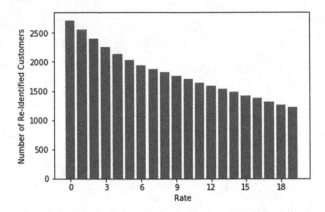

Fig. 3. Re-identification without Test

5 Conclusion

In this paper, we have shown that the recently proposed security definition *plausible deniability* has a limitation. To show this, we have proposed a new algorithm, named the *greedy elimination* attack, and its advantageousness is demonstrated using a real-world dataset. We have also shown the power of this algorithm by attacking an anonymized dataset that is not protected by Test, and it was shown that more than 50% of customers can be re-identified.

These results show that even though the plausible deniability seems useful it does not ensure the hardness of re-identification and there is a need to be careful for the practical use.

References

1. Bindschaedler, V., Shokri, R., Gunter, C.A.: Plausible deniability for privacy-preserving data synthesis. Proc. VLDB Endow. **10**(5), 481–492 (2017)
2. Chen, D., Sain, S., Guo, K.: Data mining for the online retail industry: a case study of RFM model-based customer segmentation using data mining. J. Database Mark. Custom. Strategy Manag. **19**, 197–208 (2012). https://doi.org/10.1057/dbm.2012.17
3. Dwork, C.: Differential privacy. In: Bugliesi, M., Preneel, B., Sassone, V., Wegener, I. (eds.) ICALP 2006. LNCS, vol. 4052, pp. 1–12. Springer, Heidelberg (2006). https://doi.org/10.1007/11787006_1
4. El Emam, K., Arbuckle, L.: Anonymizing Health Data: Case Studies and Methods to Get You Started, 1st edn. O'Reilly Media Inc., Newton (2013)
5. Li, N., Li, T., Venkatasubramanian, S.: t-closeness: privacy beyond k-anonymity and l-diversity, vol. 2, pp. 106–115, May 2007
6. Machanavajjhala, A., Kifer, D., Abowd, J., Gehrke, J., Vilhuber, L.: Privacy: theory meets practice on the map. In: 2008 IEEE 24th International Conference on Data Engineering, pp. 277–286 (2008)

7. Machanavajjhala, A., Kifer, D., Gehrke, J., Venkitasubramaniam, M.: l-diversity: privacy beyond k-anonymity. ACM Trans. Knowl. Discov. Data (TKDD) $1(1)$, 3–es (2007)
8. Narayanan, A., Shmatikov, V.: Robust de-anonymization of large sparse datasets. In: Proceedings of the 2008 IEEE Symposium on Security and Privacy, SP 2008, pp. 111–125. IEEE Computer Society (2008)
9. Sweeney, L.: K-anonymity: a model for protecting privacy. Int. J. Uncertain. Fuzziness Knowl.-Based Syst. $10(5)$, 557–570 (2002)

Model Extraction Oriented Data Publishing with k-anonymity

Takeru Fukuoka$^{(\boxtimes)}$, Yuji Yamaoka$^{(\boxtimes)}$, and Takeaki Terada$^{(\boxtimes)}$

Fujitsu Laboratories Ltd., Kawasaki, Japan
{fukuoka.takeru,yamaoka.yuji,terada.takeaki}@fujitsu.com

Abstract. Machine learning with personal data has been successfully employed in recent years. Protecting the privacy of a given personal dataset with utilities is therefore a major subject within the privacy community. The classifier trained on an anonymized dataset typically has poorer generalization performance than the classifier trained on the original dataset. We adopt the concept of Tramer et al.'s Model Extraction attack to place models trained on anonymized datasets similar to the original model. This approach also prevents the target variable from being published as it is. Using three open datasets, we do experiments to determine how close the original model is to the model trained on a dataset constructed by our method. Particularly when using Nursery Data set, the model trained on our anonymized dataset with $k = 20$-anonymity gives a model that has almost the same (95%) predictions on a given test dataset as the original model.

Keywords: Privacy · k-anonymity · Machine learning

1 Introduction

Nowadays, using artificial intelligence such as machine learning, individuals or companies sometimes derive new patterns and information from big data. Data collection is necessary and is a major bottleneck in machine learning. However, where data is confidential, publishing such data is sometimes illegal. Hence, in the sense of privacy-protecting Data Mining/Publishing (PPDM or PPDP), many processing/synthesizing technologies have been studied until now.

For example, we consider the following scenario. A big corporation A has a medical test result dataset of employees and a trained model that will detect employees who have cancer. Since A has a reasonable number of employees, the trained model has good predictive performance. Then another corporation B, which does not have such datasets, decides to acquire such a model for detection. However, if A directly transfers his/her model to B, there could be a violation of the personal data set's privacy. For example, the membership inference attack [18] infers from the given model whether a record belongs to the training dataset. Recently, such attacks for machine learning models are actively studied. At the moment, it is too early to establish a standard method for calculating how models

© Springer Nature Switzerland AG 2020
K. Aoki and A. Kanaoka (Eds.): IWSEC 2020, LNCS 12231, pp. 218–236, 2020.
https://doi.org/10.1007/978-3-030-58208-1_13

contain personal data. In other words, to the best of the author's knowledge, there are so far no commonly used approaches in industrial communities for processing models against privacy breaches.

Another way to give a service to B is that A passes an anonymized dataset, and B retains a model on that dataset. In such a case, k-anonymization [19,20] is one of the best approaches, as k-anonymity is easily verified by only checking the output dataset. Moreover, several researchers including the authors of [8–11,15–17], studied applying k-anonymized datasets to machine learning.

A target variable is regarded as a sensitive attribute in these studies and hence not anonymized since the values of a target variable are valuable for machine learning. However, [14] pointed out that such determination of a sensitive attribute may be a source of infringement of privacy. Thus, there is a certain risk of publishing target attribute values. Moreover, a model trained on an anonymized dataset often also has weaker results on minority class detection. For example, according to the papers [15,16] by Malle et al.'s, the F-score of the gradient boosting decision tree classifier trained on a k-anonymized Adult Data set is 0.15 lower than the classifier trained on the original dataset when $k = 19$.

In this paper, we focus on these two issues: publishing datasets without protection on sensitive attributes, and decreasing the F-score for the minority class of the model trained on anonymized datasets. We are inspired by the model extraction attack [22] to solve these issues and propose a way to generate datasets with k-anonymity, where the trained models are similar to the original one. Our proposed approach follows two steps:

Step 1. We create multiple k-anonymized datasets whose quasi-identifiers are the explanatory variables and concatenate them row-wise.

Step 2. In the last step, we replace target attribute values by the expected values by the model trained on the original dataset with anonymized inputs.

Unlike previous researches [8–11,15–17], this procedure does not publish the target attribute as it is. This replacement of the target attribute also reflects the relationship between the explanatory and target variables in the original classifier. Therefore we expect this dataset with k-anonymity will return us the original classifier.

As for experiments, we will use three open personal datasets; Adult Data Set, Nursery Data Set, and Contraceptive Method Choice Data Set. One of our major contributions is the discovery of the relationship between the number of unique records of our dataset with k-anonymity and the concordance rate of the predictions of the model trained on our dataset and that on the original dataset given. Moreover, to find out whether a dataset produced by our method preserves the usefulness as a training dataset, we will compare the F-score for the minority class of the model trained on our dataset with k-anonymity to that by the original dataset. When using Adult Data Set, the F-score for the minority class of the gradient boosting classifier trained on our dataset with k-anonymity is higher than that of [16] even if $k = 20$. Especially for Nursery Data Set, when we produce a dataset from 20 k-anonymized datasets with $k = 20$ and train a model, the predictions with the test dataset of that model coincides with the original prediction of 95% and the F-score for the minority class is 0.90 as encouraging results.

2   Related Works

In this section, we review some anonymity scales and known results for k-anonymization methods preserving utility as a training dataset.

2.1 k-anonymity vs. Differential Privacy

Roughly speaking, there are two widely used scales for anonymity; k-anonymity and ϵ-differential privacy.

k-anonymization is initially introduced by [19, 20] to prevent re-identification by making another dataset from an original dataset. We say that a dataset satisfies k-anonymity concerning given some attributes, which is called *quasi-identifier attributes*, if for an arbitrary given record, there exist at least $(k - 1)$ other records having the same values of the quasi-identifier attributes as the given records (for more precise definition, see Definition 2). By this definition, nobody can characterize an arbitrary record in the given quasi-identifier attributes. This anonymity metric is already common and used in Canada [6], Korea [2], and NHS in the UK [1].

On the other hand, ϵ-differential privacy is a privacy metric for a given non-deterministic query. In our scenario, ϵ-differential privacy for publication of the whole dataset would be in the scope. Adding noise is one of the main methods to archive ϵ-differential privacy. This anonymity metric is also common and used in Apple [21].

In this paper, we employ k-anonymity as a metric. One of the main reasons is explainability. For example, we can show k-anonymity from only the output tabular dataset. In contrast, it is difficult to show a given dataset is an output of an ϵ-differential private mechanism. From this viewpoint, k-anonymity is more explainable for the anonymity of a given dataset. Such a difference between k-anonymity and differential privacy is also reported by ENISA [3, § 4.1.4]. Moreover, it figured out other merits of k-anonymity and reported that using k-anonymity has a dominant role in data releases. This is one of the reasons why some publish institutions employ k-anonymity for privacy evaluation [1, 2, 6].

2.2 k-anonymity and Machine Learning

Previous Researches. One of the main themes of k-anonymization is the trade-off between utility and privacy. Especially in machine learning on a k-anonymized dataset, utility is regarded as a generalization performance of the model trained on a k-anonymized dataset.

The study of the k-anonymization method preserving the utility as a training dataset is started by Iyenger [11] in 2002. Until now, many k-anonymization methods are proposed and applied to learning algorithms including decision tree

[8, 9, 11, 13], Naive Bayes [8, 9, 13], logistic regression [13, 16], Linear-SVC [10, 15, 16], k-NN [17], and some ensemble methods such as random forest and gradient boosting decision tree [15, 16]. Rodríguez-Hoyos et al. [17] also listed up recent works related to k-anonymization and machine learning [17, Table 1].

Table 1. The known differences in the accuracy scores of the model trained on anonymized datasets and the original dataset. They used Adult Data Set [5]. The columns named "attributes" and "QIs" mean the number of attributes (including the target attribute) and the number of quasi-identifiers respectively. The target variable is always assumed not to be a quasi-identifier. "DT" and "LR" mean decision tree and logistic regression respectively. Note that this table is just a partial summary of [8–11, 13, 17].

Paper	Attributes	QIs	k	Model	Accuracy (Original)	Accuracy (k-anonymized)	Difference
[11]	9	8	25	DT	0.829	0.820–0.825	<0.01
[8,9]	15	9	20	DT	0.853	0.845–0.850	<0.01
[13]	15	14	20	DT	0.853	0.845–0.850	<0.01
				LR	0.8692	0.8480	0.0212
[10]	15	8	32	Linear-SVM	0.84–0.85	0.81–0.82	0.02–0.04
				RBF-SVM	0.82–0.83	0.82–0.83	<0.01
[17]	15	6	20	k-NN	0.8463	0.8415	<0.01

We pick up the known experimental result and summarize it in Table 1. From this table, we may conclude that k-anonymization does not have a bad inference on the accuracy score, at least when Adult Data Set is chosen as a dataset. As a reason for this accuracy retention, Rodríguez-Hoyos et al. [17] pointed out that k-anonymization may work as a noise removal filter and hence preserve machine-learned macro trends.

This hypothesis was also observed in their experiments about the F-score for the majority class. Actually, as a result of their experiments on Adult Data Set, the F-score for the majority class of the model trained on a k-anonymized dataset is only 0.003 less than the original model when $k = 20$ [17, Table 4].

An Issue in Utility. On the other hand, it was reported by [16] that k-anonymization has a bad inference on the F-score for the minority class. We review a part of their experimental results on Adult Data Set. According to the graph in [16, Figures 8, 10], the F-score of the minority class of the original gradient boosting classifier is in the interval $(0.71, 0.72)$. In their experiments, they at least used 6 attributes as quasi-identifiers. Then the F-score for the minority class of the model trained on their k-anonymized dataset is less than 0.55 when $k = 19$.

From these experimental results, we infer that predictions of models trained on k-anonymized datasets may be biased to the majority class. We regard this phenomenon as an issue. More precisely, an issue in our scope is to construct a dataset with k-anonymity such that the F-scores for non-majority labels of the trained model on the dataset with k-anonymity are close to those of the model trained on a given original dataset.

An Issue in Privacy. Another issue in our scope is how to avoid publishing the values of the target variable as it is. Actually, in most of the previous researches including [8–11,13,15–17], the target attribute is always assumed to be a sensitive attribute. This assumption is natural for the sake of keeping the utility as a training dataset. However, it is pointed out by [14] that any separation between quasi-identifiers and sensitive attributes essentially makes assumptions on the adversary's background knowledge. Therefore, defining the sensitive attribute to be the target variable might be a cause of privacy breach.

3   Our Approach

In this section, we give an explanation of our approach for making k-anonymized data which is suitable for machine learning. We will make such a dataset by making a lot of anonymized datasets and labeling it by using the model which is trained on the original dataset.

3.1   Notation and Setting

Tabular Datasets and k-anonymity: In this paper, we treat only tabular datasets. Our definitions of tabular datasets and k-anonymity are as follows.

Definition 1. *A tabular dataset T is a matrix $(c_{ij})_{i \in I, j \in J}$, where c_{ij} is a real number, a character string, or the missing value, which is denoted by n/a. We call I the* record set *of T and J the* attribute set. *For $j \in J$, we say j is* numerical *if c_{ij} is a real number or n/a for every i and say j is* categorical *is j is not numerical.*

Definition 2. *Let $T = (c_{ij})_{i \in I, j \in J}$ be a tabular dataset. Let k be a positive integer and* QI *a subset of J. We say that a tabular dataset T satisfies k-anonymity* with respect to the quasi-identifier attributes *QI if $\#\{i' \in I \mid c_{i',j} = c_{i,j} \text{ for all } j \in \text{QI}\} \geq k$ for every $i \in I$.*

Generalization vs. Suppression. Until now, many k-anonymization methods – which are namely algorithms to make k-anonymized datasets from given datasets – have been studied. These methods are classified into the following two approaches.

- Generalization: k-anonymizing a dataset by replacing cells with ambiguous ones. For anonymization in this approach, it is necessary to prepare a tree structure of the values of cells called *value generalization hierarchies (VGH)*.

Table 2. (a) Original table (b) Generalized table (c) Suppressed table

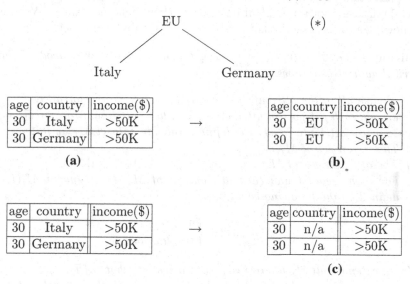

(a)   →   **(b)**

age	country	income($)
30	Italy	>50K
30	Germany	>50K

→

age	country	income($)
30	n/a	>50K
30	n/a	>50K

(c)

- Suppression: k-anonymizing a dataset by replacing cells with the missing value n/a.

For example, to 2-anonymize Table 2a in a generalization approach, we replace "Italy" and "Germany" with "EU" as in Table 2b by using the VGH ($*$). In a suppression approach, Table 2a could be anonymized to Table 2c.

Each of these two approaches has its merits and demerits. Compared to k-anonymization in a suppression approach, k-anonymization by a generalization approach keeps an amount of information if we use a non-trivial VGH. However, it is already pointed out by [4] that making a non-trivial VGH is difficult. In contrast, some k-anonymization algorithms in the suppression approach require only naive extra inputs and hence are easy to handle.

Machine Learning. In this paper, we focus on (multi-label) classification problems. We briefly review the aim of multi-label classification problems and a framework of machine learning. Let $d \in \mathbb{Z}_{>0}$, $l \in \mathbb{Z}_{>1}$, and $D = \{(x_i, y_i) \mid i \in I\} \subset \mathbb{R}^d \times \{1, \ldots, m\}$ a finite set, which is considered to be a sampling dataset of random variables. Set $\Delta^{m-1} = \{(z_l) \in [0,1]^m \mid \sum z_l = 1\}$. The goal is to pick a function $F_\theta \colon \mathbb{R}^d \to \Delta^{m-1}$ in a space of functions $\{F_\theta \mid \theta \in \Theta\}$ such that the prediction $\mathrm{argmax}_{l \in \{1,\ldots,m\}} F_\theta(x)_l$ coincides with y for another sample (x, y). To achieve this, we use D as a training dataset and obtain such a model F_θ by finding a minimizer $\theta \in \Theta$ of $\frac{1}{\#D} \sum_{(x,y) \in D} L(F_\theta(x), y)$, where L is a given loss function. Here we identify the set $\{1, \ldots, m\}$ with the standard basis of $\mathbb{R}^m$.

To pass (anonymized) datasets to these frameworks, we need to decide how to encode datasets into numerical datasets without missing values. We employ the following standard methods to encode a given tabular dataset.

Definition 3. *Let $T = (c_{i,j})_{i \in I, j \in J}$ be a tabular dataset. We encode T into a numerical dataset as follows.*

1. *We remove all of the attribute $j \in J$ satisfying $c_{i,j}$ is n/a for all i.*
2. *We encode each categorical attribute by one-hot encoding. More precisely, for a categorical attribute $j \in J$, we define a tabular dataset M_j as follows.*
   (a) *The record set of M_j is I.*
   (b) *The attribute set of M_j is the set $\{c_{i,j} \mid i \in I\} \setminus \{n/a\}$.*
   (c) *For each record i and each attribute v of M_j, the value at $M_j(i,v)$ is defined by the following equality:*

$$M_j(i,v) := \begin{cases} 1 & \text{if } c_{i,j} = v \\ 0 & \text{otherwise.} \end{cases}$$

3. *We concatenate all M_j where j is a categorical attribute of T and all $(c_{i,j})_{i \in I}$ where j is a numerical attribute column-wise. We call this concatenation D'.*
4. *We fill the missing values of D' by mean imputation and obtain a dataset D.*

We call D the encoded dataset from T.

Remark 1. We give a few remarks on this encoding.

1. This encoding method does not change the set of records.
2. The second step of this encoding is one of the most common methods for treating categorical variables as continuous (c.f. [26]). If $\{c_{i,j} \mid j \in J\}$ has no missing values, this is nothing but the standard one-hot encoding. If not, this is the dummy coding treating "n/a" as the reference category.
3. Let T_{orig} be a tabular dataset and T_{ano} be an anonymized dataset in a suppression approach. Let D_{orig} and D_{ano} be the encoded datasets from T_{orig} and T_{ano} respectively. Then the attribute set of D_{ano} must be contained the attribute set of D_{orig}.

3.2 Our Method

Let T_{orig} be a given dataset. As in explained in Sect. 2, we aim to create an algorithm producing an anonymized dataset T_{syn} with k-anonymity satisfying the following two properties.

- The F-score for the minority class of the model trained on T_{syn} is close to that on T_{orig}.
- T_{syn} satisfies k-anonymity treating all attributes as quasi-identifiers.

Roughly speaking, our approach is to make a "model extractable" dataset from a given dataset. To archive this, we label the target attribute of multiple anonymized datasets by using the model trained on the original dataset. In other words, this method is a variant of a black-box model extraction attack [22] with restricted queries obtained by anonymization.

We explain Algorithm 1 and the notation as follows.

Algorithm 1: Main Algorithm

Input: tabular dataset T, target attribute j_0, $k \in \mathbb{Z}_{>0}$, suppression algorithms $A_1, \ldots, A_N$

Output: a dataset T_{syn} with k-anonymity

begin

1    $T' \leftarrow T|_{J_T \setminus j_0}$;

2   D': the encoded dataset from T';

3   **for** $n \in \{1, \ldots, N\}$ **do**

4      $T'_{\mathrm{ano},n}$: the anonymized dataset given by applying A_n to T';

5      $D'_{\mathrm{ano},n}$: the encoded dataset from $T'_{\mathrm{ano},n}$;

6   F_n: the model trained on the concatenation $(D'|_{J_{D'_{\mathrm{ano},n}}}, T_{\{j_0\}})$;

7      $(z_i)_{i \in I_{D'_{\mathrm{ano},n}}}$: the prediction of F_n of the explanatory variables in $D'_{\mathrm{ano},n}$;

8      $T_{\mathrm{syn},n} \leftarrow (T', (z_i))$: the concatenation. (Remark 1 (1)));

9   T_{syn}: the row-wise concatenation of $T_{\mathrm{syn},1}, \ldots, T_{\mathrm{syn},N}$;

   return T_{syn}

- In our algorithm, we fix a machine learning algorithm as a hidden input. For a dataset D, let J_D denotes the attribute set and I_D the record set. For $C \subset J_D$, $D|_C$ denotes the dataset obtained by considering only the columns belonging to C.
- The inputs are a tabular dataset T, a target attribute j_0 of T, a positive integer k, and suppression algorithms $A_1, \ldots, A_N$.
- The output is a dataset with k-anonymity.
- In l.1, we set T' as the tabular dataset consisting of the explanatory variables.
- In l.2, we encode T' into the numerical data D' in the same manner as Definition 3.
- In l.3–l.8, we k-anonymize the dataset D into $D'_{\mathrm{ano},n}$ by using the anonymization algorithm A_n for each $n \in \{1, \ldots, N\}$.
- In l.4, we simply anonymize the explanatory variables T' into $T'_{\mathrm{ano},n}$ by the algorithm A_n.
- In l.5, we encode $T'_{\mathrm{ano},n}$ into $D'_{\mathrm{ano},n}$
- In l.6, we restrict the original explanatory variables D' to the attribute dataset of $D'_{\mathrm{ano},n}$. $J_{D'_{\mathrm{ano},n}}$ is a subset of $J_{D'}$ by Remark 1 (3). Then we train on the dataset with the dataset for restricted explanatory variables $D'|_{J_{D'_{\mathrm{ano},n}}}$ and the target $T_{\{j_0\}}$.

- In 1.7, we obtain the query result (z_i) by the model F_n trained on the (restricted) original dataset with the anonymized input $D'_{\text{ano},n}$.
- In 1.8, we take the column-wise concatenation $T_{\text{syn},n}$ of T' with (z_i). If giving labels is a deterministic system, $T_{\text{syn},n}$ is k-anonymized since so is T'.
- In 1.9, we take the row-wise concatenation of $T_{\text{syn},1}, \ldots, T_{\text{syn},n}$. The reason why we take multiple anonymized datasets is to increase the number of unique records that we throw into the model. Note that the concatenated data T_{syn} is k-anonymized since so is $T_{\text{syn},i}$ for every i.

Possible Variants. As a variant of our method, it is possible to change the values of a given target variable by not the predictions but the confidence vectors of the respective labels. This method is closer to the approach in [22] and hence may produce more useful datasets than our method. However, datasets produced by this alternative method also have more information on its attribute set. Since this process releases the confidence value of each class, the attribute set of the released dataset includes the range of the values of a given target attribute. This might cause another breach of privacy, which is difficult to estimate. One of the merits of our method is that this leakage cannot happen since our method preserve the attribute set of a given dataset.

Another possible variant is to use anonymization algorithms in not suppression approaches but generalization approaches. A reason why we only treat suppression approaches is to put our algorithm into practice without many auxiliary inputs depending on tabular datasets. Indeed, when we employ anonymization algorithms in generalization approaches, we must prepare algorithms for producing VGHs, which is difficult, as we pointed out in Sect. 3.1. Also, we need to encode datasets anonymized by generalization approaches. Encoding algorithms for an anonymized dataset in a generalization approach was studied by Inan et al. [10]. However, at this moment, there is no established standard encoding method independent of a given dataset. In conclusion, if we seriously apply a given dataset to our algorithm with generalization approaches, we may spend a lot of time for preparation of VGHs and encoding methods. This is another task, which is out of our scope. In contrast, the auxiliary inputs of suppression algorithms are not very dependant on a given dataset. Moreover, there are standard encoding methods for suppressed datasets as in Definition 3. Thus we employ anonymized algorithms in suppression approaches.

4   Experiments

In this section, we experimentally confirm whether our dataset with k-anonymity enables us to reconstruct the model which is trained on the original dataset. We also see the F-score for the minority class of the model trained on our dataset with k-anonymity.

4.1 Datasets

For our experiments, we will use the following three open personal datasets. Each dataset is taken from UCI Machine Learning Repository [5] and its explanatory variables consist of demographic variables of individuals.

Adult Data Set This dataset consists of a training dataset with 32561 records and a test dataset with 16281 records. The attribute set consists of 8 categorical attributes, 6 numerical attributes, and the target attribute with 2 classes. The classification task is to predict whether the annual income is higher than $50K. As a preprocessing, we remove the numerical attribute "education-num" since this is just a numeric representation of the categorical attribute "education". We also remove the numerical attribute "fnlwgt" since this is not a demographic attribute such as "age" or "education". Finally, we remove the records containing the missing value. As a result, we use a training dataset with 30162 records and a test dataset with 15060 records such that both of them have 12 attributes (including 4 numerical attributes) as the explanatory variables. The minority class is ">$50K" whose percentage is 24.8922% in the training dataset and 24.5684% in the test dataset.

Nursery Data Set This dataset consists of 12960 records, 7 explanatory categorical attributes, and the target attribute with 5 classes. The task is to predict the rank of an application for a nursery school. The ranks are divided into the following 5 classes: "not_recom", "very_recom", "priority", "spec_prior", or "recommend". As a preprocessing, we remove the records whose target class is "recommend" since the amount of such records is only two. Then the minority class is "very_recom", whose percentage is 2.53%. We split this data into a training dataset (9070 records) and a test dataset (3888 records) in the stratified fashion concerning the target attribute with 4 classes.

Contraceptive Method Choice Data Set (CMC) This dataset consists of 1473 records, 9 explanatory attributes (including 2 numerical attributes), and the target attribute with 3 classes. The task is to predict a contraceptive method divided into 3 classes: "1" = No-use, "2" = Long-term, "3" = Short-term. The minority class is "2" whose percentage is 22.6%. We split this data into a training dataset (1031 records) and a test dataset (442 records) in the stratified fashion concerning the target attribute.

4.2 k-anonymization Algorithm

In this experiment, we employ Yamaoka et al.'s *simple k-anonymization algorithm* [24] in a suppression approach. One of the reasons is that this algorithm prevents some information losses (NCP and KLD) more than the generalization algorithm proposed by Xu et al. [23]. Here we give the definitions for these information losses only for suppressed datasets for simplicity. Let T be a tabular dataset and T' a suppressed dataset. In this situation, the *normalized certainly penalty (NCP)* for T' is the product of the number of the records of T' and the percentage of the missing values in T'. The *Kullback-Leibler divergence (KLD)* is

$$\sum_{i \in I} P_T(i) \log \frac{P_T(i)}{P_{T'}(i)},$$

where I is the record set of T and P_T (resp. $P_{T'}$) is the probability distribution given by T (resp. T') with the finite support I.

In addition, Yamaoka et al.'s algorithm needs a total order on the attribute set of a given dataset as an extra input. Thus we can prepare many different k-anonymizers by producing total orders on the attribute set randomly.

4.3 Machine Learning Algorithm

As reported in [17], the prediction accuracy of the model trained on a k-anonymized dataset is sometimes better than the model trained on the original dataset. A considerable cause is that the training algorithm is not suitable for the original dataset. Hence, we need a suitable machine learning algorithm for Adult, Nursery, and CMC. In our experiments, we use LightGBM [12] to obtain a classifier, which is based on the gradient tree boosting method. The accuracy score and the F-score for the minority classes of each dataset are given in Table 3.

Table 3. The accuracy score and the F-score for the minority class of the model trained on original datasets.

Name of dataset	Accuracy score	F-score for the minority
Adult	0.8671	0.7670
Nursery	0.9985	1.0
CMC	0.5068	0.3980

As in the table, the classification task on Nursery Data Set is well-solved thanks to LightGBM. The test result on Adult Data Set is also better than the benchmarks reported in the description of Adult Data Set [5]. However, it seems difficult to solve the classification task on CMC Data Set. At this moment, the authors cannot improve these scores even if they use another machine learning process, such as a multilayer perceptron.

4.4 Experiment

In this experiment, we measure how the dataset with k-anonymity made by our method enables us to reconstruct the model trained on a given original dataset. Let T be a given tabular dataset, which is one of Adult, Nursery, or CMC. We divide T into two datasets: the training dataset T_{train} and the test dataset T_{test}. Using the training dataset T_{train}, we will construct a model F_{orig}. We also prepare suppression algorithms $A_1, \ldots, A_{20}$, which are based on Yamaoka et al.'s algorithm with picking 20 total orders of attributes randomly.

Then for each $k \in \{2, \ldots, 20\}$ and $N \in \{1, \ldots, 20\}$, we produce another dataset $T_{\text{train,syn}}^{k,N}$ with k-anonymity by applying Algorithm 1 to the inputs $T = T_{\text{train}}$, the target attribute j_0 which we want to classify, the anonymity parameter k, and suppression algorithms $A_1, \ldots, A_N$. Using the training dataset $T_{\text{train,syn}}^{k,N}$, we will construct a model $F_{\text{syn}}^{k,N}$. Since $2 \le k \le 20$ and $1 \le N \le 20$, we obtain 380 different datasets $T_{\text{train,syn}}^{k,N}$ with k-anonymity and 380 different models $F_{\text{syn}}^{k,N}$.

Test Error Rate. In the same way as [22], we measure how our model $F_{\text{syn}}^{k,N}$ is close to the original model F_{orig} trained on T_{train} by using the following *test error rate*

$$R_{\text{test}} = R_{\text{test}}(F_{\text{orig}}, F_{\text{syn}}, D_{\text{test}}) := \frac{\#\{i \in I_{D_{\text{test}}} \mid F_{\text{orig}}(x_i) \ne F_{\text{syn}}(x_i)\}}{\#I_{D_{\text{test}}}},$$

where $D_{\text{test}} = \{(x_i, y_i)\}$ is the encoded data obtained from T_{test} and $I_{D_{\text{test}}}$ denotes the record set of D_{test}. R_{test} is in the interval $[0,1]$. Note that $1 - R_{\text{test}}$ is the concordance rate between the predictions of F_{orig} and F_{syn} on the test dataset.

In Fig. 1, we observe a certain relationship between the test error rate $R_{\text{test}}^{k,N}$ of $F_{\text{syn}}^{k,N}$ and the number of unique records $U^{k,N}$ of $T_{\text{train,syn}}^{k,N}$. Figure 1 is the scatter plots $\{(U^{k,N}, R_{\text{test}}^{k,N}) \mid 2 \le k \le 20$ and $1 \le N \le 20\}$. Note that $R_{\text{test}}^{k,N} = R_{\text{test}}(F_{\text{orig}}, F_{\text{syn}}^{k,N}, D_{\text{test}})$ in our notation.

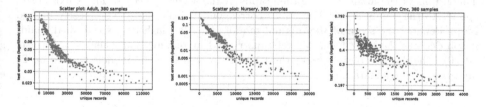

Fig. 1. The scatter plots for Adult, Nursery, and CMC Data Set. The x-axis denotes the number of unique records and the y-axis denotes the test error rate. The y-axis of the above tables is on a logarithmic scale.

Predictive Performance: F-Scores for the Minority Class and Accuracy Scores. To measure the utility of datasets constructed by our method, we simply compare the model trained on our dataset to that on a single anonymized dataset. As we create single k-anonymized datasets in 1.4 of Algorithm 1, we obtain 380 single k-anonymized datasets $T_{\text{ano}}^{k,n}$ of T by A_n, where $k \in \{2, \ldots, 20\}$ and $n \in \{1, \ldots, 20\}$. The quasi-identifier attributes of $T_{\text{ano}}^{k,n}$ are nothing but the explanatory attributes. Let $F_{\text{ano}}^{k,n}$ be the model trained on $T_{\text{ano}}^{k,n}$ for each k and n. For each $k \in \{2, \ldots, 20\}$, we compare the maximum of the F-score for the minority class of the models $\{F_{\text{ano}}^{k,n} \mid n = 1, \ldots, 20\}$ to the F-score of $F_{\text{syn}}^{k,N}$ for $N = 5, 10, 20$. The results are represented as Figs. 2 and 3.

Our experiments were conducted on a PC with Intel(R) Core(TM) i7-8700 3.20 GHz CPU and 16 GB main memory, running Microsoft Windows 10. Our algorithms except for the k-anonymization algorithm were implemented in Python 3.7.3. The implementation of the k-anonymization algorithm [24] that we employed was provided by the authors of [ibid.] and written in Java 8. For the implementation of the machine learning process, we used LGBMClassifier in lightgbm 2.3.1 Python package as a model [12].

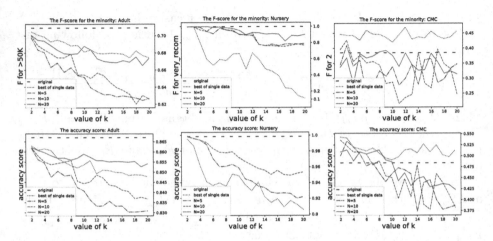

Fig. 2. The graphs in the upper part are the graphs of the F-scores for the minorities. The graphs in the lower part are the graphs of the accuracy scores. The x-axis corresponds to the number of k. The y-axis corresponds to the score. The loosely dashed graph denotes the score of the original model. The dot-dashed (resp. dashed, solid) graph denotes the score for a dataset constructed by our method when $N = 5$ (resp. 10, 20). The dotted graph denotes the best of the scores of the models trained on 20 anonymized single datasets.

4.5   Considerations

Test Error Rate. In Fig. 1, the test error rates seem to be subject to exponential decay. The minimum error rate is 0.023 (resp. 0.0005, 0.197) for Adult (resp. Nursery, CMC) Data Set. Although the order of these minimums coincides with the order of the accuracies of the original models, we do not know the reason for this phenomenon.

Compared to the CMC Data Set, our reconstruction process is successful for Nursery Data Set and Adult Data Set. On Nursery Data Set, if a dataset constructed by our method has 5000 unique records, then the predictions of the trained model on the test dataset coincide with the original model in 95%. Even if $k = 20$, the number of unique records is more than 5000 records when $N \geq 18$. For Adult Data Set, the concordance rate of the predictions is always greater than 89%. Moreover, 30000 unique records are sufficient to make the concordance rate of the predictions greater than 95%. The number of unique records exceeds 30000 if $k = 10$ and $N = 20$ for example.

F-Scores for the Minority Class. We discuss predictive performance by seeing the F-score for the minority class of each dataset.

For Adult Data Set, the F-scores of the models trained on our datasets constructed by our method are actually better than the F-scores that are reported in [16]. Although the F-score trained on a dataset constructed by our method is slightly less than the best of the F-scores of single k-anonymized datasets for $k \neq 10$, the difference of these F-scores is bounded by only 0.013 from above for each k. Note that anonymizing single dataset is not a solution for this problem since the algorithm in $\{A_1, \ldots, A_{20}\}$ which attains the best F-score depends on k.

For Nursery Data Set, our method successfully preserves the utility. In this case, the best of the F-scores of the models trained on 20 k-anonymized datasets $\{T_{\text{ano}}^{k,n} \mid n = 1, \ldots, 20\}$ quickly decreases as k increases. When $k = 20$ for example, that score is 0.1148. In contrast, the F-scores for the minority class of our models keep even if $k = 20$. When $k = N = 20$ for example, that score is 0.9005. This result encourages the effectiveness of our method for keeping the utility of a given dataset.

For CMC Data Set, the F-score trained on the original dataset is relatively low (0.3980). The original F-score is lower than the best of the F-score of the models trained on single k-anonymized datasets $\{T_{\text{ano}}^{k,n} \mid n = 1, \ldots, 20\}$. Thus our models do not have well generalization performance and the F-score does not make remarkable progress as N increases. We also note that, as in the case when we treat Adult Data Set, the algorithm in $\{A_1, \ldots, A_{20}\}$ which attains the best F-score depends on k and hence releasing a single anonymization dataset do not satisfy our purpose.

Accuracy Scores. We discuss on the accuracy scores of our models.

First, we see the result on Adult Data Set. As we saw in Sect. 2.2, there are some papers reporting that the accuracy scores of models trained on single k-anonymized datasets are not so different from the model trained on the original dataset, which is Adult Data Set. A new observation is that the accuracy scores of our models become better as N, which is the number of used single anonymized datasets in Algorithm 1, increases. Especially, the average of the accuracy scores of our models with $N = 20$ is better than that of models trained on single k-anonymized datasets.

When we treat Nursery Data Set, the accuracy scores are getting better as N increases, which was already observed when we treat Adult Data Set. Let us focus on the model trained on a single $k = 20$-anonymized dataset. This model has 0.906 as its accuracy score and 0.115 as its F-score for the minority class. These scores indicate that this model still may be used as a detector of non-minority classes, but not as a detector of a minority, which is the same conclusion as [17]. On the other hand, the model trained on a dataset constructed by our method when $N = k = 20$ has 0.979 as its accuracy score and 0.901 as its F-score for the minority class. These results also indicate that this improvement of the accuracy scores is actually caused by the improvement of predictive performance as a detector of the minority class.

The result for CMC Data Set showed the same tendency as in the case when we treated F-scores. The accuracy scores of models trained on single k-anonymized datasets are better than the original accuracy score, which is relatively low (0.5068). The accuracy scores of the models trained on datasets constructed by our method are not better than the original accuracy score. However, as discussed at the beginning of Sect. 4.4, the predicted results of the original model and our model with $N = 20$ are 80% consistent with each other. These results may indicate that the model trained on a single k-anonymized dataset gives predictions that are significantly different from those of the original model.

4.6   Conclusion of This Experiment

We give a conclusion of our experiments. In our method explained in Sect. 3.2, we create datasets with k-anonymity whose values of the target attributes are predictions of the model trained on the original dataset. Thus we can expect that predictions of the model trained on a dataset with k-anonymity by our methods become to resemble those of the original model as N increase. This expectation is encouraged by the result in Fig. 1 when we treat the 3 datasets; Adult Data Set, Nursery Data Set, and CMC Data Set.

From our method, we can also expect that the predictive performance of models trained on datasets by our method depends on that of the original model. We observed from the results in Figs. 2 and 3 that this expectation is fulfilled when we treat the above 3 datasets. Thus, when we use Nursery Data Set or Adult Data Set (resp. CMC Data Set), the models trained on our datasets have well (resp. poor) predictive performance since so do the original model.

5   Discussions and Future Works

5.1   Safety of Datasets Constructed by Our Method: A Risk Caused by Concatenation

In our method, some distinct k-anonymized datasets are created and concatenated row-wise. Thus, datasets constructed by our method have more information about the explanatory variables of a given original dataset than k-anonymized datasets in the ordinary sense.

For example, we consider the two $k = 2$-anonymized datasets in Fig. 3. If an adversary knows the published dataset is the concatenation of two anonymized datasets, then the original dataset can be recovered as follows. First, it is easily shown that the deleted two cells in the attribute "age" consist of a single "30" and a single "40". Since the number of the records of the original dataset is known to be 6, the original dataset consists of three "30" and three "40" as its "age" attribute and has at least ("30", "US"), ("30", "JP"), ("40", "US"), and ("40", "JP") as records. Since the published dataset is known to be the concatenation

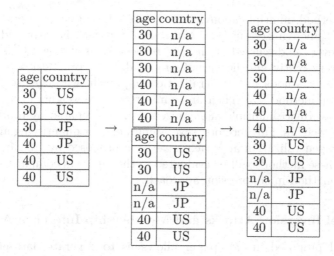

Fig. 3. Two 2-anonymization of a given dataset and the concatenation of them. An adversary might recover the original dataset from the rightmost table if he/she knows the rightmost table is the concatenation of two anonymized datasets coming from the same dataset.

of two anonymized datasets, two ("30","US") records in the published dataset come from a single anonymized dataset, which implies the original dataset has two ("30", "US"). By the same argument, the original dataset has two ("40", "US") records. Thus an adversary can recover the original dataset.

This example shows our method might have a risk of breach of privacy if the number of records of a given original dataset was published. To avoid an adversary inferring the number of the record of a given original dataset, we may delete records from the concatenation until the number of the records is a prime number. Estimation and mitigation of this risk like this countermeasure are remained to be future works.

5.2   Our Algorithm in a Completely Black Box Setting

Our algorithm does not work in the perfect black-box setting since we re-train the model in (1.6)–(1.7) in Algorithm 1. The reason is that some k-anonymization may completely delete the cells in a numerical attribute. As future work, producing numerical cells deleted in k-anonymization is necessary for achieving our method with black-box-only access.

5.3   Our Algorithm with Anonymizers in a Generalization Approach

In this paper, we mainly treat anonymization in a suppression approach. On the other hand, it is important to use anonymization in a generalization approach for our method.

In our method, multiple anonymizers are required. One of the ways to prepare multiple anonymizers in a generalization approach is to provide multiple VGHs. However, as discussed at the end of Sect. 3, providing VGHs is considered to be very costly and hence not practical. As a practical way to do our anonymization methods in a generalization approach, we may use Xu et al.'s anonymization method [23]. Their anonymizers require weights for attributes of given datasets. Hence multiple anonymizers can be prepared by randomly generating these weights. Furthermore, several methods for quantifying anonymized datasets in a generalization approach have been proposed by [10]. Implementations using these methods will be evaluated in the future in comparison with the present our method in suppression approach.

5.4 Model Inversion Attacks and Membership Inference Attacks

The method proposed in this paper allows us to generate datasets with k-anonymity such that predictions of the model trained on these datasets are close to those of the original model. We hope to evaluate in the future whether releasing these datasets with k-anonymity is safer than releasing the original model. The potential for breach of privacy when releasing original models has been evaluated by the model inversion attack [7] and the membership inference attack [18]. We can use these attacks to evaluate the security of models trained on anonymized datasets constructed by our method.

However, there are several issues with these assessments at present. First, we give considerations for model inversion attacks. Until now, model inversion attacks have been considered mainly against models trained on image data [7]. On the other hand, our anonymization deals only with tabular datasets, which makes it difficult to make accurate assessments. Next, we also give considerations for membership inference attacks. It is known that the success of membership inference attacks is related to the generalization performance of the model [18, 25]. Using three open datasets, we experimentally confirmed that the model trained on a dataset constructed by our method gives almost the same predictions as the original model. Thus, it is unclear whether the security of our method can be accurately assessed since this could result in a privacy assessment that relies on the generalization performance of the original model.

If the above issues can be resolved in the future, it will be possible to compare the safety of releasing the original model to that of releasing dataset with k-anonymity constructed by our methods.

6 Conclusion

In this paper, we propose a method to create a dataset with k-anonymity, which can be used to reproduce the original model. Our method produces such a dataset by replacing the original target variable by the prediction of the original model on the anonymized explanatory variables. This method is inspired by Tramér et al.'s model extraction attacks [22]. In the experiment, we observe how this method enables us to reproduce the original model and improve the F-score for the minor label from the ordinary anonymization. For Adult, Nursery, and CMC Data Set, we see that there is a notable relationship between the amount of the unique records of a dataset constructed by our method and the concordance rate of the prediction of the original model and that of the model trained on our dataset. For Nursery Data Set, we observe that our method improves the F-score for the minority class, although using an ordinary k-anonymized dataset as a training dataset has a bad influence on the F-score. The main reason for this improvement is that the model trained on our dataset is similar to the original model, whose predictive performance is good enough.

References

1. Anonymisation standard for publishing health and social care data specification (2013). https://digital.nhs.uk/
2. Guidelines for de-identification of personal data (2016). https://www.privacy.go.kr/
3. Privacy by design in big data (2016). https://op.europa.eu/
4. Ayala-Rivera, V., McDonagh, P., Cerqueus, T., Murphy, L., Thorpe, C.: Enhancing the utility of anonymized data by improving the quality of generalization hierarchies. Trans. Data Privacy **10**(1), 27–59 (2017)
5. Dua, D., Graff, C.: UCI machine learning repository (2017). http://archive.ics.uci.edu/ml
6. El Emam, K., Dankar, F.K.: Protecting privacy using k-anonymity. J. Am. Med. Inform. Assoc. **15**(5), 627–637 (2008)
7. Fredrikson, M., Jha, S., Ristenpart, T.: Model inversion attacks that exploit confidence information and basic countermeasures. In: Proceedings of the 22nd ACM SIGSAC Conference on Computer and Communications Security, CCS 2015, pp. 1322–1333. Association for Computing Machinery, New York (2015). https://doi.org/10.1145/2810103.2813677
8. Fung, B.C., Wang, K., Philip, S.Y.: Anonymizing classification data for privacy preservation. IEEE Trans. Knowl. Data Eng. **19**(5), 711–725 (2007)
9. Fung, B.C., Wang, K., Yu, P.S.: Top-down specialization for information and privacy preservation. In: 21st International Conference on Data Engineering, ICDE 2005, pp. 205–216. IEEE (2005)
10. Inan, A., Kantarcioglu, M., Bertino, E.: Using anonymized data for classification. In: 2009 IEEE 25th International Conference on Data Engineering, pp. 429–440. IEEE (2009)
11. Iyengar, V.S.: Transforming data to satisfy privacy constraints. In: Proceedings of the Eighth ACM SIGKDD International Conference on Knowledge Discovery and Data Mining, KDD 2002, pp. 279–288. Association for Computing Machinery, New York (2002). https://doi.org/10.1145/775047.775089
12. Ke, G., et al.: LightGBM: a highly efficient gradient boosting decision tree. In: Guyon, I., et al. (eds.) Advances in Neural Information Processing Systems 30, pp. 3146–3154. Curran Associates, Inc. (2017). http://papers.nips.cc/paper/6907-lightgbm-a-highly-efficient-gradient-boosting-decision-tree.pdf
13. Kisilevich, S., Rokach, L., Elovici, Y., Shapira, B.: Efficient multidimensional suppression for k-anonymity. IEEE Trans. Knowl. Data Eng. **22**(3), 334–347 (2009)

14. Li, N., Qardaji, W., Su, D.: On sampling, anonymization, and differential privacy or, k-anonymization meets differential privacy. In: Proceedings of the 7th ACM Symposium on Information, Computer and Communications Security, ASIACCS 2012, pp. 32–33. Association for Computing Machinery, New York (2012). https://doi.org/10.1145/2414456.2414474

15. Malle, B., Kieseberg, P., Holzinger, A.: Interactive anonymization for privacy aware machine learning. In: European Conference on Machine Learning and Knowledge Discovery ECML-PKDD, 18–22 September 2017, p. 15 (2017). http://ecmlpkdd2017.ijs.si/

16. Malle, B., Kieseberg, P., Weippl, E., Holzinger, A.: The right to be forgotten: towards machine learning on perturbed knowledge bases. In: Buccafurri, F., Holzinger, A., Kieseberg, P., Tjoa, A.M., Weippl, E. (eds.) CD-ARES 2016. LNCS, vol. 9817, pp. 251–266. Springer, Cham (2016). https://doi.org/10.1007/978-3-319-45507-5_17

17. Rodríguez-Hoyos, A., Estrada-Jiménez, J., Rebollo-Monedero, D., Parra-Arnau, J., Forné, J.: Does k-anonymous microaggregation affect machine-learned macrotrends? IEEE Access **6**, 28258–28277 (2018)

18. Shokri, R., Stronati, M., Song, C., Shmatikov, V.: Membership inference attacks against machine learning models. In: 2017 IEEE Symposium on Security and Privacy (SP), pp. 3–18. IEEE (2017)

19. Sweeney, L.: Achieving k-anonymity privacy protection using generalization and suppression. Int. J. Uncertain. Fuzziness Knowl.-Based Syst. **10**(5), 571–588 (2002). https://doi.org/10.1142/S021848850200165X

20. Sweeney, L.: K-anonymity: a model for protecting privacy. Int. J. Uncertain. Fuzziness Knowl.-Based Syst. **10**(5), 557–570 (2002). https://doi.org/10.1142/S0218488502001648

21. Team ADP: Learning with privacy at scale. Apple Mach. Learn. J. **1**(8) (2017)

22. Tramér, F., Zhang, F., Juels, A., Reiter, M.K., Ristenpart, T.: Stealing machine learning models via prediction APIs. In: Proceedings of the 25th USENIX Conference on Security Symposium, SEC 2016, pp. 601–618. USENIX Association, USA (2016)

23. Xu, J., Wang, W., Pei, J., Wang, X., Shi, B., Fu, A.W.C.: Utility-based anonymization using local recoding. In: Proceedings of the 12th ACM SIGKDD International Conference on Knowledge Discovery and Data Mining, KDD 2006, pp. 785–790. Association for Computing Machinery, New York (2006). https://doi.org/10.1145/1150402.1150504

24. Yamaoka, Y., Itoh, K.: k-presence-secrecy: practical privacy model as extension of k-anonymity. IEICE Trans. Inf. Syst. **E100.D**(4), 730–740 (2017). https://doi.org/10.1587/transinf.2016DAP0015

25. Yeom, S., Giacomelli, I., Fredrikson, M., Jha, S.: Privacy risk in machine learning: analyzing the connection to overfitting. In: 2018 IEEE 31st Computer Security Foundations Symposium (CSF), pp. 268–282 (2018)

26. Zheng, A., Casari, A.: Feature Engineering for Machine Learning: Principles and Techniques for Data Scientists, 1st edn. O'Reilly Media Inc., Newton (2018)

Pairing-Based Cryptography

Efficient Forward-Secure
Threshold Signatures

Rafael Kurek[✉]

Group of IT Security and Cryptography,
University of Wuppertal, Wuppertal, Germany
kurek@uni-wuppertal.de

Abstract. Forward-secure threshold signatures are useful to mitigate
the damage of secret key exposure. Constructions based on bilinear pairings are particularly interesting because they achieve shorter signatures
than RSA-based constructions.

We construct a forward-secure threshold signature scheme based on
bilinear pairings. Compared to existing schemes, our scheme is much
more efficient since it has a non-interactive key update and signing procedure. Additionally, our scheme does not require a trusted dealer and
has optimal resilience as well as small signatures. Our scheme is the first
one which achieves all of these and that can also be implemented on
standardized curves.

We prove our scheme EUF-CMA secure against adaptive malicious
adversaries. Our technical approach is a combination of the forward-
secure single user signature scheme by Drijvers and Neven with a slightly
modified version of the distributed key generation protocol by Gennaro
et al. This modified version allows the participating parties to adjust
their secret key shares in a forward secure way.

1 Introduction

Forward-Secure Threshold Signatures. In a standard digital signature scheme,
exposure of the secret key results in the adversary being able to sign arbitrary
messages and all hope of security is lost. There are different approaches to mitigate the damage due to an adversary that gains access to stored keys. Two
of these approaches are *forward-secure* digital signature schemes and *threshold*
signature schemes. The *forward-secure* digital signature scheme allows to evolve
the secret key in regular intervals, while the public key remains fixed. Thus,
every adversary with an outdated secret key cannot forge signatures for time
periods in the past. In an (n, k)-*threshold* signature scheme the secret key is distributed among n shares and it requires the presence of at least $k + 1$ key shares

R. Kurek—Supported by the European Research Council (ERC) under the European
Union's Horizon 2020 research and innovation programme, grant agreement 802823,
and by the German Research Foundation (DFG) within the Collaborative Research
Center "On-The-Fly Computing" (SFB 901/3).

K. Aoki and A. Kanaoka (Eds.): IWSEC 2020, LNCS 12231, pp. 239–260, 2020.
https://doi.org/10.1007/978-3-030-58208-1_14

to sign a message, whereas any subset of k key shares is insufficient. Compared to standard digital signatures, both of these primitives deliver improved security guarantees against secret key exposure in a different manner. Thus, the combination of these two primitives to a *forward-secure threshold* (FST) signature scheme can even reinforce these guarantees. Given a forward-secure threshold signature scheme, an adversary that aims at forging a signature for time period t has not only to compromise $k+1$ of the stored keys to gain sufficient key material but it also has to gain all of this key material until time period t expires. Depending on the scheme, the adversary has to gain all of this key material even in one specific time period. Since the capacities of an adversary can be assumed to be restricted, this combination provides additional security.

Beyond the generic protection against key exposure there are further use cases of forward-secure threshold signatures. In general, every use case of threshold signatures applies also to forward-secure threshold signatures as the time component adds only security, and vice versa. However, one can also imagine systems where both properties are required. For instance, imagine a company A which is going to sell one of its divisions to company B if at least k out of n managers agree on the sale. If a competing company C also wants to buy this division from A, it might try to forge a contract which says that A sells to C. However, such a contract would only be valid if A was still in possession of this division, that is if the time period of the forgery was prior to the time period of signing the original contract.

Difficulties of Constructing Forward-Secure Threshold Signatures. Unfortunately, the added benefits of combining such schemes invoke some technical challenges. These challenges occur especially in regard to efficiency.

Necessity of a trusted dealer. There is a potential risk in relying on trusted dealers to distribute the secret key shares among all parties such that they should be avoided.

Necessity of secret point-to-point connections. Due to the design of the protocol, secret point-to-point connections might be required for key generation, key update or even signing. Since these connections are expensive and might be prone to attacks they should be avoided.

Communication rounds. The efficiency of a scheme is crucially determined by the number of communication rounds. Whereas the key generation happens only once and is not a major issue, the costs for signing and especially key update play a much bigger role. In signing, the optimum would be that valid signature shares can be computed non-interactively. That is, a signature is requested and the signature shares are sent back without further interaction among the parties. Thus, there is only one communication round and no overhead. In literature, such signature schemes are also called non-interactive threshold signature schemes [15,16,20]. [1]For key update, it is

---

[1] The term "non-interactive" stems from the fact that users are able to deliver valid signature shares without interacting with each other. The communication round we count here is still there.

desirable to have no communication at all, i.e. a non-interactive procedure. Besides efficiency, the reason is that some key storage hosts might be offline or temporary unavailable. In the case of interactive key update this unavailability could block the update procedure entirely or exclude the unavailable parties from further signing procedures because of outdated key material.

Signature and key sizes. As for ordinary digital signature schemes, the challenge to construct a scheme with small signatures and small keys also arises and seems to be even harder. To illustrate the difficulties it suffices to take a look at naïve solutions for both of these primitives: a naïve solution to create a (n, k)-threshold signature scheme would be to define a signature as valid if and only if at least $k + 1$ out of n parties sign a message with a single user scheme. However, this would not only increase the total signature size but also leak which parties signed and which refused to do so. In terms of forward security, a naïve solution would be to generate and define a pair of public and secret key for each time period and then to delete the secret keys successively. Though in practice, this would yield huge parameters. Consequently, both of these solutions, especially the combination of them, are highly undesirable. For this reason, more effort is required to construct a satisfactory solution.

Our Contribution. We present a highly efficient *forward-secure threshold* signature scheme based on bilinear pairings, which can be implemented on standardized pairing-friendly curves. In this scheme, we improve the state of the art on almost all of the above dimensions. More precisely. It requires *no trusted dealer.* Secret channels are only required during the key generation, i.e. there are *no secret channels for signing and key updating* required. It provides a *non-interactive key update and signing procedure.* In addition, the scheme provides *short signatures*: one bit string of length $\log T$, where T is the maximum number of supported time periods, and two group elements. The scheme has *optimal resilience*, i.e., it can tolerate $(n-1)/2$ compromised parties and is proved secure against adaptive malicious adversaries.[2]

The (Im-)Possibility of Mobile Adversaries and Non-interactive Key Update. A mobile adversary can switch between the parties it corrupts.[3] We want to emphasize that in general, it is not possible to tolerate such adversaries while having non-interactive key update. The reason is that an adversary could for instance compromise all parties but only one party per time period. Thus, it could update the secret key shares to the time period of the last compromise and reconstruct the secret key without ever exceeding the threshold during one time period, which by security definition basically means that the adversary broke the scheme without having $k + 1$ key shares for one time period. This attack is even possible for interactive key updates that require interaction of fewer parties

---

[2] An adaptive adversary can corrupt the parties at any time. A malicious adversary is allowed to divert from the protocol in any possible fashion.

[3] A mobile adversary can switch between the parties it corrupts. For a proper overview see [1].

than the threshold. However, prevention against this attack can be given by proactive security. In a nutshell, proactive security means that we can refresh the secret key shares in a way such that all shares which were *not* refreshed cannot be used to reconstruct the secret key anymore (as long as the amount of these shares do not exceed the threshold). Unfortunately, this refreshing requires interaction between the parties or between each party and a trusted dealer, such that allowing mobile adversaries or having non-interactive key updates can be seen as a trade-off. Indeed, our FST scheme can be proactivized. We show how to add proactive security to our FST scheme and explain the differences between proactive and forward security in more details in the appendix.

Related Work. The first works on threshold signature schemes are due to Boyd [6] and Desmedt and Frankel [8]. In [16], Libert and Yung construct a non-interactive threshold-signature scheme based on bilinear pairings with groups of composite order, which is secure against adaptive malicious adversaries. Further, they suggest how a forward-secure threshold signature scheme with these properties could be built in composite order groups. In [15], Libert et al. construct a non-interactive threshold-signature scheme, which is secure against adaptive malicious adversaries and requires only groups of prime order. The first forward-secure signature scheme is presented by Bellare and Miner [3] and later improved by Abdalla and Reyzin [2]. Krawczyk [14] presents a general framework to make a signature scheme forward secure. However, the extension to forward-secure threshold signatures is restricted to eavesdropping adversaries and lacks efficiency. Drijvers and Neven [9] propose a forward-secure single user signature scheme and a forward-secure multi user signature scheme in the random oracle model [4]. These schemes are based on bilinear pairings. The first forward-secure threshold signature schemes are due to Abdalla et al. [1] and Tzeng and Tzeng [21]. The latter is broken by Wang et al. [22]. In [17], Liu et al. propose a forward-secure threshold scheme based on the standard single user signature scheme by Guillou and Quisquater [11]. Unfortunately, Liu et al. do not provide a security proof for their scheme. Chow et al. [7] present a forward-secure threshold scheme based on the forward-secure scheme by Abdalla and Reyzin [2]. Yu and Kong [23] propose a forward-secure threshold signature scheme based on bilinear pairings. In our work, we managed to achieve a forward-secure threshold signature scheme with the same properties as in the suggestion by Libert and Yung [16] but in a group of prime order. Using prime order groups increases efficiency and allows implementation on standardized pairing-friendly curves. In Fig. 1 we compare the existing FST schemes in more detail. We only analyze the second scheme from Abdalla et al. since the first one requires all parties to be available for signing. The scheme by Liu et al. is omitted since it cannot be properly specified without a security proof. The scheme by Tzeng and Tzeng was broken and is omitted aswell.

	AMN [1]	CGHY [9]	YK [25]	ours
Type	RSA	RSA	pairing	pairing
Trusted dealer	yes	yes	yes	no
Adversary type	mobile halting	adaptive malic.	static malic.	adaptive malic.
Key update	interactive	non-int.	interactive	non-int.
Compromised parties tolerated	$(n-1)/3$	$(n-1)/2$	$(n-1)/2$	$(n-1)/2$
Uncompromised parties for signing	$2k+1$	$k+1$	$k+1$	$k+1$
Communication rounds in signing	$2L$	2	4 +1 private	1
Number of signature elements	3	3	3	3

Fig. 1. L denotes the security parameter, n the number of parties, k the threshold. Malic. and non-int. abbreviate malicious and non-interactive, respectively. For a proper overview of the adversary types see [1]. One communication round is defined as sending one message and getting one message back. If not specified, the communication rounds are broadcasts. The number of signature elements also includes one element for the time as it is needed for verification. We reach adaptive security due through complexity leveraging.

2 Forward-Secure Signature Schemes

In this section, we provide definitions of forward-secure (threshold) signature schemes as well as the corresponding security definitions.

Forward-Secure Signatures For Single Users. The following definitions of forward-secure digital signatures and its security are due to Bellare and Miner [3].

Definition 1. *Forward-secure digital signatures. A forward-secure digital signature scheme Σ for T time periods and message space $\mathcal{M}$ is defined as a quadruple of algorithms: $\Sigma = (KeyGen, KeyUpdate, Sign, Verify)$, where:*

- *$KeyGen(T) \rightarrow (pk, sk_0)$. On input the maximum number of time periods T it outputs a public key pk and an initial secret key sk_0.*
- *$KeyUpdate(sk_t) \rightarrow sk_{t+1}$. If the input is a secret key for a time period $t < T$, it outputs a secret key for the next time period $t+1$ and deletes the input from its storage. Else it outputs $\perp$.*
- *$Sign(t, sk_t, m) \rightarrow \sigma$. On input a time period t with the corresponding secret key sk_t and a message m from the message space $\mathcal{M}$ it outputs a signature σ together with the time period t.*
- *$Verify(pk, t, m, \sigma) \rightarrow b$, where $b \in \{0, 1\}$. If σ is a valid signature for m at time period t and under public key pk, then $Verify$ outputs 1, else 0.*

The EUF-CMA security for forward-secure signatures is similar to the one for standard digital signatures. In the case of forward-secure signatures, we allow the adversary not only to query signatures, but also to update the secret key to the next time period and to obtain the secret key at a time period of its choice. The adversary has two ways to win. First, by delivering a valid signature for a time period prior to the one of compromising the secret key. Second, by delivering a valid signature for an arbitrary time period if it never compromised the secret key. In both cases, the adversary cannot win by delivering a message and signature for a specific time period if it had queried a signature for this message during this time period. The EUF-CMA security experiment for a forward-secure signature scheme Σ is defined as follows: The challenger defines an (initially) empty set S and runs the **KeyGen** algorithm to obtain a pair of public and initial secret key (pk, sk_0). Then, it sends the public key pk to the adversary $\mathcal{A}$. The adversary has access to the following oracles:

- **KeyUpdate.** For all time periods $t < T - 1$ it updates the current time period t and the secret key sk_t to $t + 1$ and sk_{t+1}, respectively.
- **Signing**(t, m). On input the current time period t and a message m from the message space it adds (t, m) to the set S and runs **Sign**(t, sk_t, M). Then, it returns the resulting signature σ to $\mathcal{A}$.
- **Break-In.** The challenger records the break-in time $\tilde{t} \leftarrow t$ and sends the secret key $sk_{\tilde{t}}$ to $\mathcal{A}$. This oracle can only be queried once. Afterwards, **KeyUpdate** and **Sign** cannot be queried anymore.
- **Finalize**(t^*, m^*, σ^*). If $(t^*, m^*) \in S$, then it returns 0. If $\tilde{t}$ is defined and $t^* > \tilde{t}$, then it returns 0. If $\tilde{t}$ is defined and $t^* < \tilde{t}$, then it returns **Verify**(pk, t^*, m^*). If $\tilde{t}$ is not defined (i.e. Break-In was never queried), then it returns **Verify**(pk, t^*, m^*). Afterwards, the game terminates.

Definition 2. *EUF-CMA forward security.* *Let $\mathcal{A}$ be an adversary playing the EUF-CMA security experiment for a forward-secure digital signature scheme Σ for T time periods. It $(t_{\mathcal{A}}, \varepsilon_{\mathcal{A}})$-breaks the EUF-CMA forward security of Σ for T time periods, if it runs in time $t_{\mathcal{A}}$ and*

$$\Pr[\textbf{\textit{Finalize}}(t^*, m^*, \sigma^*) = 1] \geqslant \varepsilon_{\mathcal{A}}.$$

Forward-Secure Threshold Signatures. The first definition of forward-secure threshold signatures was introduced by Abdalla et al. [1]. Here, we adopt the definition by Chow et al. [7]. The only difference between these two is that updating the secret key shares does not require an interactive protocol between all parties and can be accomplished by each party on its own.

Definition 3. *Forward-secure threshold signatures.* *A forward-secure threshold signature scheme (T, n, k)-Σ_{fst} for message space $\mathcal{M}$ is defined as a quadruple of the following components:*

- ***KeyGen***$(1^\lambda, T, n, k) \rightarrow (pk, pk_1, sk_{0,1}, \ldots, pk_n, sk_{0,n})$. *On input the security parameter λ in unary, the maximum number of time periods T, the total number of parties n, and the threshold k, this protocol produces a common public key pk and user public keys pk_i and initial secret key shares $sk_{0,i}$ for all parties $i \in [n]$. The secret shares are only known to the belonging parties.*
- ***KeyUpdate***$(sk_{t,j}) \rightarrow sk_{t+1,j}$. *If the input is a secret key share for a time period $t < T - 1$, it outputs a secret key share for the next time period $t + 1$ and deletes the input from its storage. Else it outputs $\bot$.*

- **Sign**$(t, m) \rightarrow (t, \sigma)$. *If run by at least $k + 1$ honest and uncompromised signers on input the current time period t and a message m from the message space this protocol outputs a signature σ together with the time period t.*
- **Verify**$(pk, t, m, \sigma) \rightarrow b$, *where $b \in \{0, 1\}$. If σ is a valid signature for m at time period t and under public key pk, then **Verify** outputs 1, else 0.*

The signing procedure is a protocol and contains of various steps: share-sign, share-verify, and combine. For simplicity we defined the input only as a time period and message and omit the key material held by all participating parties

Definition 4. Correctness. *Correctness can be defined in the as usual. We omit it due to space limits.*

EUF-CMA security against adaptive (static) adversaries is defined by the following security experiment between a challenger and an adversary $\mathcal{A}$. Let $\mathcal{S}$ be an (initially) empty set, which denotes the signature queries and let $\mathcal{B}$ and $\mathcal{G}$ be the sets of indices, which denote the corrupted and uncorrupted parties, respectively. At the beginning $\mathcal{B}$ is empty and $\mathcal{G} = \{1, \dots, n\}$. The challenger (on behalf of the uncorrupted parties) and the adversary (on behalf of the corrupted parties) run the key generation protocol **KeyGen**(n, k). The adversary gets the common public key pk, all user public keys $(pk_i)_{i \in [n]}$ as well as the initial secret key shares of the corrupted parties $(sk_{0,j})_{j \in \mathcal{B}}$. The adversary has access to the following oracles: i

- **Break-In**(t, j). On input the current time period t and index $j \in \mathcal{G}$ the challenger checks if $|\mathcal{B}| < k$. If this holds, the challenger removes j out of $\mathcal{G}$ and adds it to $\mathcal{B}$. If $sk_{t,j}$ is already defined, it is delivered to $\mathcal{A}$. If $|\mathcal{B}| = k$, the challenger sets $\tilde{t} \leftarrow t$ and outputs $(sk_{\tilde{t},j})_{j \in \mathcal{G}}$. [4]Afterwards, this oracle cannot be queried anymore.
- **KeyUpdate.** For all time periods $t < T - 1$ it updates the current time period t and the secret key shares $(sk_{t,j})_{j \in \mathcal{G}}$ to $t+1$ and $sk_{t+1,j}$, respectively.
- **Signing**(t, m). On input the current time period t and a message m from the message space it adds (t, m) to the set $\mathcal{S}$. Then, the challenger (on behalf of the uncorrupted parties) and the adversary $\mathcal{A}$ (on behalf of the corrupted parties) run the signing protocol **Sign**. The output of this execution is delivered to $\mathcal{A}$.
- **Finalize**(t^*, m^*, σ^*). If $(t^*, m^*) \in \mathcal{S}$, then it returns 0. If $\tilde{t}$ is defined and $t^* > \tilde{t}$, then it returns 0. If $\tilde{t}$ is defined and $t^* < \tilde{t}$, then it returns **Verify**(pk, t^*, m^*). If $\tilde{t}$ is not defined (i.e. Break-In was never queried), then it returns **Verify**(pk, t^*, m^*). Afterwards, the game terminates.

---

[4] Note that this case is only possible for time periods $t > 0$, i.e. after **KeyGen** had finished. Else, the adversary would have no way to win the security experiment.

Definition 5. *EUF-CMA forward security against adaptive (static) adversaries. Let $\mathcal{A}$ be an adaptive (a static) adversary playing the EUF-CMA security experiment for a forward-secure threshold signature scheme (T, n, k)-Σ_{fst}. It $(t_{\mathcal{A}}, \varepsilon_{\mathcal{A}})$-breaks the EUF-CMA security of (T, n, k)-Σ_{fst}, if it runs in time $t_{\mathcal{A}}$ and*

$$\Pr[\textbf{Finalize}(t^*, m^*, \sigma^*) = 1] \geqslant \varepsilon_{\mathcal{A}}.$$

We extend the robustness notion of threshold signature schemes by Gennaro et al. [10] to forward-secure threshold signature schemes. Essentially, the difference is the added **KeyUpdate** procedure.

Definition 6. *Robustness. A forward-secure threshold signature scheme Σ_{fst} is (n, k_1, k_2)-robust if in a group of n parties, even in the presence of an adversary who halts up to k_1 and corrupts maliciously k_2 parties, **Keygen**, **KeyUpdate**, and **Sign** complete successfully.*

3   Distributed Key Generation

Here, we introduce a modified variant of the distributed key generation (**DKG**) protocol by Gennaro et al. [10], which will be a major building block of our FST scheme. The basic idea behind the **DKG** protocol by Gennaro et al. [10] is to make use of Shamir's secret sharing scheme [19] in the exponent of a cyclic group. In the original **DKG** protocol a set of n parties generate a pair of secret and public key $(x, g^x) \in \mathbb{Z}_q \times \mathbb{G}$, where $\mathbb{G}$ is a multiplicative group of prime order q and generated by g. The public output of the protocol provides not only the common public key g^x, but also user public keys g^{x_i}, where x_i is the secret share of party P_i. This protocol does not require a trusted dealer and is robust against malicious behavior. We will make small modifications to the original **DKG** protocol to satisfy the requirements for forward security.

Modifications. We instantiate the protocol with the groups $\mathbb{G}_1$ and $\mathbb{G}_2$ from the bilinear pairing we will use in our threshold signature scheme. Therefore, it provides $g_2^x \in \mathbb{G}_2$, which will serve as the public key for our threshold signature scheme, as well as the values $g_2^{x_i} \in \mathbb{G}_2$ for all parties P_i, which will serve to verify the partial signatures and provide robustness of our signature scheme. Furthermore the secret is defined as $h^x \in \mathbb{G}_1$ instead of $x \in \mathbb{Z}_q$ as in the original protocol. The corresponding secret key shares are $h^{x_i} \in \mathbb{G}_1$ instead of $x_i \in \mathbb{Z}_q$ and in order to fulfill the requirements of our FST scheme, they are updated to the first time period. To guarantee forward security it is crucial that the plain values h^{x_i} and x_i for $i = 1, \dots, n$ are erased from every storage.

Note that the public keys $pk_j, j \in [n]$ equal:

$$\prod_{i \in QUAL} \prod_{k=0}^{t} (A_{ik})^{j^k} = \prod_{i \in QUAL} g_2^{s_{ij}} = g_2^{x_j}.$$

4   New Forward-Secure Threshold Signature Scheme

In this section, we introduce our forward-secure threshold signature scheme. We show how simple modifications of the **DKG** protocol, which are shown in Fig. 2, allow to create a forward-secure threshold signature scheme, which is much more efficient than the state of the art. This scheme is basically a threshold-version of the single user scheme of Drijvers and Neven [9], which is proven secure in the random oracle model. For the reader's convenience we rephrase the scheme from [9] in the supplementary material. We prove our FST scheme secure and robust against adaptive malicious adversaries.

For simplicity, we assume the common parameters to be given in our scheme. Note that this assumption does not contradict no need of a trusted dealer as such a dealer is not required for generation and sharing the public and secret key material. The common parameters could be either from a proposed standardization or commonly generated by all parties. For instance, this can be achieved by a coin-flipping protocol as in [5].

Let $(T, n, k)\text{-}\Sigma_{fst} = (\textbf{KeyGen}, \textbf{KeyUpdate}, \textbf{Sign}, \textbf{Verify})$ be a forward-secure threshold signature scheme defined as follows:

- **Common parameters.** Let $\mathcal{M}$ be the message space and let $H_q : \mathcal{M} \rightarrow \{0,1\}^\kappa$ be a hash function mapping messages to bits strings of length κ such that $2^\kappa < q$. The common parameters consist of $\mathcal{PG}$, the description of a cryptographic Type-3 pairing group, the description of H_q, the maximum number of time periods $T = 2^\ell$ as well as random group elements $g_1, h, h_0, \ldots, h_{\ell+1} \leftarrow \mathbb{G}_1$, and $g_2, \tilde{h} \leftarrow \mathbb{G}_2$, where g_1 and g_2 are generators of $\mathbb{G}_1$ and $\mathbb{G}_2$, respectively.

- **KeyGen**(1^λ). The n parties run the **DKG**(n, k) protocol from Fig. 2. Subsequently each party P_i holds an initial secret key share $sk_{0,i} = \left(g_2^{r_i}, h^{x_i} h_0^{r_i}, h_1^{r_i}, \ldots, h_{\ell+1}^{r_i}\right) \in \mathbb{G}_2 \times \mathbb{G}_1^{\ell+2}$ as well as the public keys $pk_j = g_2^{x_j}$ for all $j \in [n]$. The common public key $pk = g_2^x \in \mathbb{G}_2$ is published.

- **KeyUpdate**$(sk_{t,i})$. We assume the time periods $0, \ldots, 2^\ell - 1$ are organized as leaves of a binary tree of depth ℓ, sorted in increasing order from left to right. That is, $000 \ldots 0$ is the first and $111 \ldots 1$ is the last time period. Further, we interpret the path from the root of the tree to a leaf node t as binary representation $t = t_1 \ldots t_\ell$, where we take the left branch for $t_z = 0$ and the right one for $t_z = 1$. We proceed in the same way for internal nodes $\omega = \omega_1 \ldots \omega_s$, where $s < \ell$. Let $r_i \leftarrow \mathbb{Z}_q$ be picked uniformly at random. Then, we associate to each party P_i and each node ω a secret key:

$$(c_i, d_i, e_{i,s+1}, \ldots, e_{i,\ell+1}) = \left(g_2^{r_i}, h^{x_i} (h_0 \prod_{v=1}^{s} h_v^{w_v})^{r_i}, h_{s+1}^{r_i}, \ldots, h_{\ell+1}^{r_i} \right).$$

Protocol DKG(n, k):

Generation of shared secret x:

1. (a) Each party P_i chooses two random polynomials $a_i(z)$ and $b_i(z)$ over $\mathbb{Z}_q$ of degree k:

$$a_i(z) = a_{i0} + a_{i1}z + \cdots + a_{ik}z^k \text{ and}$$
$$b_i(z) = b_{i0} + b_{i1}z + \cdots + b_{ik}z^k.$$

   (b) P_i computes and broadcasts $C_{is} = g_2^{a_{is}}\tilde{h}^{b_{is}} \in \mathbb{G}_2$ for $s = 0, \ldots, k$.

   (c) P_i computes $s_{ij} = a_i(j)$ and $s'_{ij} = b_i(j) \mod q$ for $j = 1, \ldots, n$ and sends s_{ij}, s'_{ij} secretly to P_j.

   (d) For $i = 1, \ldots, n$ each party P_j checks whether or not

$$g_2^{s_{ij}}\tilde{h}^{s'_{ij}} = \prod_{s=0}^{k}(C_{is})^{j^s}. \tag{1}$$

   If there is an $i \in [n]$ such that the check fails, P_j broadcasts a *complaint* against P_i.

   (e) If a dealer P_i receives a complaint from P_j, he broadcasts the values s_{ij} and s'_{ij} satisfying Equation 1.

   (f) Each party disqualifies any player that either received more than k *complains* or answered to a complaint with values that does not satisfy Equation 1.

2. Each party defines the set $QUAL$, which indicates all non-disqualified parties.

3. The shared secret is defined as $h^x = h^{\sum_{i \in QUAL} a_{i0}} \in \mathbb{G}_1$. Each party P_i computes $h^{x_i} := h^{\sum_{j \in QUAL} s_{ij}} \in \mathbb{G}_1$ and sets its initial share of this secret as

$$sk_{0,i} := \left(g_2^{r_i}, h^{x_i}h_0^{r_i}, h_1^{r_i}, \ldots, h_{\ell+1}^{r_i}\right) \in \mathbb{G}_2 \times \mathbb{G}_1^{\ell+2},$$

where $r_i \leftarrow \mathbb{Z}_q$ is picked uniformly at random.

Extracting $y := g_2^x \in \mathbb{G}_2$:

4. (a) Each party $P_i, i \in QUAL$ computes and broadcasts the values $A_{is} = g_2^{a_{is}} \in \mathbb{G}_2$ for $s = 0, \ldots, k$.

   (b) For each $i \in QUAL$, each party P_j checks whether or not

$$g_2^{s_{ij}} = \prod_{s=0}^{k}(A_{is})^{j^s}. \tag{2}$$

   If there is an $i \in QUAL$ such that the check fails, P_j *complaints* about P_i by broadcasting s_{ij} and s'_{ij} that satisfy Eq. 1 but not Eq. 2.

   (c) For all parties P_i who received at least one valid complaint in this phase, the other parties run a reconstruction of $a_i(z)$ and A_{is} for $s = 0, \ldots, k$ in the clear, using the values s_{ij}.

   (d) Each party computes the common public key as $y = \prod_{i \in QUAL} A_{i0} \in \mathbb{G}_2$ and the user public keys pk_j as $g_2^{x_j} = \prod_{i \in QUAL} \prod_{k=0}^{t}(A_{ik})^{j^k}$ for all $j \in [n]$. Except of all public keys and the initial secret share all parties erase all other values from their storage.

Fig. 2. Our modified version of the **DKG** protocol due to Gennaro et al..

Given such a secret key, we produce a secret key for a descendant node $\omega' = \omega_1 \ldots \omega_{s'}$, where $s' > s$ as

$$(c_i', d_i', e_{i,s'+1}', \ldots, e_{i,\ell+1}')$$

$$= \left(c_i \cdot g_2^{r_i'}, d_i \cdot \prod_{v=s+1}^{s'} e_{i,v}^{w_v} (h_0 \prod_{v=1}^{s'} h_v^{w_v})^{r_i'}, e_{i,s'+1} \cdot h_{s'+1}^{r_i'}, \ldots, e_{i,\ell+1} \cdot h_{i,\ell+1}^{r_i'} \right),$$

where $r_i' \leftarrow \mathbb{Z}_q$ is picked uniformly at random.

Let C_t be the smallest subset of nodes that contains for each time period $t, \ldots, T-1$ an ancestor or the leaf itself, but no nodes of ancestors or leafs for time periods $0, \ldots, t-1$. For time period t, we define the secret key $sk_{t,i}$ of party P_i as the set of its secret keys associated to all nodes in C_t. In order to update the secret key to time period $t+1$ it determines C_{t+1} and computes the secret keys for all nodes in $C_{t+1} \setminus C_t$. Afterwards, it deletes $sk_{t,i}$ and all used re-randomization exponents r_i'.

- **Sign**(m). Let $M := h_q(m)$ be the hash value of message $m \in \mathcal{M}$ and $t = t_1 \ldots t_\ell$ the bit representation of time period t. Let $\mathcal{W}$ be the set of indices of all parties participating in signing M. W.l.o.g. we assume that $\mathcal{W}$ contains at least $k+1$ distinct indices. The participating parties run the signing protocol from Fig. 3.

Remark 1. Note that the set $\mathcal{V}$ might be of size greater than $k+1$, while $k+1$ partial signatures are sufficient to construct the final signature. Hence, the final signature is not unique if not every party takes all partial signatures for constructing it. However, all signatures constructed in Step 4 are nevertheless indistinguishable from a signature created in a single user protocol because it is easy to re-randomize both σ_1 and σ_2. Especially seeing two valid signatures (σ_1, σ_2) and (σ_1', σ_2') it cannot be deduced how many signers were involved in signing. For this reason we do not have to force the parties to aggregate all partial signatures and thus, avoid overhead in computation.

- **Verify.** On input $(\sigma_1, \sigma_2) \in \mathbb{G}_1 \times \mathbb{G}_2$ message m, public key pk and time period t compute $M = h_q(m)$ and output 1 if

$$e(\sigma_1, g_2) = e(h, pk) \cdot e(h_0 \cdot \prod_{v=1}^{\ell} h_v^{t_v} \cdot h_{\ell+1}^M, \sigma_2) \tag{4}$$

else output 0.

Proof of Correctness. In order to show that (σ_1, σ_2) is a valid signature for message M at time period t under the common public key $pk = g_2^x$ we have to show first that we can determine the set $\mathcal{V}$, which indicates the correct signature shares. That

---

Sign$(t, M, P_1, ..., P_n)$:

1. **Share-Sign.** At request of a signature for message M at time $t = t_1 \ldots t_\ell$, each party $P_i, i \in \mathcal{W}$ signs M under its signing key $(c_i, d_i, e_{i,\ell+1})$ derived from $sk_{t,i}$. The resulting signatures are

$$(\sigma_{1,i}, \sigma_{2,i}) = \left(d_i \cdot e_{i,\ell+1}^M \cdot (h_0 \cdot \prod_{v=1}^{\ell} h_v^{t_v} \cdot h_{\ell+1}^M)^{r_i'}, c_i \cdot g_2^{r_i'} \right),$$

where $r_i' \leftarrow \mathbb{Z}_q$ is picked uniformly at random. Each party $P_i, i \in \mathcal{W}$ sends its signature to all other parties.

2. **Share-Verify.** All parties in $\mathcal{W}$ use the public keys $pk_i, i \in \mathcal{W}$ to verify if all the received signatures are valid. That is,

$$e(\sigma_{1,i}, g_2) = e(h, pk_i) \cdot e(h_0 \cdot \prod_{v=1}^{\ell} h_v^{t_v} \cdot h_{\ell+1}^M, \sigma_{2,i}). \tag{3}$$

3. **Combine.** Let $\mathcal{V} \subseteq \mathcal{W}$ indicate a set of users sending valid signatures. Assuming $\mathcal{V}$ contains at least $k + 1$ distinct indices. Each party can now compute the Lagrange coefficients L_i and aggregate the signatures as follows:

$$(\sigma_1, \sigma_2) := (\prod_{i \in \mathcal{V}} \sigma_{1,i}^{L_i}, \prod_{i \in \mathcal{V}} \sigma_{2,i}^{L_i}).$$

Fig. 3. The signing protocol of our FST scheme.

is, we have to show that we can check whether the partial signatures $(\sigma_{1,i}, \sigma_{2,i})$, $i \in \mathcal{W}$ are correct. Let $(\sigma_{1,i}, \sigma_{2,i})$ be an honestly generated signature. Then,

$$\sigma_{1,i} = d_i \cdot e_{i,\ell+1}^M (h_0 \prod_{v=1}^{\ell} h_v^{t_v} \cdot h_{\ell+1}^M)^{r_i'}$$

$$= h^{x_i} (h_0 \prod_{v=1}^{\ell} h_v^{t_v})^{r_i} \cdot e_{i,\ell+1}^M \cdot (h_0 \prod_{v=1}^{\ell} h_v^{t_v} \cdot h_{\ell+1}^M)^{r_i'}$$

$$= h^{x_i} (h_0 \prod_{v=1}^{\ell} h_v^{t_v})^{r_i} \cdot h_{\ell+1}^{r_i \cdot M} \cdot (h_0 \prod_{v=1}^{\ell} h_v^{t_v} \cdot h_{\ell+1}^M)^{r_i'} = h^{x_i} (h_0 \prod_{v=1}^{\ell} h_v^{t_v} \cdot h_{\ell+1}^M)^{r_i + r_i'},$$

$$\tag{5}$$

where we used the fact that $e_{i,\ell+1} = h_{i,\ell+1}^{r_i}$. Furthermore, $\sigma_{2,i} = g_2^{r_i+r_i'}$. The signature $(\sigma_{1,i}, \sigma_{2,i})$ with $\sigma_{1,i}$ as in (5) and with $\sigma_{2,i}$ satisfies (3), since

$$
e(h^{x_i}(h_0 \prod_{v=1}^{\ell} h_v^{t_v} \cdot h_{\ell+1}^M)^{r_i+r_i'}, g_2) = e(h^{x_i}, g_2) \cdot e((h_0 \prod_{v=1}^{\ell} h_v^{t_v} \cdot h_{\ell+1}^M)^{r_i+r_i'}, g_2)
$$

$$
= e(h, g_2^{x_i}) \cdot e(h_0 \cdot \prod_{v=1}^{\ell} h_v^{t_v} \cdot h_{\ell+1}^M, g_2^{r_i+r_i'}).
$$

For this reason, we can indeed check whether a signature $(\sigma_{1,i}, \sigma_{2,i})$ for message M at time period t is valid under public key $g_2^{x_i}$ and thus include i into set $\mathcal{V}$. It remains to show that all partial signatures $(\sigma_{1,i}, \sigma_{2,i})$, $i \in \mathcal{V}$ interpolate to a valid signature under the common public key g_2^x. For this purpose we set $R := \sum_{i \in \mathcal{V}} L_i(r_i + r_i')$. Then,

$$
\sigma_1 = \prod_{i \in \mathcal{V}} \sigma_{1,i}^{L_i} = h^{\sum_{i \in \mathcal{V}} L_i \cdot x_i}(h_0 \prod_{v=1}^{\ell} h_v^{t_v} \cdot h_{\ell+1}^M)^{\sum_{i \in \mathcal{V}} L_i(r_i+r_i')}
$$

$$
= h^x(h_0 \prod_{v=1}^{\ell} h_v^{t_v} \cdot h_{\ell+1}^M)^R,
$$

where $\sum_{i \in \mathcal{V}} L_i \cdot x_i$. Furthermore, $\sigma_2 = \prod_{i \in \mathcal{V}} \sigma_{2,i}^{L_i} = g_2^{\sum_{i \in \mathcal{V}} L_i(r_i+r_i')} = g_2^R$. Overall, we have

$$
e(\sigma_1, g_2) = e(h^x(h_0 \prod_{v=1}^{\ell} h_v^{t_v} \cdot h_{\ell+1}^M)^R, g_2) = e(h^x, g_2) \cdot e((h_0 \prod_{v=1}^{\ell} h_v^{t_v} \cdot h_{\ell+1}^M)^R, g_2)
$$

$$
= e(h, g_2^x) \cdot e((h_0 \prod_{v=1}^{\ell} h_v^{t_v} \cdot h_{\ell+1}^M), \sigma_2),
$$

which shows that (σ_1, σ_2) fulfills (4) and therefore is a valid signature for message M at time period t under public key $pk = g_2^x$.

Proof of Security. As preparation for the security reduction we describe in Fig. 4 the simulation of the key generation protocol **DKG** and in Fig. 5 the simulation of the signing protocol **Sign**. The simulation of the **DKG** protocol is basically due to Gennaro et al. [10]. As the **DKG** protocol we instantiate the simulation with the groups $\mathbb{G}_1$ and $\mathbb{G}_2$ from the bilinear pairing we use in our FST signature scheme and make the same adjustments in order to enable forward security. We explain these adjustments in Sect. 3.

Simulation of DKG. During key generation, the adversary is allowed to control at most k parties. Otherwise, it would gain access to the secret key at time period 0 and by definition it would have no possibility to win the security experiment of the signature scheme. First, we assume a static adversary as in the proof in [10].

Then, we show how to extend the security to adaptive adversaries. We explain in Sect. 5 why this approach is reasonable. W.l.o.g. we assume the compromised parties to be $P_1, \ldots, P_k$. Let $\mathcal{B} := \{1, \ldots, k\}$ indicate the set of parties controlled by the adversary $\mathcal{A}$ and let $\mathcal{G} := \{k+1, \ldots, n\}$ indicate the set of honest parties, which are run by the simulator.

Protocol DKGSim$(y = g_2^x, n, k)$:

1. The simulator performs the Steps 1a-1f, 2, and, 3 on behalf of the uncorrupted parties exactly as in the **DKG**(n, k) protocol. Additionally, it reconstructs the polynomials $a_i(z), b_i(z)$ for $i \in \mathcal{B}$. Then:
   - The set $QUAL$ is well-defined and $\mathcal{G} \subseteq QUAL$ and all polynomials are random for all $i \in \mathcal{G}$.
   - The adversary sees $a_i(z), b_i(z)$ for $i \in \mathcal{B}$, the shares $(s_{ij}, s'_{ij}) = (a_i(j), b_i(j))$ for $i \in QUAL$, $j \in \mathcal{B}$ and C_{is} for $i \in QUAL$, $s = 0, \ldots, k$.
   - The simulator knows all polynomials $a_i(z), b_i(z)$ for $i \in QUAL$ as well as all shares s_{ij}, s'_{ij}, all coefficients a_{is}, b_{is} and the public values C_{is}.
2. The simulator performs as folllows:
   - Computes $A_{is} = g_2^{a_{is}} \in \mathbb{G}_2$ for $i \in QUAL \setminus \{n\}$, $s = 0, \ldots, k$.
   - Sets $A_{n0}^* = y \cdot \prod_{i \in QUAL \setminus \{n\}} (A_{i0}^{-1})$.
   - Sets $s_{nj}^* = s_{nj} = a_n(j)$ for $j = 1, \ldots, k$.
   - Computes $A_{ns}^* = (A_{n0}^*)^{\lambda_{s0}} \cdot \prod_{i=1}^{k} (g_2^{s_{ni}^*})^{\lambda_{si}} \in \mathbb{G}_2$ for $s = 1, \ldots, k$, where the λ_{is}s are the Lagrange interpolation coefficients.
   (a) The simulator broadcasts A_{is} for $i \in \mathcal{G} \setminus \{n\}$ and A_{ns}^* for $s = 0, \ldots, k$.
   (b) It performs for all uncorrupted parties the verification of (2) on the values A_{ij} for $i \in \mathcal{B}$. In case of a fail it broadcasts a complaint (s_{ij}, s'_{ij}). Since the adversary controls at most k parties and the simulator behaves honestly, only secret shares of corrupted parties can be reconstructed.
   (c) Afterwards it performs the Steps 4c and 4d of the **DKG**(n, k) protocol.

Fig. 4. The simulation of the DKG protocol from Fig. 2.

Simulation of Sign. Note that during the simulation of the signing protocol the simulator already simulated the distributed key generation protocol and is therefore in possession of the secret shares $x_1, \ldots, x_k$ and the polynomials $a_i(z), b_i(z)$ for all $i \in [n]$.

It follows from the **DKG** protocol that the secret shares for all parties $P_j, j \in [n]$ are defined as $x_j := \sum_{i \in QUAL} s_{ij} \mod q$. For **DKGSim** these are defined as $x_j := \sum_{i \in QUAL \setminus \{n\}} s_{ij} + s_{nj}^* \mod q$, where the values s_{nj}^* for $j = k+1, \ldots, n$, i.e. for $j \in \mathcal{G}$, are not explicitly known. From **DKGSim** we also derive that the corresponding public keys equal:

$$g_2^{x_j} = \prod_{i \in QUAL \setminus \{n\}} g_2^{s_{ij}} \cdot g_2^{s_{nj}^*} = \prod_{i \in QUAL \setminus \{n\}} \prod_{s=0}^{k} (A_{is})^{j^s} \prod_{s=0}^{k} (A_{ns}^*)^{j^s},$$

SignSim$(t, M, (\sigma_1, \sigma_2))$

1. The signature is requested. The simulator is in possession of the polynomials $a_i(z), b_i(z)$ for all $i \in [n]$. At request of a signature for message M at time $t = t_1 \ldots t_\ell$ it uses these information to construct valid signature shares for M on behalf of all uncorrupted parties: for $j = k+1, \ldots, n$ it computes $\sigma'_{1,j}$ as

$$\prod_{i \in QUAL \setminus \{n\}} \prod_{s=0}^{k} (H_{is})^{j^s} \cdot (\hat{H}_{n0}) \cdot \prod_{s=1}^{k} ((\hat{H}_{n0})^{\lambda_{s0}} \cdot \prod_{i=1}^{k} (h^{s^*_{ni}})^{\lambda_{si}})^{j^s}.$$

Then, it picks $r_j \leftarrow \mathbb{Z}_q$ uniformly at random and computes $\sigma_{1,j}$ as

$$\sigma'_{1,j} \cdot (h_0 \prod_{v=1}^{\ell} h_v^{t_v} \cdot h_{\ell+1}^{M})^{r_j}.$$

Afterwards, it computes $\sigma_{2,j}$ as:

$$\sigma_2^{\sum_{s=1}^{k} \lambda_{s0} \cdot j^s + 1} \cdot g_2^{r_j}.$$

Then, the simulator sends $(\sigma_{1,i}, \sigma_{2,i})$ for all $i = k+1, \ldots, n$ to the corrupted parties $P_1, \ldots, P_k$. The simulator might receive partial signatures on behalf of the corrupted parties.
2. The simulator does nothing.
3. The adversary can use any set $\mathcal{V}$ of at least $k+1$ partial signatures to construct the final signature:

$$(\sigma_1, \sigma_2) = (\prod_{i \in \mathcal{V}} \sigma_{1,i}^{L_i}, \prod_{i \in \mathcal{V}} \sigma_{2,i}^{L_i}),$$

where L_i are Lagrange coefficients. The simulator does nothing.

Fig. 5. The simulation of the signing protocol from Fig. 3.

where the values A^*_{ns} include the common public key $y = g_2^x$. Hence, in order to compute the secret share h^{x_j} for $j \in \mathcal{G}$ either the corresponding value h^x or s^*_{nj} would be needed. Although. these values are unknown to the simulator it is possible to use a valid signature (σ_1, σ_2) for message M to extract a valid signatures for all parties $P_j, j \in \mathcal{G}$. For this purpose define:

- $H_{is} := h^{a_{is}} \in \mathbb{G}_1$ for all $i \in QUAL \setminus \{n\}, s = 0, \ldots, k$, where a_{is} are the coefficients of the polynomials computed during **DKGSim**.
- $H^*_{n0} := \prod_{i \in QUAL \setminus \{n\}} (H_{i0}^{-1}) \cdot h^x \in \mathbb{G}_1$.
- $s^*_{nj} := s_{nj} = a_n(j)$ for $j = 1, \ldots, k$.
- $H^*_{ns} := (H^*_{n0})^{\lambda_{s0}} \cdot \prod_{i=1}^{k} (h^{s^*_{ni}})^{\lambda_{si}} \in \mathbb{G}_1$ for $k = 1, \ldots, t$, where λ_{is}s are the Lagrange interpolation coefficients.
- $\hat{H}_{n0} := \prod_{i \in QUAL \setminus \{n\}} (H_{i0}^{-1}) \cdot \sigma_1 \in \mathbb{G}_1$

Analogously to $g_2^{x_j}$ the value h^{x_j} is defined as $\prod_{i \in QUAL \setminus \{n\}} \prod_{s=0}^{k} (H_{is})^{j^s} \cdot \prod_{s=0}^{k} (H_{ns}^*)^{j^s}$. To obtain a valid signature under public key pk_j compute an intermediate $\sigma'_{1,j}$ as:

$$\prod_{i \in QUAL \setminus \{n\}} \prod_{s=0}^{k} (H_{is})^{j^s} \cdot (\hat{H}_{n0}) \cdot \prod_{s=1}^{k} \left((\hat{H}_{n0})^{\lambda_{s0}} \cdot \prod_{i=1}^{k} (h^{s_{ni}^*})^{\lambda_{si}} \right)^{j^s}$$

$$= \prod_{i \in QUAL \setminus \{n\}} \prod_{s=0}^{k} (H_{is})^{j^s} \cdot \left(\prod_{i \in QUAL \setminus \{n\}} (H_{i0}^{-1}) \cdot h^x (h_0 \prod_{v=1}^{\ell} h_v^{t_v} \cdot h_{\ell+1}^M)^r \right)$$

$$\cdot \prod_{s=1}^{k} \left((\prod_{i \in QUAL \setminus \{n\}} (H_{i0}^{-1}) \cdot h^x (h_0 \prod_{v=1}^{\ell} h_v^{t_v} \cdot h_{\ell+1}^M)^r)^{\lambda_{s0}} \cdot \prod_{i=1}^{k} (h^{s_{ni}^*})^{\lambda_{si}} \right)^{j^s}$$

$$= \prod_{i \in QUAL \setminus \{n\}} \prod_{s=0}^{k} (H_{is})^{j^s} \cdot \left(\prod_{i \in QUAL \setminus \{n\}} (H_{i0}^{-1}) \cdot h^x \right) \cdot (h_0 \prod_{v=1}^{\ell} h_v^{t_v} \cdot h_{\ell+1}^M)^r$$

$$\cdot \prod_{s=1}^{k} \left((\prod_{i \in QUAL \setminus \{n\}} (H_{i0}^{-1}) \cdot h^x)^{\lambda_{s0}} \cdot \prod_{i=1}^{k} (h^{s_{ni}^*})^{\lambda_{si}} \right)^{j^s} \cdot \prod_{s=1}^{k} \left((h_0 \prod_{v=1}^{\ell} h_v^{t_v} \cdot h_{\ell+1}^M)^{r \cdot \lambda_{s0}} \right)^{j^s}$$

$$= \prod_{i \in QUAL \setminus \{n\}} \prod_{s=0}^{k} (H_{is})^{j^s} \cdot (\prod_{s=0}^{k} (H_{ns}^*)^{j^s}) \cdot (h_0 \prod_{v=1}^{\ell} h_v^{t_v} \cdot h_{\ell+1}^M)^{r \cdot \sum_{s=1}^{k} \lambda_{s0} \cdot j^s + r}$$

$$= h^{x_j} \cdot (h_0 \prod_{v=1}^{\ell} h_v^{t_v} \cdot h_{\ell+1}^M)^{r \cdot \sum_{s=1}^{k} \lambda_{s0} \cdot j^s + r}.$$

Then, pick a uniformly random $r_j \leftarrow \mathbb{Z}_p$ and re-randomize $\sigma_{1,j}$ and $\sigma_{2,j}$ as:

$$\sigma'_{1,j} \cdot (h_0 \prod_{v=1}^{\ell} h_v^{t_v} \cdot h_{\ell+1}^M)^{r_j} \quad \text{and} \quad \sigma_2^{\sum_{s=1}^{k} \lambda_{s0} \cdot j^s + 1} \cdot g_2^{r_j}. \tag{6}$$

Lemma 1. *Protocols **DKG** and **DKGSim** as well as **Sign** and **SignSim** are indistinguishable.*

PROOF. Compared to the original protocol, our modifications to **DKG** and **DKGSim** have no impact on the adversarie's view. That is, the broadcasted messages are as in the original protocol instantiated with $\mathbb{G}_2$, the view of the corrupted parties is also the same, and the storing of the secret key shares by the uncorrupted parties is done internally and cannot be seen. Thus, for static adversaries the proof is the same as in the original version and can be found in Theorem 2 of [10]. In order to manage adaptive adversaries, the simulator has to guess prior to step 1 of **DKGSim** which parties the adversary is going to corrupt. Whenever the adversary corrupts a party P_j, $j \in \mathcal{B}$ the simulator delivers all values computed and stored on behalf of this party. The adversary takes over the role of P_j. The simulator aborts if its guess was wrong. The simulation is successful with probability at least $1/\binom{n}{k}$. In the same fashion like for the Key generation protocols it can be shown that **Sign** and **SignSim** are indistinguishable as well. □

Lemma 2. *The scheme (T, n, k)-Σ_{fst} is (n, k_1, k_2)-robust, if $k_1 + k_2 \leq k$ and $n \geq 2k + 1$. In particular, the scheme is $(n, 0, k)$-robust, i.e. robust against malicious adversaries.*

PROOF. Here, we argue for the strongest case, i.e. $(n, 0, k)$. The only protocols where the adversary on behalf of the compromised parties may interact with honest ones are **KeyGen** and **Sign**. Hence, we have to show that the adversary is not able to prevent the honest parties from executing these protocols successfully. For **KeyGen**, instantiated with the **DKG** protocol, it follows from the proof in [10]. Basically, the reason is that any party who deviates from the protocol is either disqualified or its correct secret share is reconstructed by the honest majority.

For **Sign**, we make use of the fact that the **DKG** protocol delivers for all parties P_i the elements $g_2^{x_i}$, where x_i is their share of the secret. Functioning as public keys pk_i they allow the other parties to check validity in (3) of the submitted partial signatures. Hence, only signatures which are valid for message M will be aggregated. It follows that k parties can neither manipulate nor prevent the key generation or the final signature as long as $n \geq 2k + 1$.   □

Theorem 1. *Let $\mathcal{A}$ be an adaptive adversary that $(t_{\mathcal{A}}, \varepsilon_{\mathcal{A}})$-breaks the EUF-CMA security of (T, n, k)-Σ_{fst} and let Σ be the single user signature scheme from [9]. Given $\mathcal{A}$, we can build a simulator $\mathcal{R}$ that $(t_{\mathcal{R}}, \varepsilon_{\mathcal{R}})$-breaks the EUF-CMA forward security of Σ for T time periods such that*

$$t_{\mathcal{R}} = O(t_{\mathcal{A}}) \text{ and } \varepsilon_{\mathcal{R}} \geq \binom{n}{k}^{-1} \cdot \varepsilon_{\mathcal{A}}.$$

PROOF. We show how $\mathcal{R}$ simulates $\mathcal{A}$'s EUF-CMA security experiment instantiated with Σ_{fst} perfectly and how it uses the challenge provided by $\mathcal{A}$ to win its own EUF-CMA security experiment instantiated with Σ. Simulator $\mathcal{R}$ receives a public key $y \in \mathbb{G}_2$ at the beginning of its EUF-CMA forward security experiment. Then, $\mathcal{R}$ guesses the first k parties $\mathcal{A}$ might compromise. Let $\mathcal{B}'$ denote the set of indices of these parties. W.l.o.g. we assume these parties to be $P_1, \ldots, P_k$. Further let $\mathcal{G} = \{1, \ldots, n\}$ and $\mathcal{B} = \emptyset$ denote the indices of the uncompromised and compromised parties from the perspective of $\mathcal{A}$. Then, $\mathcal{R}$ and $\mathcal{A}$ continue with the key generation procedure **KeyGen**. During this procedure, the adversary is allowed to make k queries to **Break-In**. The procedures for adversary $\mathcal{A}$ are simulated by $\mathcal{R}$ as follows.

- **KeyGen.** To simulate the **KeyGen** protocol for $\mathcal{A}$ the simulator runs the **DKGSim** protocol on input (y, n, k). $\mathcal{A}$ receives all information to compute the initial secret key shares of the compromised parties as well as the common public key $pk = y$ and the user public keys pk_i for $i = 1, \ldots, n$. Additionally to all public keys, $\mathcal{R}$ holds the initial secret keys $sk_{0,i}$ for all $i \in \mathcal{B}'$.

- **KeyUpdate.** Whenever $\mathcal{A}$ asks to execute **KeyUpdate**, then $\mathcal{R}$ asks for **KeyUpdate** in the EUF-CMA forward security game of Σ.

- **Signing**(t, M). Whenever $\mathcal{A}$ sends a signing query for message M at time period t, $\mathcal{B}$ forwards this query to its own signing oracle and receives a signature (t, σ_1, σ_2). Then, $\mathcal{B}$ runs the **SignSim** protocol with input $(t, M, (\sigma_1, \sigma_2), y)$.

- **Break-In**(j, t). Adversary $\mathcal{A}$ queries the break-in oracle on input an index j and the current time period t. Simulator $\mathcal{R}$ checks if $|\mathcal{B}| < k$. If this holds and $j \notin \mathcal{B}'$, then $\mathcal{R}$ aborts. Else $\mathcal{R}$ removes j out of $\mathcal{G}$ and adds it to $\mathcal{B}$. If $sk_{j,t}$ is already defined, it is delivered to $\mathcal{A}$. If $|\mathcal{B}| = k$ and $j \in \mathcal{G}$, the challenger $\mathcal{R}$ sets $\tilde{t} \leftarrow t$ and computes the secret keys $sk_{t,j}$ for all $j \in \mathcal{G}$ as follows. First, it queries the break-in oracle in the EUF-CMA security experiment of Σ. It obtains the secret key sk_t, which consists of tuples of the form

$$(c, d, e_{s+1}, \ldots, e_{\ell+1}) = \left(g_2^r, h^x (h_0 \prod_{v=1}^s h_v^{w_v})^r, h_{s+1}^r, \ldots, h_{\ell+1}^r \right),$$

which correspond to either internal nodes $\omega = \omega_1 \ldots \omega_s$, where $s \leq \ell$ or to the leaf representing time period t.

It defines similar to **SignSim**:
- $H_{is} := h^{a_{is}}$ for all $i \in QUAL \setminus \{n\}, s = 0, \ldots, k$, where a_{is} are the coefficients of the polynomials computed during **DKGSim**.
- $H_{n0}^* := \prod_{i \in QUAL \setminus \{n\}} (H_{i0}^{-1}) \cdot h^x$.
- $s_{nj}^* := s_{nj} = a_n(j)$ for $j = 1, \ldots, k$.
- $H_{ns}^* := (H_{n0}^*)^{\lambda_{s0}} \cdot \prod_{i=1}^k (h^{s_{ni}^*})^{\lambda_{si}}$ for $s = 1, \ldots, k$, where λ_{si}s are the Lagrange interpolation coefficients.
- $\bar{H}_{n0} := \prod_{i \in QUAL \setminus \{n\}} (H_{i0}^{-1} \cdot d)$ for each tuple $(c, d, \ldots)$ separately.

Then, for all tuples on the stack it computes d_j as:

$$\prod_{i \in QUAL \setminus \{n\}} \prod_{s=0}^k (H_{is})^{j^s} \cdot (\bar{H}_{n0}) \cdot \prod_{s=1}^k \left((\bar{H}_{n0})^{\lambda_{s0}} \cdot \prod_{i=1}^k (h^{s_{ni}^*})^{\lambda_{si}} \right)^{j^s}.$$

for all values x from $\{c, e_{i+1}, \ldots, e_{\ell+1}\}$ it computes x_j as:

$$x^{\sum_{s=1}^k \lambda_{s0} \cdot j^s + 1}$$

In order to guarantee a perfect simulation $\mathcal{R}$ re-randomizes the secret keys of all parties in the same fashion as the signatures in (6). Finally, it outputs $sk_{t,j}$ for all $j \in \mathcal{G}$ as the stack of tuples of the form $(c_j, d_j, e_{j,i+1}, \ldots, e_{j,\ell+1})$. Analogously to the signature in **SignSim** it holds that

$$d_j = \prod_{i \in QUAL \setminus \{n\}} \prod_{k=0}^k (H_{is})^{j^s} \cdot (\bar{H}_{n0}) \cdot \prod_{s=1}^k \left((\bar{H}_{n0})^{\lambda_{s0}} \cdot \prod_{i=1}^k (h^{s_{ni}^*})^{\lambda_{si}} \right)^{j^s}$$

$$= h^{x_j} \cdot (h_0 \prod_{v=1}^s h_v^{w_v})^{r \cdot \sum_{s=1}^k \lambda_{k0} \cdot j^s + r}.$$

Overall, these stack form valid secret keys $sk_{t,j}$ for all $j \in \mathcal{G}$ and their simulation is perfect.

- **Finalize**$(M^*, (t^*, \sigma_1^*, \sigma_2^*))$. At the end, $\mathcal{A}$ submits the challenge $(M^*, (t^*, \sigma_1^*, \sigma_2^*))$. $\mathcal{B}$ forwards this challenge to the **Finalize** procedure in its own EUF-CMA security experiment.

Together with Lemma 1 it follows that the simulation of the security experiment for $\mathcal{A}$ is perfect. Both, $\mathcal{A}$ as well as $\mathcal{R}$ have to provide a valid forgery for the same public key and under the same restriction of the time period $\tilde{t}$ from the Break-In procedure. Hence, $\mathcal{R}$ wins its security game whenever $\mathcal{A}$ provides a valid forgery and $\mathcal{R}$ guesses the corrupted parties correctly, which happens with probability at least $\binom{n}{k}^{-1}$. Note that a forgery $(M^*, (t^*, \sigma_1^*, \sigma_2^*))$ is only valid if no signature for (t^*, M^*) was queried. The running time of $\mathcal{R}$ is the running time of $\mathcal{A}$ plus some small overhead. Overall, we have

$$t_{\mathcal{R}} = O(t_{\mathcal{A}}) \text{ and } \varepsilon_{\mathcal{R}} \geq \binom{n}{k}^{-1} \cdot \varepsilon_{\mathcal{A}}.$$

$\square$

5 Discussions

Complexity Leveraging. To prove our FST scheme secure against adaptive adversaries we used complexity leveraging. This approach results in a security loss of at most $\binom{n}{k}$, where n is the number of parties and k the threshold. Although, this loss appears quite big it is worth noting that in practice n is relatively small. For instance for a threshold scheme with $10, 20$ or 30 parties the maximum loss is $2^8, 2^{18}$ and 2^{28}, respectively. Although the suggestion from [16] does not require complexity leveraging, it is based on groups of composite order. Compared to elliptic curves of prime order these groups require a much bigger modulus to guarantee the same level of security.[5] Furthermore the known techniques to translate schemes in composite order groups into schemes in prime order groups result in bigger signatures and require a trusted dealer. Hence, to get a more efficient scheme the security loss in our scheme can be compensated by a slightly bigger modulus, which still remains much smaller compared to one of composite order as long as the number of users is not extremely large. Additionally, this approach avoids a trusted dealer.

Signature and Key Sizes. In [9], Drijvers and Neven analyzed the signature and key sizes in the context of their single user scheme. The structure of the signatures and keys in our threshold scheme is the same structure as of the signatures and keys in their single user scheme. The only difference is that the

---

[5] For comparison of the concrete sizes we refer to the common recommendations: https://www.keylength.com/.

common parameters in the threshold version have one additional element in $\mathbb{G}_2$. As pointed out in [9], a signature consists of one element in $\mathbb{G}_1$, one element in $\mathbb{G}_2$ and one bit string of length ℓ, where $T = 2^\ell$ is the maximum number of time periods. For all time periods, the secret key contains at most one node key at every level $d = 1, \ldots, \ell$. For level d the node key consists of 1 element in $\mathbb{G}_2$ and $\ell - d + 2$ elements in $\mathbb{G}_1$, which leads to at most ℓ elements in $\mathbb{G}_2$ and $\ell^2/2 + 3\ell/2$ elements in $\mathbb{G}_1$. The public key and the common parameters consist of $\ell + 4$ elements in $\mathbb{G}_1$, 3 elements in $\mathbb{G}_2$, and a description of the hash function and the pairing group. This includes the additional element in $\mathbb{G}_2$. For a BLS12-381 curve one element in $\mathbb{G}_1$ requires 32 bits and one element in $\mathbb{G}_2$ requires 40 bits. Assuming $T = 2^{30}$, this yields a signature size of 84 bytes and a secret key size of at most 16800 bytes. The elements from the public key and the common parameters require 1208 bytes.

On the Distinction Between Proactive and Forward Security. In forward security, the public key is fixed but the secret key changes in regard to the time period. The time period is also embedded in the secret key. If the secret key of time period t gets exposed, it is possible to sign signatures for all time periods $t' \geqslant t$, but it is still infeasible to do so for time periods $t' < t$. Proactive security is an additional *interactive* security mechanism for secret sharing. This mechanism changes the secret shares, but not the secret itself and as in forward security, the public key remains unchanged. Since proactive security does not embed the time period it can be seen as a parallel time line when combined with forward security. For instance, let k_1 be shares from a time period t and k_2 be shares from the same time period t but after proactivization. Further let $k_1 + k_2 \geqslant k + 1$, but $k_1, k_2 < k + 1$, where k is the threshold. Then, it is *not* possible to reconstruct the secret from the shares k_1 and k_2, although they belong to the same time period. Overall, proactivization can provide additional security but it must be executed carefully since every set of players of size at most k which did not participate in proactivizing is forever excluded from signing. In order to proactivize the key material in our scheme the users had to run the **DKG** protocol where each party P_i sets the constant term of polynomial a_i to 0. It is also worth mentioning that in order to tolerate mobile adversaries, having a non-interactive key update procedure and a separate protocol for proactivization is still preferable to having an interactive key update procedure. The reason is that the former allows different levels of granularity. For instance, key update could happen every hour and proactivization once per day. Proactive security was introduced by Ostrovsky and Yung [18]. Herzberg et al. showed techniques to achieve robust proactivization for polynomial secret sharing [12,13].

Conclusion. We proposed a *forward-secure threshold signature scheme*, which improves the state of the art in many aspects. The main advantages of our scheme are the *non-interactive key update and signing procedure*, the fact that it can be implemented on *standardized pairing-friendly curves* and, that *no trusted dealer* is required. Our signature and key sizes are also quite short. Drijvers and Neven [9] analyzed the concrete sizes for their single user scheme, which hold also for our threshold version except of one additional element. We reproduced this analysis in the appendix. We proved our scheme secure against adaptive malicious adversaries. Also mobile adversaries can be tolerated. This requires proactivization of our scheme, which we explained in the appendix.

References

1. Abdalla, M., Miner, S., Namprempre, C.: Forward-secure threshold signature schemes. In: Naccache, D. (ed.) CT-RSA 2001. LNCS, vol. 2020, pp. 441–456. Springer, Heidelberg (2001). https://doi.org/10.1007/3-540-45353-9_32
2. Abdalla, M., Reyzin, L.: A new forward-secure digital signature scheme. In: Okamoto, T. (ed.) ASIACRYPT 2000. LNCS, vol. 1976, pp. 116–129. Springer, Heidelberg (2000). https://doi.org/10.1007/3-540-44448-3_10
3. Bellare, M., Miner, S.K.: A forward-secure digital signature scheme. In: Wiener, M. (ed.) CRYPTO 1999. LNCS, vol. 1666, pp. 431–448. Springer, Heidelberg (1999). https://doi.org/10.1007/3-540-48405-1_28
4. Bellare, M., Rogaway, P.: Random oracles are practical: a paradigm for designing efficient protocols. In: Proceedings of the 1st ACM Conference on Computer and Communications Security, CCS 1993, New York, NY, USA, pp. 62–73. ACM (1993)
5. Ben-Or, M., Goldwasser, S., Wigderson, A.: Completeness theorems for non-cryptographic fault-tolerant distributed computation (extended abstract). In: STOC (1988)
6. Boyd, C.: Digital multisignatures. In: Cryptography and Coding, pp. 241–246 (1986)
7. Chow, S.S.M., Go, H.W., Hui, L.C.K., Yiu, S.-M.: Multiplicative forward-secure threshold signature scheme. Int. J. Netw. Secur. **7**, 397–403 (2008)
8. Desmedt, Y., Frankel, Y.: Threshold cryptosystems. In: Brassard, G. (ed.) CRYPTO 1989. LNCS, vol. 435, pp. 307–315. Springer, New York (1990). https://doi.org/10.1007/0-387-34805-0_28
9. Drijvers, M., Neven, G.: Forward-secure multi-signatures. Cryptology ePrint Archive, Report 2019/261 (2019). http://eprint.iacr.org/2019/261
10. Gennaro, R., Jarecki, S., Krawczyk, H., Rabin, T.: Secure distributed key generation for discrete-log based cryptosystems. J. Cryptol. **20**, 51–83 (2007). https://doi.org/10.1007/s00145-006-0347-3
11. Guillou, L.C., Quisquater, J.-J.: A "Paradoxical" indentity-based signature scheme resulting from zero-knowledge. In: Goldwasser, S. (ed.) CRYPTO 1988. LNCS, vol. 403, pp. 216–231. Springer, New York (1990). https://doi.org/10.1007/0-387-34799-2_16
12. Herzberg, A., Jakobsson, M., Jarecki, S., Krawczyk, H., Yung, M.: Proactive public key and signature systems. In: Proceedings of the ACM Conference on Computer and Communications Security, January 1997
13. Herzberg, A., Jarecki, S., Krawczyk, H., Yung, M.: Proactive secret sharing or: how to cope with perpetual leakage. In: Coppersmith, D. (ed.) CRYPTO 1995. LNCS, vol. 963, pp. 339–352. Springer, Heidelberg (1995). https://doi.org/10.1007/3-540-44750-4_27
14. Krawczyk, H.: Simple forward-secure signatures from any signature scheme. In: Proceedings of the 7th ACM Conference on Computer and Communications Security, CCS 2000, New York, NY, USA, pp. 108–115. ACM (2000)

15. Libert, B., Joye, M., Yung, M.: Born and raised distributively: fully distributed non-interactive adaptively-secure threshold signatures with short shares. Theor. Comput. Sci. **645**, 1–24 (2016)
16. Libert, B., Yung, M.: Adaptively secure non-interactive threshold cryptosystems. Theor. Comput. Sci. **478**, 76–100 (2013)
17. Liu, L.-S., Chu, C.-K., Tzeng, W.-G.: A threshold GQ signature scheme. In: Zhou, J., Yung, M., Han, Y. (eds.) ACNS 2003. LNCS, vol. 2846, pp. 137–150. Springer, Heidelberg (2003). https://doi.org/10.1007/978-3-540-45203-4_11
18. Ostrovsky, R., Yung, M.: How to withstand mobile virus attacks (extended abstract). In: Proceedings of the Tenth Annual ACM Symposium on Principles of Distributed Computing, PODC 1991, New York, NY, USA, pp. 51–59. ACM (1991)
19. Shamir, A.: How to share a secret. Commun. ACM **22**(11), 612–613 (1979)
20. Shoup, V.: Practical threshold signatures. In: Preneel, B. (ed.) EUROCRYPT 2000. LNCS, vol. 1807, pp. 207–220. Springer, Heidelberg (2000). https://doi.org/10.1007/3-540-45539-6_15
21. Tzeng, W.-G., Tzeng, Z.-J.: Robust forward-secure signature schemes with proactive security. In: Kim, K. (ed.) PKC 2001. LNCS, vol. 1992, pp. 264–276. Springer, Heidelberg (2001). https://doi.org/10.1007/3-540-44586-2_19
22. Wang, H., Qiu, G., Feng, D., Xiao, G.-Z.: Cryptanalysis of Tzeng-Tzeng forward-secure signature schemes. IEICE Trans. **89-A**, 822–825 (2006)
23. Yu, J., Kong, F.: Forward secure threshold signature scheme from bilinear pairings. In: Wang, Y., Cheung, Y., Liu, H. (eds.) CIS 2006. LNCS (LNAI), vol. 4456, pp. 587–597. Springer, Heidelberg (2007). https://doi.org/10.1007/978-3-540-74377-4_61

Accelerating Beta Weil Pairing with Precomputation and Multi-pairing Techniques

Kai Kinoshita$^{(\boxtimes)}$ and Koutarou Suzuki

Toyohashi University of Technology, Toyohashi, Aichi, Japan
kinoshita.kai.ty@tut.jp, suzuki@cs.tut.ac.jp

Abstract. In this paper, we present the efficient computation methods of β Weil pairing with the precomputation and multi-pairing techniques. We use the following two ideas to facilitate applying those techniques to β Weil pairing.

1. Elimination of denominators of β Weil pairing: The original β Weil pairing proposed by Aranha et al. is the products of quotients of extended Miller functions. Then, we propose the method to eliminate denominators of β Weil pairing.

2. Elimination of exponents of β Weil pairing: The original β Weil pairing has distinct exponent in each term. Then, we propose the method to eliminate exponents of the β Weil pairing. Thereby, we can apply the precomputation and multi-pairing technique to β Weil pairing in order to accelerate the computation.

Moreover, we estimate the computational costs of the proposed methods for the BLS-48 curve with 256 bit level of security against the Kim-Barbulescu attack, proposed by Kiyomura et al. Then, we compare the results with the normal β Weil pairing and the optimal ate pairing. Furthermore, we also provide implementation results.

Keywords: β Weil pairing $\cdot$ Precomputation $\cdot$ Multi-pairing $\cdot$ BLS-48 curve

1 Introduction

Since ID-based cryptography [9,34] have been proposed, many pairing-based cryptographic applications such as group signature schemes [32], attribute-based encryption [33] and functional encryption [28] have been introduced and have received much attention. All pairing-based cryptography currently used in practice are based on bilinear pairings on elliptic curves, requiring both elliptic curve operations and function computation and evaluation to compute the pairing of two points on an elliptic curve [30]. Generally, a pairing on the elliptic curve is a non-degenerate bilinear map $e : \mathbb{G}_1 \times \mathbb{G}_2 \to \mathbb{G}_3$, where $\mathbb{G}_1$ and $\mathbb{G}_2$ are additive cyclic sub-groups on a certain elliptic curve E over a finite extension field $\mathbb{F}_{p^k}$

© Springer Nature Switzerland AG 2020
K. Aoki and A. Kanaoka (Eds.): IWSEC 2020, LNCS 12231, pp. 261–281, 2020.
https://doi.org/10.1007/978-3-030-58208-1_15

and $\mathbb{G}_3$ is a multiplicative cyclic group in $\mathbb{F}_{p^k}^*$, where p is a prime and $k \geq 1$ is an embedding degree. $\mathbb{G}_1, \mathbb{G}_2, \mathbb{G}_3$ are a group with order r respectively.

So far, in order to construct practical pairing-based cryptographic applications, many researchers have improved efficiency of pairing computation and proposed several methods of calculating pairings. In representative pairings, there are Weil, Tate, Eta [6], (twisted) ate [21], R-ate [27], optimal ate [38] pairings and their generalizations [20]. Currently, the most mainstream pairing computation method is optimal ate pairing, which is a Tate-type pairing made of the Miller function and the final exponentiation. There are many implementation results of the optimal ate pairing [1,10,11,24,26,29,31,37]. In recent years, various platforms such as PCs, smartphones and embedded systems equipped with multi-core processors are gradually increasing. The parallel computation in such platforms can expect further efficiency improvement for single pairing but the efficient method for parallelizing the final exponentiation is still unknown. Therefore, the optimal ate pairing is not suitable in multi-core environments.

On the other hand, there is the β Weil pairing [3] proposed by Aranha et al., which is not necessary to compute the final exponentiation. Moreover, in [1], it is reported that the β Weil pairing is more efficient than optimal ate pairing using multi-core processors. The β Weil pairing is made of the products of quotients of Miller functions. Several pairings, which also contain some Miller functions like β Weil pairing, exist and have been proposed the efficient computational methods [15,35,40,41] by applying the multi-pairing technique [16]. However, we did not find the result of applying multi-pairing technique for the original β Weil pairing.

In this paper, we present the efficient computation methods of β Weil pairing with the precomputation and multi-pairing techniques. We use the following two ideas to facilitate applying those techniques to β Weil pairing.

1. Elimination of denominators of β Weil pairing: The original β Weil pairing proposed by Aranha et al. is the products of quotients of extended Miller functions. Then, we propose the method to eliminate denominators of β Weil pairing.
2. Elimination of exponents of β Weil pairing: The original β Weil pairing has distinct exponent in each term. Then, we propose the method to eliminate exponents of the β Weil pairing. Thereby, we can apply the precomputation and multi-pairing technique to β Weil pairing in order to accelerate the computation.

Moreover, we estimate the computational costs of the proposed methods and give comparisons with conventional methods. For comparisons, we estimate the costs for the BLS-48 curve parameter proposed by Kiyomura et al. [26] with 256 bit level of security against the Kim-Barbulescu attack [25]. So far, other parameters [4,5,14,18,19,22] against the Kim-Barbulescu attack are proposed, but we mainly deal with BLS-48 in this paper.

Finally, we also provide implementation results.

2   Preliminaries

This section reviews Barreto-Lynn-Scott (BLS) curve, the optimal ate pairing, the β Weil pairing, precomputation and multi-pairing techniques.

2.1   Barreto-Lynn-Scott (BLS) Curve

In [7], Barreto, Lynn and Scott proposed a family of non super-singular pairing-friendly elliptic curves for specific embedding degrees. In what follows, we consider the curve of embedding degree $k = 48$, named BLS-48. The BLS-48 curve is defined over field $\mathbb{F}_p$ as follows:

$$E/\mathbb{F}_p : y^2 = x^3 + b, \quad (b \neq 0) \tag{1}$$

where $x, y \in \mathbb{F}_{p^k}$. For the BLS-48 curve, characteristic $p(\kappa)$, Frobenius trace $t(\kappa)$, order $r(\kappa)$ and the specific integer variable κ are as shown below, where κ is such that $6 \mid (p(\kappa) - 1)$.

$$p(\kappa) = (\kappa - 1)^2(\kappa^{16} - \kappa^8 + 1)/3 + \kappa,$$
$$r(\kappa) = (\kappa^{16} - \kappa^8 + 1),$$
$$t(\kappa) = \kappa + 1,$$
$$\kappa = -2^{32} - 2^{30} - 2^{10} + 2^7 - 1 \text{ [26]},$$

2.2   Optimal Ate Pairing and β Weil Pairing

The optimal ate pairing proposed by Vercauteren [38] is the most efficient method of computing the pairing. Let $E[r]$ be an r-torsion subgroup and π_p be the Frobenius endomorphism, i.e. $\pi_p : E \to E : (x, y) \mapsto (x^p, y^p)$. Define $\mathbb{G}_1 = E[r] \cap Ker(\pi_p - [1])$, $\mathbb{G}_2 = E[r] \cap Ker(\pi_p - [p])$ as the subgroup of rational points of order r in $E[r]$. We denote scalar s multiplication for a rational point R by $[s]R$. Let E' be a twist of degree d of E with $\phi : E' \to E$ defined over $\mathbb{F}_{p^d}$, and define $\phi^{-1} : E \to E'$. Let $s \in \mathbb{Z}, R \in E[r]$. A function $f_{s,R}$ is the rational function in $\mathbb{F}_{p^k}(E)$ with divisor

$$div(f_{s,R}) = s(R) - ([s]R) - (s-1)(\mathcal{O}),$$

which is called Miller function [30]. The Miller function computation is made of multiple (vertical)line functions, multiplications and squarings in $\mathbb{F}_{p^k}$. We denote the line through points R and S by $\ell_{R,S}$ and the vertical line through points R and $-R$ by v_R. For $R \in \mathbb{G}_1$, $S \in \mathbb{G}_2$(or $R \in \mathbb{G}_2, S \in \mathbb{G}_1$), $s \in \mathbb{Z}$, $f_{s,R}(S)$ is computed by Algorithm 1. Here, we assume that $f_{s,R}(S)$ is raised to the power of $p^{k/2} - 1$ after computing itself.

Algorithm 1: Compute Miller function.

Input: $R \in \mathbb{G}_1, S \in \mathbb{G}_2 (\text{or } R \in \mathbb{G}_2, S \in \mathbb{G}_1), s \in \mathbb{Z}$.
Output: $f_{s,R}(S), [s]R$

$\mu \leftarrow 1, \quad T \leftarrow R$;
for $i \leftarrow \lfloor \log_2 s \rfloor - 1$ *to 0* **do**
$\quad \mu \leftarrow \mu^2$;
$\quad \mu \leftarrow \mu \cdot \ell_{T,T}(S), \quad T \leftarrow [2]T$;
$\quad$ **if** *n-th bit of* $s = \pm 1$ **then**
$\quad\quad | \quad \mu \leftarrow \mu \cdot \ell_{T,R}(S), \quad T \leftarrow T + R$;
$\quad$ **end**
end
return μ, T

The following are three well-known useful results for the Miller functions. For all $a, b \in \mathbb{Z}$ and $R \in E[r]$, we have following relations,

$$f_{a+b,R} = f_{a,R} \cdot f_{b,R} \cdot \ell_{[a]R,[b]R} / v_{[a+b]R}, \tag{2a}$$

$$f_{ab,R} = f_{b,R}^a \cdot f_{a,[b]R} = f_{a,R}^b \cdot f_{b,[a]R}, \tag{2b}$$

$$f_{r,R}^a = f_{ar,R}, \tag{2c}$$

Let $h(x) = \sum_{i=0}^{\omega} h_i x^i \in \mathbb{Z}[x]$ be an optimal polynomial obtained by using a lattice–based method such that $h(p) \equiv 0 \pmod r$. Let $m = h(p)/r$ and we assume that $r \nmid m$. For $R \in E[r]$, from Eqs. (2c), we have

$$f_{r,R}^m = f_{mr,R} = f_{\sum_{i=0}^{\omega} h_i p^i, R}.$$

From Eqs. (2a) and Eqs. (2b), we obtain the following formula as shown by Theorem 1 in [38],

$$f_{r,R}^m = \left(\prod_{i=0}^{\omega} f_{h_i,[p^i]R} \cdot \prod_{i=0}^{\omega-1} \frac{\ell_{[h_i p^i]R, [\tau_{i+1}]R}}{v_{[\tau_i]R}} \right) \cdot \prod_{i=0}^{\omega} f_{p^i,R}^{h_i} \tag{3}$$

where $\tau_i = \sum_{j=i}^{\omega} h_j p^j$.

Let $f_{p,h,R}$ denote the expression within the parenthesis in Eqs. (3);

$$f_{p,h,R} = \prod_{i=0}^{\omega} f_{h_i,[p^i]R} \cdot \prod_{i=0}^{\omega-1} \frac{\ell_{[h_i p^i]R, [\tau_{i+1}]R}}{v_{[\tau_i]R}} \tag{4}$$

$f_{p,h,R}$ is called *extended Miller function* to be the normalized rational function with divisor $div(f_{p,h,R}) = \sum_{i=0}^{\omega} h_i(([p^i]R) - (\mathcal{O}))$. $f_{p,h,R}$ has different formulae depending on curve parameters and has one Miller function for almost parameters. Here, the optimal ate pairing a_{opt} is defined by

$$a_{opt} : \mathbb{G}_1 \times \mathbb{G}_2 \to \mathbb{G}_3, (P,Q) \mapsto f_{p,h,Q}(P)^{(p^k-1)/r}. \tag{5}$$

Moreover, β Weil pairing is defined by

$$\beta : \mathbb{G}_1 \times \mathbb{G}_2 \to \mathbb{G}_3, \ (P,Q) \mapsto \left[\prod_{i=0}^{e-1} \left(\frac{f_{p,h,Q}([p^i]P)}{f_{p,h,[p^i]P}(Q)} \right)^{p^{\delta_i}} \right]^{(p^{k/2}-1)}, \tag{6}$$

where $e = k/gcd(k,d)$ and $\delta_i = e - 1 - i$.

2.3 Precomputation Technique

A bilinear map e is calculated for inputs of rational points $P \in \mathbb{G}_1$ and $Q \in \mathbb{G}_2$. If either P or Q is a fixed argument in a particular protocol, it is known that we can precompute a part of the Miller function. This technique is called precomputation technique, which is first pointed out by Scott [36] and analysed in more detail by Costello et al. [12]. The computation of a Miller function $f_{s,Q}(P)$ is made of the computation of line functions depended on Q, substitutions of P for computed line functions and so on. In general pairing computation, those operations are executed at the same time, but the line functions can be computed independently because they only depend on Q as can be seen from Algorithm 1. After that, we can compute $f_{s,Q}(P)$ by substituting P for stored line functions. These algorithms are shown below.

Algorithm 2: CSL: Calculate and store line functions.

Input: $R \in \mathbb{G}_2$(or $R \in \mathbb{G}_1$), integer s
Output: An array g of $\lfloor \log_2 s \rfloor + HW(s) - 1$ line functions and sR.
   $HW(s)$ is the hamming weight of s

$T \leftarrow R, j \leftarrow 1$;
for $i \leftarrow \lfloor \log_2 s \rfloor - 1$ *to 0* **do**
 | $g[j] \leftarrow \ell_{T,T}, \ T \leftarrow 2T, \ j \leftarrow j + 1$;
 | **if** i-*th bit of* $s = \pm 1$ **then**
 | | $g[j] \leftarrow \ell_{T,R}, \ T \leftarrow T + R, \ j \leftarrow j + 1$;
 | **end**
end
return $g, \ T$

Algorithm 3: EM: Evaluate Miller function with stored line functions.

Input: An array g of line functions in $f_{s,R}$, $S \in \mathbb{G}_1$(or $\mathbb{G}_2$) and $s \in \mathbb{Z}$.
Output: $f_{s,R}(S)$

$\mu \leftarrow 1, \ j \leftarrow 1$;
for $i \leftarrow \lfloor \log_2 s \rfloor - 1$ *to 0* **do**
 | $\mu \leftarrow \mu^2$;
 | $\mu \leftarrow \mu \cdot g[j](S), \ j \leftarrow j + 1$;
 | **if** i-*th bit of* $s = \pm 1$ **then**
 | | $\mu \leftarrow \mu \cdot g[j](S), \ j \leftarrow j + 1$;
 | **end**
end
return μ

In the case of Q is known in advance or it is necessary to compute multiple $f_{s,Q}(\cdot)$ in single pairing computation, we once compute and store the line functions, then we can reuse them. Since the β Weil pairing include multiple $f_{s,Q}(\cdot)$, this technique is expected to accelerate the β Weil pairing computation.

2.4 Multi-pairing Technique

For the sets of rational points $P_1, P_2, \cdots, P_N \in \mathbb{G}_1$ and $Q_1, Q_2, \cdots, Q_N \in \mathbb{G}_2$, the evaluation of the products of the form $\prod_{i=1}^{N} e(P_i, Q_i)$ is required in many protocols. Granger et al. [16] have proposed an efficient algorithm for calculating the products, namely the multi-pairing technique. The computation of a single Tate-like pairing $e(P_i, Q_i)$ require to compute a Miller function including M squarings. Accordingly, the computation of N pairings require $N \cdot M$ squarings in the naive computation. On the other hand, by using this technique, the computation of N pairings require only M squarings from the simple power law that $(a_1^2 \cdot a_2^2 \cdots a_N^2) = (a_1 \cdot a_2 \cdots a_N)^2$. This computation algorithm is given in [35, Algorithm 1]. This technique is used for the computation of products of pairings in general, but there are the few works [15,35,40,41] that have applied this technique for a single pairing computation. Some of the pairing computation methods have two or more Miller functions in a single pairing, so that this technique also can be applied to the β Weil pairing.

3 Proposed Computation Methods for β Weil Pairing

In this section, we propose the formula Eqs. (8) for β Weil pairing computation. We also propose the application of precomputation and multi-pairing techniques for Eqs. (8).

3.1 Elimination of Denominators of β Weil Pairing

If we apply multi-pairing technique to $\frac{f_{p,h,Q}([p^i]P)}{f_{p,h,[p^i]P}(Q)}$, we need to compute conjugation for line function in each step of loops in the denominator Miller function. Note that we can compute conjugations instead of inversions [2]. The computational cost of conjugation is negligible, but the occurrence of special operations in each step of loops is redundant and complicates implementation. To avoid the conjugations, we propose the method to eliminate denominators of the β Weil pairing in order to facilitate applying the multi-pairing technique. To do this, we show some useful results.

Lemma 1. *Assume that vertical lines can be regarded as 1. For all $a \in \mathbb{Z}$ and $R \in E$, we obtain the following two relations:*

(i). $f_{a,R}^{-1} = f_{a,-R}$
(ii). $f_{p,h,R}^{-1} = f_{p,h,-R}$

Proof. (*i*). Equations (2b) gives that

$$f_{a,R}^{-1} = \frac{f_{-1,R}^a \cdot f_{a,[-1]R}}{f_{-1,[a]R}}.$$

Then, we have that $div(f_{-1,[a]R}) = -([a]R) - ([-a]R) + 2(\mathcal{O}) = -(([a]R) + ([-a]R) - 2(\mathcal{O})) = div(v_{[a]R}^{-1})$ and $div(f_{-1,R}^a) = div(v_R^{-a})$. From the above, we have that

$$f_{a,R}^{-1} = \frac{v_R^{-a} \cdot f_{a,[-1]R}}{v_{[a]R}^{-1}}.$$

From the assumption, so that we have that

$$f_{a,R}^{-1} = f_{a,[-1]R}.$$

(*ii*). Equations (3) gives that

$$f_{p,h,R} = \frac{f_{rm,R}}{\prod_{i=1}^{\omega} f_{p^i,R}^{h_i}}.$$

Given the above equation to -1 power and we have that

$$f_{p,h,R}^{-1} = \frac{f_{rm,R}^{-1}}{\prod_{i=1}^{\omega} (f_{p^i,R}^{h_i})^{-1}} = \frac{f_{rm,R}^{-1}}{\prod_{i=1}^{\omega} (f_{p^i,R}^{-1})^{h_i}}.$$

Then, (*i*) gives that

$$f_{p,h,R}^{-1} = \frac{f_{rm,-R}}{\prod_{i=1}^{\omega} f_{p^i,-R}^{h_i}} = f_{p,h,-R}.$$

$\square$

By applying Lemma 1 to Eqs. (6), we obtain the following formula.

$$\beta(P,Q) = \left[\prod_{i=0}^{e-1} \left(f_{p,h,Q}([p^i]P) \cdot f_{p,h,[p^i]\overline{P}}(Q) \right)^{p^{\delta_i}} \right]^{(p^{k/2}-1)}, \tag{7}$$

where $\overline{P} = [-1]P$. We can apply the multi-pairing technique to compute $f_{p,h,Q}([p^i]P) \cdot f_{p,h,[p^i]\overline{P}}(Q)$ without conjugations for line functions. However, we still can not apply its technique to distinct exponent terms in Eqs. (7). In the next section, we eliminate this problem.

3.2   Elimination of Exponents of β Weil Pairing

If we try to apply the multi-pairing technique to $\prod_{i=0}^{e-1} \left(f_{p,h,Q}([p^i]P) \cdot f_{p,h,[p^i]\overline{P}}(Q) \right)^{p^{\delta_i}}$ in Eqs. (7), we can not apply its technique to Miller functions of different i's, since each term has exponent p^{δ_i}. To extend the applicable scope of the multi-pairing technique, we propose the method to eliminate exponents of Eqs. (7) for all $i = 0, 1, ..., e - 1$. To do this, we show the useful results.

From the definition of $\mathbb{G}_1$ and $\mathbb{G}_2$, we have that

$$f^{p^i}_{p,h,P}(Q) = f_{p,h,P}(\pi_{p^i}(Q)), \quad f^{p^i}_{p,h,Q}(P) = f_{p,h,\pi_{p^i}(Q)}(P).$$

From the above relations, we obtain the following new formula.

$$\beta(P,Q) = \left[\prod_{i=0}^{e-1} f_{p,h,\pi_{p^{\delta_i}}(Q)}([p^i]P) \cdot f_{p,h,[p^i]\overline{P}}(\pi_{p^{\delta_i}}(Q)) \right]^{(p^{k/2}-1)} \tag{8}$$

All extended Miller functions in Eqs. (8) have the same exponent for regardless of i, so that we can apply the multi-pairing technique to all Miller functions. We show the efficient computation method for Eqs. (8) by using the precomputation and multi-pairing techniques below.

3.3   Application of the Precomputation Technique

Before evaluating Eqs. (8) by using multi-pairing technique, we compute and store all line functions in Miller functions by using the precomputation technique CSL in Algorithm 2.

We assume that a Miller function in $f_{p,h,[p^i]\overline{P}}$ is $f_{s,[p^i]\overline{P}}$ and a Miller function in $f_{p,h,\pi_{p^{\delta_i}}(Q)}$ is $f_{s,\pi_{p^{\delta_i}}(Q)}$ for some integer s.

For $f_{s,[p^i]\overline{P}}$, we normally compute $[p^i]\overline{P}$ and $\mathrm{CSL}([p^i]\overline{P}, s)$ for each i respectively. For $f_{s,\pi_{p^{\delta_i}}(Q)}$, we compute $\pi_{p^{\delta_i}}(Q)$ and $\mathrm{CSL}(\pi_{p^{\delta_i}}(Q), s)$ for each i respectively. However, in depending on the number of processors, it is efficient by using the following different method.

From the definition of $\mathbb{G}_2$, $f_{s,\pi_{p^{\delta_i}}(Q)}$ is the same as the function raised all line functions in $f_{s,Q}$ to the power of p^{δ_i}. For operations on the extension field, p^i-th Frobenius map's cost is cheaper than elliptic curve operations' cost, so that we select its way in fewer cores environment for the computation of $f_{s,\pi_{p^{\delta_i}}(Q)}$ for each $i (\geq 1)$. This method named CSLFrob is as shown below.

Algorithm 4: CSLFrob: p^n-th Frobenius map for stored line functions

---

Input: An array g of line functions, integer n.

Output: An array g' of line functions raised line functions in g to power of p^n.

for $j \leftarrow 1$ *to length of g* **do**
  | $g'[j] \leftarrow g[j]^{p^n}$;
end
return g'

3.4   Application of the Multi-pairing Technique

After computing and storing all line functions by using the above section's technique, we compute the products of Miller functions in Eqs. (8) by using the multi-pairing technique.

We assume that a Miller function in $f_{p,h,\pi_{p^{\delta_i}}}(Q)$ is $f_{s,\pi_{p^{\delta_i}}}(Q)$ and a Miller function in $f_{p,h,[p^i]\overline{P}}$ is $f_{s,[p^i]\overline{P}}$ for some integer s. The products of Miller functions in Eqs. (8) is as follows.

$$\prod_{i=0}^{e-1} f_{s,\pi_{p^{\delta_i}}}(Q)([p^i]P) \cdot f_{s,[p^i]\overline{P}}(\pi_{p^{\delta_i}}(Q)) \tag{9}$$

Let $g_i = \mathrm{CSL}(\pi_{p^{\delta_i}}(Q), s)$ and $h_i = \mathrm{CSL}([p^i]\overline{P}, s)$ for $0 \leq i \leq e-1$. Moreover, let $P_i = [p^i]P$ and $Q_i = \pi_{p^{\delta_i}}(Q)$. Equations (9) can be computed by using the following method named EMM.

Algorithm 5: EMM: Evaluate product of multiple Miller functions

---

Input: $[(g_1, S_1), (g_2, S_2), \cdots, (g_N, S_N)]$ and $s \in \mathbb{Z}$, where g_i is an array of
line functions and S_i is a rational point in $\mathbb{G}_1$ or $\mathbb{G}_2$.
Output: $\prod_{i=1}^{N} EM(g_i, S_i, s)$

$\mu \leftarrow 1,\ j \leftarrow 1$;
for $n \leftarrow \lfloor \log_2 s \rfloor - 1$ **to** *0* **do**
$\quad \mu \leftarrow \mu^2$;
$\quad \mu \leftarrow \mu \cdot \prod_{i=1}^{N} g_i[j](S_i),\ j \leftarrow j+1$;
$\quad$**if** *n-th bit of s* $= \pm 1$ **then**
$\quad\quad \mu \leftarrow \mu \cdot \prod_{i=1}^{N} g_i[j](S_i),\ j \leftarrow j+1$;
$\quad$**end**
end
return μ

We can execute the following EMM to evaluate Eqs. (9).
$\mathrm{EMM}([(g_0, P_0), (h_0, Q_0), (g_1, P_1), (h_1, Q_1), \cdots, (g_{e-1}, P_{e-1}), (h_{e-1}, Q_{e-1})], s)$.

4   Proposed Methods in the Case of BLS-48

In this section, firstly we describe the basic operations for the β Weil pairing on BLS-48. Then, we show details of the proposed methods for serial and, 2 and 4 parallel computations.

4.1   Basic Operations for BLS-48 β Weil Pairing

The BLS-48 curve $E : y^2 = x^3 + b$ is defined over $\mathbb{F}_p$ and its twist $E' : y^2 = x^3 - b/w$ defined over $\mathbb{F}_{p^8} = \mathbb{F}_{p^4}(w)$, where $b = 1$ and prime p is defined with the parameter $\kappa = -2^{32} - 2^{30} - 2^{10} + 2^7 - 1 \equiv p \pmod{r}$ proposed by [26]. Moreover, we can take that $h(p) = \kappa - p$ and we can obtain the following relations. Its details are in [38].

$$f_{p,h,P} = f_{\kappa,P}, \quad f_{p,h,Q} = f_{\kappa,Q}.$$

Accordingly, by applying the above relations to Eqs. (8), the following formula is given by

$$\beta(P,Q) = \left[\prod_{i=0}^{7} \left(f_{\kappa,\pi_{p^7-i}(Q)}([p^i]P) \cdot f_{\kappa,[p^i]\overline{P}}(\pi_{p^7-i}(Q))\right)\right]^{(p^{24}-1)}.$$

We use the projective coordinates for the computation of point doubling and addition with associated line functions in $f_{\kappa,P}$ with reference to [17]. Also, we use the affine coordinates for the computation of point doubling and addition with associated line functions in $f_{\kappa,Q}$ with reference to [17] and [26].

Towering of $\mathbb{F}_{p^{48}}$ Extension Field. Let $6|(p-1)$, where p is the characteristics of the finite field underlying BLS-48 curve and -1 is a quadratic and cubic non-residue in $\mathbb{F}_p$ since $p \equiv 3 \pmod 4$. An element in $\mathbb{F}_{p^{48}}$ can be represented using the following towering scheme:

$$\mathbb{F}_{p^2} = \mathbb{F}_p[u]/(u^2+1),$$
$$\mathbb{F}_{p^4} = \mathbb{F}_{p^2}[v]/(v^2+u+1),$$
$$\mathbb{F}_{p^8} = \mathbb{F}_{p^4}[w]/(w^2+v),$$
$$\mathbb{F}_{p^{24}} = \mathbb{F}_{p^8}[z]/(z^3+w),$$
$$\mathbb{F}_{p^{48}} = \mathbb{F}_{p^{24}}[s]/(s^2+z).$$

We give the computational costs of the tower extension field arithmetic and special operations in the pairing computations in Table 1. The cost of arithmetic operations in $\mathbb{F}_{p^j}$ are denoted as M_j for a multiplication, S_j for a squaring and I_j for an inversion. In particular, the cost of arithmetic operations in $\mathbb{F}_p$ are denoted as M, S, I for a multiplication, a squaring and an inversion respectively. We assume that $M = S$. Moreover, we regard costs of addition, subtraction and basis multiplication as negligible in a customary way.

p^i-th Frobenius Map for a Line Function. A line function in $f_{\kappa,Q}$ and its p^i-th Frobenius map are represented as below:

$$\ell(x,y) = y + xC_1 + C_2, \quad C_1, C_2 \in \mathbb{F}_{p^{48}}, \quad x, y \in \mathbb{F}_p,$$
$$\ell(x,y)^{p^i} = y^{p^i} + x^{p^i}C_1^{p^i} + C_2^{p^i} = y + xC_1^{p^i} + C_2^{p^i}.$$

Here, C_1 and C_2 each have only one element in $\mathbb{F}_{p^8}$ [26]. The cost of Frobenius map for the extension field element is at most the degree of field extension, so that the cost of p^i-th Frobenius map for C_1 and C_2 is $16M$. From that κ is $-2^{32} - 2^{30} - 2^{10} + 2^7 - 1$, $f_{\kappa,Q}$ is made of 36 line functions. Therefore, the cost of one CSLFrob execution for $f_{\kappa,\pi_{p^7-i}(Q)}$ is $36(16M) = 576M$.

Table 1. Costs of arithmetic operations in a tower extension field $\mathbb{F}_{p^{48}}$ [8,13] and special operations in the β Weil pairing computations for BLS-48.

Field	Mult.	Squaring	Inversion
$\mathbb{F}_{p^2}$	$M_2 = 3M$	$S_2 = 2M$	$I_2 = 4M + I$
$\mathbb{F}_{p^4}$	$M_4 = 9M$	$S_4 = 6M$	$I_4 = 14M + I$
$\mathbb{F}_{p^8}$	$M_8 = 27M$	$S_8 = 18M$	$I_8 = 44M + I$
$\mathbb{F}_{p^{24}}$	$M_{24} = 162M$	$S_{24} = 108M$	$I_{24} = 341M + I$
$\mathbb{F}_{p^{48}}$	$M_{48} = 486M$	$S_{48} = 324M$	$I_{48} = 881M + I$
$\mathbb{F}_{p^{48}}$ **Arith.**		**Operation Count**	
Affi. sparse multiplication [17]		$10(M_8) + 3(8M) = 294M$	
Proj. sparse multiplication (Appendix A)		$313M$	
p^i power Frobenius		$47M$	
$E'(\mathbb{F}_{p^8})$ **Arith.**		**Operation Count**	
Point doubling with line		$I_8 + 2S_8 + 3M_8 = 161M + I$	
Point addition with line		$I_8 + S_8 + 3M_8 = 143M + I$	
Substitution P for line		$8M$	
$\pi_p^i(Q)$		$16M$	
$E(\mathbb{F}_p)$ **Arith.**		**Operation Count**	
Point doubling with line		$5M + 6S = 11M$	
Mixed point addition with line		$11M + 2S = 13M$	
Substitution Q for line		$16M$	
Scalar κ/p multiplication		$32(11M) + 4(13M) = 404M$	

Sparse Multiplication for Projective Coordinates. The sparse multiplication formula for projective coordinates on BLS-48 is that

$$(a_0 + a_1 z + a_2 zs) \cdot (b_0 + b_1 s),$$

where $a_0 \in \mathbb{F}_p, a_1, a_2 \in \mathbb{F}_{p^8}, b_0, b_1 \in \mathbb{F}_{p^{24}}$. However, we did not find the efficient computation method for this expression. Therefore, we show details about the using method in Appendix A.

4.2 Serial Computation

We compute the following formula for β Weil pairing in serial computation.

$$
\begin{aligned}
\beta(P,Q) = [&f_{\kappa,\pi_{p^7}(Q)}(P) \cdot f_{\kappa,\overline{P}}(\pi_{p^7}(Q)) \cdot f_{\kappa,\pi_{p^6}(Q)}([p]P) \cdot f_{\kappa,[p]\overline{P}}(\pi_{p^6}(Q)) \\
&\cdot f_{\kappa,\pi_{p^5}(Q)}([p^2]P) \cdot f_{\kappa,[p^2]\overline{P}}(\pi_{p^5}(Q)) \cdot f_{\kappa,\pi_{p^4}(Q)}([p^3]P) \cdot f_{\kappa,[p^3]\overline{P}}(\pi_{p^4}(Q)) \\
&\cdot f_{\kappa,\pi_{p^3}(Q)}([p^4]P) \cdot f_{\kappa,[p^4]\overline{P}}(\pi_{p^3}(Q)) \cdot f_{\kappa,\pi_{p^2}(Q)}([p^5]P) \cdot f_{\kappa,[p^5]\overline{P}}(\pi_{p^2}(Q)) \\
&\cdot f_{\kappa,\pi_p(Q)}([p^6]P) \cdot f_{\kappa,[p^6]\overline{P}}(\pi_p(Q)) \cdot f_{\kappa,Q}([p^7]P) \cdot f_{\kappa,[p^7]\overline{P}}(Q)]^{(p^{24}-1)}
\end{aligned}
$$

First, we compute all line functions in Miller functions in order to apply the multi-pairing technique to all $2e$ Miller functions. κ is $-2^{32} - 2^{30} - 2^{10} + 2^7 - 1$, so that each Miller function is made of 32 doubling steps and 4 (mixed) addition steps. The computational costs of $\mathrm{CSL}([p^i]\overline{P}, \kappa) = h_i$ for computing $f_{\kappa,[p^i]\overline{P}}$ for $0 \le i \le 7$ is $32(11M) + 4(13M) = 404M$ for each i. Here, we do not require to compute extra $[p^i]\overline{P}$ because we also obtain $[p^i]\overline{P}$ after computing $\mathrm{CSL}([p^{i-1}]\overline{P}, \kappa)$ from a relation $\kappa \equiv p \pmod{r}$. Here, it is necessary to convert $[p]\overline{P}$ from projective coordinates to affine coordinates for mixed addition step for a cost of $I + 2M$. The computational costs of $\mathrm{CSL}(Q, \kappa) = g_0$ for $f_{\kappa,Q}$ is $32(161M+I)+4(143M+I) = 5724M+36I$. Then, we compute $\mathrm{CSLFrob}(g_0, i) = g_i$ for computing $f_{\kappa,\pi_{p^i}(Q)}$ for each i. The computational costs of $\mathrm{CSLFrob}(g_0, i)$ is $576M$ for each i. Hence, the total cost of the all line functions computation is $8(404M) + 7(I + 2M) + (5724M + 36I) + 7(576M) = \mathbf{13002M + 43I}$.

Second, we compute all Miller functions evaluations by using multi-pairing technique. We first compute $\pi_{p^i}(Q)$ for each of i, for a cost of $7(16M) = 112M$. Then, we compute $\mathrm{EMM}([(g_7, P_0), (g_6, P_1), (g_5, P_2), (g_4, P_3), (g_3, P_4), (g_2, P_5),$ $(g_1, P_6), (g_0, P_7), (h_7, Q_0), (h_6, Q_1), (h_5, Q_2), (h_4, Q_3), (h_3, Q_4), (h_2, Q_5), (h_1, Q_6),$ $(h_0, Q_7)], \kappa)$, where $[p^i]P = P_i$ and $\pi_{p^i}(Q) = Q_i$.

The computational costs of all substitutions of points for line functions is $8 \cdot 36(16M)+8\cdot36(8M) = 6912M$ and the computational costs of squarings, sparse multiplications in EMM is $31S_{48} + 8 \cdot 36(294M) + 8 \cdot 36(313M) = 184860M$. Hence, the total cost of the all Miller functions evaluations is $112M + 6912M + 184860M = \mathbf{191884M}$.

Finally, we compute the power of $(p^{24} - 1)$. Its computation is made of 1 conjugation(the cost is negligible), 1 inversion and 1 multiplication in $\mathbb{F}_{p^{48}}$, for a cost of $I_{48} + M_{48} = 881M + I + 486M = \mathbf{1367M + I}$.

The Total Cost of Serial Computation. From the above, we conclude that the estimated cost of serial computing the β Weil pairing is $(13002M + 43I) + 191884M + (1367M + I) = \mathbf{206253M + 44I}$.

4.3   Parallel Computation Using 2 Processors

For parallel computation using 2 processors, we divide Eqs. (10) into 2 groups A, B and assign each group to each processor.

$$\beta(P,Q) = (\ A^p \cdot B\ )^{(p^{24}-1)}$$
$$A = f_{\kappa,\pi_{p^6}(Q)}(P) \cdot f_{\kappa,\overline{P}}(\pi_{p^6}(Q)) \cdot f_{\kappa,\pi_{p^4}(Q)}([p^2]P) \cdot f_{\kappa,[p^2]\overline{P}}(\pi_{p^4}(Q))$$
$$\cdot f_{\kappa,\pi_{p^2}(Q)}([p^4]P) \cdot f_{\kappa,[p^4]\overline{P}}(\pi_{p^2}(Q)) \cdot f_{\kappa,Q}([p^6]P) \cdot f_{\kappa,[p^6]\overline{P}}(Q)$$
$$B = f_{\kappa,\pi_{p^6}(Q)}([p]P) \cdot f_{\kappa,[p]\overline{P}}(\pi_{p^6}(Q)) \cdot f_{\kappa,\pi_{p^4}(Q)}([p^3]P) \cdot f_{\kappa,[p^3]\overline{P}}(\pi_{p^4}(Q))$$
$$\cdot f_{\kappa,\pi_{p^2}(Q)}([p^5]P) \cdot f_{\kappa,[p^5]\overline{P}}(\pi_{p^2}(Q)) \cdot f_{\kappa,Q}([p^7]P) \cdot f_{\kappa,[p^7]\overline{P}}(Q)$$

First, we compute all line functions in Miller functions as shown below:

Step 1.

1. The 1st processor computes $CSL(Q, \kappa) = g_0$ for computing $f_{\kappa,Q}$, for a cost of **$5724M + 36I$**.
2. The 2nd processor computes $CSL([p^i]\overline{P}, \kappa) = h_i$ for computing $f_{\kappa,[p^i]\overline{P}}$ for $(0 \leq i \leq 7)$, for a cost of $8(404M) + 7(I + 2M) = 3246M + 7I$.

Step 2.

1. The 1st processor computes $CSLFrob(g_0, 2) = g_2$ for computing $f_{\kappa,\pi_{p^2}(Q)}$, for a cost of $36(16M) = 576M$. In addition, this processor computes $\pi_{p^2}(Q)$, $\pi_{p^4}(Q)$ and $\pi_{p^6}(Q)$, for a cost of $54M$.
2. The 2nd processor computes $CSLFrob(g_0, 4) = g_4$ and $CSLFrob(g_4, 2) = g_6$ for computing $f_{\kappa,\pi_{p^4}(Q)}$ and $f_{\kappa,\pi_{p^6}(Q)}$, for a cost of $2(576M) = 1152M$.

Second, we compute all of Miller functions evaluations with 2 processors as shown below, where we denote by P_i $[p^i]P$ and by Q_i $\pi_{p^i}(Q)$.

Step 3.

1. The 1st processor computes $A = EMM([(g_6, P), (h_0, Q_6), (g_4, P_2), (h_2, Q_4),$ $(g_2, P_4), (h_4, Q_2), (g_0, P_6), (h_6, Q)], \kappa)$, for a cost of $31S_{48} + 4 \cdot 36(8M + 294M) + 4 \cdot 36(16M + 313M) = 100908M$.
2. The 2nd processor computes $B = EMM([(g_6, P_1), (h_1, Q_6), (g_4, P_3), (h_3, Q_4),$ $(g_2, P_5), (h_5, Q_2), (g_0, P_7), (h_7, Q)], \kappa)$, for the same cost as 1st processor.

Finally, we compute $(A^p \cdot B)^{(p^{24}-1)}$.

Step 4.

1. One processor computes 1 Frobenius map, 2 multiplications and 1 inversion in $\mathbb{F}_{p^{48}}$, for a cost of $M_{48} + 1(47M) + (M_{48} + I_{48}) = 1900M + I$.

The Total Cost of Parallel Computation Using 2 Processors. The total cost is the sum of max values in each step. Therefore, we conclude that the estimated cost of parallel computing the β Weil pairing using 2 processors is $(5724M + 36I) + (1152M) + (100908M) + (1900M + I) = 109684M + 37I$.

4.4 Parallel Computation Using 4 Processors

For parallel computation using 4 processors, we divide Eqs. (10) into 4 groups A, B, C, D and assign each group to each processor.

$$\beta(P,Q) = (A^{p^3} \cdot B^{p^2} \cdot C^p \cdot D)^{(p^{24}-1)}$$
$$A = f_{\kappa,\pi_{p^4}(Q)}(P) \cdot f_{\kappa,\overline{P}}(\pi_{p^4}(Q)) \cdot f_{\kappa,Q}([p^4]P) \cdot f_{\kappa,[p^4]\overline{P}}(Q)$$
$$B = f_{\kappa,\pi_{p^4}(Q)}([p]P) \cdot f_{\kappa,[p]\overline{P}}(\pi_{p^4}(Q)) \cdot f_{\kappa,Q}([p^5]P) \cdot f_{\kappa,[p^5]\overline{P}}(Q)$$
$$C = f_{\kappa,\pi_{p^4}(Q)}([p^2]P) \cdot f_{\kappa,[p^2]\overline{P}}(\pi_{p^4}(Q)) \cdot f_{\kappa,Q}([p^6]P) \cdot f_{\kappa,[p^6]\overline{P}}(Q)$$
$$D = f_{\kappa,\pi_{p^4}(Q)}([p^3]P) \cdot f_{\kappa,[p^3]\overline{P}}(\pi_{p^4}(Q)) \cdot f_{\kappa,Q}([p^7]P) \cdot f_{\kappa,[p^7]\overline{P}}(Q)$$

First, we compute all line functions in Miller functions with 3 processors as shown below:

Step 1.

1. The 1st processor computes $\mathrm{CSL}(Q, \kappa) = g_0$ for computing $f_{\kappa,Q}$, for a cost of $5724M + 36I$.
2. The 2nd processor computes $\pi_{p^4}(Q)$ and $\mathrm{CSL}(\pi_{p^4}(Q), \kappa) = g_4$ for computing $f_{\kappa,\pi_{p^4}(Q)}$, for a cost of $16M + 5724M + 36I = \mathbf{5740M + 36I}$.
3. The 3rd processor computes $\mathrm{CSL}([p^i]\overline{P}, \kappa) = h_i$ for computing $f_{\kappa,[p^i]\overline{P}}$ for $(0 \leq i \leq 7)$, for a cost of $8(404M) + 7(I + 2M) = 3246M + 7I$.

Second, we compute all of Miller functions evaluations with 4 processors as shown below, where we denote by P_i $[p^i]P$ and by Q_i $\pi_{p^i}(Q)$.

Step 2.

1. The 1st processor computes $A = \mathrm{EMM}([(g_4, P), (g_0, P_4), (h_0, Q_4), (h_4, Q)], \kappa)$, for a cost of $31S_{48} + 2 \cdot 36(8M + 294M) + 2 \cdot 36(16M + 313M) = \mathbf{55476M}$.
2. The 2nd processor computes $B = \mathrm{EMM}([(g_4, P_1), (g_0, P_5), (h_1, Q_4), (h_5, Q)], \kappa)$, for the same cost as 1st processor.
3. The 3rd processor computes $C = \mathrm{EMM}([(g_4, P_2), (g_0, P_6), (h_2, Q_4), (h_6, Q)], \kappa)$, for the same cost as 1st processor.
4. The 4th processor computes $D = \mathrm{EMM}([(g_4, P_3), (g_0, P_7), (h_3, Q_4), (h_7, Q)], \kappa)$, for the same cost as 1st processor.

Finally, we compute $(((A^p \cdot B)^p \cdot C)^p \cdot D)^{(p^{24}-1)}$.

Step 3. One processor computes 3 Frobenius maps, 3 multiplications and 1 inversion in $\mathbb{F}_{p^{48}}$, for a cost of $3M_{48} + 3(47M) + 1(M_{48} + I_{48}) = \mathbf{2966M + I}$.

The Total Cost of Parallel Computation Using 4 Processors. The total cost is the sum of max values in each step. Therefore, we conclude that the estimated cost of parallel computing the β Weil pairing using 4 processors is $(5740M + 36I) + (55476M) + (2966M + I) = \mathbf{64182M + 37I}$.

5   Comparisons

In this section, we compare the computational costs of the proposed methods obtained in Sect. 4 with the costs of optimal ate pairings and normal β Weil pairings. The cost of the optimal ate pairing for BLS-48 is found in [29]. However, the computational costs of the normal β Weil pairings for new security parameters proposed by Kiyomura et al. are not estimated in existing research. Therefore, we estimate the costs of the normal β Weil pairings in Appendix B. We summarise those results in Table 2. In Table 2, we assume that $I = 50M$ as in [29]. For future reference, in Table 3, we show required storage for precomputation technique in proposed methods. We also provide implementation results for the proposed methods and the normal β Weil pairings in Sect. 5.1.

Table 2. Computational costs of the optimal ate pairings, the normal β Weil pairings and the proposed methods for BLS-48 per processor.

Pairings	Overall costs		
	1 processor	2 processors	4 processors
Optimal ate pairings	$145,940M$ [29]	$128,551M^{\dagger}$	$119,857M^{\dagger}$
Normal β Weil pairings	$414,892M$	$209,990M$	$108,268M$
Proposed methods	$208,453M$	$111,534M$	$66,032M$

† These costs are not given in existing researches. We estimate the costs by dividing a Miller loop computational cost $34778M$ in [29] by the number of processors. Note that the way to parallelize final exponentiation is not known.

Table 3. Storage costs of precomputation technique in proposed methods for BLS-48.

	Storage [number of F_p elements]		
	1 processor	2 processors	4 processors
Proposed methods	$8 \cdot 36 \cdot 3 + 8 \cdot 36 \cdot 16$ $= 5472$	$8 \cdot 36 \cdot 3 + 4 \cdot 36 \cdot 16$ $= 3168$	$8 \cdot 36 \cdot 3 + 2 \cdot 36 \cdot 16$ $= 2016$

* The number of $\mathbb{F}_p$ elements is obtained by $a_1 \cdot b_1 \cdot c_1 + a_2 \cdot b_2 \cdot c_2$.
a_1/a_2: the number of precomputed extended Miller functions $f_{p,h,P_i}/f_{p,h,Q_i}$.
b_1/b_2: the number of stored lines in $f_{p,h,P_i} / f_{p,h,Q_i}$.
c_1/c_2: the number of $\mathbb{F}_p$ elements of line coefficients in $f_{p,h,P_i}/f_{p,h,Q_i}$.

5.1 Implementation Results

We implemented the proposed methods and the normal β Weil pairings on BLS-48 curve based on libsnark, a cryptographic open source library used in blockchain ZCash. We also measured on Raspberry Pi 4 Model B, CPU: Broadcom 2711, 1.5 GHz quad-core ARM Cortex-A72, RAM: 2 GB, OS: Raspbian GNU/Linux 10 (buster), Compiler: gcc 8.3.0, Library: OpenMP 2.0 (for parallel computing). We show the experimental results in Table 4. Note that the state of the art implementation comparison of the optimal ate pairing on BLS-48 is left for future work.

Table 4. Timings of the normal β Weil pairings and the proposed methods for BLS-48 per number of processors. Timings are 100 time execution averages.

Pairings	Time [second]		
	1 processor	2 processors	4 processors
Normal β Weil pairings	2.28	1.15	0.59
Proposed methods	1.19	0.62	0.36

6   Application to Other Curves

In this section, we apply the proposed formula Eqs. (8) to several pairing friendly curves. Concrete computations and efficiency evaluations are left for future work.

KSS Curve with $k = 16$. KSS curves are available for several embedding degrees [23]. In particular, the curve with $k = 16$, named KSS-16, is known as the most efficient for the curve ensuring 128 bits of security [4]. The parametrization in [4] is as follows:

$$p(\kappa) = (\kappa^{10} + 2\kappa^9 + 5\kappa^8 + 48\kappa^6 + 152\kappa^5 + 240\kappa^4 + 625\kappa^2 + 2398\kappa + 3125)/980,$$
$$r(\kappa) = (\kappa^8 + 48\kappa^4 + 625)/61250, \quad \kappa = 2^{35} - 2^{32} - 2^{18} + 2^8 + 1.$$

Here, polynomial $h(x) \in \mathbb{Z}[x]$ required for extended Miller functions $f_{p,h,R}$ in β Weil pairing formula is given by $h(x) = \kappa + x - 2x^5$ [39]. Therefore, the extended Miller function for KSS-16 β Weil pairing is given as follows:

$$f_{p,h,R} = f_{\kappa,R} \cdot \ell_{[\kappa]R,[p]R} \cdot \ell_{[-p^5]R,[-p^5]R}.$$

Since the curve has degree 4 twist and $e = gcd(32, 4) = 4$, the proposed β Weil pairing formula for KSS-16 is given as follows:

$$
\begin{aligned}
\beta(P, Q) = [&f_{\kappa,Q_3}(P) \cdot f_{\kappa,\overline{P}}(Q_3) \cdot f_{\kappa,Q_2}(P_1) \cdot f_{\kappa,\overline{P_1}}(Q_2) \cdot f_{\kappa,Q_1}(P_2) \cdot f_{\kappa,\overline{P_2}}(Q_1) \\
&\cdot f_{\kappa,Q}(P_3) \cdot f_{\kappa,\overline{P_3}}(Q) \cdot \ell_{[\kappa]Q_3,Q_4}(P) \cdot \ell_{[\kappa]Q_2,Q_3}(P_1) \cdot \ell_{[\kappa]Q_1,Q_2}(P_2) \\
&\cdot \ell_{[\kappa]Q,Q_1}(P_3) \cdot \ell_{\overline{Q_8},\overline{Q_8}}(P) \cdot \ell_{\overline{Q_7},\overline{Q_7}}(P_1) \cdot \ell_{\overline{Q_6},\overline{Q_6}}(P_2) \cdot \ell_{\overline{Q_5},\overline{Q_5}}(P_3) \\
&\cdot \ell_{[z]\overline{P},\overline{P_1}}(Q_3) \cdot \ell_{[z]\overline{P_1},\overline{P_2}}(Q_2) \cdot \ell_{[z]\overline{P_2},\overline{P_3}}(Q_1) \cdot \ell_{[z]\overline{P_3},\overline{P_4}}(Q) \\
&\cdot \ell_{P_5,P_5}(Q_3) \cdot \ell_{P_6,P_6}(Q_2) \cdot \ell_{P_7,P_7}(Q_1) \cdot \ell_{P_8,P_8}(Q)]^{(p^8-1)} \quad (10)
\end{aligned}
$$

BLS Curves with $k = 12, 24$. BLS curves are also available for several embedding degrees [7]. In particular, the curve with $k = 12$, named BLS-12, is known as having almost the same efficiency as the KSS-16 ensuring 128 bits of security [4]. And the curve with $k = 24$, named BLS-24, is known as one of the candidates for the efficient pairing ensuring 192 bits of security [4]. Both curves have the same degree 6 twist, the same polynomial $h(x) = \kappa - x$ for extended Miller functions and the same extended Miller function $f_{p,h,R} = f_{\kappa,R}$. Thus, the proposed β Weil pairing formulas for BLS-12 and BLS-24 are given as follows:

$$\beta(P, Q) = \left[\prod_{i=0}^{e-1} f_{\kappa,Q_{\delta_i}}(P_i) \cdot f_{\kappa,\overline{P_i}}(Q_{\delta_i}) \right]^{(p^{k/2}-1)}.$$

7   Conclusion

In this paper, we presented the efficient computation methods of the β Weil pairing with the precomputation and multi-pairing techniques. Firstly, in order to facilitate applying those techniques, we showed two ideas which are 1. the elimination of denominators of the β Weil pairing and 2. the elimination of exponents of the β Weil pairing. Moreover, we provide the methods of applications those techniques to the β Weil pairing. Then, we estimated computational costs of the proposed methods and the normal β Weil pairings for a BLS-48 curve parameter with 256 bit level of security [26] and compared them and the optimal ate pairings cost [29]. Finally, we also provided implementation results for the proposed methods and the normal β Weil pairings.

A   Sparse Multiplication for Projective Coordinates

In projective coordinates, the following line function is obtained from the elliptic curve doubling and addition steps.

$$\ell(x, y) = C_1 + C_2 x + C_3 y, \ C_1, C_2, C_3 \in \mathbb{F}_p$$

The isomorphic mapping ϕ from twist E' to E is given as follows:

$$\phi : E' \to E : (x, y) \mapsto (zx, uzsy).$$

For $Q' = (x_Q, y_Q) \in E'$, $\phi(Q') = Q = (zx_Q, uzsy_Q) \in \mathbb{G}_2$.
Then, we substitute Q for $\ell(x, y)$ and we obtain that

$$\ell(Q) = C_1 + C_2 x_Q z + C_3 y_Q uzs \in \mathbb{F}_{p^{48}}, \ C_1, C_2, C_3 \in \mathbb{F}_p.$$

By rearranging the above formula, we obtain that

$$\ell(Q) = C_1 + D_1 z + D_2 zs \in \mathbb{F}_{p^{48}}, \ C_1 \in \mathbb{F}_p, D_1, D_2 \in \mathbb{F}_{p^8}.$$

The sparse multiplication $f \cdot \ell(Q)$ can be calculated by Algorithm 6 and Algorithm 7, where $f \in \mathbb{F}_{p^{48}}$.

The cost of Fq6SparseMul is $5M_8 = 135M$, or $3M_8 + 2(8M) = 97M$ in case of $a_0 \in \mathbb{F}_p$. The cost of PSM is $97M + 3M_8 + 135M = 313M$.

Algorithm 6: PSM: Projective sparse multiplication in $\mathbb{F}_{p^{48}}$

Input:

$\qquad a = a_0 + a_1 z + a_2 zs; a_0 \in \mathbb{F}_p, a_1, a_2 \in \mathbb{F}_{p^8}, \ b = b_0 + b_1 s; b_0, b_1 \in \mathbb{F}_{p^{24}}$
Output: $ab \in \mathbb{F}_{p^{48}}$

$A \leftarrow b_0, \ B \leftarrow b_1, \ C \leftarrow a_0 + a_1 z, \ D \leftarrow a_2 z, \ e \leftarrow \text{Fq6SparseMul}(C, A)$
$f \leftarrow a_2 \cdot Bz, \ g \leftarrow \text{Fq6SparseMul}(C + D, A + B) - e - f$
$c_0 \leftarrow e + f \cdot (-z), c_1 \leftarrow g$
return $c = c_0 + c_1 s$

Algorithm 7: Fq6SparseMul [17], used in Algorithm 6

Input: $a = a_0 + a_1 z; a_0, a_1 \in \mathbb{F}_{p^8}, \ b = b_0 + b_1 z + b_2 z^2; b_0, b_1, b_2 \in \mathbb{F}_{p^8}$
Output: $ab \in \mathbb{F}_{p^{24}}$

$A \leftarrow a_0 \cdot b_0, \ B \leftarrow a_1 \cdot b_1, \ C \leftarrow a_1 \cdot b_2(-w), \ D \leftarrow A + C, \ e \leftarrow a_0 + a_1$
$f \leftarrow b_0 + b_1, \ E \leftarrow e \cdot f, G \leftarrow E - (A + B), \ H \leftarrow a_0 \cdot b_2, \ I \leftarrow H + B$
return $D + Gz + Iz^2$

B   BLS-48 Normal β Weil Pairing

We compute the following formula for β Weil pairing.

$$
\beta(P,Q) = \left[\left(\frac{f_{\kappa,Q}(P)}{f_{\kappa,P}(Q)} \right)^{p^7} \left(\frac{f_{\kappa,Q}([p]P)}{f_{\kappa,[p]}P(Q)} \right)^{p^6} \left(\frac{f_{\kappa,Q}([p^2]P)}{f_{\kappa,[p^2]}P(Q)} \right)^{p^5} \left(\frac{f_{\kappa,Q}([p^3]P)}{f_{\kappa,[p^3]}P(Q)} \right)^{p^4} \right.
$$
$$
\left. \left(\frac{f_{\kappa,Q}([p^4]P)}{f_{\kappa,[p^4]}P(Q)} \right)^{p^3} \left(\frac{f_{\kappa,Q}([p^5]P)}{f_{\kappa,[p^5]}P(Q)} \right)^{p^2} \left(\frac{f_{\kappa,Q}([p^6]P)}{f_{\kappa,[p^6]}P(Q)} \right)^{p} \left(\frac{f_{\kappa,Q}([p^7]P)}{f_{\kappa,[p^7]}P(Q)} \right) \right]^{(p^{k/2}-1)}
\tag{11}
$$

B.1   Serial Computation

Normal β Weil pairing computation in serial computation are 8 $f_{\kappa,Q}(P)$, 8 $f_{\kappa,P}(Q)$, 16 multiplications in $\mathbb{F}_{p^{48}}$, 9 conjugates, 7 Frobenius maps and 1 inversion in $\mathbb{F}_{p^{48}}$. The costs for each of computations are as follows. The cost of $f_{\kappa,Q}(P)$ is $32(161M+I+8M+294M)+4(143M+I+8M+294M)+31(324M) = 26640M+36I$. The cost of $f_{\kappa,P}(Q)$ is $32(11M+16M+313M)+4(13M+16M+313M)+31(324M) = 22292M$. The total cost is $8(26640M+36I)+8(22292M)+16(486M) + 7(47M) + 1(881M + I) = 400442M + 289I$.

B.2   Parallel Computation Using 2 Processors

1st processor computes $\prod_{i=0}^{3} \left(\frac{f_{\kappa,Q}([p^i]P)}{f_{\kappa,[p^i]}P(Q)} \right)^{p^{7-i}}$.

2nd processor computes $[p^i]P$ for $(1 \leq i \leq 4)$ and $\prod_{i=4}^{7} \left(\frac{f_{\kappa,Q}([p^i]P)}{f_{\kappa,[p^i]}P(Q)} \right)^{p^{7-i}}$.

In the last process, one processor multiply the two results and computes $p^{k/2-1}$ power. In first parallel computation, 2nd processor's cost is greater than 1st processor's cost because 2nd processor require the extra computation of $[p^i]P(1 \leq i \leq 4)$ which does not require in 1st processor. Therefore, total computation cost is the sum of 2nd processor's cost and the last process cost. The 2nd processor's cost is $4(404M) + 4(26640M + 36I) + 4(22292M) + 7(486M) + 3(47M) = 200887M + 144I$. The last process cost is $2(486M) + 1(881M + I) = 1853M + I$. Therefore, the total cost is $200887M + 144I + 1853M + I = 202740M + 145I$.

B.3   Parallel Computation Using 4 Processors

1st processor computes $\prod_{i=0}^{1} \left(\frac{f_{\kappa,Q}([p^i]P)}{f_{\kappa,[p^i]}P(Q)} \right)^{p^{7-i}}$.

2nd processor computes $[p^i]P$ for $(2 \leq i \leq 3)$ and $\prod_{i=2}^{3} \left(\frac{f_{\kappa,Q}([p^i]P)}{f_{\kappa,[p^i]}P(Q)} \right)^{p^{7-i}}$.

3rd processor computes $[p^i]P$ for $(4 \leq i \leq 5)$ and $\prod_{i=4}^{5} \left(\frac{f_{\kappa,Q}([p^i]P)}{f_{\kappa,[p^i]}P(Q)} \right)^{p^{7-i}}$.

4th processor computes $[p^i]P$ for $(6 \leq i \leq 7)$ and $\prod_{i=6}^{7} \left(\frac{f_{\kappa,Q}([p^i]P)}{f_{\kappa,[p^i]}P(Q)} \right)^{p^{7-i}}$.

In the last process, one processor multiply the four results and computes $p^{k/2-1}$ power. In the first parallel computation, 4th processor's cost is greater than 1st, 2nd and 3rd processor's cost because 4th processor require the extra computation of $[p^6]P$. Therefore, total computation cost is the sum of 4th processor's cost and the last process cost. The 4th processor's cost is $6(404M)+2(26640M+36I)+2(22292M)+3(486M)+1(47M) = 101793M+72I$. The last process cost is $4(486M) + 1(881M + i) = 2825M + I$. Therefore, the total cost is $101793M + 72I + 2825M + I = 104618M + 73I$.

References

1. Aranha, D.F., Fuentes-Castañeda, L., Knapp, E., Menezes, A., Rodríguez-Henríquez, F.: Implementing pairings at the 192-bit security level. In: Abdalla, M., Lange, T. (eds.) Pairing 2012. LNCS, vol. 7708, pp. 177–195. Springer, Heidelberg (2013). https://doi.org/10.1007/978-3-642-36334-4_11
2. Aranha, D.F., Karabina, K., Longa, P., Gebotys, C.H., López, J.: Faster explicit formulas for computing pairings over ordinary curves. In: Paterson, K.G. (ed.) EUROCRYPT 2011. LNCS, vol. 6632, pp. 48–68. Springer, Heidelberg (2011). https://doi.org/10.1007/978-3-642-20465-4_5
3. Aranha, D.F., Knapp, E., Menezes, A., Rodríguez-Henríquez, F.: Parallelizing the Weil and Tate pairings. In: Chen, L. (ed.) IMACC 2011. LNCS, vol. 7089, pp. 275–295. Springer, Heidelberg (2011). https://doi.org/10.1007/978-3-642-25516-8_17
4. Barbulescu, R., Duquesne, S.: Updating key size estimations for pairings. J. Cryptol. **32**, 1298–1336 (2019). https://doi.org/10.1007/s00145-018-9280-5
5. Barbulescu, R., Mrabet, N.E., Ghammam, L.: A taxonomy of pairings, their security, their complexity. Cryptology ePrint Archive, Report 2019/3485 (2019)
6. Barreto, P.S.L.M., Galbraith, S.D., Ó'hÉigeartaigh, C., Scott, M.: Efficient pairing computation on supersingular Abelian varieties. Des. Codes Cryptogr. **42**, 239–271 (2007). https://doi.org/10.1007/s10623-006-9033-6
7. Barreto, P.S.L.M., Lynn, B., Scott, M.: Constructing elliptic curves with prescribed embedding degrees. In: Cimato, S., Persiano, G., Galdi, C. (eds.) SCN 2002. LNCS, vol. 2576, pp. 257–267. Springer, Heidelberg (2003). https://doi.org/10.1007/3-540-36413-7_19
8. Beuchat, J.-L., González-Díaz, J.E., Mitsunari, S., Okamoto, E., Rodríguez-Henríquez, F., Teruya, T.: High-speed software implementation of the optimal ate pairing over Barreto–Naehrig curves. In: Joye, M., Miyaji, A., Otsuka, A. (eds.) Pairing 2010. LNCS, vol. 6487, pp. 21–39. Springer, Heidelberg (2010). https://doi.org/10.1007/978-3-642-17455-1_2
9. Boneh, D., Franklin, M.: Identity-based encryption from the Weil pairing. In: Kilian, J. (ed.) CRYPTO 2001. LNCS, vol. 2139, pp. 213–229. Springer, Heidelberg (2001). https://doi.org/10.1007/3-540-44647-8_13
10. Bos, J.W., Costello, C., Naehrig, M.: Exponentiating in pairing groups. Cryptology ePrint Archive, Report 2013/458 (2013)
11. Costello, C., Lauter, K., Naehrig, M.: Attractive subfamilies of BLS curves for implementing high-security pairings. In: Bernstein, D.J., Chatterjee, S. (eds.) INDOCRYPT 2011. LNCS, vol. 7107, pp. 320–342. Springer, Heidelberg (2011). https://doi.org/10.1007/978-3-642-25578-6_23

12. Costello, C., Stebila, D.: Fixed argument pairings. Cryptology ePrint Archive, Report 2010/342 (2010)
13. Devegili, A.J., Ó'hÉigeartaigh, C., Scott, M., Dahab, R.: Multiplication and squaring on pairing-friendly fields. Cryptology ePrint Archive, Report 2006/471 (2006)
14. Duquesne, S., Mrabet, N.E., Haloui, S., Rondepierre, F.: Choosing and generating parameters for pairing implementation on BN curves. Appl. Algebra Eng. Commun. Comput. **29**, 113–147 (2018). https://doi.org/10.1007/s00200-017-0334-y
15. Fouotsa, E., Pecha, A., Mrabet, N.E.: Beta Weil pairing revisited. Afrika Mathematika **30**, 371–388 (2019). https://doi.org/10.1007/s13370-019-00653-8
16. Granger, R., Smart, N.P.: On computing products of pairings. Cryptology ePrint Archive, Report 2006/172 (2006)
17. Grewal, G., Azarderakhsh, R., Longa, P., Hu, S., Jao, D.: Efficient implementation of bilinear pairings on ARM processors. In: Knudsen, L.R., Wu, H. (eds.) SAC 2012. LNCS, vol. 7707, pp. 149–165. Springer, Heidelberg (2013). https://doi.org/10.1007/978-3-642-35999-6_11
18. Guillevic, A.: A short-list of STNFS-secure pairing-friendly curves at the 128-bit security level. Cryptology ePrint Archive, Report 2019/1371 (2019)
19. Guillevic, A., Masson, S., Thomé, E.: Cocks-pinch curves of embedding degrees five to eight and optimal ate pairing computation. Cryptology ePrint Archive, Report 2019/431 (2019)
20. Hess, F.: Pairing lattices. In: Galbraith, S.D., Paterson, K.G. (eds.) Pairing 2008. LNCS, vol. 5209, pp. 18–38. Springer, Heidelberg (2008). https://doi.org/10.1007/978-3-540-85538-5_2
21. Hess, F., Smart, N.P., Vercauteren, F.: The Eta-pairing revisited. IEEE Trans. Inf. Theory **52**(10), 4595–4602 (2006)
22. Housni, Y.E., Guillevic, A.: Optimized and secure pairing-friendly elliptic curves suitable for one layer proof composition. Cryptology ePrint Archive, Report 2020/351 (2020)
23. Kachisa, E.J., Schaefer, E.F., Scott, M.: Constructing Brezing-Weng pairing-friendly elliptic curves using elements in the cyclotomic field. In: Galbraith, S.D., Paterson, K.G. (eds.) Pairing 2008. LNCS, vol. 5209, pp. 126–135. Springer, Heidelberg (2008). https://doi.org/10.1007/978-3-540-85538-5_9
24. Khandaker, M.A.-A., Nanjo, Y., Ghammam, L., Duquesne, S., Nogami, Y., Kodera, Y.: Efficient optimal ate pairing at 128-bit security level. In: Patra, A., Smart, N.P. (eds.) INDOCRYPT 2017. LNCS, vol. 10698, pp. 186–205. Springer, Cham (2017). https://doi.org/10.1007/978-3-319-71667-1_10
25. Kim, T., Barbulescu, R.: Extended tower number field sieve: a new complexity for the medium prime case. In: Robshaw, M., Katz, J. (eds.) CRYPTO 2016. LNCS, vol. 9814, pp. 543–571. Springer, Heidelberg (2016). https://doi.org/10.1007/978-3-662-53018-4_20
26. Kiyomura, Y., Inoue, A., Kawahara, Y., Yasuda, M., Takagi, T., Kobayashi, T.: Secure and efficient pairing at 256-bit security level. In: Gollmann, D., Miyaji, A., Kikuchi, H. (eds.) ACNS 2017. LNCS, vol. 10355, pp. 59–79. Springer, Cham (2017). https://doi.org/10.1007/978-3-319-61204-1_4
27. Lee, E., Lee, H.S., Park, C.M.: Efficient and generalized pairing computation on Abelian varieties. Cryptology ePrint Archive, Report 2008/040 (2008)
28. Lewko, A., Okamoto, T., Sahai, A., Takashima, K., Waters, B.: Fully secure functional encryption: attribute-based encryption and (hierarchical) inner product encryption. In: Gilbert, H. (ed.) EUROCRYPT 2010. LNCS, vol. 6110, pp. 62–91. Springer, Heidelberg (2010). https://doi.org/10.1007/978-3-642-13190-5_4

29. Mbiang, N.B., Aranha, D.F., Fouotsa, E.: Computing the optimal ate pairing over elliptic curves with embedding degrees 54 and 48 at the 256-bit security level. Int. J. Appl. Cryptogr. (2019). 1753-0536
30. Miller, V.: The Weil pairing, and its efficient calculation. J. Cryptol. **17**, 235–261 (2004). https://doi.org/10.1007/s00145-004-0315-8
31. Mitsunari, S.: A fast implementation of the optimal ate pairing over BN curve on Intel Haswell processor. Cryptology ePrint Archive, Report 2013/362 (2013)
32. Nakanishi, T., Funabiki, N.: Verifier-local revocation group signature schemes with backward unlinkability from bilinear maps. IEICE Trans. **90-A**(1), 65–74 (2007)
33. Sahai, A., Waters, B.: Fuzzy identity-based encryption. In: Cramer, R. (ed.) EURO-CRYPT 2005. LNCS, vol. 3494, pp. 457–473. Springer, Heidelberg (2005). https://doi.org/10.1007/11426639_27
34. Sakai, R., Kasahara, M.: Cryptosystems based on pairing. In: SCIS 2000 C20 Okinawa, Japan (2000)
35. Sakemi, Y., Takeuchi, S., Nogami, Y., Morikawa, Y.: Accelerating twisted ate pairing with Frobenius map, small scalar multiplication, and multi-pairing. In: Lee, D., Hong, S. (eds.) ICISC 2009. LNCS, vol. 5984, pp. 47–64. Springer, Heidelberg (2010). https://doi.org/10.1007/978-3-642-14423-3_4
36. Scott, M.: Computing the Tate pairing. In: Menezes, A. (ed.) CT-RSA 2005. LNCS, vol. 3376, pp. 293–304. Springer, Heidelberg (2005). https://doi.org/10.1007/978-3-540-30574-3_20
37. Scott, M.: On the efficient implementation of pairing-based protocols. In: Chen, L. (ed.) IMACC 2011. LNCS, vol. 7089, pp. 296–308. Springer, Heidelberg (2011). https://doi.org/10.1007/978-3-642-25516-8_18
38. Vercauteren, F.: Optimal pairings. IEEE Trans. Inf. Theory **56**(1), 455–461 (2010)
39. Zhang, X., Lin, D.: Analysis of optimum pairing products at high security levels. In: Galbraith, S., Nandi, M. (eds.) INDOCRYPT 2012. LNCS, vol. 7668, pp. 412–430. Springer, Heidelberg (2012). https://doi.org/10.1007/978-3-642-34931-7_24
40. Zhang, X., Wang, K., Lin, D.: On efficient pairings on elliptic curves over extension fields. In: Abdalla, M., Lange, T. (eds.) Pairing 2012. LNCS, vol. 7708, pp. 1–18. Springer, Heidelberg (2013). https://doi.org/10.1007/978-3-642-36334-4_1
41. Zhao, C.A., Xie, D., Zhang, F., Zhang, J., Chen, B.L.: Computing bilinear pairings on elliptic curves with automorphisms. Des. Codes Cryptogr. **58**, 35–44 (2011). https://doi.org/10.1007/s10623-010-9383-y

Machine Learning

Timing Attack on Random Forests for Generating Adversarial Examples

Yuichiro Dan[✉], Toshiki Shibahara, and Junko Takahashi

NTT Secure Platform Laboratories, 3-9-11, Midori-cho,
Musashino-shi, Tokyo 180-8585, Japan
{yuuichirou.dan.xd,toshiki.shibahara.de,junko.takahashi.fc}@hco.ntt.co.jp

Abstract. The threat of implementation attacks to machine learning has become an issue recently. These attacks include side-channel attacks that use information acquired from implemented devices and fault attacks that inject faults into implemented devices using external tools such as lasers. Thus far, these attacks have targeted mainly deep neural networks; however, other popular methods such as random forests can also be targets. In this paper, we investigate the threat of implementation attacks to random forests. Specifically, we propose a novel timing attack that generates adversarial examples, and experimentally evaluate its attack success rate. The proposed attack exploits a fundamental property of random forests: the response time from the input to the output depends on the number of conditional branches invoked during prediction. More precisely, we generate adversarial examples by optimizing the response time. This optimization affects predictions because changes in the response time imply changes in the results of the conditional branches. For the optimization, we use an evolution strategy that tolerates measurement error in the response time. Experiments are conducted in a black-box setting where attackers can use only prediction labels and response times. Experimental results show that the proposed attack generates adversarial examples with higher probability than a state-of-the-art attack that uses only predicted labels. This suggests the attacker motivation for implementation attacks on random forests.

Keywords: Side-channel attack · Black-box attack · Evolution strategy

1 Introduction

While machine learning is expected to become common by 2024 [9], novel attacks on machine learning have become an issue since the work by Szegedy et al. [21] in 2013. The most representative of these attacks is evasion, hereinafter referred to as an adversarial example [4,5,10–12,16,21]. In an adversarial example, the attacker deceives the prediction model by adding small perturbations to the input data. Another representative attack is model extraction, which extracts

© Springer Nature Switzerland AG 2020
K. Aoki and A. Kanaoka (Eds.): IWSEC 2020, LNCS 12231, pp. 285–302, 2020.
https://doi.org/10.1007/978-3-030-58208-1_16

or learns prediction models in machine-learning-based systems and constructs substitute models using input and output data of the systems [22].

Until recently, researchers have investigated attacks exploiting weaknesses in algorithms such as the fact that gradients of loss functions indicate directions for misclassification, and the fact that a good approximation of a prediction model can be generated using a set of its input and output data (algorithm attacks) [4,5,8,10–12,15,16,20–23]. From around 2017, some researchers have indicated attacks that use weaknesses in devices that employ prediction models (implementation attacks) [1,2,7,14,17,24,25]. For example, an attack was proposed that generates faults through laser injection causing misclassification [2]. Additionally, several attacks were discovered that extract prediction models by measuring physical quantities such as timing and electromagnetic radiation [1,7,14,25]. These implementation attacks pose significant threats especially when attackers have easy access to prediction models as edge AIs.

The target of these implementation attacks has been limited to deep neural networks. In other words, implementation attacks on tree-based methods have not been reported even though such methods include practical machine learning methods [18] such as XGBoost [6] and random forests [3]. Thus, in this paper, we address the threat of implementation attacks to random forests. In particular, we propose a novel attack exploiting the response time from the input to the output (timing) for generating adversarial examples, and evaluate its attack success rate experimentally. We focus on the attack using the timing among implementation attacks (timing attacks) because measuring the timing does not require expensive equipment or advanced skills. Consequently, timing attacks are easy to execute, and more tractable for many attackers than other implementation attacks.

There are two challenges in generating adversarial examples using the timing: building a strategy required to cause misclassification using the timing, and mitigating the measurement error of the timing. In regard to the former challenge, drastic changes in the timing can cause misclassification due to the following reason. Because the timing correlates with the number of conditional branches invoked in a random forest during prediction, drastic changes in the timing imply drastic changes in the results of the invoked branches. These changes in the results of the branches can ruin prediction results. The latter challenge requires a noise-tolerant optimization method to change the timing appropriately even if measurement errors exist. Such optimization methods include evolution strategies. When updating an optimum once, evolution strategies evaluate multiple candidates close to the current optimum and obtain a new optimum using a weighted average of the candidates. In this way, evolution strategies can robustly find a good optimum even if each of the evaluation results of candidates contains measurement errors. For this reason, we use the covariance matrix adaptation evolution strategy (CMA-ES), one of the most popular evolution strategies.

We evaluate the threat of the proposed attack in a black-box setting where attackers can use only prediction labels and the timing. Note that we assume a victim system that conceals parameters of the prediction model and confidence values of predictions in this setting. The evaluation results show that the proposed attack generates adversarial examples with higher probability than a low frequency boundary attack (LFBA) [11], a state-of-the-art algorithm attack. This suggests the attacker motivation for timing attacks on random forests.

The remainder of this paper is structured as follows. Section 2 introduces related work regarding implementation attacks and algorithm attacks on machine learning. Section 3 reviews random forests, CMA-ES, and LFBA as research background. Section 4 describes the assumption of the threat in this paper. In Sect. 5, we propose the novel timing attack. Section 6 describes the setting and the results of the experiments along with their interpretations. In Sect. 7, we discuss some risky situations involving timing attacks, and some possible directions for countermeasures against the attacks. Section 8 presents our conclusions.

2   Related Work

This section describes representative attacks on algorithms and implementations of machine learning.

2.1   Implementation Attacks on Machine Learning

Implementation attacks on machine learning have received interest since 2017 [17]. Thus far researchers have shown a few attacks such as fault attacks [2,17] and side-channel attacks [1,7,14,24,25]. A fault attack injects faults into implemented devices using external tools such as lasers. A side-channel attack uses information acquired from implemented devices.

For example, Liu et al. [17] conceptually advocated a fault attack causing misclassification. Although their research avoided referring to practical methods that cause faults, another research [2] specified such a method that causes faults by injecting a laser into devices that run prediction models. As for side-channel attacks, there are a few attacks that extract prediction models using information on timing [7], cache hits [14,25], or electromagnetic waves [1]. Additionally, Wei et al. [24] proposed an attack using information on power consumption for extracting input data.

As mentioned above, several studies have already addressed implementation attacks on machine learning. However, these studies mainly target deep neural networks. Regarding other popular methods such as random forests [3], revealing the threat of implementation attacks to such methods requires further investigation.

2.2   Algorithm Attacks on Machine Learning

Unlike implementation attacks, algorithm attacks on machine learning have attracted attention since 2013 [21]. There are many attacks such as poisoning [15], evasion [4,5,10–12,16,21], model extraction [22], model inversion [8], membership inference [20], and hyperparameter stealing [23]. A poisoning attack forces a prediction model to learn inappropriately by mixing tampered data into the training dataset. An evasion attack deceives a trained prediction model by adding small perturbations to the input data. A model extraction attack extracts a prediction model from the input and output data of the model. An inversion attack restores the training data of a prediction model. A membership inference attack judges if given data belong to the training dataset of a prediction model. A hyperparameter stealing attack extracts hyperparameters that tune the training algorithm of a prediction model.

Among these attacks, evasion attacks, also known as adversarial examples, are one of the most well-known attacks on machine learning, which were first proposed in 2013 [21]. This triggered a series of studies on attacks on machine learning as mentioned above. Evasion attacks are broadly divided into white-box [10,16,21] and black-box attacks [4,5,11,12] depending on information used for the attacks. White-box attacks use information on prediction models such as the architecture, parameters, and output data of the models. Black-box attacks use only the output data. Black-box attacks are further divided into score-based [5,12] and label-based [4,11] attacks. Score-based attacks use prediction labels and confidence values, whereas label-based attacks use only prediction labels.

To evaluate the threat posed by these attacks, three metrics are used generally: the misclassification rate, perturbation size, and number of queries. The misclassification rate is the percentage of original input data that successfully cause misclassification through perturbation addition by attackers. The perturbation size is the magnitude of the perturbation generally calculated using mean squared errors (MSEs) of perturbed data to original data. The number of queries is the number of trials conducted by an attacker to obtain the output of the prediction model. In terms of these metrics, attacks with a high misclassification rate, small perturbation size, or low number of queries pose severe risk because they represent a high probability for misclassification to occur, difficulty to notice perturbations with the human eye, or low cost and high stealthiness, respectively.

These metrics generally have a trade-off relationship. Mitigating this trade-off is a focus of adversarial example generation methods. For example, in the case of label-based attacks, LFBA [11], a state-of-the-art algorithm attack, limits the perturbation search to the region consisting only of low frequency components in the frequency space of the input images, and generates adversarial examples with smaller perturbation and fewer queries than do previous methods.

3   Background

This section briefly reviews random forests [3], CMA-ES [13], and LFBA [11].

3.1   Random Forests

Random forests represent a supervised machine learning algorithm consisting of multiple decision trees. A decision tree is a prediction model that has a tree structure. It receives input data at the root node, invokes conditional branches at intermediate nodes depending on the value of each element of the data, and outputs prediction results corresponding to a leaf node to which the data finally reach. Accurate prediction requires appropriate branch conditions at the root and intermediate nodes. For each node, training algorithms search for the best condition that divides the training data subset reaching the node into two subsets whose label homogeneity improves the most. To measure this homogeneity, these algorithms usually use metrices such as entropy and Gini index.

In a random forest, decision trees are trained separately but work together as one prediction model. This makes the prediction accuracy higher than that of a single decision tree. Data input to a random forest are received by each decision tree, and the output value from each decision tree is aggregated as a prediction result. This aggregation involves majority vote using the output values for classification cases, and average calculation using these values for regression cases. This paper focuses on classification cases below.

3.2   CMA-ES

CMA-ES is an evolution strategy. Evolution strategies utilize a biological evolution mechanism to optimize objective functions defined on real vector spaces. Generally speaking, evolution strategies are tolerant of noisy objective functions. These methods update tentative optima based on objective function values of multiple candidates for optima. This reduces susceptibility of tentative optima to noise in objective function values. In this category, CMA-ES [13] is a representative method that efficiently solves optimization problems with a low number of iterations. Here, we review $(\mu/\mu_w, \lambda)$-CMA-ES, a typical variation of CMA-ES.

CMA-ES optimizes a function by iterating the next three steps (a generation). In this subsection, we explain these steps by considering minimizing objective function $f(x)$, where x is a multidimensional real vector (e.g. an input image to prediction models).

Step 1 A normal distribution with mean m (centroid) and covariance matrix C generates λ candidates for the optimum (individuals).
Step 2 The value of $f(x)$ of each individual is calculated, and μ individuals are selected in ascending order with respect to the function values.
Step 3 A weighted average of the μ individuals is obtained, and centroid m and covariance matrix C are updated based on this result.

This method generally requires tuning the initial values of m and C, and designing the objective function. Moreover, designing a conversion function often facilitates the optimization. The conversion function maps the space where individuals are expressed to the space where objects (i.e., inputs to the objective function) is expressed. This function is useful because spaces suitable for individuals are often different from spaces suitable for objects. For example, when objects are gray scale images, a suitable space for objects is two-dimensional real space, but the frequency space transformed from real space with a discrete cosine transform can be suitable for individuals. This is true if the low frequency components dominate changes in the objective function value. Other parameters such as λ and μ have default values depending on dimensions of individuals as recommended in [13].

3.3   LFBA

LFBA [11] is a state-of-the-art label-based algorithm attack that generates adversarial examples. This attack is derived from the Boundary Attack [4]. Below, we review the Boundary Attack before LFBA, considering the generation of an adversarial example of original image x_O with $d \times d$ pixels.

The Boundary Attack begins with initializing tentative image x_A, which already causes misclassification. An attacker chooses an initial image, or simply generates random noise otherwise. Then, the attacker iterates the update of x_A by adding small perturbations. An iteration comprises the following four steps.

Step 1 The attacker generates perturbation η from a normal distribution over the real space of the image, and rescales it to a small perturbation.

Step 2 Perturbation η undergoes projection onto the sphere around x_O with radius $\|x_A - x_O\|_2$.

Step 3 Adversarial example candidate $\tilde{x}$ is obtained as $x_A + \eta$, and this candidate subsequently approaches slightly closer directly toward x_O.

Step 4 If $\tilde{x}$ causes misclassification, it takes the place of the current x_A; otherwise x_A remains unchanged.

LFBA improves the efficiency of the above attack by restricting the search space to the low frequency region. In particular, in Step 1 above, it generates a perturbation only with low frequency components. To generate such a perturbation, LFBA uses a normal distribution over the low frequency subspace in the frequency space of the image. An inverse discrete cosine transform is used to convert the perturbation to a perturbation in real space. This restriction to the low frequency region effectively reduces the dimensions of the search space. Thus, LFBA requires fewer queries than the Boundary Attack.

4   Threat Model

In this section, we describe the threat model assumed in this paper in terms of the victim and attacker. First, in regard to the victim, we assume a service provider that receives query x from a user and responds with a corresponding prediction label, l. The prediction is carried out by prediction model $F(x; w)$, where parameter w is trained with labeled training dataset $D = \{(x, l)\}$. As a countermeasure to algorithm attacks, the victim conceals model $F(x; w)$, dataset D, and the confidence values of the predictions. This is because disclosure of such information makes generating adversarial examples more effective [10, 12]. On the other hand, the victim does not know of the threat of the timing attacks, and no countermeasures for such attacks are applied. Thus, the victim unintentionally leaks information regarding the internal processing in the prediction model through the response time for query.

Second, the assumption of the attack is as follows. As described in Subsection 2.2, adversarial example attacks are broadly divided into white-box and black-box attacks. In this paper, we focus on label-based attacks among the black-box attacks. This is because it is difficult to use directly the prediction model and confidence values, which are both concealed by the victim. Instead, the attacker attempts to generate adversarial examples by efficiently exploiting the response time (i.e., timing).

5   Timing Attack on Random Forests

In this section, we describe how the proposed attack generates adversarial examples using the timing. There are two challenges in generating adversarial examples: building a strategy required to cause misclassification using the timing, and mitigating the measurement error of the timing. In regard to the former challenge, an appropriate change in the timing can cause misclassification, considering the internal processing in a random forest. This is because changes in the timing imply changes in the sum of the distance from the root node to the leaf node to which input data reach through conditional branches in each decision tree (depth). To change the timing appropriately, we should know the relationship between the timing and the possibility of misclassification. In this paper, this relationship is discussed in Subsect. 5.2, and experimentally confirmed in Subsect. 6.1. Note that this is not a part of the attack, but simply a preliminary experiment to design the proposed attack.

The latter challenge requires a noise-tolerant optimization method. This is because the timing must be changed along the appropriate direction even if measurement error in the timing exists. To confront this problem, we apply CMA-ES [13] in this paper. CMA-ES is a popular method in evolution strategy, which is a category of optimization methods employing noise tolerance.

The reminder of this section overviews the proposed attack, the objective function, and the conversion function. We originally designed the last two functions for the application of CMA-ES to the proposed attack. Hereinafter, we consider attacking gray scale images expressed in $[0,1]^{d \times d}$ for simplicity.

5.1   Notation and Flow of Proposed Attack

In this subsection, we describe the notation and flow in the algorithm of the proposed attack. The notation is defined as follows: x_O is the original non-adversarial image before the attack; l_O is its label; Γ is the distribution that generates individuals of CMA-ES; m_O is the initial value of the centroid of Γ; C_O is the initial value of the covariance matrix of Γ; λ is the number of individuals generated per generation; $gen_{\max}$ is the upper limit of the generation; $f(x; x_O, l_O)$ is the objective function of x when x_O and l_O are given; $\tilde{\phi}$ is the tentative minimum value of $f(\boldsymbol{x}; \boldsymbol{x}_O, l_O)$; $\tilde{z}$ is the tentative optimum individual corresponding to $\tilde{\phi}$; $g(\boldsymbol{z}; \boldsymbol{x}_C, \boldsymbol{z}_C)$ is the conversion function that outputs the image corresponding to individual $\boldsymbol{z}$ when central image $\boldsymbol{x}_C$ and individual offset $\boldsymbol{z}_C$ are given; $\text{LFBA}(\boldsymbol{x}, N; \boldsymbol{x}_O, l_O)$ is the result of LFBA after N iterations starting from initial image $\boldsymbol{x}$ to generate an adversarial example of $\boldsymbol{x}_O$; and $\boldsymbol{x}_A$ is the generated adversarial example.

Algorithm 1 shows the flow of the proposed attack. First, we initialize Γ with $\boldsymbol{m}_O$ and C_O in line 1. We also initialize $\boldsymbol{x}_C$ with $\boldsymbol{x}_O$, $\boldsymbol{z}_C$ with $\boldsymbol{m}_O$, $\tilde{\phi}$ with ∞, $\tilde{z}$ with $\boldsymbol{m}_O$ in line 2. Next, CMA-ES repeats the optimization at most $gen_{\max}$ times in the following flow. To begin with, Γ generates λ individuals $\boldsymbol{z}_1, \boldsymbol{z}_2, \cdots, \boldsymbol{z}_\lambda$ in line 4. Then, we evaluate value ϕ_i of the objective function of each individual in line 6. Subsequently, we update Γ based on $\boldsymbol{z}_i$ and ϕ_i according to the procedure of CMA-ES in line 8. At this point, if $\phi_\iota < \tilde{\phi}$ for $\iota = \text{argmin}_i \phi_i$, ϕ_ι and $\boldsymbol{z}_\iota$ respectively replace $\tilde{\phi}$ and $\tilde{z}$ in line 10. Additionally, we substitute $g(\tilde{z}; \boldsymbol{x}_C, \boldsymbol{z}_C)$ for $\boldsymbol{x}_A$ in line 11. Simultaneously, in line 12, we replace $\boldsymbol{x}_C$ with the image converted from the post-update centroid of Γ when pre-update $\boldsymbol{x}_C$ and $\boldsymbol{z}_C$ are given. In this line, we also replace $\boldsymbol{z}_C$ with the updated centroid of Γ. Then, if $\boldsymbol{x}_A$ causes misclassification, the timing attack with CMA-ES halts and LFBA assumes the attack in line 18; otherwise, the timing attack continues returning to line 3. This is because after misclassification, we only have to optimize a noiseless quantity, that is, the distance between $\boldsymbol{x}_A$ and $\boldsymbol{x}_O$. Such a task is more suitable for LFBA. Finally, we obtain $\boldsymbol{x}_A$ as the output of this attack in line 19.

In the above attack, we need to design the objective function $f(\boldsymbol{x}; \boldsymbol{x}_O, l_O)$ and the conversion function $g(\boldsymbol{z}; \boldsymbol{x}_C, \boldsymbol{z}_C)$ for applying CMA-ES to the timing attack. Additionally, changing the arguments of the conversion function (line 12) is an original contrivance. The reminder of this section describes the details of their designs and intensions.

5.2   Design of Objective Function

The objective function for CMA-ES used in this paper is:

$$f(\boldsymbol{x}; \boldsymbol{x}_O, l_O) = \begin{cases} S(t(\boldsymbol{x})) & (l(\boldsymbol{x}) = l_O) \\ \text{MSE}(\boldsymbol{x}, \boldsymbol{x}_O) - 1 & (l(\boldsymbol{x}) \neq l_O) \end{cases}. \tag{1}$$

Here, $l(\boldsymbol{x})$ is the prediction label obtained by inputting $\boldsymbol{x}$ to the prediction model, $t(\boldsymbol{x})$ is the time spent from the query of $\boldsymbol{x}$ to the response of $l(\boldsymbol{x})$, $S(t)$ is a function that estimates the possibility of misclassification from t, and $\text{MSE}(\boldsymbol{x}, \boldsymbol{x}_O)$ is the mean squared error of $\boldsymbol{x}$ to $\boldsymbol{x}_O$ (i.e., the perturbation size). In this expression, it may seem that the case where $l(\boldsymbol{x}) \neq l_O$ is unnecessary, when the attack is assumed by LFBA. However, we consider this case to select the best solution even when multiple individuals cause misclassification at the same time.

Algorithm 1. Proposed timing attack for generating adversarial examples

Input:

x_O: original image

l_O: original label

Γ: distribution that generates individuals of CMA-ES

m_O: initial centroid of Γ

C_O: initial covariance matrix of Γ

$f(x; x_O, l_O)$: objective function of generated image x when x_O and l_O are given

$\tilde{\phi}$: tentative minimum value of $f(x; x_O, l_O)$

$\tilde{z}$: tentative optimum individual corresponding to $\tilde{\phi}$

$g(z; x_C, z_C)$: transformer of individual z when x_C and z_C are given

LFBA$(x, N; x_O, l_O)$: the result of LFBA with N iterations starting from initial image x to generate an adversarial example of pair (x_O, l_O)

Output:

x_A: an adversarial example of x_O

1: Initialize Γ with m_O and C_O
2: $x_C \leftarrow x_O$, $z_C \leftarrow m_O$, $\tilde{\phi} \leftarrow \infty$, $\tilde{z} \leftarrow m_O$
3: **for** $gen = 1$ to $gen_{\max}$ **do**
4:     Generate λ individuals z_i $(i = 1, \cdots, \lambda)$ with Γ
5:     **for** $i = 1$ to λ **do**
6:         $\phi_i \leftarrow f(g(z_i; x_C, z_C); x_O, l_O)$
7:     **end for**
8:     Update Γ by z_i and ϕ_i $(i = 1, \cdots, \lambda)$
9:     **if** $\phi_\iota < \tilde{\phi}$ for $\iota = \mathrm{argmin}_i \phi_i$ **then**
10:         $\tilde{\phi} \leftarrow \phi_\iota$, $\tilde{z} \leftarrow z_\iota$
11:         $x_A \leftarrow g(\tilde{z}; x_C, z_C)$
12:         $x_C \leftarrow g(m; x_C, z_C)$, $z_C \leftarrow m$ (m is the centroid of Γ)
13:     **end if**
14:     **if** x_A is misclassified **then**
15:         Break this loop
16:     **end if**
17: **end for**
18: $x_A \leftarrow$ LFBA$(x_A, gen_{\max} - gen; x_O, l_O)$
19: **return** x_A

In Eq. (1), $S(t)$ adheres to the two conditions below.

Condition 1. The possibility of misclassification increases as $S(t)$ decreases.
Condition 2. $S(t)$ is always positive.

Condition 1 is to cause misclassification by maximizing the possibility of its occurrence. Condition 2 always makes the function value in cases where $l(x) \neq l_O$ smaller than that in cases where $l(x) = l_O$. This ensures that misclassified images become the optimum solutions. Indeed, under the assumption that each pixel value is in $[0, 1]$, MSE(x, x_O) is less than 1. Therefore, it is true under Condition 2 that the function value becomes smaller in cases of misclassification than otherwise.

Strictly speaking, the above conditions are not sufficient to specify $S(t)$. In this paper, we infer that $S(t) = t$. The reason for this inference is twofold.

First, from Condition 1, the simplest and most plausible forms of $S(t)$ are $\pm t$. This is because if we change t monotonically to a drastic extent, the internal processing also drastically changes. Second, maximizing t is likely to be more difficult than minimizing it. This difficulty can be derived from the fact that each conditional branch divides the space expressing images into two portions. This division shrinks the volume of subspaces consisting of images of deep depth, making such subspaces difficult to find. Indeed, we experimentally observed the difficulty as described in Subsect. 6.1. Here, note that $S(t) = t$ meets Condition 2.

5.3   Design of Conversion Function

The conversion function for CMA-ES used in this paper is

$$g(\boldsymbol{z}; \boldsymbol{x}_C, \boldsymbol{z}_C) = \mathrm{clip}(\boldsymbol{x}_C + \epsilon \tanh(\mathrm{IDCT}_r(\boldsymbol{z} - \boldsymbol{z}_C))). \tag{2}$$

Here, $\boldsymbol{z}$ is an individual, $\boldsymbol{x}_C$ is the central image to add perturbation, $\boldsymbol{z}_C$ is an offset of the individual, $\mathrm{clip}(\boldsymbol{x})$ is a function to clip $\boldsymbol{x}$ within $[0,1]^{d \times d}$, $\epsilon \ll 1$ is a constant to limit the perturbation size, and $\mathrm{IDCT}_r(\boldsymbol{z})$ is an inverse discrete cosine transform from the low frequency region of the frequency space to real space. Below, we describe the roles of $\boldsymbol{z}_C$ and $\boldsymbol{x}_C$, as well as the definition and reason for adopting $\mathrm{IDCT}_r(\boldsymbol{z})$.

First, the definition of $\mathrm{IDCT}_r(\boldsymbol{z})$ is

$$\mathrm{IDCT}_r(\boldsymbol{z}) = \mathrm{IDCT}(\boldsymbol{\eta}),$$

where IDCT is the inverse discrete cosine transform for the vertical and horizontal axes, and

$$\eta_{i,j} = \begin{cases} z_{i,j} & (1 \leq i, j \leq rd) \\ 0 & \text{otherwise} \end{cases}.$$

Here, r is a constant corresponding to the reduction rate of the dimension. We introduce this transformation to improve the efficiency of the optimization by the dimension reduction, based on an idea from previous research [11].

Finally, the roles of $\boldsymbol{z}_C$ and $\boldsymbol{x}_C$ are described with the reasons for their introduction and validity in line 12 in Algorithm 1. Equation (2) means that at most $\pm\epsilon$ perturbations are added to image $\boldsymbol{x}_C$. On the other hand, as shown in line 2 of Algorithm 1, because $\boldsymbol{x}_C$ is initialized by $\boldsymbol{x}_O$, the proposed attack initially searches for adversarial examples in the vicinity of $\boldsymbol{x}_O$. Therefore, if we fix $\boldsymbol{x}_C$ to $\boldsymbol{x}_O$, this limits the search for adversarial examples to a narrow region around $\boldsymbol{x}_O$. Thus, we intended to expand the search area by replacing $\boldsymbol{x}_C$ with the image generated with the centroid of Γ when $\tilde{\boldsymbol{z}}$ changes in line 10. This is what line 12 in Algorithm 1 represents. More precisely, in order for CMA-ES to operate properly, the image transformed from individual $\boldsymbol{z}$ under post-update $\boldsymbol{x}_C$ must be at least approximately the same as the image transformed from the same individual $\boldsymbol{z}$ under pre-update $\boldsymbol{x}_C$. Therefore, in line 12, $\boldsymbol{z}_C$ simultaneously shifts to the centroid of Γ as $\boldsymbol{x}_C$ changes. Indeed, suppose the old $\boldsymbol{x}_C$ is $\boldsymbol{x}_{\text{old}}$, the new x_C is x_{new}, the old z_C is z_{old}, and the new z_C is z_{new}, then the following equation holds if the effect of clipping and terms $O(||z_{new} - z_{old}||^2)$ are ignored:

$$g(z; x_{new}, z_{new}) \simeq g(z; x_{old}, z_{old}).$$

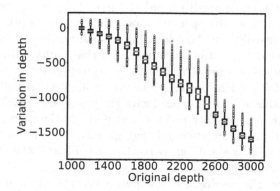

Fig. 1. Boxplot of variations in depth caused by adding perturbations to input images to a random forest. Original depth of the images without perturbations is represented on horizontal axis. Variation in depth caused by adding perturbations to the images is represented on vertical axis. Regardless of the original depth, the variations in depth tend to be negative.

6 Experiments

To prove the threat of the timing attack to random forests, we conducted two experiments described in the following subsections. More specifically, we first verify the difficulty in finding images of deep depth to support presumption $S(t) = t$. Then, we evaluate the threat of the proposed attack by comparing the proposed attack to LFBA [11].

The victim environment prepared for these experiments comprises a machine, an OS, a machine learning framework, a prediction model, and a dataset. The machine is an HP ProDesk 600 G2 SFF with an Intel Core i5 -6500 CPU and 16.0 GB memory. The OS is Windows 7 Professional. The machine learning framework is scikit-learn [19]. The prediction model is RandomForestClassifier with 100 decision trees, and other parameters are set to default values. The dataset is the Modified National Institute of Standards and Technology (MNIST) database. The MNIST training dataset is used to train the prediction model, whereas the MNIST test dataset is used in the following experiments. By combining these components, we prepared the victim environment in which depths are leaked from the timing. The correlation coefficient between the timing and the depth is 0.89.

As for the proposed attack, parameters $\epsilon = 0.05$, $r = 1/4$, $z_O = 0$, $C_O = 25.0 I_{rd}$ are set based on preliminary experiments, where I_{rd} is an $rd \times rd$ identity matrix. The other parameters of CMA-ES are set to the default values as recommended in [13].

6.1   Verification of Difficulty in Finding Images of Deep Depth

This subsection describes the experiment to verify the difficulty in finding images of deep depth. This difficulty supports presumption $S(t) = t$ as mentioned in Subsect. 5.2. In this experiment, we examined the distribution of depth variations caused by adding random small perturbations to original images. We conduct this experiment to show that perturbations shorten the depths for almost all original images regardless of the original depths of the images without perturbations. Below, we describe the procedures and the results of this experiment.

The experiment procedure is as follows. First, to each of 10,000 images in the test dataset, 10,000 random perturbations are generated and added. Each perturbation has a value of ± 0.01 per pixel with the probability of 50% for each sign. Next, depths of the images with and without perturbations are recorded. Then, variations in depth are calculated and aggregated to each bin with the width of 100 by depth of the images without perturbations. Finally, the distributions are expressed as a boxplot.

Figure 1 shows the results of this experiment. The original depth is represented on the horizontal axis, and the variation in depth when perturbations are added is represented on the vertical axis. Regardless of the original depths, the variations in depth tend to be minus. This shows the difficulty in finding perturbations that make depths deep. The cause of this difficulty can be the smallness of the subspaces that comprises images of deep depth in the space expressing images, as is explained in Subsect. 5.2. Hereinafter, considering this difficulty, $S(t) = t$ is assumed because the optimization in this direction is easier than that in the opposite direction.

6.2   Threat Evaluation of Proposed Attack

This section describes the experiment to evaluate the threat of the proposed attack. In this experiment, we compare the proposed attack to LFBA [11], a state-of-the-art algorithm attack, to show the superiority of the proposed attack to algorithm attacks. Additionally, we compare the proposed attack to an invalid timing attack. We define an invalid timing attack as an attack that uses the same algorithm as the proposed attack but substitutes a constant value of 1 for t in Eq. (1) instead of the valid timing. This invalidates the optimization of the timing. Comparison of these two attacks is expected to indicate that the valid timing critically contributes to the superiority of the proposed attack.

In this experiment, we measure the following four metrics: the misclassification rate, average perturbation size, attack success rate, and Simpson coefficient between two sets of original images successfully attacked by the proposed attack and by LFBA. The definitions and the meanings of the first two metrics are mentioned in Subsect. 2.2. The attack success rate is defined as the ratio of misclassified images with MSEs less than 0.001. This perturbation size is sufficiently small for human eyes to overlook according to literature [11]. The Simpson coefficient is an indicator measuring the overlap of two sets, say A and B, defined as

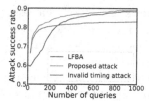

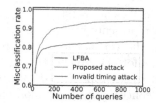

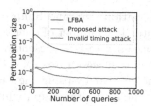

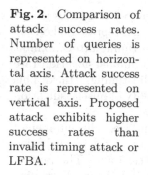

Fig. 2. Comparison of attack success rates. Number of queries is represented on horizontal axis. Attack success rate is represented on vertical axis. Proposed attack exhibits higher success rates than invalid timing attack or LFBA.

Fig. 3. Comparison of misclassification rates. Number of queries is represented on horizontal axis. Misclassification rate is represented on vertical axis. LFBA, proposed attack, and invalid timing attack exhibit high rates in this order.

Fig. 4. Comparison of perturbation sizes. Number of queries is represented on horizontal axis. Average perturbation size of misclassified images is represented on vertical axis. LFBA exhibits the worst size of the three attacks.

$|A \cap B| / \min(|A|, |B|)$. We use this indicator to evaluate quantitatively differences in characteristics between the proposed attack and LFBA.

Among these metrics, we mainly compare the attack success rate. In particular, if the success rate of the proposed attack is higher than the success rate of the invalid timing attack and LFBA, we judge that the timing attack is a threat at least to the victim environment we prepared. In such a case, using the timing weakens the effect of the countermeasure that conceals the prediction models and the confidence values. We use the remaining metrics to analyze the results in detail.

The procedure for this experiment is described below. First, we extract 1,000 original images correctly classified without attacks from the test MNIST dataset, which constitutes a victim dataset to be attacked. Second, we record the results of the three attacks for each image in the victim dataset. The procedure in each attack is as follows. To begin with, for each image, we execute the attack program that repeats queries. After a certain number of queries, the attack program updates the solution once considering the responses. At this time, three values are recorded: the boolean value if a misclassification occurred, the perturbation size, and the number of queries so far. The attack program iterates this procedure comprising a certain number of queries and an update. When the attack completes, we aggregate these records per query and calculate three metrics for each query: the misclassification rate, the average perturbation size of the misclassified images, and the attack success rate. Note that we aggregate the records every 15 queries. This query interval is the largest number of queries required for an iteration of all the attacks. Third, the Simpson coefficient is similarly calculated depending on these records of the proposed attack and LFBA.

The remainder of this subsection describes the results and the interpretation of the data in the order of the attack success rate, misclassification rate, perturbation size, and Simpson coefficient. First, Fig. 2 shows the attack success rate. The number of queries is represented on the horizontal axis and the attack success rate is represented on the vertical axis. The proposed attack exhibits higher success rates than those for the invalid timing attack and LFBA. This means that by using the timing, the proposed attack decreases the effectiveness of the countermeasure, which conceals the prediction model and the confidence values.

Second, Fig. 3 shows the misclassification rate. The number of queries is represented on the horizontal axis and the misclassification rate is represented on the vertical axis. LFBA, the proposed attack, and the invalid timing attack exhibit high misclassification rates in this order. Particularly, the misclassification rate is higher for the proposed attack than that for the invalid timing attack. This indicates that optimizing the timing increases the probability of misclassification and contributes to high attack success rates.

Third, Fig. 4 shows the average of the perturbation size. The number of queries is represented on the horizontal axis and the average of the perturbation size of the misclassified images is represented on the vertical axis. The perturbation size remains much smaller in the proposed attack and the invalid timing attack than in that for LFBA by an order of magnitude. The difference between the proposed attack and the invalid timing attack increased as the number of queries increased, and the perturbation size of the former became larger than that for the latter. This means that optimizing the timing yields a negative effect on the perturbation size. However, this causes only slight deterioration in the success rate and the increase in misclassification rate compensates for the negative effect. This effect results from the design of the objective function. Before misclassification, the function forces the optimization to reduce only the timing and to ignore the perturbation size according to Eq. (1).

Fourth, Fig. 5 shows the Simpson coefficient. The number of queries is represented on the horizontal axis. The Simpson coefficient, which indicates the degree of overlap of the sets of images successfully attacked by the proposed attack and LFBA, is represented on the vertical axis. The coefficient is 1 if and only if (iff) one set includes the other; 0 iff the two sets are exclusive; and in the middle if they partially overlap. Overall, as the figure shows, the Simpson coefficient remains at nearly 1 during the attacks. In conjunction with the fact that the success rate is higher in the proposed attack than in LFBA, this means that the set successfully attacked by the proposed attack includes almost all of the set that can be attacked by LFBA. This suggests that there are only a few incorrigible images such that LFBA can attack but the proposed attack cannot.

7   Discussion

In this section, we discuss risky situations involved with the timing attack, limitations of the proposed attack, and some possible directions for countermeasures.

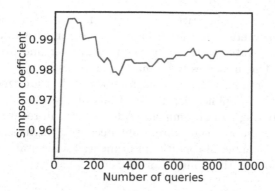

Fig. 5. Simpson coefficient, which indicates the degree of overlap of image sets successfully attacked by the proposed attack and LFBA. Number of queries is represented on horizontal axis. Simpson coefficient is represented on vertical axis. Overall, the Simpson coefficient remained at almost 1 during the attacks. In addition to the results in Fig. 2, this means that the set of the proposed attack includes the set of LFBA.

7.1 Risky Situations and Limitations of Timing Attack

In this subsection, we discuss situations where the risk of the timing attack increases, along with limitations of the proposed attack. This discussion considers two viewpoints: the viewpoint of the manner for mutual communication between the victim and the attacker, and that of the victim environment. First, the manner of communications includes local or remote communications. Here, remote communications means the case where the victim environment and the attacker program are on different machines and communicate through a network. Local communications means the case where they are on the same machine and communicate locally. Between these cases, local communications can be more risky due to the absence of measurement errors resulting from communications delay. For example, local communications is actualized when the attacker has the prediction model readily available in the case of an edge AI.

Second, the victim environment comprises a machine, an OS, a framework, a prediction model, and a dataset. Among these, a case in which the machine or OS cause fewer interruptions can increase the risk due to a decrease in measurement errors of the timing. Such a situation can occur when the machine has many CPU cores and the OS executes few processes simultaneously. This also means the proposed attack is invalidated when the victim environment is busy. However, the attacker may efficiently circumvent this difficulty by outlier detection in the timing because interruptions can cause jumps in the timing.

Regarding the framework, the programing language used in the framework can affect the risk. For example, a framework based on C++ may be easier to attack than a framework based on Python due to the absence of interpreters, which can generate superfluous measurement errors in the timing. This also means that the proposed attack may fail more often when the victim environment uses a framework based on a language executed on a complex software stack. This limitation can be critical unlike the interruptions mentioned above because measurement errors in the timing will be continuous in this case. Thus, the attacker must iterate the timing measurement over and over for the same perturbed image. This increases the number of queries.

As for the prediction model, a large number of decision trees can increase the risk because this amplifies depth variations of the random forest, making variations in the timing more prominent. Additionally, in regard to the dataset, the diversity of the dataset can be relevant because a high degree of diversity will require a large number of conditional branches for accurate prediction. This also makes variations in the timing more salient.

7.2   Possible Directions for Countermeasures

There are two possible directions for countermeasures for the timing attack in principle: taking measures subsequent to or prior to training. The first direction includes the following two strategies, which are popular in the context of timing attacks on cryptographic systems: making the processing time constant, and limiting the attacker ability to control queries. For example, in the former case, there is a method that waits to respond until a predetermined fixed time elapses. In the latter case, there is a method that adds random perturbation to input data. In the former example, the prediction accuracy does not deteriorate, but the average processing time increases. This is because the fixed time must be longer than the processing time required for the maximum depth. This is inconvenient to users. In the latter case, the average processing time does not deteriorate, but the prediction accuracy decreases due to the perturbation.

The second direction can lead to a method that aligns the depths of leaf nodes using a contrivance in a training algorithm. This reduces the width of variations in the timing, making the timing attack difficult. This strategy will mitigate the trade-off between the prediction accuracy and processing time mentioned above. A simple idea for this strategy is to restrict the maximum depth of the trees. Tightening this restriction aligns the depths of leaf nodes. `RandomForestClassifier` can readily adopt this idea because this prediction model has a parameter for such restriction. However, this restriction can conflict with prediction accuracy. Mitigating this confliction may require a novel training algorithm. This will be a topic for future work.

8   Conclusion

In this paper, to prove the threat of implementation attacks to random forests, we presented a novel timing attack to generate adversarial examples, and evaluated its threat experimentally. The proposed attack searches for a misclassified image in the vicinity of the normal one by optimizing the timing using CMA-ES, a typical method in evolution strategies.

In the experiment, we compared the proposed timing attack with a state-of-the-art algorithm attack. The results show that the attack success rate of the former exceeded that of the latter in the black-box setting where attackers can use only prediction labels and the timing. This suggests the threat of implementation attacks to random forests in the sense that such attacks can make it less effective to conceal the prediction model and the confidence values as a countermeasure to adversarial example generation. In the future, we investigate countermeasures to defend random forests from timing attacks.

References

1. Batina, L., Bhasin, S., Jap, D., Picek, S.: CSI NN: reverse engineering of neural network architectures through electromagnetic side channel. In: Proceedings of the 28th USENIX Security Symposium, USENIX Security 2019, pp. 515–532 (2019)
2. Breier, J., Hou, X., Jap, D., Ma, L., Bhasin, S., Liu, Y.: Practical fault attack on deep neural networks. In: Proceedings of the 2018 ACM SIGSAC Conference on Computer and Communications Security, CCS 2018, pp. 2204–2206 (2018)
3. Breiman, L.: Random forests. Mach. Learn. **45**(1), 5–32 (2001)
4. Brendel, W., Rauber, J., Bethge, M.: Decision-based adversarial attacks: reliable attacks against black-box machine learning models. In: Proceedings of the 6th International Conference on Learning Representations. ICLR 2018 (2018)
5. Chen, P.Y., Zhang, H., Sharma, Y., Yi, J., Hsieh, C.J.: Zoo: zeroth order optimization based black-box attacks to deep neural networks without training substitute models. In: Proceedings of the 10th ACM Workshop on Artificial Intelligence and Security, AISec 17, pp. 15–26 (2017)
6. Chen, T., Guestrin, C.: XGBoost: a scalable tree boosting system. In: Proceedings of the 22nd ACM SIGKDD International Conference on Knowledge Discovery and Data Mining, KDD 2016, pp. 785–794 (2016)
7. Duddu, V., Samanta, D., Rao, D.V., Balas, V.E.: Stealing neural networks via timing side channels. arXiv preprint arXiv:1812.11720 (2018)
8. Fredrikson, M., Jha, S., Ristenpart, T.: Model inversion attacks that exploit confidence information and basic countermeasures. In: Proceedings of the 22nd ACM SIGSAC Conference on Computer and Communications Security, CCS 2015, pp. 1322–1333 (2015)
9. Gartner: Top Trends on the Gartner Hype Cycle for Artificial Intelligence (2019). https://www.gartner.com/smarterwithgartner/top-trends-on-the-gartner-hype-cycle-for-artificial-intelligence-2019/
10. Goodfellow, I.J., Shlens, J., Szegedy, C.: Explaining and harnessing adversarial examples. arXiv preprint arXiv:1412.6572 (2014)
11. Guo, C., Frank, J.S., Weinberger, K.Q.: Low frequency adversarial perturbation. In: Proceedings of the 35th Conference on Uncertainty in Artificial Intelligence. UAI 2019 (2019)
12. Guo, C., Gardner, J., You, Y., Wilson, A.G., Weinberger, K.: Simple black-box adversarial attacks. In: Proceedings of the 36th International Conference on Machine Learning, ICML 2019, pp. 2484–2493 (2019)
13. Hansen, N., Ostermeier, A.: Completely derandomized self-adaptation in evolution strategies. Evol. Comput. **9**(2), 159–195 (2001)
14. Hong, S., et al.: Security analysis of deep neural networks operating in the presence of cache side-channel attacks. arXiv preprint arXiv:1810.03487 (2018)

15. Jagielski, M., Oprea, A., Biggio, B., Liu, C., Nita-Rotaru, C., Li, B.: Manipulating machine learning: poisoning attacks and countermeasures for regression learning. In: Proceedings of the 2018 IEEE Symposium on Security and Privacy, S&P 2018, pp. 19–35 (2018)
16. Kantchelian, A., Tygar, J.D., Joseph, A.: Evasion and hardening of tree ensemble classifiers. In: Proceedings of the 33rd International Conference on Machine Learning, ICML 2016, pp. 2387–2396 (2016)
17. Liu, Y., Wei, L., Luo, B., Xu, Q.: Fault injection attack on deep neural network. In: Proceedings of the 2017 IEEE/ACM International Conference on Computer-Aided Design. pp. 131–138. ICCAD '17 (2017)
18. Oracle: An introduction to building a classification model using random forests in python. https://blogs.oracle.com/datascience/an-introduction-to-building-a-classification-model-using-random-forests-in-python
19. Pedregosa, F., et al.: Scikit-learn: machine learning in Python. J. Mach. Learn. Res. **12**, 2825–2830 (2011)
20. Shokri, R., Stronati, M., Song, C., Shmatikov, V.: Membership inference attacks against machine learning models. In: Proceedings of the 2017 IEEE Symposium on Security and Privacy, S&P 2017, pp. 3–18 (2017)
21. Szegedy, C., et al.: Intriguing properties of neural networks. arXiv preprint arXiv:1312.6199 (2013)
22. Tramèr, F., Zhang, F., Juels, A., Reiter, M.K., Ristenpart, T.: Stealing machine learning models via prediction APIs. In: Proceedings of the 25th USENIX Security Symposium, USENIX Security 2016, pp. 601–618 (2016)
23. Wang, B., Gong, N.Z.: Stealing hyperparameters in machine learning. In: Proceedings of the 2018 IEEE Symposium on Security and Privacy. S&P 2018, pp. 36–52 (2018)
24. Wei, L., Luo, B., Li, Y., Liu, Y., Xu, Q.: I know what you see: power side-channel attack on convolutional neural network accelerators. In: Proceedings of the 34th Annual Computer Security Applications Conference, ACSAC 2018, pp. 393–406 (2018)
25. Yan, M., Fletcher, C.W., Torrellas, J.: Cache telepathy: leveraging shared resource attacks to learn DNN architectures. arXiv preprint arXiv:1808.04761 (2018)

Correction to: Detection of Running Malware Before it Becomes Malicious

Sergii Banin and Geir Olav Dyrkolbotn

Correction to:
Chapter "Detection of Running Malware Before it Becomes Malicious" in: K. Aoki and A. Kanaoka (Eds.): *Advances in Information and Computer Security*, **LNCS 12231,**
https://doi.org/10.1007/978-3-030-58208-1_4

Some errors were present in the originally published Chapter 4. The following modifications were made:

Page 67, line 16 has been corrected to: "switching from BEP behavior to AEP it is relatively low".
Page 67, line 22 has been corrected to: "selects more features for AEP data than for BEP data".

The updated version of this chapter can be found at
https://doi.org/10.1007/978-3-030-58208-1_4

K. Aoki and A. Kanaoka (Eds.): IWSEC 2020, LNCS 12231, p. C1, 2020.
https://doi.org/10.1007/978-3-030-58208-1_17

Author Index

Printed in the United States
By Bookmasters